PLANNING

Buildings for Habitation, Commerce and Industry

PLANNING, Ninth edition

Other volume titles

Architects Technical Reference Data

Buildings for Administration, Entertainment and Recreation

Buildings for Health, Welfare and Religion

Buildings for Education, Culture and Science

PLANNING

Buildings for Habitation, Commerce and Industry

Edited by
EDWARD D. MILLS, C.B.E., F.R.I.B.A., F.S.I.A.

NEWNES-BUTTERWORTHS

LONDON—BOSTON
SYDNEY-WELLINGTON-DURBAN-TORONTO

THE BUTTERWORTH GROUP

UNITED KINGDOM   Butterworth & Co (Publishers) Ltd
London: 88 Kingsway, WC2B 6AB

AUSTRALIA   Butterworths Pty Ltd
Sydney: 586 Pacific Highway, NSW 2067
Also at Melbourne, Brisbane,
Adelaide and Perth

CANADA   Butterworth & Co (Canada) Ltd
Toronto: 2265 Midland Avenue, Scarborough, Ontario M1P 4S1

NEW ZEALAND   Butterworths of New Zealand Ltd
Wellington: 26–28 Waring Taylor Street, 1

SOUTH AFRICA   Butterworth & Co (South Africa) (Pty) Ltd
Durban: 152–154 Gale Street

USA   Butterworth (Publishers) Inc
Boston: 19 Cummings Park, Woburn, Mass 01801, USA

First published in 1936 by Architect & Building News
Second edition 1937
Third edition 1938
Fourth edition 1939
Fifth edition published for Architect & Building News
by Gilbert Wood & Co Ltd 1947
Sixth edition 1949
Seventh edition published for Architect & Building News
by Iliffe & Sons Ltd 1953
Eighth edition published for Architect & Building News
by Iliffe Books Ltd 1959
Ninth edition published by Newnes-Butterworths, 1976

© E. D. Mills and the several contributors named in the list of contents, 1976

ISBN 0 408 00226 3

Filmset by Ramsay Typesetting (Crawley) Ltd

Printed in Scotland by Thomson Litho Ltd, East Kilbride

FOREWORD

By Gontran Goulden, O.B.E., T.D., F.R.I.B.A.
Deputy Chairman, The Building Centre Group

The construction industry becomes daily more complicated and to attempt to abstract the relevant information from the mass of literature available is no easy task. It is now almost impossible for one man to know even the main sources of technical information by heart.

For nearly forty years *Planning* has been a leader among the books that list, discuss and illustrate all those vital facts and figures that are not to be found in one place elsewhere. The man on the drawing board, whether a beginner, experienced in general or specialised practice, or about to burst into computerised building design will always need simple basic information of the kind that packs the pages of this entirely new edition of *Planning* which has been expanded and now comprises five volumes.

The whole question of information for the construction industry still awaits a satisfactory solution. It is doubtful even whether it is capable of being solved to meet everyone's demands. At one end of the scale there are those who demand comprehensive lists of manufacturers and products, corrected up to the minute and covering every conceivable detail of each item. Others require research information in the greatest depth with all available sources equally up to date and comprehensive. We know that this problem can be dealt with by computers, at a price. We know too that various attempts and exercises have been and are being made to turn this major undertaking into a financially possible service.

Only time will show whether the user can be trained to realise that time spent in his office on research costs money and that the answer could be available in less time, thereby saving him money. A small proportion of users are prepared to pay for information, most still think it should be free and paid for by the other fellow. Comprehensive information for the industry will require a nationally co-ordinated effort. So far there is little or no sign of this.

In the meantime the need for the right information continues in all branches of the industry. In addition to major outside-the-office sources each one of us has his own particular favourite reference books and catalogues. This personal preference will always be there wherever comprehensive systems develop.

Planning has filled many people's personal information needs for years. With a mass of useful data, and as a guide to the form of construction industry information generally, this new edition should, like its predecessors, prove invaluable and I wish it every success.

Gontran Goulden

CONTENTS

INTRODUCTION

Planning first appeared as a weekly feature in the Architect & Building News and was contributed by two architects under the pseudonym of E. & O.E. In 1936 the first bound volume was published and the authors were subsequently revealed as Roland Pierce and Patrick Cutbush, later to be joined by Anthony Williams. Since that date eight editions have appeared at frequent intervals and the general pattern has changed little over the years. Today, *Planning* is recognised throughout the world as one of the standard reference books for architects. There can be few architects offices in the UK which do not possess and constantly use at least one copy, and in many architects offices in the remote parts of the world a much used copy still holds pride of place on the bookshelf. Architectural students have always found this to be an essential work of reference and many have started their architectural libraries with *Planning* and one or two of the other well known books of reference.

The radical changes which are taking place in the world of building has led to a reappraisal of the place of *Planning* in the technical information field and in the way in which the valuable material it contained is presented. New techniques and disciplines are being developed in the building industry and these must be reflected in the technical information available. The building industry is becoming more closely integrated and *Planning* must inevitably reflect this. It has, therefore, been restructured so that it appeals to a wider cross-section of the industry including architects, builders, quantity surveyors, engineers, planners and students. With these considerations in mind, together with the change to metric in the building industry, the publishers Newnes-Butterworth and Building and Contract Journals who have taken over the publishing responsibilities of the Architect & Building News, decided that a completely new approach should be adopted and this volume is one of a series which reflect the new pattern.

The previous edition consisted of three sections; a general section dealing with information applicable to more than one type of building; a section dealing with information applicable to specific building types and metrication information to aid the conversion of imperial units to metric ones. In essence the new edition accepts this broad classification and although the work has been conceived in metric, the conversion material is retained in part.

The volume entitled *Planning—Architects' technical reference data* includes sections dealing with legislation, British Standards, materials etc. as well as basic planning data which concerns all types of building, such as landscaping, car parking, circulation, sanitary requirements, storage requirements etc., together with the metric conversion material originally in the eighth edition. All information contained in earlier editions that is still valid has been retained and a considerable amount of new material has been added. Other volumes deal with specific building types and cover a wide range of subjects, some of these building types have not been dealt with in previous editions.

The unique characteristic of this series of volumes is that it indicates how various types of buildings are planned by supplying information and data which are essential before planning can begin. It does not deal with the aesthetics of design, although in the volumes dealing with particular building types illustration is not only by means of diagrams but by plans and photographs of actual completed buildings, either in part of whole showing the way in which particular problems have been solved.

The endeavour throughout all sections of the new edition has been to provide a ready reference of basic information, or guidance as to where more detailed information can be obtained. One book can never hope to provide all the facts, and inevitably information will be omitted or given in part but it is hoped that readers will find this new method of presentation useful, and that it will carry on the long tradition of *Planning* as an essential publication for all concerned with building.

The volumes dealing with specific building types are sub-divided as follows: *Habitation, Commerce and Industry; Health, Welfare and Religion; Administration, Entertainment and Recreation; Education, Culture and Science.* Each building type is covered by the following subsections to ensure uniform treatment and to facilitate ease of reference. These are—Introduction; siting; planning; space requirements; data; accommodation; statutory requirements, legislation and Authorities; examples; bibliography.

Whenever possible diagrams and tables have been used and the bibliography lists the important books and publication that will aid further research. Unlike previous editions, the material for each specialist section has been prepared by architects with a special knowledge and experience in the particular category of building, and the range of building types has been considerably extended. By this means it is hoped that the 9th edition will be even more useful to architects and others than its predecessors.

The sources from which the material for the present edition has been gathered have been many and varied. The Editor greatly appreciates the willing co-operation of the various contributors and a biography of the author is given at the end of each section. Books, periodicals, people and associations have all contributed in a very practical way and because it is impossible to set out a complete list of those concerned, this general acknowledgement is addressed to all who have been associated with the preparation of the book and is an expression of the sincere thanks of both the Editor and publishers.

Finally, special thanks are due to Gontran Goulden who has contributed the foreword in his private and personal capacity. He has been intimately concerned with all aspects of building information in this country and abroad for the past twenty-five years and his continued interest is greatly appreciated.

The Editor would welcome any constructive criticism or comments, as the work will be constantly revised and kept up to date, and every effort will be made to take account of suggestions which may be made, so that they can be applied to future editions.

Edward D. Mills
Editor

Edward D. Mills, *CBE, FRIBA, FSIA, Architect, lecturer and broadcaster, RIBA Alfred Bossom Research Fellow 1953, Churchill Research Fellow, 1969, a member of the RIBA Council from 1955–1962 and from 1963–1969. Senior partner in the architectural practice of Edward D. Mills & Partners, whose works include industrial buildings, schools and research laboratories as well as the Cathedral of St. Andrew, Mbale, Uganda and the National Exhibition Centre, Birmingham.*

Member of the Design Council Farm Buildings Advisory Committee, a member of Uganda Society of Architects and Chairman of the Faculty of Architecture of the British School at Rome. Author of The Modern Factory *(2nd Edition 1959) and* The Modern Church *(1952) published by the Architectural Press;* The New Architecture in Great Britain, *Whitefriars Press (1953);* Factory Building in Great Britain, *Leonard Hill Books (1967);* The Changing Workplace, *George Godwin Ltd. (1972).*

1 HOUSES AND FLATS

ALFRED J. ROWE, A.R.I.B.A.

INTRODUCTION

This section deals primarily with dwellings intended for letting whether in the form of houses or flats but reference is also made to houses for the individual client. An important consideration which has to be borne in mind in the planning of 'housing' as opposed to 'houses' is that the occupier is individually unknown and, therefore, the planning must be concerned with providing the best possible solution for the probable needs of an average family in the particular area in which the dwellings are to be built. A further and more difficult factor is the need to anticipate as accurately as possible future trends and changing patterns of living.

The principles of good house and flat planning are the same whether the accommodation is large or small, expensive or low-cost. Different categories of accommodation occur at all levels; e.g. homes for families, for single people, for elderly people and for the disabled. Further detailed information on the last category is given in *Planning: Buildings for Health, Welfare and Religion*.

The planning of houses and flats is a complex operation because of the wide range of activities to be provided for. The nature of these activities changes from family to family and as the occupants grow older and the plan must allow for flexibility to provide for this.

Apart from the information contained in this section, reference should also be made for specialised aspects of housing layout and design Sections 2 and 3 in this volume and to the following *Planning* volumes.

Planning: Architects' Technical Reference Data
 Human dimensions and common sizes
 Internal and external circulation
 External works and landscape, including road services
 Dimensional co-ordination
 Metrication

Planning: Buildings for Health, Welfare and Religion
 Homes for the aged
 Housing for the disabled

SITING

GROUPING

Housing accommodation today is provided in numerous types of building, including single storey, two-storey and three-storey houses as well as low rise and high rise blocks of maisonettes and flats. This provides great scope in the layout and grouping of units, relating them both to existing development and to future development. Mixed forms of development including houses, low blocks and high blocks are often desirable from both the architectural and the social points of view. The manner in which the particular site can be developed is controlled by the Local Planning Authority who stipulate the density of development in terms of unit per hectare or sometimes habitable rooms per hectare. When this criterion is used to establish the density, half the width of the roads up to a maximum of 6 m may be included for the purpose of calculating area, site cover and the number of dwellings.

Houses may be built singly, in pairs or in terraces. Detached houses are the most popular due to the increase in privacy provided but the cost is greater due to increased lengths of roads, sewers and services and to the increased amount of external wall.

The space between buildings can be considered from several viewpoints but they must be considered together and not in isolation. These can be grouped under the following headings and are described in detail below:
 Access (vehicles and pedestrians)
 Garaging and parking
 Communal spaces
 Private spaces

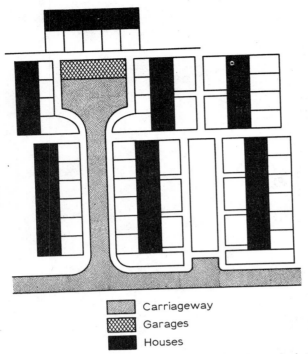

Carriageway

Garages

Houses

Fig. 1.1   The vehicle cul-de-sac. With a turning circle or hammer-head at the end of the carriageway and with individual or grouped garages

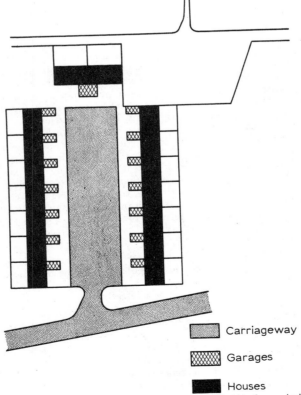

Carriageway

Garages

Houses

Fig. 1.2   The garage court. With the carriageway widened to form a single large enclosure for vehicles and grouped for individual garages

ACCESS (FOR VEHICLES AND/OR PEDESTRIANS)

Recommended widths for roads serving housing estates are as given in Table 1.1.

Table 1.1 WIDTH OF ACCESS ROADS

Type of road	Width in m
Access road serving more than 300 dwellings (where the road is a bus route the width should be increased to 6.75 m)	6.00
Access road including culs-de-sac serving 150–300 dwellings	5.50
Access road including culs-de-sac serving up to 150 dwellings	5.00 to 5.50
Secondary means of access limited to cars only (e.g. to garage courts)	up to 4.00
Access to parking or garages for	
1 car	2.30
up to 10 cars	3.00
over 10 cars	4.00
Footways where provided alongside carriageways	1.80
Main pedestrian ways or routes (segregated footway systems)	2.50

The most important consideration in planning access routes for cars and pedestrians is that of safety and this is best achieved by complete segregation on Radburn principles. This requires:

(a) Roads for motor vehicles only.
(b) A separate footpath system.
(c) Houses specially designed and grouped with separate access for pedestrians and cars.

Layouts based on these Radburn principles generally conform to one of three basic types, illustrated in Figs. 1.1 to 1.3.

In practice it is never possible completely to separate cars from pedestrians (even drivers' walk) but the layout should be prepared in such a way as to discourage pedestrians from walking along or crossing roads.

In layouts which provide such separation the house must be planned in such a way that the main entrance to the house is clear, particularly to visitors. It is also necessary that access to houses can be achieved without sacrifice of privacy to other adjoining property.

GARAGING AND PARKING

In housing estates, space must be provided not only for the parking or garaging of residents' and visitors' cars but also vans and lorries some of which are parked near drivers' homes overnight.

The amount of parking/garaging is controlled by the planning authority and depends on the type of housing it serves.

If cars are not parked or garaged integrally with the house or flat, a close and preferably covered access way should be provided. Consideration must also be given to the needs of frequent and regular visits by vehicles such as refuse lorries and tradesmen and those of infrequent and irregular visits by emergency services and removal vehicles.

Turning circles must be adequate for fire appliances and hard standing provided adjacent to tall blocks of flats for wheeled escape appliances. Requirements for this vary from one authority to another and the Fire Brigade should be consulted at an early stage. It is not always necessary for such areas to be hard paved and various open concrete paving blocks are available which, at the same time, provide a hard standing for occasional use with the visual amenity of soft landscaping.

Individual garages should be based on a minimum internal size of 5000 mm by 2500 mm which will comfortably house the majority of cars available. Where the garage is adjacent to or integral with the house, space must also be provided outside the garage and clear of the open door for a car to stand when being cleaned or unloading and for visitors to park clear of the road. Where the garage is in a block with others, adequate space must be provided to enable a car to enter and leave and to see other cars or pedestrians in the vicinity. Recommended dimensions are shown in Figs 1.4 and 1.5.

COMMUNAL SPACES

The communal spaces between houses, block of flats, etc include areas of hard and soft landscaping, sitting areas and children's playspaces. These areas are particularly important for flat dwellers who do not normally have private gardens.

Hard landscaping is essential where there is much pedestrian traffic such as in the vicinity of entrances to flats or where paths meet, to avoid muddy patches. Large areas of soft landscaping such as grass or planting need careful and constant attention but can do much to soften the prospect particularly for those living on the lower floors of high-rise developments. Planting can also be used functionally to give privacy or, on a larger scale, to provide protection against noise from busy roads, railways, etc. Shrubs and climbing plants can also be used to cover unsightly garage blocks, refuse chambers, etc.

Sitting areas should be provided for elderly people and housewives where they can meet their neighbours. They can be sited in a quiet corner away from the noise of play areas

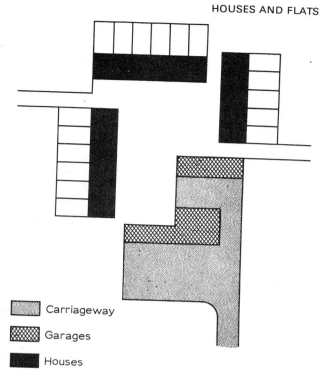

▨	Carriageway
▩	Garages
■	Houses

Fig. 1.3 The pedestrian forecourt. The head of the cul-de-sac or garage court is extended to form a paved pedestrian area from which each house is entered. Garages are grouped away from the houses

and should be protected against the wind either by shrubs or walls or in a sunny area.

If an area is not set aside for children to play they will find their own playspace often to the detriment of other residents' amenities. The area to be provided is set out in a Government circular as 3 m² per child bedspace. Play areas should be sited near family homes so that children, especially young ones, can be kept under supervision. Areas should be provided for children of all ages and, in larger schemes, separated so that older children are discouraged from using equipment provided for younger ones.

The play equipment provided should include popular and traditional items (swings, roundabouts, see-saws and slides). Static architectural equipment (tunnels, mazes, climbing blocks, etc) is generally less popular with children and, although some psychologists consider such equipment to be advantageous educationally, experience shows that

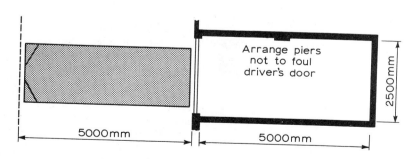

Arrange piers
not to foul
driver's door

2500mm

5000mm   5000mm

Fig. 1.4 Recommended dimensions for garage

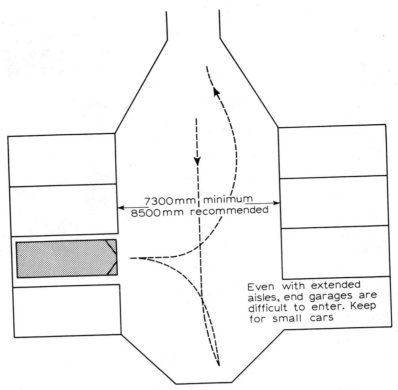

Fig. 1.5 Recommended dimensions for manoeuvring to enter and leave garages

they are little used by children. In large schemes the roof-space can sometimes be used for a playspace but supervision is difficult. Care must also be taken in the detail design of parapets.

PRIVATE SPACE

This can be anything from the small paved courtyard of a patio house to a large garden of a house designed for an individual client. It is used for general outdoor living, children's play area, baby's sleep and gardens, decorative or produce.

It is important that wherever possible, some private outdoor space is provided, even for the smallest unit although this is difficult in the case of high rise flats where a balcony often provides the only opportunity for the occupants to sit outdoors in conditions of privacy. It is preferable to avoid soft landscaping in small private spaces which are best completely paved with planting in tubs. Even in large gardens, an area of hard landscaping adjacent to the house is desirable in the form of paths or a terrace to avoid excessive wearing of grassed areas.

PLANNING

Houses and flats are today designed in such variety that it is impossible to divide them into hard and fast categories. Some characteristics (e.g. of frontage or number of storeys)

have such a strong influence on internal planning that some generalisations can be made.

NARROW FRONTAGE HOUSES

Where houses have to be provided in a high density scheme, narrow frontage plans with a frontage of between 3.5 m and 5.5 m are very useful. However, these have many disadvantages and problems arising from the small proportion of external wall in relation to the area of each floor—privacy, satisfactory through access, versatile orientation, natural lighting to all living areas, kitchen and bathroom are difficult to achieve economically. Narrow frontage plans, however, make maximum use of road and footpath frontage and the space required for daylighting between blocks. Because of the need to light the rearmost parts of living areas, external walls are often extensively glazed and privacy is sometimes prejudiced. Because gardens are narrow and easily over-looked from the sides, substantial screening is essential but privacy can be improved by staggering the terraces.

Access to the garden has often to be through the main living room, although a lobby on the garden side can be provided to keep the living room free from muddy shoes, etc. This problem can be avoided by building three-storey houses with the main living accommodation on the first floor and a throughway provided at ground floor level. Narrow frontage plans have a little choice of orientation as it is virtually impossible to provide a through living room.

Internally, the main difficulty in planning a narrow

frontage house arises from the fact that the centre of the house is so far from the windows. With houses designed for more than three people where a separate living space is required, it is difficult to achieve this without sacrificing the daylighting and ventilation of other areas.

The bathroom, which is usually provided at first floor level, can be internal and lit and ventilated artificially or by means of a clerestory window.

MEDIUM FRONTAGE HOUSES

Most of the problems set out for narrow frontage houses can be solved by increasing the frontage of the house to between 5.5 m and 7.3 m. It is usually more difficult to achieve high densities with medium frontage plans because they take up more road and footpath frontage.

With plans of this type it is possible to arrange two living rooms side by side, away from the front door, ensuring greater privacy for the living areas. It is still difficult, however, to provide a through living room to give a versatile orientation.

It is also possible for two-storey medium frontage terraced houses to have an attached or integral garage. This type of plan probably offers the best compromise between a convenient internal plan and an economical site layout.

WIDE FRONTAGE HOUSES

With wide frontage terrace houses over 7.3 m, costs are increased. Circulation areas tend to be high but privacy, through access, space for the car, natural lighting to all spaces and versatile orientation are all relatively easy to provide. With these plans, arrangements can be made for all the habitable rooms to face away from the access side of the house ensuring greater privacy and protection from noise where this is a particular problem. This can only be done, however, at the expense of orientation.

It is also possible, with wide frontage house plans, to arrange for access lobbies at front and back and access to the garden through the main living spaces can be completely avoided. It is desirable to provide integral or attached garages. Good relationships between all internal rooms can be achieved with this type of plan. It is also possible to provide a plan with some flexibility to enable, for example, a double bedroom to be sub-divided into two single bedrooms, or vice versa.

PATIO HOUSES

Apart from the traditional terrace layout of house, it is often possible to design accommodation around a patio to give greater privacy; houses can also be joined in various ways to suit differing conditions of access, level and orientation. Patio houses are, however, more expensive than terrace houses because of their greater wall/floor area ratio. The plans take up more frontage than terrace houses and their ground coverage is usually greater than that of terrace houses. It is still possible, however, to achieve high densities.

The disadvantage of patio house plans is their extended circulation areas and increased costs for services, particu-

larly heating. It is generally possible, however, for the plumbing services to be centralised.

CLUSTER HOUSES

Houses can be designed in cluster blocks with plans not unlike the forms used for multi-storey flats. Some terrace and patio house plans can be grouped into clusters, but such a grouping usually results in extravagant use of the site if privacy is not to be sacrificed.

The cluster is a plan type which makes it relatively easy to ensure privacy between houses in the same cluster, but it is difficult to achieve economically between a cluster group and other adjacent buildings. It is a plan form that lends itself to a single access layout off an internal pedestrian route. With such a plan it is difficult to provide attached or integral garages, but covered routes to blocks of garages can be provided.

Cluster plans generally are more versatile in orientation than normal terrace housing. For typical plans see Figs 1.6 to 1.10.

FLATS

The flat is primarily a type of dwelling for urban development for crowded areas and expensive sites. Its use enables more people to live in towns and therefore close to centres of work and entertainment with corresponding avoidance of loss of time in travelling from suburban houses. Flats can be planned as low rise with heights up to three storeys. For flats above this height lifts are necessary, unless the levels of the site allow an entrance at a level other than ground level.

A criticism frequently levelled against flats is a possible lack of privacy, but it is doubtful if this lack is greater than in ordinary town houses, planned in terraces, for each flat can be self-contained and approached from a staircase and lift hall which are, in fact a vertical extension of the street. High rise buildings generally cost more than low rise, largely owing to the high cost of vertical circulation.

Four types of access can be considered as follows. Examples of these types are shown in Fig. 1.11.

(a) *Balcony (or gallery) access.* This access type is suitable for either flats or maisonettes but balconies tend to be noisy, exposed to the weather, potentially dangerous for young children and can induce giddiness in some occupants. With maisonettes, balconies occur only at alternate floors and overshadowing of the floor below is reduced. One advantage of this type of access is the encouragement it gives to social contact.

(b) *Access from the cross-ventilated lobby or small semi-private balcony open to the air.* This has developed from the acceptance of one common staircase in high buildings with entrances to individual flats in the cross ventilated lobby. It provides a good degree of privacy but the cross-ventilated lobby is draughty.

(c) *Internal Lobby Access.* This is suitable for flats and comprises an internal lobby served by lifts and an adjoining

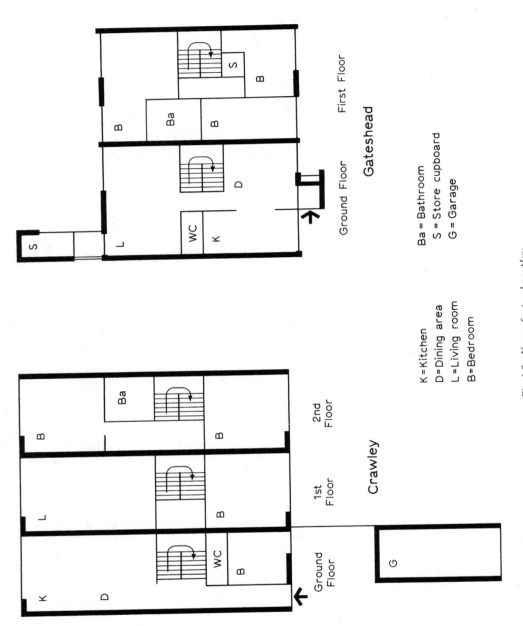

K = Kitchen
D = Dining area
L = Living room
B = Bedroom

Ba = Bathroom
S = Store cupboard
G = Garage

Fig. 1.6   Narrow frontage house plans

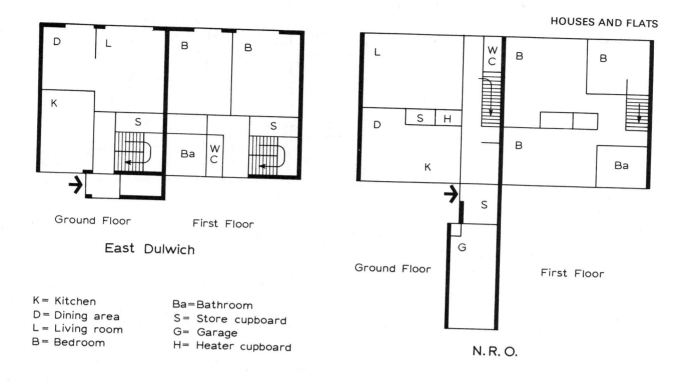

Ground Floor   First Floor

East Dulwich

K = Kitchen   Ba = Bathroom
D = Dining area   S = Store cupboard
L = Living room   G = Garage
B = Bedroom   H = Heater cupboard

Ground Floor   First Floor

N. R. O.

Fig. 1.7   Medium frontage house plans

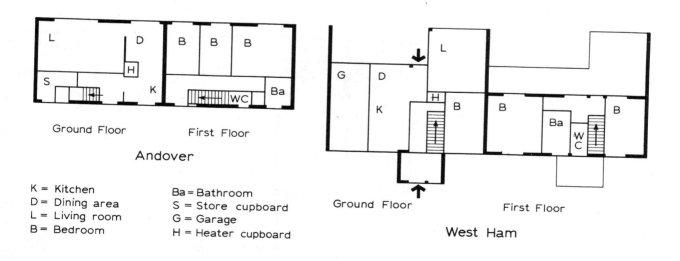

Ground Floor   First Floor

Andover

K = Kitchen   Ba = Bathroom
D = Dining area   S = Store cupboard
L = Living room   G = Garage
B = Bedroom   H = Heater cupboard

Ground Floor   First Floor

West Ham

Fig. 1.8   Wide frontage house plans

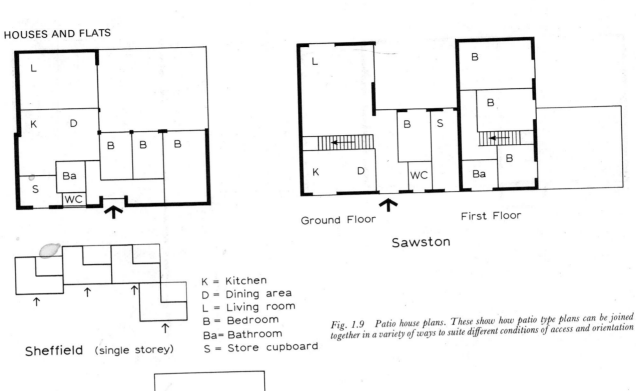

K = Kitchen
D = Dining area
L = Living room
B = Bedroom
Ba= Bathroom
S = Store cupboard

Sawston

Sheffield (single storey)

Fig. 1.9   Patio house plans. These show how patio type plans can be joined together in a variety of ways to suite different conditions of access and orientation

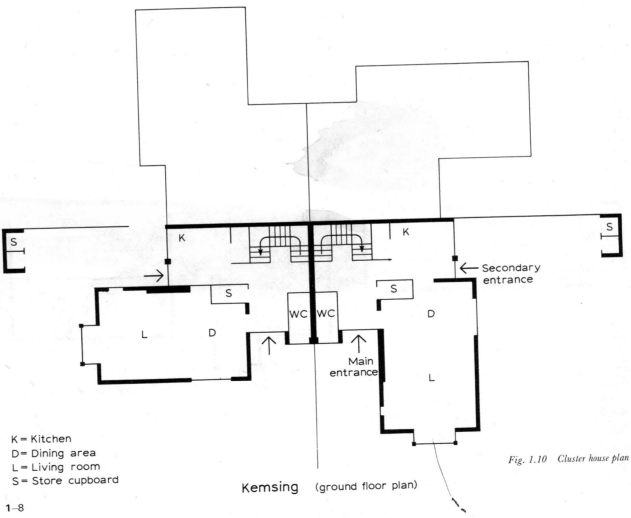

K = Kitchen
D = Dining area
L = Living room
S = Store cupboard

Kemsing   (ground floor plan)

Fig. 1.10   Cluster house plan

1—8

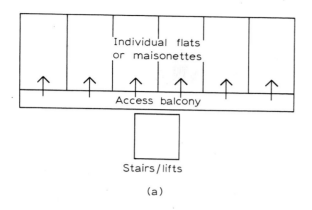

(a)

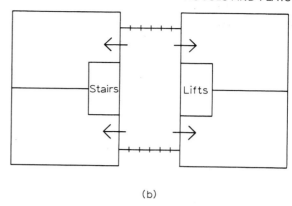

(b)

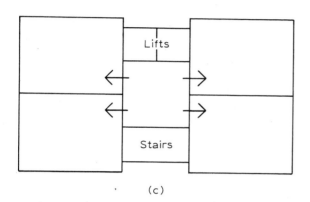

(c)

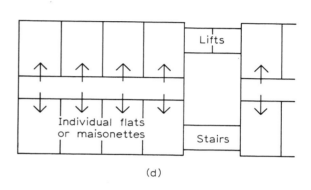

(d)

Fig. 1.11   Methods of access
(a) Balcony (or gallery) access.
(b) Access from cross-ventilated lobby (stairs and lifts can be in
a separate block externally).
(c) Access from internal lobby.
(d) Secondary access from internal corridors.

staircase with individual entrances to flats. It gives full protection from the weather and a high degree of privacy but can create a sense of isolation.

(d) *Common hall or corridor access.* This is suitable for flats or maisonettes and permits a larger number of units to be served by the common lifts and stairs and is particularly suited to smaller flats.

SPACE REQUIREMENTS

A.   SPACE

So far as the sizes of local authority housing units are concerned, this is generally controlled by legislation. There is, of course, a tendency for this legislation to be revised from time to time but the Table 1.2 which is based on 'Homes for today and tomorrow' can be used to establish the recommended size for units of differing types. This shows the minimum floor area (in m²) which should be allowed for occupation by 1–6 people.

Table 1.2 MINIMUM FLOOR AREAS FOR HOMES BUILT IN THE FUTURE

No. of people	6	5	4	3	2	1
3 storey house*	98	94	—	—	—	—
2 storey centre terrace	92.5	85	74.5	—	—	—
2 storey semi or end	92.5	82	72	—	—	—
Maisonette	92.5	82	72	—	—	—
Flat	86.5	79	70†	57	44.5	30
Single storey house	84	75.5	66	57	44.5	30

All dimensions in m².
*These figures will require modification if a garage is built-in.
†67 if balcony access.

Net floor area is the area of one or more floors enclosed by the walls of a dwelling, including the area occupied by partitions, staircases and any external w.c. It excludes the floor area of general stores, bin store, fuel store, garage or balcony. The general storage space which should be allowed is shown in Table 1.3.

The general storage area is taken to exclude floor areas occupied by bin store, fuel store or pram space and any space required inside houses as access from one side of the house to the other. Where the garage is integral with or joins the

Table 1.3 GENERAL STORAGE AREA ALLOWED FOR HOMES
BUILT IN THE FUTURE

No. of people	6	5	4	3	2	1
Houses*	4.5	4.5	4.5	4	4	3
Flats and maisonettes:						
Inside the dwelling	2	2	2	1.5	1.5	1
Outside the dwelling	1.5	1.5	1.5	1.5	1.5	1.5

All dimensions in m².
* Some of this may be on an upper floor; but at least 2.5 m²
  should be at ground level.

house, any area in excess of 12 m² can count towards the general storage provision.

B. PLAN ARRANGEMENTS (LOCAL AUTHORITY)

A dwelling shall have (i) an entrance hall or lobby with space for hanging outdoor clothes and (ii) for three-person and larger houses and three-person and larger dwellings served by a lift or ramp a space for a pram (1400 mm × 700 mm).

Except in one-person or two-person dwellings access to the bathroom and w.c. shall be arranged without having to pass through another room.

The kitchen in a dwelling for two or more persons must provide a space where casual meals may be taken by a minimum of two persons.

In addition to kitchen storage, the sink and space for a cooker, a minimum of two further spaces shall be provided in convenient positions to accommodate a refrigerator and a washing machine. The latter may be in the kitchen or in a convenient position elsewhere. These spaces may be provided under work top surfaces.

Most house layouts now provide for public access to both sides of the house but where public access to a house of three or more persons is from one side only, a way through the house from front to back shall be provided and this must not be through the living room. In such cases the dustbin compartment shall be on the front entrance doors.

C. FITTINGS AND EQUIPMENT (LOCAL AUTHORITY)

1. W.C.'s

The w.c. and washbasin provision shall be as set out below:
(a) In one-, two-, and three-person dwellings, one w.c. is required and may be in the bathroom.
(b) In four-person two-storey or three-storey houses and two-level maisonettes and in four-person and five-person flats and single-storey houses, one w.c. is required in a separate compartment.
(c) In two- or three-storey houses and two-level maisonettes at or above the minimum area for five persons and in flats and single-storey houses at or above the minimum floor area for six persons, two w.c.'s are required, one of which may be in the bathroom.
(d) Where a separate w.c. does not adjoin a bathroom, it must contain a washbasin.

2. Linen Storage

A cupboard shall be provided giving 0.6 m³ of clear storage space in four-person and larger dwellings or 0.4 m³ in smaller dwellings.

3. Kitchen Fitments

Kitchen fitments comprising enclosed storage space in connection with preparation and serving food and washing up, cleaning and laundry operations, and food, shall be provided as follows:

Three-person and larger dwellings   2.3 m³
One- and two-person dwellings   1.7 m³

Part of this provision shall comprise a ventilated, cool larder and a broom store. This can be in the form of a cupboard provided elsewhere than in the kitchen.

Where standard fitments are used the cubic capacity should be measured overall for the depth and width and from the underside of the worktop to the top of the plinth for the height.

Worktops shall be provided on both sides of the sink and on both sides of the cooker position. Kitchen fitments shall be arranged to provide a work sequence comprising work top/cooker/work top/sink/work top (or the same in reverse order) unbroken by a door or other traffic way.

PRIVATE HOUSING

Where private housing is concerned there are no statutory requirements for overall floorspace except those laid down by The National House-Builders Registration Council as applied to kitchen layout, w.c.'s and storage accommodation. These requirements are as follows:

Kitchen Layout

Every kitchen shall be so designed as to provide the following:
(i) Either (a) a clear space not less than 600 mm wide, together with such piping, cables or other apparatus as may be necessary to enable a gas, electric or oil cooker to be installed; such space shall not be under a window; or (b) A solid-fuel cooker designed for continuous burning with adequate constructional provision for the disposal of the products of combustion and not located under a window.
(ii) A sink with at least one drainer (independently or as a combined unit), the whole being not less than 1000 mm wide.
(iii) Space for work surfaces, not less than 500 mm from front to back, as follows. A work surface on each side of and immediately adjacent to the sink (the drainer may be included as a work surface), and a work surface on each side of the cooker. However, one work surface may be common to sink and cooker.

The aggregate width of the space available for work surfaces, including the drainer, shall be not less than 1500 mm and no single space shall be less than 300 mm wide. Through access between sink and cooker should be avoided.

(iv) Two clear spaces for storage or installation of other appliances, one space being not less than 600 mm wide and one space being not less than 800 mm wide. These spaces may be incorporated with those required for work spaces on the assumption that the appliances will fit under any work surfaces ultimately installed. This requirement may be waived if appliances are provided and built in by the builder or where suitable space is provided elsewhere (such as the provision of space for a washing machine in a utility room).

W.C.'s

In any dwelling with an internal staircase whose floor area exceeds 80 m² or any dwelling on one floor whose area exceeds 75 m² if only one appliance is provided, this shall be in a separate compartment. Every compartment containing a w.c. appliance shall also contain a washbasin unless the w.c. compartment immediately adjoins a bathroom or other compartment containing a washbasin.

Storage Accommodation

Every dwelling shall be provided with:

(i) Enclosed domestic storage accommodation in or easily accessible to the kitchen in accordance with the following:

In a dwelling where the total floor area is less than 60 m²	1.3 m² min
In a dwelling where the floor area exceeds 60 m² but is less than 80 m²	1.7 m² min
In a dwelling where the floor area exceeds 80 m²	2.3 m² min

(ii) A cupboard positioned adjacent to or enclosing the hot water cylinder or with an alternative method of heating for the airing of domestic linen, etc.

DATA

For local authority work all plans must now show the furniture drawn on and should be designed to accommodate furniture as set out below.

Kitchen. Small table unless one is built-in.

Meals space. Dining table and chairs.

Living areas. Two or three easy chairs; settee; TV set; small tables; reasonable quantities of other possessions, such as radiogram, bookcase.

Single bedrooms. Bed or divan (2000 mm × 900 mm); bedside table; chest of drawers; wardrobe space for cupboard to be built-in.

Main bedrooms. Double bed (2000 by 1500 mm) or alternatively two single beds each 2000 mm × 900 mm; bedside tables; chest of drawers; double wardrobe or space for cupboard to be built-in; dressing table.

Other double bedrooms. Two single beds (2000 mm × 900 mm); bedside tables; chest of drawers; double wardrobe

or space for cupboard to be built-in; small dressing table.

Where bedrooms are designed as study/bedrooms or bed-sitting rooms, space must also be provided for such additional furniture as tables, desks and easy chairs. The scale of provision depending on the nature of the activity and the age of the occupant.

ELECTRIC SOCKET OUTLETS

Requirements for the provision of electric sockets are generally the same for local authority housing and for that built to correspond with the requirements of the National House-Builders Registration Council as follows:

Working area of kitchen	4
Dining area (local authority)	1
Dining area (private)	2
Living area	3
Bedroom	2
Hall or landing	1
Bed-sitting room in family dwellings	3
Bed-sitting room in one-person dwellings	5
Integral or attached garage	1
Walk-in general store (in house only)	1

Any sockets required for night store space or water heating are in addition to the above.

ACCOMMODATION

The scale of accommodation to be provided is sometimes governed by statutory requirements, as in the case of local authority housing or, in the private sector by the Technical Requirements of the National House Builders Registration Council.

In all but the most elaborate and expensive house designed for the individual client, this accommodation has to be put to different and often conflicting uses to provide for the complex range of activities in the home. For convenience this accommodation can be listed under the following headings:

Food preparation/laundry
Refuse disposal
Eating
Leisure
Circulation
Sleeping
Personal care

These are covered in detail in the following paragraphs.

FOOD PREPARATION/LAUNDRY

A kitchen plan is a complex problem. It is the workshop in which the housewife performs many operations of widely differing natures. Good and expensive equipment in itself does not guarantee a solution, for unless the equipment is properly arranged and the space planned as a whole, labour and effort is not reduced. It is the relationship with equipment to use and the sequence of operations that are the important factors. The three main groups of work to be planned for in the kitchen are

(a) Food preparation.
(b) Washing up.
(c) Laundry.

It is preferable if this last function is carried out in a separate room (e.g. Utility Room) but this is only possible in the larger house.

Certain units of equipment particularly the sink are used for more than one of these groups of work but broadly each group has special units associated with it. It is therefore of the utmost importance to consider carefully the sequence of work and the fittings involved in order to plan the whole correctly. In the course of a day's work, the housewife is constantly changing from one type to another and compromises are therefore necessary in the types, position and working heights of fitments.

The sequence of operations in connection with meal preparation is:

1. Delivery or collection of goods together with storage.
2. Preparation of food.
3. Cooking.
4. Preparation of the dining table.
5. Distribution of food to the table.
6. Return of food and crockery from the table.
7. Washing up.
8. Putting away of washed-up crockery, glass and cutlery.

Item 1 involves the larder, store cupboards, refrigerator and freezer. In small houses and flats, the larder is often omitted and there is rarely room for a large freezer. There is, however, a tendency for housewives to buy food in bulk and provision for its storage is becoming more necessary, both in the form of dry storage and freezer accommodation.

Item 2 needs the use of worktop surfaces together with the sink and these must be closely related to each other and to the larder and cooker which is the major feature of Item 3. It is essential that proper workspace is provided at both sides of the cooker.

Item 4 requires linen and tableware to be taken from storage to the table, partly by way of the worktop or in the case of hot plates and dishes, by way of the cooker. This cannot be completely separated from Item 5 which involves the conveyance of food from cooker and worktop together with some food directly from storage to the dining table.

Item 6 reverses the processes of Items 4 and 5 so that surplus food is returned to storage, dirty china and cutlery to the sink, clean china and cutlery together with linen to storage.

Item 7 involves the sink or a dish-washing machine. If this is to be provided, consideration must be given to its plumbing.

The work sequence recommended in the Parker, Morris Report is 'work surface/cooker/work surface/sink/work surface' (or the same in reverse order) unbroken by a door or other traffic way and arranged in either a straight line or in an 'L' or in a 'U' (see Figs. 1.12 and 1.13).

There can be a variety of relationships between the working area and the dining area of the home, but they can generally be divided into:

(a) Working kitchen with a separate dining room.
(b) Working kitchen with dining space incorporated; and
(c) Dining/Kitchen.

In all cases it is important that the kitchen is designed so that natural light is available, preferably from a window, although this is not a requirement so far as Building Regulations is concerned. Kitchens without windows are acceptable only in very small units of accommodation such as one or two persons flats where the housewife is unlikely to spend long periods of time in the kitchen.

It is important that the kitchen is placed in a convenient position relative to the entrance doors so that the housewife can see visitors and also so that she can control children playing outside.

The other main work apart from food preparation and serving in which the kitchen is involved, is that of laundry. This may be divided into three sub-groups—washing, drying and ironing—of which the first is in itself a series of separate operations. It is better if laundry work can be kept apart from that of cooking, for example in a Utility Room, owing to the heat, steam and smell involved. Although with the increasing popularity of automatic washing machines, this is less necessary if the kitchen is large enough to accommodate the extra equipment. Provision has to be made for storage of dirty washing. If a Utility Room is not provided, this is best done in a laundry basket in the bathroom or one of the bedrooms. It should, however, be in the position where it is available for all members of the household.

Where an external drying space is provided, the housewife should have direct access to this from the kitchen or laundry room without negotiating other rooms. Because the housewife spends so much time in the kitchen, consideration should be given to the view. Traditionally, kitchens were planned on the cool side of the house so as to compensate for large heat-producing stoves but, with better ventilation and smaller electric and gas cookers, this is not so necessary and the kitchen can face the sun providing that some protection from over-heating in the summer can be provided (e.g. blinds). Large windows facing south or west should be avoided.

REFUSE DISPOSAL

The collection and disposal of refuse of all types needs careful consideration, particularly with the increasing amount of packaging for disposal. For individual houses and small groups of flats the dustbin or sack remains the only practical solution. The placing of the dustbin should be given proper attention as part of the planning so that it is conveniently sited relative to the refuse producing area (kitchens, etc) and to the access for the refuse collecting vehicles.

With larger blocks of flats, chutes are normally installed, usually in one of two forms:

(a) Separate chutes from each flat to individual dustbins at ground level, and
(b) Chutes serving a number of flats and delivering to a main container at ground or basement level.

The second type is more common and usually has hoppers at all floors. The room to accommodate these containers can often be grouped with stores but the weight and size of the containers makes it necessary for the collector's vehicle to obtain easy access.

Activity sequences

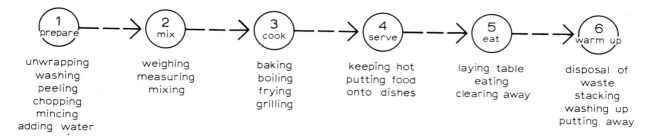

1 prepare	2 mix	3 cook	4 serve	5 eat	6 warm up
unwrapping washing peeling chopping mincing adding water	weighing measuring mixing	baking boiling frying grilling	keeping hot putting food onto dishes	laying table eating clearing away	disposal of waste stacking washing up putting away

Arrangement of activity zones

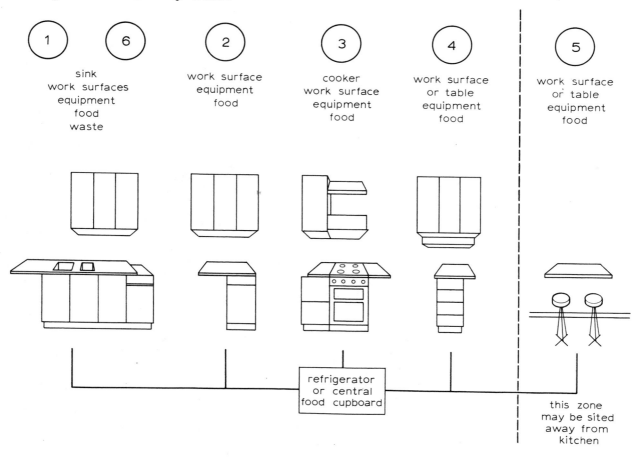

Fig. 1.12   Meal preparation process

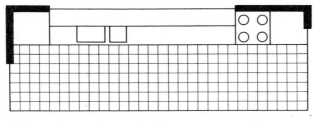

Straight-line assembly

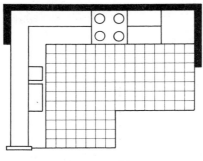

L assembly

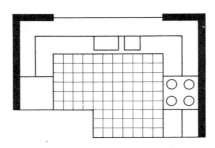

U assembly

Fig. 1.13 Meal preparation assemblies
Straight-line assembly. This is the simplest combination of the meal preparation zone. It can be accommodated in a width of 1800 mm.
L *assembly. The counter frontage is the same as in the straight-line assembly but the corner provides extra 600 mm for wall cupboards.*
U *assembly. Two corners in this assembly provide an extra 1200 mm of wall storage.*

The chutes must be planned conveniently for the flat and preferably in its own open lobby with adequate natural ventilation. For reasons of economy, a single chute can be planned to serve a number of flats at each floor level. With large scale developments it may be possible to incorporate incinerators or a water-borne system of waste disposal.

Detailed information on sizes of bins and containers is given in the volume *Planning: Architects' Technical Reference Data.*

EATING

This activity can, in the smaller home, take place either in the leisure area or be associated with food preparation. It is preferable, if possible, for a separate area to be provided particularly so that it may then be used for other purposes (children's homework, sewing, etc).

A separate dining room is necessary only in larger houses than those of the minimum area for the 3-bedroom local authority house, but is usually required in houses for the individual client. Apart from the use of the area for eating, it also provides greater flexibility in the use of space for the other activities referred to above.

Wherever the eating area is situated it is essential that it is closely related to the food preparation area with direct access by door for the serving of meals and subsequent clearing away. A service hatch can be provided but it should have shelf space on both sides.

The space required for the eating area depends on the nature of the meal and the number of people to be accommodated. Breakfast bars can be provided in a limited space sometimes by using drop-down tables. Where main meals are eaten at a table, a space of at least 3000 mm × 3000 mm will be necessary to accommodate the average family and occasional visitors. A larger area is necessary if a separate room is provided or if any additional furniture is to be accommodated other than table and chairs.

LEISURE

Leisure activities in the home include those which are normally carried out with the family, such as watching TV and other activities which require quieter conditions (e.g. playing chess). Activities may also include those which, in themselves, are noisy, (e.g. listening to pop-records); these are best carried out away from main leisure areas.

It is important, therefore, that rooms set aside for leisure are flexible and can provide for different arrangements of furniture to suit changing activities. The room should be large enough to accommodate comfortably all the occupants, or, in the case of young families, the eventual number of occupants of the house.

The room must provide sufficient space for two or three easy chairs, a settee, a TV set, a small table, a reasonable quantity of other possessions such as a radiogram and bookcase. With the gradual disappearance of the open fire, more formal arrangements of the furniture are less necessary and the design of the room should allow for flexibility in the layout.

Consideration must also be given to the occasion when a very large floor space is required for parties, etc when it might be possible to combine the leisure area with other parts of the accommodation. Some form of folding partition is the obvious way of doing this, but it does not provide good sound insulation when the secondary room is required for study, etc.

CIRCULATION

Economies of internal planning and space saving are gained by the reduction of corridor and connecting spaces to a reasonable minimum but excessive elimination generally reduces privacy and comfort. It is important however that the widths of circulation spaces should not be reduced so that they are inconvenient for people to pass each other, particularly in public areas such as lobbies and common stairs which can be intensively used at peak hours. It is also necessary for circulation areas to be properly lit, both naturally and artificially. Doors, particularly to cupboards, should not obstruct circulation spaces when open.

In addition to circulation within the house or flat, consideration must also be given to entering and leaving and to everything that happens in the immediate vicinity of the home, such as putting out washing, fetching fuel (if stored externally) etc.

Main entrances must be planned to provide for safe and clear access for both pedestrian and vehicular traffic, for people and goods. In multi-unit developments it is best to separate people from vehicles as far as possible.

Single steps in circulation areas should be avoided, particularly where they occur unexpectedly for no apparent reason. Ramps are sometimes necessary to provide convenient access for disabled people or for mothers pushing prams. These ramps should not, however, be so steep as to be dangerous when icy. Access stairs should, wherever possible, be covered and, preferably, totally enclosed. Where fire prevention legislation requires an alternative means of escape it is sometimes possible to arrange for the secondary stair to provide a service access. Detailed information on planning data for corridors, stairways and lifts is given in the volume *Planning Architects' Technical Reference Data* (section 2 Internal Circulation).

A porch or lobby serves several functions. It can be looked on as a neutral area where occasional callers can be met without taking them into the privacy of the family. It can act as a draught lobby and it can also act as a space where outdoor clothing can be removed and stored. A house or flat designed for family accommodation must provide space for storing a pram and pushchair. This accommodation is sometimes provided in external stores, but these are most unpopular with mothers, as such stores are generally cold and damp and mothers tend to use the pram indoors as a cot during the day where the baby can be properly supervised.

Requirements for general storage as required by the Parker Morris report have been given previously under 'Space Requirements'.

Storage for garden equipment, bicycles and other purposes is also required for four/five person houses at the rate of 4.5 m² per dwelling clear of refuse containers, fuel bins and access ways. The storage space need not all be on the same floor so long as there is at least 2.25 m² on the ground floor.

Flats and maisonettes should have storage comparable to that in a house. Four or more persons require 1.4 m² of general storage within the flat. There should be a separate store elsewhere of 2.0 m² for each flat whatever size of family. If the flat has a garden, additional storage is required for garden tools.

Every home must have a cupboard for the storage of linen, that can also be used for airing or keeping dry. It is preferable for this to be sited off a circulation space so that it is always available without having to enter another room such as a bedroom or bathroom.

Bedrooms should be provided so that each member of the family other than the parents, can have a single bedroom to him/herself. This need not apply to very young children. Bedrooms should have direct access from landings or corridors and should in no circumstances be inter-communicating.

Double bedrooms should be planned to accommodate two single beds and the parents' bedroom should be large enough for a cot occasionally. Children's bedrooms can sometimes be planned to accommodate bunk beds thus releasing some of the floor area for other furniture such as tables and easy chairs.

There is a school of thought which suggests that, owing to the limitation of space in many houses, certain of the bedrooms should be planned and equipped as bed-sitting rooms. If this suggestion is to be adopted, special consideration should be given to the floor area, of which such a large proportion is generally occupied by the bed and circulation space.

Most bedrooms should be provided with built-in cupboards allowing not less than 600 mm run of hanging space per person. Cupboards should be at least 550 mm deep internally and doors 2000 mm high with extra cupboards above reaching to the ceiling for the storage of the less frequently required articles. The provision of adequate built-in cupboards is more economical in floor-space than the provision of equivalent areas of storage in the form of loose furniture. By careful planning of cupboards, the partition between two rooms may be formed entirely of such cupboards.

By using lightweight or demountable partitions a double bedroom can be designed so that it can be divided into two single bedrooms or vice versa. This flexibility is particularly desirable to accommodate the needs of a changing family.

PERSONAL CARE

Accommodation listed under this heading refers generally to bathrooms, w.c.'s and cloakrooms, but it also covers activities normally carried out elsewhere (e.g. changing, hair-drying, washing at basins in bedrooms, kitchen sinks, etc.).

The position of the bathroom in the home is generally preferred on the upper floor or in close relationship to the sleeping accommodation. Bathrooms are, however, also used by some housewives for small-scale laundry and drying clothes, but where the status of the accommodation allows, this is best provided elsewhere. If adequate lighting and artificial ventilation can be provided, bathrooms can be internal. Because of the need to economise on service installations this is particularly suited to blocks of flats. It also allows greater versatility in the orientation of habitable rooms. In positioning the bathroom, the possibility of noise affecting other rooms must be taken into consideration.

Appliances to be provided in the bathroom include bath, shower (separate or over bath), washbasin, w.c. and bidet. If no other w.c. is provided elsewhere it should be in a compartment separate from the bath and preferably have an additional washbasin. It is desirable that two w.c.'s should be provided in homes having three or more bed-rooms. The second w.c. is best provided near the entrance to the home so that it can be used immediately on entering. It is then also conveniently placed for children playing outdoors or for the garden or other outdoor leisure areas.

Planning is dependent on the proper relationship of rooms and of various services required by different rooms or portion of the house and, therefore, each problem should be analysed to show fundamental relationships and circulations.

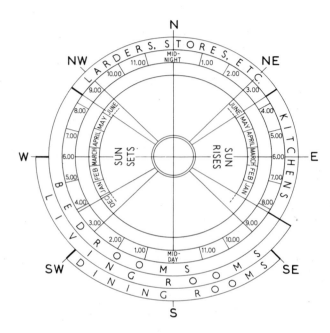

Fig. 1.14   Recommended aspects in relation to the sun

STATUTORY REQUIREMENTS LEGISLATION AND AUTHORITIES

A new 'two-tier' system of local government came into force in England and Wales on 1st April, 1974.

In London, local government is controlled by the Greater London Council (first tier) and by London Borough Councils (second tier). In England and Wales (outside London), local government is controlled by County Councils (first tier) and District Councils (second tier).

Six new counties (apart from London) have the status of Metropolitan Counties and the districts within these are Metropolitan Districts. The Metropolitan Counties are Greater Manchester, Merseyside, South Yorks, Tyneside, West Midlands and West Yorkshire.

In Scotland, local government is divided into counties, counties of cities (Aberdeen, Dundee, Edinburgh and Glasgow), large burghs and small burghs.

PLANNING

In general terms overall planning is the responsibility of the first tier while development control is that of the second tier councils.

All Town and Country Planning law in England and Wales is based on the Town and Country Planning Act, 1947. This Act has been modified on various occasions and current Acts relating to housing are:

Town and Country Planning Act, 1959
Town and Country Planning Act, 1962
Town and Country Planning Act, 1968
Town and Country Planning Act, 1971
Town and Country Planning Act, 1972
Town and Country Planning Act, 1974

CONSTRUCTION REGULATIONS

Statutory controls over the construction of housing are as follows:

(a) Inner London
The design, construction and use of buildings in the City of London and the Inner London Boroughs is controlled by legislation made under the London Building Acts, 1930–1939 and in By-laws made under these Acts. These Acts and By-laws are enforced by the G.L.C. through District Surveyors.

(b) England and Wales (outside the 12 Inner London Boroughs)
Construction regulations are based on the Public Health Acts 1939 and 1961 and, apart from certain minor local by-laws, are contained in the Building Regulations 1972 (with Amendments). Responsibility for the enforcement of these Regulations is that of the District Council.

(c) Scotland
Building Control is based on the Building (Scotland) Act, 1959 as amended by the Buildings (Scotland) Act, 1970. Various Regulations have been made under these Acts. Building Control is by a building authority appointed by the local authority.

OTHER LEGISLATION

Other legislation affecting housing includes:

(a) The Fire Precautions Act 1971. This currently applies to certain kinds of residential accommodation and is controlled by the fire authority (in consultation with the local authority).

(b) The Clean Air Acts 1956 to 1968. Where dwellings are within a designated smoke control area, grants may be obtained towards the cost of adapting any fireplace to burn only 'authorised fuels'.

(c) Housing Acts 1969 and 1974. Under this Act and subject to certain conditions, grants may be obtained towards the cost of providing new dwellings by conversion of existing buildings or for improving the standard of amenity of existing dwellings.

Under these Acts local authorities have the power to make grants or loans to Housing Associations towards the cost of the construction or improvement of dwellings.

(d) Airport Authority Act, 1965. Grants may be obtained towards the cost of insulating dwellings near airports against noise.

(e) Highways Acts 1959 and 1971.

(f) Noise Regulations 1973. The Highway Authority has a duty to pay a grant towards the cost of insulating a dwelling against noise arising from the use of a new highway.

DIRECTORY OF AUTHORITIES AND ORGANISATIONS

Building Centre Limited,
26, Store Street,
London WC1E 7BR

Building Societies Association,
14, Park Street,
London W.1.

Commission for the New Towns,
Glen House,
Stag Place,
London, S.W.1.

Council of Scientific Management in the Home,
26, Bedford Square,
London, W.C.1.

Department of the Environment,
Marsham House,
Marsham Street,
London, S.W.1.

Design Centre,
28, Haymarket,
London, SW1Y 4SU

Federation of Registered House Builders,
82, New Cavendish Street,
London, W.1.

Housing Centre Trust,
13, Suffolk Street,
London, S.W.1.

Housing Corporation,
Sloane Square House,
London, S.W.1.

Institute of Housing Managers,
Victoria House,
Southampton Row,
London, W.C.1.

National Building Agency,
NBA House,
Arundel Street,
London, WC2 3DZ

National Federation of Housing Societies,
86, Strand,
London, W.C.2.

National House Builders Registration Council,
58, Portland Place,
London, W1N 4BU

Scottish Home and Health Department,
St. Andrew's House 1,
Edinburgh EH7 5DG

For names and addresses of other organisations see volume on *Planning: Architects Technical Reference Data* (Directory section).

EXAMPLES

The following examples are typical of the types referred to in the text.

Brandon Estate, Southwark, London.
Architect: Hubert Bennett, Architect to L.C.C. (in succession to Sir Leslie Martin).
Mixed development including 18-storey point blocks, 7-storey slab blocks of maisonettes, 3-storey maisonettes over shops integrated with rehabilitated houses.
Architects' Journal (1st November, 1961).

Park Hill, Sheffield.
Architect: J.L. Womersley, City Architect.
Major redevelopment of central area site with flats and maisonettes varying in height from 4-storey to 14-storeys. A system of horizontal decks has been used as the main method of access which also retains the social virtues which existed in the old houses from which the tenants have moved. Completed 1960.
RIBA Journal (December, 1962).

Frome, Somerset.
Architects: Whicheloe and Macfarlane.
Small estate of courtyard houses. Winning design in a regional competition. Completed 1964.

Ravenscroft Road, West Ham, London.
Architect: Cleeve Barr.
Designed by MOHLG Development Group, to demonstrate Parker Morris standards in low cost 2-storey houses. Completed 1964.
Architects' Journal (28th October, 1964).

HOUSES AND FLATS

Canada Estate, Bermondsey, London.
Architect: Hubert Bennett, Architect to the L.C.C.
High density development 21-storey point blocks, 4-storey and 3-storey blocks of maisonettes and flats.
Architects' Journal (3rd February, 1965).

Dundee, Scotland.
Architects: Baxter, Clark & Paul.
Courtyard housing. A large development including single storey courtyard houses.
Architects' Journal (14th January, 1970).

Warley, Smethwick.
Architects: National Building Agency (R.C. Purdew, Chief Executive, Architectural Division).
Medium density 2-storey houses and flats. N.B.A.'s first metric housing development project based on recommendations of MHLG Design Bulletin 16. Completed 1971.
Architects' Journal (8th September, 1971).

Cheltenham Estate, North Kensington, London.
Architect: Erno Goldfinger.
Mixed development including high-rise and low-rise flats and communal facilities.
Architects' Journal (10th January, 1973).

Westminster and Southwark, London.
Architects: A. Rigby, Chief Architect, City of Westminster and Neylan & Ungless.
Small flats for couples and single people. This scheme demonstrates what can be done on a restricted urban site and is a good example of urban infill.
Architects' Journal (21st February, 1973).

Palace Fields, Runcorn, Cheshire.
Architect: R.L.E. Harrison, Chief Architect, Runcorn Development Corporation.
Single and two-storey houses all with garages attached or close to dwelling and with individual private garden.
Architects' Journal (9th October, 1974).

BIBLIOGRAPHY

Collymore, Peter *House conversion and renewal*, Architectural Press.
Hole, W.V. and Attenburrow, J.J. *Houses and people*, Building Research Station.
Donnison, D.V. *The Government of housing*, Penguin Books.
Goldsmith, Selwyn, *Wheelchair housing*, Architects' Journal (25th June 1975).

Homes for today and tomorrow (Parker Morris Report), H.M.S.O.
Home Storage, House and Garden.
Bathrooms, House and Garden.
Kitchens, House and Garden.
Housing the Elderly, M.T.P. Construction.
Housing the Family, M.T.P. Construction.
Metric House Shells, National Building Agency.
Single Storey Housing: Design Guide, National Building Agency.
Architects' Journal Design Guides on Housing and related subjects.
Published by the Architectural Press.

Design Bulletins. Published by Department of the Environment. (Some of these have been superseded by later Bulletins but much of the background information still holds good.)
1. Some aspects of designing for old people.
2. Grouped flatlets for old people.
3. Service cores in high flats.
5. Landscaping for flats.
6. Space in the home.
7. Housing cost yardstick.
10. Cars in housing (1).
11. Old people's flatlets at Stevenage.
12. Cars in housing (2).
13. Safety in the home.
14. House planning.
15. Family houses at West Ham.
16. Co-ordination of components in housing.
17. The family at home.
18. Designing a low rise housing system.
19. Living in a slum.
20. Moving out of a slum.
21. Families living at high density.
22. New housing in a cleared area.
23. Housing single people (1).
24. Spaces in the home.
25. The estate outside the dwelling.
26. New housing and road traffic noise.
27. Children and play.
28. Multi-purpose halls.
29. Housing single people (2).
30. Services for housing.
31. Housing for the elderly.

Architects' Journal Design Guides on Housing and related subjects published by Architectural Press.

Alfred J. Rowe ARIBA, *has been responsible for many housing projects both for a large commercial undertaking snd in private practice. He was previously with Edward D. Mills & Partners and worked with them on the National Exhibition Centre in Birmingham. He is now in private practice on his own account and has been responsible for many schemes of housing rehabilitation and projects involving the motor car.*

2 RESIDENTIAL HOSTELS

ANTHONY WYLSON, F.R.I.B.A., A.A. Dip. (Hons)

INTRODUCTION

Residential hostel accommodation is a wide ranging term covering communal living accommodation particularly in respect to single people. This covers a diversity of uses including accommodation for people in relation to temporary academic, employment or holiday situations, accommodation for single people in residential areas (for example unmarried or widowed people), accommodation close to employment or leisure facilities, residential clubs, serviced suites of rooms, and children's hostels, hostels for the physically or mentally handicapped and accommodation for homeless families.

In each category, there is a growing demand for single person accommodation and a dissatisfaction with present institutional or makeshift arrangements. The early independence of young people and changing social patterns are creating a great need for single person serviced accommodation that provides privacy and independence. There are factors governed by economic and social context, management, location and size. In many cases, provision of accommodation for single people will be of a modest scale through the conversion of existing houses.

ECONOMIC LEVEL

The method of financing a residential hostel is fundamental to the initial briefing. A local authority hostel for single people or a hostel run by a charitable organisation, will have a particular significance in the community structure. The former may be related to other local authority services (library, community club, clinic, senior citizens organisations); the latter may be related to church or synagogue.

The financing will determine the degree of independence of occupants, the use of dormitories or single rooms, communal facilities such as dining and leisure rooms, heating, hot water, maintenance, linen, clothes mending, laundry, shop, mail, car maintenance and recreational facilities.

MANAGEMENT

The method of controlling access, the degree of independence within the building and the general use of facilities will affect planning; for example, communal washing facilities as opposed to individual bathrooms, cooking facilities as opposed to cafeteria or restaurant, room key control, arrangements regarding cleaning and linen, maintenance of furniture and rooms, method of heating. The form of management will influence the optimum size of the hostel.

LOCATION

The function of the hostel will determine the most suitable location. A location that is sympathetic to the quality of life to be achieved within the hostel is important. Attachment to the local community should be considered if the hostel is providing an environment in place of family life.

A children's hostel would be away from a dangerous traffic situation, accessible to schools or closely associated with the particular school it aims to serve. It would also be related to recreational facilities. At the same time, consideration would be given to location in respect of staff accommodation and amenities.

A young single persons' hostel would be located near to the college, work catchment area or leisure activity that it serves. Consideration should also be given to the amenities available to the occupants. Where shift work is concerned a quiet situation is of great importance (i.e. a nurses' hostel).

An old persons' hostel requires careful siting, to be protected from unnecessary noise but at the same time to be part of the life of the community. Hostels for old people should be reasonably close to shops and such leisure facilities as cinemas. As most hostels are provided for those of lower income-groups it is important to avoid sites which are expensive, either in first cost or in maintenance or annual outgoings, in order to keep down rents.

SIZE

This will be determined by Clients' brief and site capacity. However, each hostel type has an optimum size in relation to construction, management, running and maintenance costs. The height of the building is significant to age of occupants and site location.

One particular study carried out by the Department of the Environment suggests that for middle-aged single person housing, 80 units is the maximum to make certain communal services economic, whereas personal contact between management and residents became difficult with over 200 people in a scheme.

SITING

SITES

Criteria vary with the particular type of hostel, though there are, however, common factors for most sites. Proximity to public transport linking hostel to places of work is of first importance.

Traffic access is necessary to service parts of all hostels for delivery of food, fuel and laundry and the collection of refuse. In most types of hostel no other traffic access facilities are needed beyond the occasional car or ambulance at main entrances.

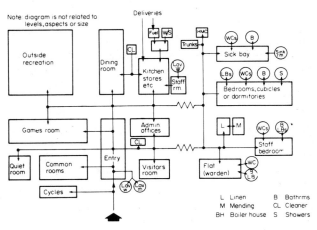

Fig. 2.1. General analysis

Sites need not necessarily be level; good use may often be made of falls or half-levels for storage and similar accommodation. Where outdoor recreational facilities are provided some reasonably level portions of the site are needed to avoid excessive installation costs. Terraces attached to the buildings can be a great summer asset.

ASPECT

As hostels are domestic buildings in continuous occupation for all seasons of the year, the aspects given to the various rooms should follow normal domestic allocations. Living-rooms and bedsitting-rooms should have positions receiving some sunlight even during the winter months. Less good aspects may be given up to kitchens, although pleasant working conditions should be achieved. Games rooms may be given the less sunny aspects, being mainly used during wet weather or in the evenings.

When hostels are planned in less crowded areas, it is desirable to include sufficient site area for a garden and for games (i.e. tennis), unless such facilities are already available in the neighbourhood or at the places of work to which the hostels may be attached.

Adequate public services such as drainage, water and power are essential. In the case of a few special situations, such as accommodation for agricultural or factory workers,

services would be provided within the site (e.g. a septic tank, a generator). A good water supply or ample water storage is important.

PLANNING

The basic planning, similar to hotels, must relate accommodation rooms or dormitories to service rooms and common facilities. Common rooms such as reception, adminstrative offices, dining room, cafeteria, kitchens, sick room, lounge, and leisure activities would be near the ground floor (Fig. 2.1).

In relation to bedrooms or dormitories, there would be service rooms (wash rooms, linen store, pantry or utility rooms) and common rooms to serve groups of bedrooms. Servicing the building will include vertical circulation, heating, ventilation, water supply, communications and fire protection and storage. Except where large dormitories are included, the planning problem is similar to hotels providing a structure that will suit small units of accommodation on the upper floors with the large spaces of communal rooms on the ground floor. Various types of basic plan are· shown in Figs. 2.2 and 2.3.

ENTRANCE

The entrance hall will serve as a reception and waiting area. Entrance from the street or drive should be provided with a draught lobby. It is normal for the purposes of control to have only one entrance. Consideration should be given to immediate needs of people using the hostel, such as changing rooms from dirty or wet clothes and boots, lavatory accommodation, telephone facilities, mail distribution, messages etc.

ADMINISTRATIVE OFFICES

Hostels are generally run by a manager, warden, matron or bursar. The office requires a central position which can supervise the main entrance. In small hostels, the office serves also as the warden's or matron's sitting room. The office should provide space for room keys, letter rack, desk, files, and a safe. In some cases the warden may have a separate suite, the general office being used by clerical staff.

In large hostels, a separate reception office and inquiry counter may be needed, as in a hotel. The office or enquiry counter should be at one side of the entrance hall and should have a counter or hatch. Where the hostel accommodates short-stay visitors, the entrance planning can be treated similar to that of a hotel. In some hostels the office also serves as a shop for articles such as stamps, toilette requirements, cigarettes and stationery.

VISITORS' ROOM

This is usually approached directly from the entrance hall and furnished as a normal sitting-room. It is generally used for the reception of residents' guests of the opposite sex or as a room where visitors may be taken for private and quiet conversation. Such a room is especially necessary where hostels provide only bedroom and dining-room accommodation.

COMMON ROOMS

All hostels need common rooms for day and/or evening use by residents, but areas and types may vary considerably. In common lodging-houses and those for very low income-groups a combined lounge-dining-room for each sex may be all that is provided; it may be based on an area of as little as 1m² per bed. In normal hostels for lower- and middle-income groups, a total area for common rooms, including dining-room, will usually amount to 1·8 m² per bed as a minimum. If it is desired to seat all the residents for meals at the same time, considerably more may be required. It can be assumed that a proportion of the residents will be out at any one time, except in hostels for old people and children. This may well affect the total space for these communal rooms. In general, smaller hostels need more common-room space per bed than larger ones.

Common-room space, apart from dining-rooms, should be divided between a number of areas for particular purposes such as sitting-rooms, quiet rooms and games rooms, the demand for which varies according to the type of resident. Common rooms are normally planned on the ground floor, although lower ground floors and even basements may be used for some purposes such as games rooms. In hostels for old people all rooms should be on the same level to avoid steps and, similarly, in children's hostels supervision is simplified if all the rooms are planned together in a group on one level. Common rooms should have plan shapes for a variety of uses. They should be well lit, with pleasant outlooks wherever this is possible.

It is not possible to give a proportional distribution of common-room space between various uses, as this varies according to the situation of site, type of hostel and residents' ages and occupations. (See Fig. 2.2).

LOUNGES

Several small rooms are more useful and better appreciated by users than one large room. Such rooms are more homely and less institutional. It should, however, be possible to open two or more rooms together for formal or larger social occasions. (See Fig. 2.2). Common rooms can, therefore, be planned *en suite*, but every effort should be made to check noise between them when in normal use, either by acoustic treatment or by initial planning.

The common rooms should be varied in shape and size and suitable for furnishing with normal domestic types of easy chairs and occasional tables arranged in groups. A piano is usually required in one room and provision should be made for radio and television. In some hostels television is confined to a special room. Some facilities should be provided near the lounges for the storage of part of the furniture when it is necessary to clear the rooms for dances, receptions, etc.

QUIET ROOMS

At least one room should be set aside for reading and writing, except perhaps in hostels with bed-sitting-rooms or study-bedrooms. The position of quiet rooms should ensure the maximum cut-off from other common rooms and par-ticularly any which may be the source of noise, such as games rooms. Good natural and artificial-lighting is essential.

The rooms are usually furnished with easy chairs and writing tables with suitable chairs.

OTHER COMMON-ROOM FACILITIES

Some hostels provide library facilities in the quiet room or provide for the loan of books from the office. In some hostels and especially those attached to teaching-establishments, a properly equipped library may be needed for the storage of books and for study purposes. Quite large areas may be needed and the plan should follow the lines given in the Sections 3 and 4 in *Planning: Buildings for Education, Culture and Science*.

Some hostels provide music practice-rooms. These can be small rooms, about 2.7 m by 1.8 m; they must be well insulated, by acoustic materials and by planned isolation, to avoid the transmission of sound to other parts of the building.

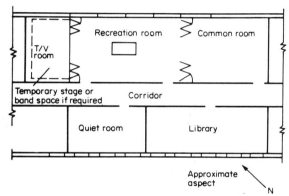

Fig. 2.2.   *Layout of common rooms in a hostel*

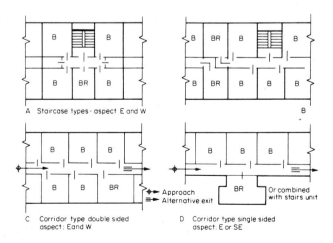

Fig. 2.3.   *Floor layouts for multi-storeyed hostels*
B. Bedrooms
Br. Baths, W.C.'s and L.B.'s.

GAMES ROOMS

In hostels for older residents, rooms may be needed for cards, chess and similar games. For younger people, rooms for more strenuous games such as table tennis, darts and even squash, are likely to be required. Billiards rooms are sometimes provided. In some large hostels facilities for swimming and physical training are provided.

Games rooms are sometimes used for dances and practice dances and should have a flooring material suitable for this use. Except where facilities such as a gymnasium or swimming pools are provided, it is often convenient to plan one large room for use for a variety of games.

FOOD SERVICE

Facilities may vary greatly. Many organisations do not provide midday meals for residents, except at week-ends, but provide midday meals for the staff only. Some hostels, however, such as those for old people, children and those attached to educational organisations have to provide for all meals, including afternoon tea. Other hostels, while not providing midday meals have to be prepared to issue packed lunches. Many have to provide meals spread over long periods of the day, as residents leave for or arrive from work at irregular times of both day and night.

Except in higher-rental types and those for old people and children, self-service is becoming general; this has considerable bearing on the planning of kitchens and serveries as it is then virtually essential that they are planned on the same floor level as the dining-rooms or canteens. The type of meal served also greatly affects kitchen layout, but generally hostels have set meals with only a small choice of dishes which simplifies the amount of room and equipment necessary.

In scholastic hostels or halls of residence there is an increasing tendency to provide all meals in a central dining-room, or college hall, although, in some cases, provision is made for students to take dinner and sometimes lunch in a main dining-hall and to provide other light meals or refreshments in their rooms. This arrangement necessitates more elaborate pantries and storage facilities associated with living-accommodation.

Before making detailed plans for catering facilities, it is important to consider the various requirements. These will include:

(a) *Meal patterns.* Establish the types of meals to be provided and whether there is a need to cater for special occasions. Also if any meals are served in a different location (i.e. midday meals).

(b) *Staffing.* It is important to provide good accommodation and attractive and efficient working conditions to attract high quality staff. Due to the high cost of efficient staff it may be necessary to have larger units.

(c) *Siting.* The kitchen should be kept near the main road to keep the access short. It should also be near the boiler house for the efficient supply of hot water.
Staff accommodation should be kept apart from the kitchens, so that staff off duty do not overlook their work.

When the positions of the kitchen and dining room (Figs. 2.4 and 2.5) have been established on the site, the following points should be considered before any detailed planning.

(a) *Relationship of kitchen, servery and dining room.* A single storey building is the most economical to operate and maintain and every attempt should be made to have the kitchen and dining areas at the same level.

(b) *Aspect.* A pleasant outlook for staff is desirable, especially in the preparation areas of the kitchen. If windows are at a high level worktops should be arranged so that staff can be looking across the room. Good lighting is important. Top lighting and ventilation can provide pleasant conditions as well as keeping the floor area free. The morning sun can make the area more cheerful without adding excessive solar heat. If possible the dining room should be free from columns to allow for flexibility in table layouts.

(c) *Plan.* The general circulation is an important factor in planning. Service entrances at the back of the kitchen, a square kitchen, a rectangular dining room with the entrance at one end and servery along one side, seem to provide the best arrangement.

(d) *Kitchen yard.* This must allow for turning space for the largest vehicles and possibly staff car parking. Refuse disposal units, sufficient bin storage, storage of returnable containers should be allowed for and the whole area well screened. Bins should be protected against dogs and it is advisable to provide a standpipe and hose near the bins for hosing down the area. Also a heavy duty gully should be provided.

Deliveries → Store → Prep. → Cooking → Serv. → Dining

Fig. 2.4.   Relationship of kitchen, servery and dining areas

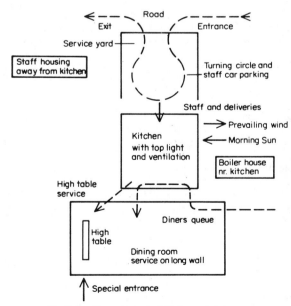

Fig. 2.5.   General layout of kitchen and dining room

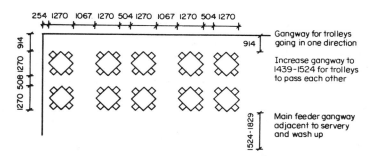

Fig. 2.6. Spacings for tables and chairs (informal dining)
Tables (914 × 914) each seating 4 people

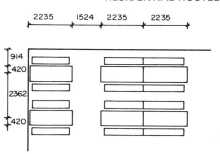

Fig. 2.7. Spacings for tables and benches (formal dining)
2 tables (2235 × 828) for 8 people
2 tables (1652 × 828) for 6 people

DINING ROOMS

Dining rooms for students, old people and children may have to seat the whole of the residents at one sitting. In other types of hostel, meals are programmed over longer periods and the dining room may be smaller as it is used in relays. Generally a floor area of at least 0·937 m² to 1·390 m² per person is necessary to permit table space and adequate gangways. This area has to be varied according to the type of table adopted as it will only be adequate if long tables seating eight or ten persons are used. (See Section 7 'Factories'). Tables for two or four persons are generally used in the higher rental types and these will require more space (Figs. 2.6 and 2.7). Detailed information on dining-room seating is given in Section 3 'Hotels, Motels and Camps for the Motorist'. The reader is referred to the same sources for various requirements for kitchens, cafeteria service, serveries, etc.

THE DINING AREA

Kitchen and dining room staff normally eat in the main dining room before or after the main meal service, so are not included in the total number for the purpose of calculating dining space.

The type of service to be used and the dining arrangements must be established before a satisfactory plan can be worked out. These types can be summarised under the following headings:

(a) *Continuous dining.* All meals are informal i.e. there is no formal start or finish to a meal. Diners are free to come or go within a given time and have a choice of menu. Either waiter or self service or a mixture of both may be used.

(b) *Single dining.* Certain meals are regularly eaten formally with everyone eating together. This is not true for all meals and can be just for formal occasions. As all food is required at the same time extra equipment and servery space would be needed.

(c) *Waiter service.* Usually only for special occasions. If more frequent, allowance must be made for waiters to come and go easily from the servery.

(d) *Family service.* Diners sit in 'family' groups. The food is brought to the table by one of the group or a waiter. Groups are usually 8 in number.

(e) *Mixed dining.* When one sitting is formal and another informal, usually the formal is the second sitting. When two dining rooms are served by one kitchen, one can be formal and the other informal. If this is considered it must be planned for both to be used continuously, or the informal dining becomes overloaded.

(f) *Service of informal meals.* Factors affecting efficient service include:

1. Number of meals.
2. Length of dining period.
3. Rate of service. Between 6 and 8 meals per minute can be assumed.
4. Time of meal. This may vary between 10 and 25 minutes.
5. Number of sittings.

Allow an approximate area for dining of 1·2 m² per diner. Seating can be in the form of benches or chairs along refectory tables, or chairs around tables.

Consider gangway spacings for movement of people and trolleys. Allow for spacings for a High Table if needed (Fig. 2.8) and general arrangements for cash payments, either at the end of the servery or near the exit depending on the type of service provided.

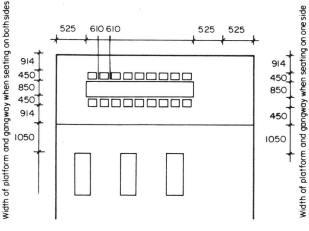

Fig. 2.8. Spacing for high table

KITCHEN AREA

The kitchen area comprises all the areas occupied by equipment, offices, stores, access, circulation etc. Kitchen planning (see Fig. 2.9) will depend on a variety of requirements including:

    (a) Number of meals.
    (b) Length of dining period.
    (c) Form of service.
    (d) Type of meal.
    (e) Range of menu.
    (f) Staff available.
    (g) Choice of equipment.

A detailed analysis of the equipment and accommodation requirements is vital. It is important to find out about any new kitchen equipment as this is continually being developed. It is then important to arrange the items in correct relationship to each other allowing for adequate access space.

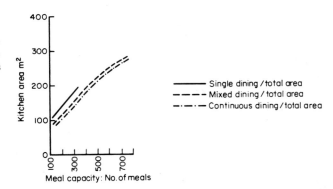

Fig. 2.9.   *Kitchen area related to meal capacity*

Staff accommodation

Staff are divided into two groups, kitchen and dining room staff. The total number of kitchen staff is approx. 1 person to 20 main meals served. But the number of people working in the kitchen at one time is 1 person for 25 main meals. The dining staff consists of waiters and dining room cleaners.
Staff lockers and lavatories. Each member of staff should have a locker, high enough to hang a coat and with a shelf. The locker should be well ventilated. The locker room should have a bench, not more than 600 mm run to every 8 lockers, and a mirror and a shelf.
1 wc for every 15 staff and 1 wash hand basin for each wc. It is a statutory requirement that one further wash hand basin should be in the working part of the kitchen.

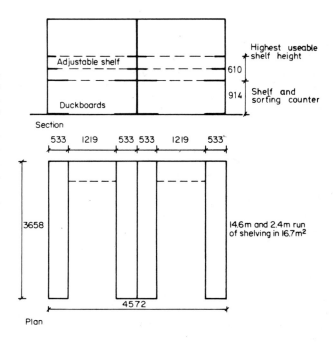

Offices

Cook Caterer. Office of not less than 3·7 m². This should have a view of working parts of kitchen.
Manager. With a meal capacity of 350 or more a manager and chef are needed; the manager's office should be at least 9·3 m² and the chef, 5·6 m².
With very large establishments an *assistant manager* and *clerk* would be employed each with an office about 5·6 m².
Storekeeper. If there is a storekeeper he would need at least 1·1 m² of space near the dry store from where he can check deliveries and keep records.

Storage

Stores should be planned close to their appropriate preparation area (see Fig. 2.10). Methods of storage consist of racks and shelves, which should be arranged for easy access.
    Sizes of stores vary with the number of meals to be served.
    Types of store: dry store; vegetable store; cold store; cool store; bread store; deep freeze.

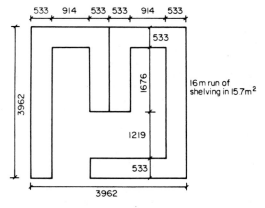

Fig. 2.10   *Dry store and vegetable store shelving*

Preparation

This covers the process between taking goods from the stores to the cooking, and can be divided as follows:
Vegetable preparation.
Preparation of pastry and sweets.
Meat and fish preparation.
Cold preparation.
Adequate worktop space must be allowed for in each area, also sinks, and refuse bins or bags.
The various items of equipment needed take up a lot of space. These items include, mincers, peelers, mixers, slicers etc.

Cooking

The various methods of cooking, requiring different equipment, are: Roasting or baking; Boiling; Steaming; Frying; Grilling.

Pre-service operations

This requires carefully positioned worktops for draining, mashing, straining of vegetables and slicing meat.

Service

The type of servery will depend on the type of service, queue speed, number of meals, range of menu, method of payment and whether beverages are served.
The counter should be able to be used for cafeteria service, family service and occasional waiter service. Therefore consideration should be given to display that can be screened, a top that can be cleared and access for people with trays or trolleys. The counter usually consists of a hot and cold section, a section for serving bread and butter etc. and a section for beverages.
The length of counter space for every 20 meals is 150 mm for each section in cafeteria service and 300 mm for 'family service.' If a bainmarie is incorporated in the hot section, the length allowed should be doubled.

Washing-up

The sequence of the washing up operation is as follows:

Arrival of clearing trolleys.
Stripping and stacking.
Racking and pre-rinsing.
Wash and rinsing.
Drying.
Returning to use or store.
There are many types of washing up and rinsing machines and racks. Allowance should be made for the washing of cooking equipment away from the preparation area.

Refuse disposal

Refuse can be as much as 0·03 m³ per week for every 8 diners. The types of refuse are:

(a) Containers. Boxes, cartons, bottles and tins, some of which are returnable to the manufacturers.

(b) Vegetable waste and unserved cooked food. This can be disposed of through a waste dilution unit discharging into a drain, or is sometimes sold as swill.

(c) Inedible preparation waste. i.e. bones, etc.

(d) Waste from washing up. This should not be added to saleable swill.

Non-returnable containers and other waste are either collected by the refuse collector, incinerated or put in a waste disposal unit.

OCCASIONAL MEALS

Since hostels must be considered as the homes of residents, some facilities for snacks and tea-making are sometimes required. These may be provided by the normal kitchen and dining-room service in those hostels which find it necessary and possible to provide staff over the long periods involved, but often alternative arrangements have to be made.
Some hostel organisers require small tea-kitchens or pantries near common rooms; others, and particularly when dealing with bed-sitting rooms or study-bedrooms, find that tea pantries are needed on bedroom or residential floors. When plans are based on the use of common staircases serving up to about four sets of rooms per floor, as in the so-called 'collegiate' type or halls of residence, one pantry will usually be found sufficient for four storeys (16 rooms). In most other types, however, one pantry per floor is the minimum needed, and it will be found that a single pantry will serve a large number of rooms in hostels of the corridor type assuming that adequate space and sufficient equipment are provided. In some schemes, cleaners' stores and even a resident's laundry may be combined in one group with the pantry and the whole service unit be placed on intermediate floors, more or less equidistant from all bedrooms.
The normal pantry equipment is two or more gas boiling-rings or electric kettles, a small griller, a sink and draining boards and a series of small ventilated lockers in which each resident may keep china and supplies. Two gas-rings will usually suffice for up to twenty persons unless whole meals such as breakfast have to be cooked. Most hostels discourage residents from keeping food, china and similar articles for meals in bedrooms or sitting-rooms.

RESIDENTS' KITCHENS, ETC.

Where these are required, for example, for single persons and in houses for the elderly, full facilities for communal meals are not provided, but the occupants do their own cooking. This is done by either planning kitchen recesses to bed-sitting rooms, as described in Section 1 'Houses and Flats', or else by providing common kitchens to house separately metered small cookers (with high-level small oven and hot-plate), etc for each person as illustrated in Figs. 2.11 and 2.12.

A series of ventilated larder and store cupboards is also needed, one for each person, and space for a number of preparation tables which may be shared by two or three persons. Several sinks are needed in order to permit several persons to wash up concurrently. It is desirable, in rooms for the able-bodied elderly, that facilities for tea-making should be available in each bed-sitting room.

STAFF MEALS

Wardens, managers and those having special rooms sometimes have meals served in their rooms and it is then necessary to plan suitable small service pantries in association with the rooms or flats in which the meals are taken. It is quite usual, however, for senior staff to take meals in the common dining-room with residents.

Domestic staff, if resident, are provided with all meals and often non-resident staff have a proportion of meals at the hostel. It is therefore essential to provide a staff dining-room near the kitchen and servery. This should not also be the staff sitting-room, for which separate provision should be made.

HEATING AND HOT WATER SUPPLY

Hot water

Constant hot water is now essential in hostels of all types. It should be borne in mind, however, that the demand may be a variable one and likely to be concentrated within early-morning and late-evening peak periods. Considerable storage may therefore be required and time-lag factors must be reduced as much as possible.

The normal demand may be taken to be at least 68 litres at 49°C per head per day and this may be much larger in high rental types or in those hostels providing large restaurant or canteen or full laundry facilities where higher temperatures may also be needed.

Heating

Some form of central heating will be required in the common rooms of practically all hostels, except the smallest types, where heat might be reasonably provided by solid fuel or gas or electric fires. Some hostels do not provide heating in bed-rooms. The demand for this service, however, is rapidly in-creasing, particularly where there are dormitories, which do not permit easy installation of alternative methods.

For bed-sitting rooms or study bedrooms central heating may be required to provide either general background heating or the sole means of heating. Where used for background heating purposes only, supplementary gas or electrical heaters are usually installed, as the demand for heating tends to be varied and intermittent. Children's hostels and those for old people should have central heating throughout.

Cold water

Cold-water storage should be designed on a basis of at least 91 litres per bed per day. It is better to allow for 136 to 180 litres, especially if a hostel is planned with fully equipped kitchens and/or laundry.

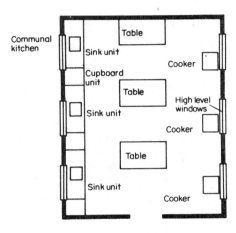

Fig. 2.11. Residents' communal kitchen

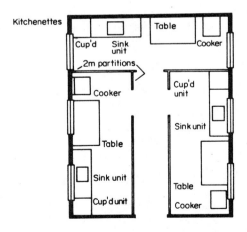

Fig. 2.12. Resident's kitchenettes

ACCOMMODATION—SLEEPING

It has already been stated that most hostels are to a greater or lesser degree affected by legislation. The over-crowding requirements of Section 57 and the Fifth Schedule of the Housing Act, 1936, and Section 10 of the Housing Act, 1949, may be assumed to control minimum floor space for all sleeping-rooms in hostels, except those which should be controlled by DES regulations for schools.

The smallest space per person required in a dormitory is 4·6 m² and 6·5 m² should be the area allowed for the smallest bedroom. Some dormitories for juveniles have been planned on an allowance of 3·7 m², but this would seem to be undesirably small.

If bedrooms are designed to accommodate more than one person, 10·2 m² should be the minimum for two adults and 14·8 m² for three adults. For any hostels other than those to be let at the lowest rentals, these minimum areas can well be increased considerably and it will be found that single rooms at 8·8 m² to 9·2 m² are often required, inclusive of fixed furniture or fittings such as cupboards.

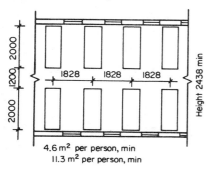

Fig. 2.13. Open dormitory

When, however, bedrooms are to serve as bed-sitting rooms, especially if they are to be occupied for long periods as in students' hostels, floor areas should be calculated at not less than 10·2 m² per person and are better if in the 11 m² to 13 m² range. Double bed-sitting rooms should be at least 16·7 m² to 18·5 m² in area. It is important that minimum room widths be considered in association with the floor areas mentioned above. Single rooms should be at least 2·4 m wide (but preferably 3 m) and double rooms at least 3·6 m, if adequate allowance for comfortable layout is to be provided.

Privacy in bedrooms depends largely on the amount of rent the occupier is willing to pay; although in some hostels for young adults, especially females, there is a preference for sharing rooms. When rooms are shared it is often necessary to provide for a minimum of three persons. The maximum number of persons in a dormitory should not generally exceed 20 and smaller numbers are to be preferred.

Sleeping accommodation also varies considerably according to the type of resident and his or her vocational activities. Dormitories are usually required in some industrial hostels, children's hostels and hostels for juveniles.

In hostels attached to educational establishments single study-bedrooms have become almost universal, but a few double rooms are sometimes included; in university hostels there is often a demand for bedrooms and sitting-rooms or studies to be separate rooms and designed as a suite. Separate bedrooms are desirable in old people's hostels and in such projects some rooms of flatlets may be needed for married couples.

It should be emphasised again that the type of sleeping-accommodation and the constructional spans involved to provide it economically have a very considerable effect on the planning of the building as a whole. In other words, the layout of upper bedroom floors tends to dictate the spans available for, and therefore the planning of, the common rooms on lower floors.

DORMITORIES

Open dormitories are needed in certain types of hostel. It will be seen from Fig. 2.13 how 4·6 m², the normal minimum floor area per person, can be set out. More area, however, is desirable if adequate space is to be provided between beds for circulation and for storage accommodation.

Dormitories or cubicles should provide a minimum of 4·6 m² of floor area per person and about 11·3 m³ of air per person. The sizes set out for dormitories in boarding schools are, perhaps, a better standard.

The use of dormitories raises storage problems for clothing and other personal property, and dressing-tables may be needed. It is desirable in all dormitories to provide a bedside locker, or alternatively a dressing-chest, and either may be built-in fitments. Dressing-tables or chests at the rate of one per person can be provided at the end of the dormitory room, in the central gangway where there is sufficient width, or adjacent to each bed where the layout permits. Facilities for hanging clothes can be provided by wardrobe cupboards at the ends of the room or in a separate locker-room adjoining the dormitory. Except in children's dormitories, a chair at least should be provided for each bed. In better types of hostels care should be taken that the placing of artificial light makes it possible to read in bed without inconveniencing adjoining occupants. It is important that opening lights in windows are close to the ceiling and any opening portion should be designed to eliminate side draughts.

Dormitories divided into cubicles with permanent part-height partitions, curtains, or a combination of the two, are needed in many hostels. This type of accommodation may be planned in a variety of ways as shown in Fig. 2.14. Type A shows a dormitory occupying the full span which may be as little as 5 m wide. Whatever span is used, the cubicle widths should not be reduced below 2·1 m and 2·4 m is better to give sufficient space for furniture and comfortable movements of the user. If tall hanging-cupboards are provided in each cubicle it is better if partitions are used in preference to curtains; this has some bearing on the type of bed-layout used. In plans of Type A, partitions are often used between units and curtains only to form the central passage division. A window should be provided for each cubicle in this type of plan.

Type B (Fig. 2.14), showing beds grouped in the centre of the dormitory, has the advantage that beds do not come immediately under windows; therefore there is less likelihood that windows will be closed and thus cut off cross-ventilation. Open dormitories are also planned on this arrangement of beds with a dwarf bulkhead partition, about 1·5 to 1·8 m in height in the centre of the room, into which the beds and dressing-chests between the beds can be recessed. In Type B it is better if the central division is always a partition rather than a curtain. This type, it should be noted, calls for wider spans than Type A owing to the double passageways. It is undesirable to use solid partitions at the front of this type of cubicle as the air circulation may be reduced excessively thereby. It will be noted also that greater latitude in window spacing is possible with Type B.

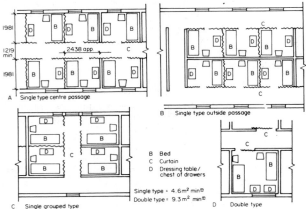

Fig. 2.14. *Layouts of dormitories. Cubicles in dormitories*

Type C is a development of grouped beds, in which the passageway is kept to one side of the room and the beds are planned parallel to the length of the room; this avoids beds facing windows. This type is best with partitions across the room and curtains parallel to the outside walls, to avoid the central cubicles being too dark or badly ventilated.

Type D shows a form of double cubicle formed entirely with partitions 1·8 m high, with curtains used at the entrance to each compartment. This is slightly more economical in floor space as the dressing space may be reduced a little. When this type is used the curtained entrances should be staggered as shown.

Another type, often used, takes the form of small cubicles, with doors, exactly similar to single bedrooms as shown in Fig. 2.17, Type A or Type D, but taking divisions to a height of only 1·8 m or 2 m instead of up to the ceiling.

Where solid partitions are used the materials used should be reasonably fire-resisting. Partitions should be at least 1·8 m high and the room height such that there is a clear 0·6 m above them. Partitions are often kept 200–300 mm clear of the floor, except at structural supports, in order to facilitate cleaning.

Fig. 2.15 shows two types of 'open' dormitory for various kinds of school and for seasonal buildings such as agricultural hostels. Type A is arranged to give 7.4 m² per person with two beds in each bay on each side of the wing or span; Type B shows six beds per compartment, two on one side and four on the other, arranged to provide the minimum area of 4·6 m² per person.

BEDROOMS

Fig. 2.16 shows separate bedrooms. Diagram A shows minimum-sized bedrooms on either side of a common corridor. Corridors serving bedrooms should not be less than 1·2 m wide for comfortable circulation and for handling baggage and furniture.

The width should be increased when longer than about 9 m. Double doors have to be accommodated to cut off stairs, etc.

Doors to rooms on opposite sides of a corridor should be staggered and not be opposite to one another.

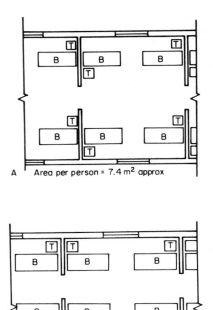

Fig. 2.15. *Layouts of dormitories. Divided dormitories*

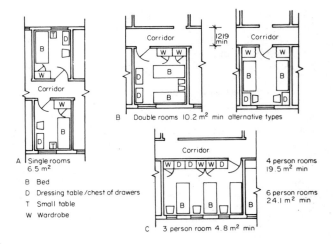

Fig. 2.16. *Bedroom layouts*

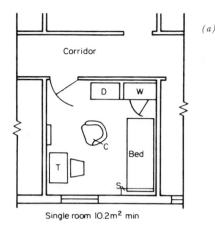

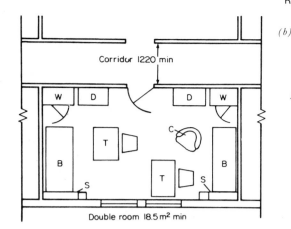

Single room 10.2m² min

Double room 18.5m² min

Fig. 2.17. *Layout of single and double bed-sitting rooms*

B. *Bed*
C. *Armchair*
D. *Dressing table/ chest of drawers*
S. *Bookshelves*
T. *Table*
W. *Wardrobe*

It will be seen that with a minimum amount of furniture, namely a single bed, bedside table, dressing-chest, hanging cupboard and a chair, very little movement space is left for the occupier in an area of 6·5 m²: thus an increase over this minimum should be provided whenever possible.

In such small rooms it is of first importance to place windows and doors carefully so as to leave adequate space for the bed; positions other than in the centre of the rooms are generally advantageous. Except in very low-rental types allowances for bed-spaces should be 1950 by 900 mm. Whenever possible beds should not have a long side against a wall as this complicates bedmaking. Bedside tables should be based on 380 × 380 mm, dressing-chests on 900 × 455 mm, wardrobes or hanging cupboards on 600 to 900 by 550 mm and chairs assumed to be 455 × 455 mm.

Diagram B shows two alternative plans for two minimum-sized bedrooms; one with the beds along the division wall and the other with bed-heads against the division wall. In each example, windows and doors are planned in relation to the beds in the room. Again it will be seen that the minimum floor space of 10·2 m² is very small for comfort and should be increased whenever possible to allow the full quota of furniture for each person being installed as recommended above for single bedrooms.

Diagram C illustrates a room for three beds based on the minimum floor area of 14·8 m²; this permits only a minimum amount of furniture and it is forced into positions which are bad in relation to daylight and windows.

It is advantageous to plan wardrobes, whether loose or built-in, against corridor walls, to reduce the incidence of noise from corridor traffic. In many schemes fanlights are required over room doors so as to light and ventilate the corridor. It is, however, better to avoid these in order to reduce noise; also, the light in one room may be disturbing to the occupants of another. As corridors are likely to serve as the main means of escape in case of fire, fanlights, when used, may be required to be fixed and glazed with wired glass, in which circumstance corridor ventilation must be obtained in other ways, for example, at the ends or by means of occasional bays opening on to windows and the open air.

STUDY BEDROOMS AND BED-SITTING ROOMS

Fig. 2.17 shows three typical study-bedrooms or bed-sitting rooms based on minimum floor areas. The rooms should be laid out to provide space for the following furniture in addition to reasonable circulation space: Bed; desk or writing table; bookshelves; a single chair; dressing-chest; wardrobe or hanging cupboards full height of room. In many schemes it is necessary to plan also for a fire; this is generally either electric or gas, either with or without slot-meters. In most modern schemes, however, a central-heating installation can be assumed, at any rate for background heating. Space must, therefore, be found for radiators and, if the latter are only to provide general background heating, space must be allowed for an electric or gas fire in addition.

Fig. 2.17(a) shows a single room in which window and door are kept to one side to avoid the bed and also to provide good working light for the desk table. The minimum area is about 10·2 m².

Fig. 2.17(b) shows double rooms with minimum floor areas of 18·5 m² and is based on using a wide frontage and narrow span.

A small but important matter connected with hostel bedrooms is accommodation for damp towels; these usually are kept in the bedrooms and not in the lavatories; rooms should therefore be provided with a towel rack or rail in such a way that dampness does not cause damage to furniture or decorations. Where hot-water radiators are installed a towel-rail can be combined.

SUITES

Where suites of rooms are required these should be planned on the recommendations given in Section 1 'Houses and Flats'. Bedrooms may lead directly out of sitting-rooms, but on no account should the approach from outside the suite be through the bedroom to the sitting-room.

STAFF BEDROOMS

These should be planned away from the general hostel bedrooms, or be cut off from them, or approached by way of separate service staircase. This accommodation may take the form of dormitories or be provided in double or single rooms (see also Section 3).

ACCOMMODATION—SPECIAL ROOMS

BAGGAGE

Storage of residents' baggage becomes an important matter if small bedrooms or studies are to be kept reasonably unencumbered. Although some accommodation for suitcases may be possible in cupboards in the rooms, it is usual to provide special baggage accommodation.

The requirements can be divided into two parts: firstly the main trunk room where large and heavy baggage is stored and to which the residents do not require frequent access; secondly, small store rooms on each bedroom floor for suitcases and similar light luggage which may be needed more frequently for week-ends and holidays. It should be remembered that frequently hostels are almost the only homes of residents, who have no other place to leave or store property. There are, of course, some types of hostel which require very little baggage-storage space, such as children's hostels and those catering mainly for visitors or workers staying for short periods.

A main baggage or trunk room should provide for storing approximately 0·5 m³ per person, in such a manner that all articles stored are accessible without need to move other property. The room can be in the basement or similar unimportant position if dry and well-ventilated.

The room should be fitted with strong shelving for trunks, etc. The width of the gangways between shelving should be sufficient to allow standing-room while withdrawing a bulky trunk from a shelf. For hand-baggage rooms near to the users' bedrooms, any unimportant space may be used, so long as it is dry and ventilated. These rooms also should be fitted with strong shelving, though it is possible to reduce the gangways by about 450 mm in width, and a third tier of shelving might be added.

CARETAKER'S CUPBOARD

A properly planned service room or caretaker's cupboard should provide for storage of supplies and materials together with all the necessary cleaning appliances, and a properly designed slop-sink with a draining-board.

These rooms should be associated with the sanitary accommodation in order to assist services; they should have daylight or ample alternative ventilation. Shelving is needed for materials and suitable racks and hooks for brooms, etc., and facilities for drying clothes, etc.

LINEN AND MENDING

Two rooms are generally needed in all larger hostels for the handling and maintenance of linen; in small hostels one room is usually adequate for storage and repairs. The main linen room has to serve for the bulk storage of linen; from it subsidiary linen rooms on the bedroom floors are supplied; it also has to serve as the space for the sorting of clean and dirty linen coming from and going to the laundry. The area is, of course, dependent on the size of the hostel and also on whether the personal laundry of the residents is also to be dealt with e.g. the larger quantities generally necessary in hostels for children or men.

A second room is required for the use of the staff which repairs linen. More space will again be wanted if residents' clothing is also repaired by the linen-room staff. (See Section 3.)

CLOAKROOM

Some cloaks space situated conveniently near the entrance and the dining-room is needed in most hostels where residents may leave outdoor clothing without the necessity of going to their bedrooms.

In hostels for children and in those where working-clothing is always changed on entering the building, cloakrooms may also be needed near secondary entrances. In hostels for students, cloakrooms may be required also to act as changing-rooms for games purposes and some bathroom or shower accommodation adjoining may become necessary.

In the normal type of cloakroom it is usual to provide racks with hat-and-coat pegs and umbrella stands, but in some, more elaborate coat-hanger equipment is installed; hat-and-coat pegs should be placed at 300 mm centres on single rows for adults and at 250 mm centres for adolescents. Cloakroom equipment for children should follow school practice. Smaller cloakrooms may also be needed in association with visitors' rooms, especially to cater for visitors of the opposite sex and for social occasions; in most cases these should have sanitary accommodation attached.

SUNDRY SPECIAL ROOMS, ETC.

The following accommodation is sometimes required in addition to that usually required and already detailed.

Room for boot and shoe cleaning: on each bedroom floor, adjacent to the personal laundry room (if provided).

Cycle storage, may be in separate closed or open sheds, or in the basement; ramps (1:12) being provided for the latter position.

Changing rooms and/or lavatories for non-resident staff, preferably on the ground floor and near staff entrance. Staff common rooms may be required in the larger type of hostels.

A male porters' changing room and/or lavatory may be a special requirement in connection with women's hostels in which only a few men are employed. Such staff may be resident or non-resident, according to circumstances.

GUEST ROOMS

Some hostels, especially those for middle and high income-groups, set aside one or two bedrooms for visitors which may be hired by the residents for their guests, but it is doubtful if space will normally be afforded for this purpose or this accommodation be sufficiently remunerative for general adoption.

SICK ROOM

In all types of hostel provision should be made for residents with minor illnesses, except perhaps for those in single rooms. Single- or double-bed wards or sick-bays are usually provided at the rate of about one bed per 50 residents. The rooms should be rather larger than the normal single hostel bedroom—about 9·2 m² for single rooms and 18·5 m² for two-bed wards. The wards should provide at least 22·6 m³ of air space per bed and beds should be planned to be at least 1·8 m apart. Sick rooms are generally planned near the sleeping accommodation of whoever may have to look after the patients, e.g., matron, warden or housekeeper. Sick rooms should have separate service and sanitary facilities comprising bathroom, wc, kitchenette, cupboard and small store room.

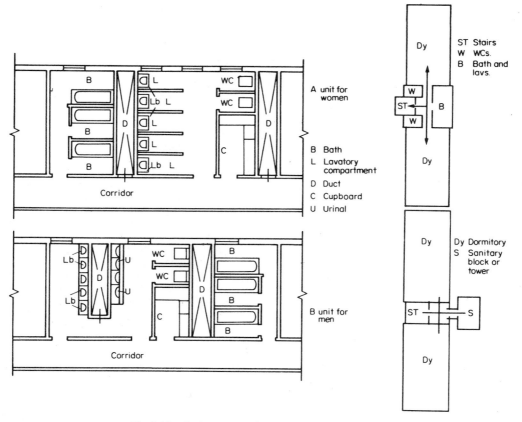

A unit for women

B Bath
L Lavatory compartment
D Duct
C Cupboard
U Urinal

B unit for men

ST Stairs
W WCs.
B Bath and lavs.

Dy Dormitory
S Sanitary block or tower

Fig. 2.18. Sanitary accommodation common to several bedrooms

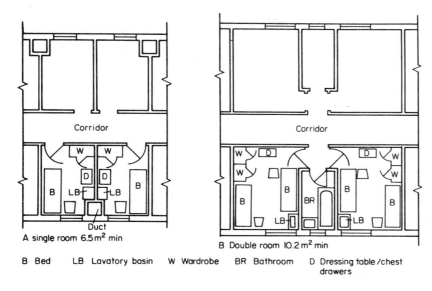

A single room 6.5 m² min

B Double room 10.2 m² min

B Bed   LB Lavatory basin   W Wardrobe   BR Bathroom   D Dressing table/chest drawers

Fig. 2.19. Lavatory basins in single rooms; sanitary accommodation shared by two rooms

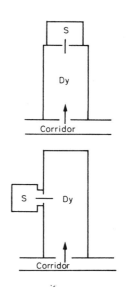

Fig. 2.20. Position of sanitary accommodation
Dy. Dormitory S. Sanitary unit

SANITARY ACCOMMODATION

Some accommodation should be planned on the ground floor or basement for daytime use and in connection with common rooms. In some types such as those for children and old people and common lodging-houses this is likely to be the greater part of the total accommodation. When bed-sitting-rooms reduce the common-room areas a larger part of the total sanitary accommodation should be distributed among the bedroom floors. In hostels for young children the ground-floor accommodation should be planned in close proximity to the day-rooms as in nursery schools.

The distribution of the necessary fittings throughout any hostel is much influenced by the type of resident and especially by whether bed-sitting rooms are provided, as these probably mean that the bedroom floors are used to a greater extent during longer hours per day; thus more fittings are needed on these floors and less on the ground-floor and/or common-room levels. It will also be obvious that the relative proportions of the bedroom and common-room accommodation will also affect plan locations.

The number of sanitary fittings required is variable, but the following figures may be taken as a general guide:

W.C.s: two per ten persons.

Baths: one per ten persons.

Basins: one per three persons (min).

A proportion of the baths may be provided in the form of showers. The installation of showers in hostels for old people is seldom required.

It is desirable that basins be provided in all single bedrooms and in bedrooms for two persons, but if bedrooms are shared by more than two persons it is better to place the basins in lavatory groups convenient to a number of rooms. Where basins are grouped it is usual to keep them separate from the baths. The entrance end of the cubicle (opposite to the basin) may be open or fitted with a curtain (see Fig. 2.18). When a number of basins is used in lavatories it is better if the basins are spaced apart to provide ample elbow-room, rather than to use ranges where the basins are abutting.

Where bed-sitting rooms or study bedrooms are used (see Fig. 2.19) opinions vary greatly as to whether or not basins should be installed, but there seems to be an increasing preference for basins where the resultant cost of widespread plumbing installation can be met. It is desirable, however, that basins should be so placed in rooms that they can be screened easily, or shut away within fitments.

Where the plumbing services are widely distributed, it is better to distribute bathrooms rather than to concentrate them in groups. The cost is not thereby increased and users have the minimum distance from bedrooms to bath and an additional degree of privacy. Such an arrangement is shown in Fig. 2.19, Diagram B, where a bathroom is planned between two adjoining bedrooms, thus the basins in the adjoining rooms and the bathroom fittings use common services.

The wc allocation may be reduced in men's hostels, if sufficient urinals are provided.

In children's hostels the number of sanitary fittings should be based on the requirements for schools, according to the age-groups to be catered for.

The placing of sanitary accommodation relative to dormitories often presents difficulties. It will be preferable to plan sanitary units between the main circulation (staircases or corridors) and the dormitories (see Fig. 2.18). Thus two dormitories may often be served by one combined unit, with corresponding simplification of plumbing and services. In such a position access from dormitory to sanitary unit does not waste space in the dormitory.

Sanitary units planned at ends of the dormitories opposite the entrance to the room or on the sides of the latter tend to cause disturbance, especially in hostels where residents get up or go to bed at widely varying times.

Staff, both resident and non-resident, must, in any large hostel, have their own sanitary accommodation located in the parts of the building most used by them. Managers, housekeepers and similar officials usually have a bathroom and wc as a unit within their flat or attached to their rooms.

LAUNDRIES

Few hostels are sufficiently large to require independent laundries. In order, however, to discourage residents from using lavatory basins for washing clothing, many hostels for women and even some of those for men provide special facilities for residents to do personal laundry. The equipment normally provided is one washtub per 25 and one ironing-board per 20 persons, and a number of small drying cabinets. Consideration should be given to the possibility of installing washing machines. Such laundry facilities are usually installed in separate rooms on bedroom floors, adjacent to the general sanitary accommodation, to simplify plumbing; in some schemes it has been found advantageous to plan the laundry in a group with the tea-pantry. Adequate electric or gas points should be provided, at suitable levels above the floors for irons, washing machines and drying machines as required.

Special hairdressing and washing facilities are often provided in women's hostels. These should take the form of one or two basins in a room of about 9·2 m² in area, in which also space should be planned for well-lit dressing-tables and mirrors; some plugs for electric hair-driers, etc., may also be needed as part of this equipment.

STUDENT HOSTELS

INTRODUCTION

Although students use a wide variety of buildings during their studies, this sub-section considers buildings used exclusively by students, i.e. student residential buildings and student union buildings. Student residential buildings can be broadly divided into two categories (i) Halls of Residence; (ii) Houses or Hostels.

HALLS OF RESIDENCE

Traditionally, apart from lodgings, Halls of Residence have been the usual accommodation provided for students. The case for Halls of Residence for university students was made in the Report of the sub-committee on Halls of Residence, in the Niblett Report published by the University Grants Committee in 1957. Niblett-type Halls are basically study-bedroom blocks off a central corridor with communal ablution facilities on each floor, usually with communal dining room, lounge, games room, laundry room, etc at ground level. The Halls were designed as single sex and sometimes sited at considerable distance from educational facilities. This type of accommodation proved to be wasteful in the overprovision of space provided for communal activities that were infrequently used.

An example of a Niblett-style residence was built at Southampton University (Fig. 2.21); adapted forms of Niblett Halls followed, including a Hall of Residence built at Reading University and designed by UGC Architects in 1964 (Fig. 2.22). In designing this building the UGC set out to demonstrate the standards of fittings, finish and design which could be achieved within its own cost limits. It housed two hundred students, forty attached students, four dons, and the administrative staff. The Hall was planned with 'groups' made up from seven to thirteen study-bedrooms in order that the student should feel he was part of a family group. All furniture in the room was loose and could be arranged in different layouts; adequate bookshelves and pin-up spaces were provided.

The Building Research Station in its Hostel User Study of 1965–66 states that 'at some of the eight schemes visited there was evidence to show that management and residents would welcome means whereby residence facilities could be broken down into smaller groups thus forming household groups of study-bedrooms for up to twelve people, some with their own lobby and entrance and kitchen/common room'.

The Report states that 'there are no ideal sizes for such household groups but twenty-five persons seems a maximum'. In addition to the changing social requirement, the trend away from Halls of Residence has been brought about by financial constraints, which have made it almost impossible for the architect to design a Niblett-type Hall of Residence; he is forced to develop new forms based on low-cost housing and a social unit of 6–8 students. It would appear that the smaller social unit is very much welcomed by some students, particularly if the unit can be provided with adequate social space.

LOAN FINANCE RESIDENCES

Loan finance residences were adopted in 1968. The principle behind loan finance residences is that the University borrows money at commercial rates of interest to make up the difference between the 25% (maximum) subsidy and the actual cost, ie on a unit costing £2000 (maximum) per student, the University has to borrow £1500 (1974 figures). The loan is then serviced from the rent income received from the student. In addition to servicing the loan the student's rent must pay for heating, lighting, cleaning, maintenance and management costs.

This method of financing has caused some Universities difficulty to achieve cost limits, and the cost control becomes apparent when compared to other prestige University buildings or to earlier subsidised Halls of Residence. Notwithstanding the financial restraints, a number of interesting schemes have been completed. (See Examples).

SITING

The siting of residential accommodation in universities is normally determined by the layout of the master plan. In this way the siting of residential buildings will be considered with the siting requirements of other buildings.

Most university buildings are on a different scale from residential buildings, and where in the past it was possible to obtain an architectural grouping between university academic buildings and Niblett-style Halls of Residence, there is a much more difficult problem of scale in siting domestic housing in close proximity to academic buildings. Many students have complained that residences are often sited much too far away from the social focus of universities, and would like to see student accommodation forming the heart of a university.

In siting residential accommodation, provision must be made for access for fire-fighting vehicles and ambulances. Easy access should also be available for the collection and containing of refuse prior to removal. Adequate provision should be made for car parking, both for students and their their visitors, although it is unlikely that any such provision can be made within a loan-financed scheme.

PLANNING

Figs. 2.23 and 2.24 show typical layouts of study bedrooms, one loan financed, the other UGC financed.

MAINTENANCE

In selecting materials and finishes the architect should go for robust construction and hard-wearing finishes, but because of the stringent cost criteria, architects are often left with no alternative but to select materials at a lower initial cost knowing that higher recurrent maintenance costs will result.

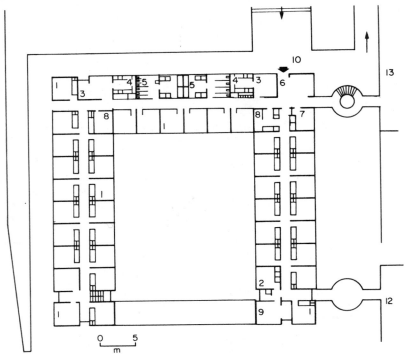

1. Study/bedroom
2. Bedroom
3. Dining
4. Kitchen
5. Lavatories
6. Waiting
7. Porter
8. Store
9. Don's flat. Living room
10. Main entrance
11. Car park
12. Future hall
13. Completed hall

Fig. 2.21.   Niblett Type Hall, Southampton University. Ground Floor plan

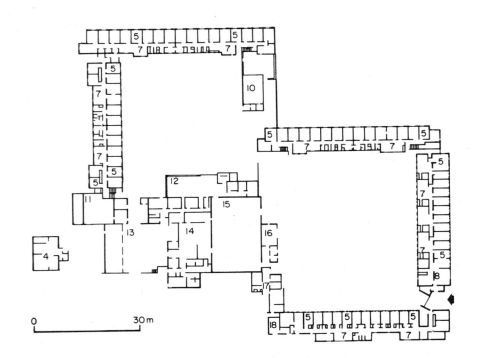

4. Staff house
5. Study/bedrooms
7. Pantry
8. Porter's room
9. Guest rooms
10. Music room
11. Boiler house
12. Junior common room
13. Kitchen yard
14. Kitchen
15. Dining hall
16. Senior common room
17. Warden's house
18. Garage

Note. Library, games room
and Don's set not shown

Fig. 2.22.   Typical Niblett type plan developed by UGC Reading University

SPACE REQUIREMENTS

The basic space provision is for a separate study-bedroom for each student, although in some cases sharing a room by two persons may be an alternative. Additional facilities required are: A kitchen for self-catering; some common room/social space; washing and sanitary accommodation; laundry facilities.

THE STUDY/BEDROOM

The area of study bedrooms provided under loan finance residences has varied from a maximum of 10·6 m² to a minimum of 7·01 m² the average size study-bedroom being 9·16 m². The architect may reduce the size of the study-bedrooms in order to provide more kitchen or social space. The small area of the study-bedrooms does restrict the arrangement of the space, and many architects have adopted room sizes with the depth greater than the width, the average dimensions of study-bedrooms being 3·50 m × 2·50 m.

If the width is reduced to under 2·25 m then problems may

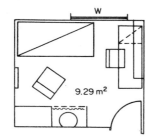

Fig. 2.23. Typical loan finance solution

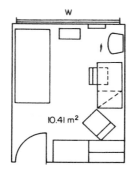

Fig. 2.24. Typical UGC finance solution

arise obtaining adequate daylighting into the rear of the room; also the room may become less flexible for the varying of furniture layouts. Design solutions which require permanent electrical lighting should be avoided because of the high maintenance costs.

THE KITCHEN/SOCIAL AREA

All student accommodation should include a self-catering kitchen where students can prepare a meal for themselves.

The role of the kitchen has considerably changed. Until quite recently the kitchen was thought of as the place where a kettle could be boiled or a tin of soup heated. There is now a very increasing emphasis on the kitchen and cooking facilities in order to meet the rise in self-catering students and to provide much needed social space where the 'family' group can meet. The provision of adequate kitchen and social space may lead to a reduction in the size of the study bedrooms.

The number of students sharing kitchens in existing student accommodation varies considerably from 6 up to about 25. Many universities have found 5–6 persons to be the ideal; this can then be developed into a family group.

With regard to the social area, many loan-financed schemes have not provided adequate space, either within the kitchen or adjacent to it, for social purposes. This is usually due to the cost restraints rather than the architect's choice; briefs request the architect to provide a design solution at a minimum capital cost in order to keep rents down to a minimum. The provision of some social space is extremely important, if a family spirit is to be generated, even if cost restraints produce smaller study-bedrooms.

SANITARY FACILITIES

The ratio of the provision of bathrooms and lavatories for students is left to the client's brief or architect's discretion within the cost limit. The ratio of sanitary provision has varied between the following:

No. of students per	w.c.	Bath	Shower	Washbasin
Minimum	2·7	3·0	3·0	0·8
Maximum	7·5	35	22	6

The average figure generally compares with the suggested ratio of one wc to every five or six students, and one bath or shower to every five or six students. If the accommodation is to be used for Conference letting during vacations, it is essential that the study-bedrooms be provided with a wash basin, as conference organisers are reluctant to accept accommodation without this amenity.

Considerable doubt exists as to whether or not students prefer baths to showers. While showers take up less space and consume less water, it is believed that there is a preference for baths, particularly if no basin is provided in the study-bedroom. The ideal is to provide the variety of a bath and a shower; and if space and/or cost prevents this, then a bath is probably likely to satisfy more needs, particularly if it has shower facilities combined over the bath.

The provision of a utility room under loan-financed arrangements is extremely difficult; particularly for the small family group of 5–6 students, although it is an essential requirement.

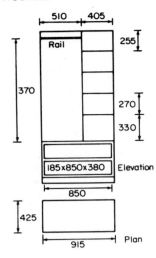

Fig. 2.25.   Typical wardrobe unit

DATA

Fig. 2.25 illustrates a typical storage unit, of which many variants are currently to be found. Surveys have shown that storage provision should satisfy the following requirements:

(a) Certain specific aspects of the storage must be satisfactory; for example, the depth of the cupboard for clothes hanging, the height of any drawers, space for a bulky garment and for a suitcase, and some lockable space.

(b) The main storage unit must provide an efficient solution, for example a built-in fitment.

(c) Other items of enclosed storage should augment provision of the main unit so that the total amount of enclosed storage is satisfactory to the individual resident.

(d) The open shelving should provide enough area for book shelving and display needs, and also help to meet any requirements outstanding from the enclosed storage provision, with any requirements outstanding from desk, table, and other putting-down places, to the satisfaction of the resident. Open shelving is the easiest to provide.

(e) Generous pinboard should be provided.

ACCOMMODATION

There have been many studies carried out on study-bedrooms. The Building Bulletin 37 (see Bibliography) states:
'The experience of students living in rooms of 8·36 m² shows that the conditions are acceptable for University or College terms. The arguments in favour of a fairly small study-bedroom are:

(a) Study can be conducted just as well in a small room.

(b) Three or four friends can be entertained in the smallest practicable study-bedroom.

(c) The saving in area will represent a saving in cost.

(d) It may well be preferable to have a higher standard of specification for a small room or, alternatively, to provide additional facilities such as a larger amenity elsewhere.

(e) Fuel costs should be reduced pro-rata to the reduction in the cube of the building.

The arguments in favour of a larger study-bedroom are:

(a) Room shape is of less crucial importance and the Architect's task becomes easier.

(b) The student has scope to move his furniture about and to give his room an individual character.

(c) There is less need for built-in, purpose-made furniture which tends to be expensive.

(d) It is only in larger rooms that an additional student can be temporarily accommodated in case of need.'

The room size for a particular scheme will be a compromise between cost, common room balance area, and study-bedroom area and specification.

GROUPING OF UNITS

The National Union of Students have stated their standards in their Briefing Document to all Student Unions, September 1971, as follows:

(a) Unit of 10–16 people. Choice of type of accommodation to meet individual need and preference can be catered for with this unit. This is borne out by other user study surveys.

(b) The household should be of a size economically determined, with socially desired limits: it may vary from 6 to 24. Provision should be made for one wc for 6 students; one bath and one shower for 12 students; one kitchen per 6 students with some social space attached.

(c) A 10% provision of double rooms must be considered as the maximum.

(d) Each single room should be not less than 9·29 m² in net floor area. Each double room should be not less than 13·93 m².

(e) A working desk space of 0·65 m².

(f) A hand basin in each double room and preferably in each single room also.

(g) Artificial lighting in each room of at least 200 W combined power.

(h) A minimum temperature of 18°C.

(i) Sound insulation between rooms, and between rooms and corridors of not less than 45 dB's.

(j) The furniture in each room should be moveable and of varying types to suit the individual student's tastes. It should consist of a bed, desk, wardrobe, adequate shelving for books, hard-backed chair and an easy chair.

(k) Openable window area of 5% of the total floor area.

The following facilities should be available for communal use:

(a) Cooking facilities.

(b) Laundry facilities.

(c) One bath and one shower to a maximum of twelve students.

(d) One wc for a maximum of six students.

(e) Telephones (at least one per fifty students).

(f) A nursery (if married students with children are catered for).

(g) Recreational rooms (dependent on the size of the hostel and its distance from the institution and local community).

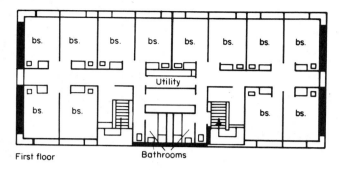

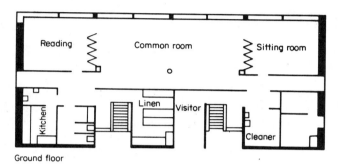

Fig. 2.26. *Nurses Hostel, Princess Margaret Hospital, Swindon*
The plan rectangle of access space necessary for each piece is associated with the plan of the furniture. Resultant rectangles are arranged together with permissible overlapping of access space to establish room proportions.

EXAMPLES

NURSES HOSTEL, PRINCESS MARGARET HOSPITAL, SWINDON (Fig. 2.26)

The hostel is within the hospital grounds and consists of three three-storey hostel blocks similar in size but differing in the ground floor accommodation. The blocks are parallel with each other and are linked with covered walks.
Architects: Powell and Moya.

CHURCHILL COLLEGE, CAMBRIDGE (Fig. 2.27)

The project was designed as a new college in an open site. The layout consists of court yard buildings grouped to form larger enclosed areas. The focal point of the complex is the communal buildings with a first floor dining hall seating 360. The common room, bar, shop and coffee bar are on the ground floor. The residential blocks have rooms arranged off staircases in groups of about 12.
Architects: Richard Sheppard, Robson and Partners

LOUGHBOROUGH COLLEGE OF EDUCATION, LEICESTERSHIRE (Fig. 2.28)

This residential building consists of a double tower block that acts as a focus to a complex of academic buildings. The sections are 22 and 18 storeys respectively, one tower for men and one for women. The towers are linked by a vertical circulation core. The study/bedrooms are arranged radially on plan. Accommodation is provided for 100 men students and 200 women students. Each study/bedroom floor has an open sitting space with a pantry adjacent.
Architects: Collins, Melvin, Ward and Partners.

Fig. 2.27. *Churchill College, Cambridge*

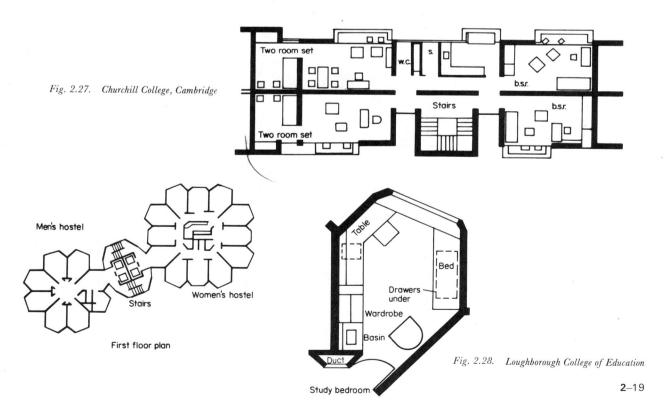

Fig. 2.28. *Loughborough College of Education*

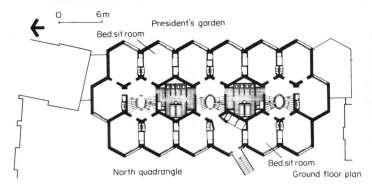

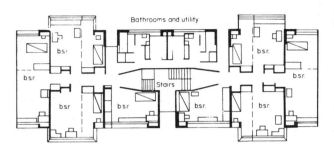

Fig. 2.29. St. John's College, Oxford

Fig. 2.30. Cripps Building, St. John's College, Cambridge

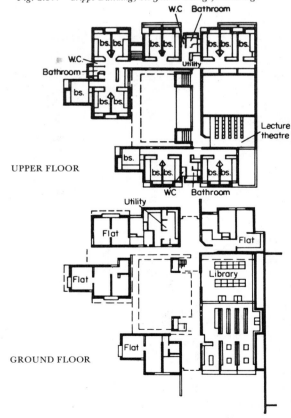

UPPER FLOOR

GROUND FLOOR

ST. JOHN'S COLLEGE, OXFORD (Fig. 2.29)

This building consists of 31 single rooms with the common and service rooms being provided in existing buildings adjacent. The centre section of the plan consists of three staircases lit by clerestory lighting. Between the staircases, there are bathrooms and lavatories. The study/bedrooms extend around this centre core the majority of which have a south facing aspect due to the hexagonal and honeycomb plan form.
Architects: Architects Co-Partnership Inc.

CRIPP'S BUILDING, ST JOHN'S COLLEGE, CAMBRIDGE (Fig. 2.30)

The site consisted of a long section of back land with a narrow approach road and a separate pedestrian access across the River Cam. A brook bisects the site. The building provides 200 sets of rooms for undergraduates of which about three quarters are two room sets, and the remainder are study/bedrooms. The rooms are arranged on each floor in groups of four off each staircase. The building is four storeys high with studio rooms and penthouse flats with access to a roof terrace. The ground floor accommodates visitors lavatories, plant rooms, changing rooms, junior common room, bar, kitchen and seminar room.
Architects: Powell and Moya.

THEOLOGICAL COLLEGE, CHICHESTER (Fig. 2.31)

The site was originally a small kitchen garden and is surrounded by scheduled trees. Within the building, study bedrooms are arranged in seven groups of five on the upper floors with the tutors flats, library and main circulation on the ground floor. Each room has a casement window and a roof light over the recess for desk and bookshelves.
Architects: Ahvends, Burton and Koralek.

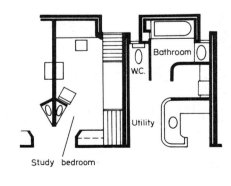

Fig. 2.31. Theological College, Chichester

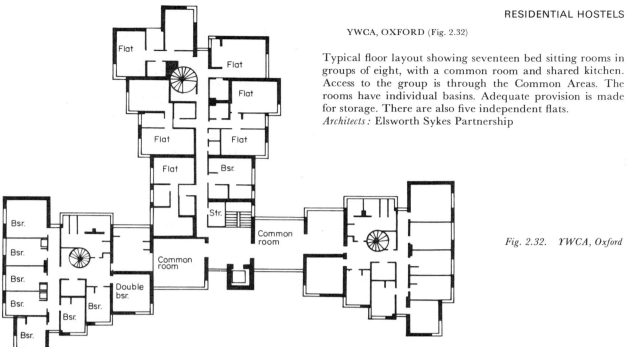

YWCA, OXFORD (Fig. 2.32)

Typical floor layout showing seventeen bed sitting rooms in groups of eight, with a common room and shared kitchen. Access to the group is through the Common Areas. The rooms have individual basins. Adequate provision is made for storage. There are also five independent flats.
Architects: Elsworth Sykes Partnership

Fig. 2.32. YWCA, Oxford

ST. JOHN'S SCHOOL, TIFFIELD (Fig. 2.33)

This building provides the accommodation of an approved school for boys aged 13–17. The accommodation is divided into house units of thirty boys each. All dormitories are on the first floor, consisting of seven rooms for four boys each and two single rooms. There is a flat for the house-master with separate external access and a smaller flat for another member of staff.

The common rooms, dining room and kitchen, washing rooms, showers and lavatories are on the ground floor, the latter adjoining the entrance.
Architects: James A. Crabtree and Associates

Fig. 2.33. St. John's School, Tiffield (approved school)

HALLS OF RESIDENCE

Norwich House and Essex House, University of Sussex, 1967.
Architects: Hubbard Ford and Partners
Brunel University Residences, Uxbridge, London.
Architects: Richard Shepphard, Robson and Partners
Trinity Hall Undergraduate House, Cambridge, U.K. 1968.
Architects: Arup Associates, London.
The Wolfson Building, Sommerville College, Oxford, U.K. 1976.
Architects: Arup Associates, London
Quincy House, Harvard University, Cambridge, Massachusetts, U.S.A. 1960.
Architects: Shepley, Bulfinch, Richardson & Abbott, Boston
Student Hostel, Amsterdam, Holland. 1966.
Architects: Herman Hertzberger, Amsterdam with T. Hazewinkel and H. A. Dicke

STUDENT HOUSING AND HOSTELS

Protestant Students' Hostel, Berlin-Grunewald, Germany. 1962.
Architect: Peter Lehrecke, Berlin
Hostels for Young People, St. Etienne, France. 1963.
Architect: Andre Wogenscky, Paris
Siegmundshof-Ost Student Hostel, Berlin, Germany. 1961.
Architect: Klaus H. Ernst, Berlin
Tempus Student Hostels, Bromma, Stockholm, Sweden. 1963.
Architects: Nilsson, Sundberg & Wiren, Stockholm
International House of South Wales, Penarth, Glamorganshire.
Architects: Edward D. Mills & Partners, London

2–21

STATUTORY REQUIREMENTS
AND LEGISLATION AND AUTHORITIES

(i) Outline Planning Approval, Town & Country planning Act, 1971 The Planning Authority will normally require details of: use of site; density; building lines; road entrances; height and bulk of building; materials; angles of light; garages and car parking provision.
(ii) Detailed Planning Approval, Town & Country Planning Act 1971.
(iii) Fire Precautions Act 1972.
(iv) Building Regulations 1972 and the first amendment 1973. Applicable throughout England and Wales except within the administrative area of the Greater London Council.
(v) Public Health Acts 1936 and 1961.
(vi) Standards of School Premises Regulations 1972.
(vii) The Building Standards (Scotland) Regulations 1971. Applicable in Scotland.
(viii) London Building Acts 1973. Applicable only in the Inner London Boroughs (i.e: the former L.C.C. area).
(ix) Means of escape as set out in Public Health Act 1936, Section 60 and Fire Precautions Act 1972. Consult the prevention officer of local fire authority or the Greater London Council Fire Brigade. Also discuss access for fire appliances and fire fighting generally.
(x) Daylighting. Consult Planning Authority.
(xi) Ministry requirements and recommendations. Official recommendations and guidance and statutory requirments are issued by:
  University Grants Committee
  Department of Education and Science
  Department of the Environment
  Department of Health & Social Security
  Home Office

BIBLIOGRAPHY

Allen P., 'Hostel Planning' *Architects' Journal*, (April 1965).
Allen, Phyllis, *Hostel User Study*, Building Research Station.
Allen P. G. and Miller A., 'Living Accommodation for Young People' Ministry of Technology, BRS Miscellaneous Papers 12.
Architectural Record Book, *Apartments and Dormitories*, Dodge Corporation, New York (1958).
Bendixson, T. M. P., *Student Rooms Design*, Council of Industrial Design (June 1962).
Brawne, M., 'Student living approaches to residential planning' *Architectural Review*, (October 1963).
Department of Education and Science, *Student Residence*, HMSO (1967).
Fengler, Max, 'Heime: Studenten—Berufstätigen und Atenheime (Hostels for Students, Nurses, Working Women and Old People)', Koch, Stuttgart (1963).
Fengler, Max, 'Students dormitories and homes for the aged' Tiranti, London, (1964).
Heigert, Hans, and Wirsurg, W., *Houses for Young People*, Juventa, Munich (1960).
Hostels and housing for students, Bouw, Rotterdam (October 1964).
'Hostels for students' *Der Architekt*, BDA (November 1961).
International Youth Hostel Federation, *Youth Hostels around the World*, Copenhagen (1963).
Krämer, Karl, *Architektur Wettbewerbe*, Karl Krämer, Stuttgart (1961).
Mullins, W. and Allen, P., *Student Housing*, Crosby Lockwood, London (1971).
Nagel, S. and Linke, S., *Heimbauten (Homes for Single People)* Bertelsmann Fachverlag, Gütersloth (1970).
Peter, P., *Wohnen in Gemeinschaft (Hostels)*, Callway, Munich (1968).
Residential Catering, University Grants Committee, University Building Notes, HMSO, London (1966).
'Residential spaces, fixtures and equipment: Hostels and halls of residence' *Architects' Journal* (March/April, 1965).
Riker, *Planning Functional College Housing*, Columbia University, New York, (1956).
Student Residence, Building Bulletin No. 37, HMSO.
'Study bedrooms: a critical appraisal', *Architects' Journal*, (April 1965).
Tolmach, Judy, *Student Housing*, Education Facilities Laboratories, New York (1972).
University Grant Committee, *Sub-committee on Halls of Residence*, HMSO (1957).
'User survey: hall of residence, Imperial College, south side of Princes Gardens, Kensington', *Architects' Journal* (April, 1965).

Published in "Architects' Journal"
'Hostels and Halls of Residence', (Issues of 10 April, 17 April, 24 April and 1st May, 1968).
'Hostel Planning', (1st May, 1968).
'Hall of Residence User Survey', (28th April, 1965).
'Noise in Student Residences', (21st April, 1965).
'Accommodation for Undergraduates and Fellows', (4th October, 1967).
'Students' Hostel, Clare Hall', (19th August, 1973).

LOAN FINANCE ACCOMMODATION

Reference should be made to U.G.C. publication 'Loan-Finance Residence in United Kingdom Universities, June 1972'. This provides a comparative analysis of 42 Loan-Finance Schemes.

Anthony Wylson, *FRIBA, A.A.Dip.(Hons) is a partner in the firm Anthony Wylson and Munro Waterson and has prepared studies on various hotel projects. These include a motel, a commercial hotel and a Mediterranean tourist complex incorporating hotel, hostel and chalets. The firm has also carried out a variety of residential schemes embracing different aspects of accommodation.*

3 HOTELS, MOTELS AND CAMPS FOR THE MOTORIST

ANTHONY WYLSON, R.I.B.A.

INTRODUCTION

The Hotel is essentially a building for providing a service to guests. The variation in hotel types is extensive ranging from the simple motel to the complexity of luxury city hotels or an extensive tourist complex. The efficient running will be generated by satisfactory planning and thus it is vitally important for the Architect to work in very close collaboration with his client and consultants. This section is in two parts the first dealing with hotels and the second covering motels and camps for the motorist. The latter are planned for people touring by car or caravan who may stop in the camp for one night only or for the duration of their holiday.

HOTELS

The life of a hotel, as it is originally planned could be no more than 30–35 years. Thus during the early stages of planning a degree of flexibility should be considered to allow for possible change at some future date.

Two principal factors govern the hotel design and hotel type; first, the type of guests to be catered for and secondly the type and location of the site.

GUEST TYPES

1. Long term guests demanding a need for more residential facilities, both in public rooms and bedrooms.
2. Holidays. Visitors such as groups on holiday either families or one age groups where recreational rooms, facilities for children and old people are important to occupy leisure time.
3. Conferences. Delegates provided by bulk bookings for short periods e.g. weekends or one week conferences. These may require suites of rooms for seminars or the exclusive use of one large room for a period.
4. Short-stay business represents a large proportion of guests in most urban hotels, needing the use of single rooms mainly during the week. This includes in-transit guests at airports, ferry terminals or motels.
5. Day visitors requiring the use of public rooms by local non-resident guests. In some areas the use by visitors may be quite extensive requiring different types of restaurant, ballroom or discotheque.

6. The nationality of guests is an important aspect. If foreign guests frequent the hotel it is important to cater for some of their requirements i.e. room temperatures, menu etc.
7. Disabled guests. Allowance should always be made for the disabled to be free to use any facility in the hotel.

Hotels may be designed with one type of guest as a priority but most hotels cater for several types simultaneously.

LOCATION

The location of the site is fundamental to the feasibility of the project, as location will either promote or obstruct the acceptability of the hotel to the guests that it aims to serve. Accessibility, surroundings, availability of transport, aspect, noise, amenities must all be equated.

PRINCIPAL FUNCTIONS

Within the planning of the hotel there are five principal functions to be related:

(i) The public areas including access for traffic, parking, loading and unloading, entrance hall, reception, access for services and refuse disposal. In large hotels the general circulation area includes small shops or space for commercial display.

(ii) Function rooms which can range from a simple dining room to an extensive complex of restaurants, cafeteria, bars, ballroom, recreational room, swimming pool, quiet rooms, TV room, cinema and discotheque.

(iii) Bedroom accommodation including washing facilities either as shared or private bathrooms, linen stores, valet services, room food service etc.

(iv) Staff facilities and administrative offices.

(v) Service rooms, boiler room, ventilation electrical intake.

These functions vary in importance and scale depending upon the size and location of the hotel. A small commercial hotel could include only sufficient dining room space for breakfast and light meals whereas a luxury tourist hotel would give importance to spacious lounge accommodation, swimming pools and recreation space in addition to adequate provision for restaurant, bar and cafeteria.

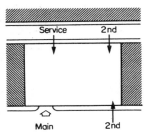 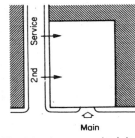 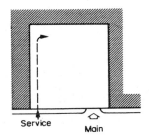

Fig. 3.1 Access to restricted sites.
Main entrance for residential guests and visitors.
2nd entrance to function rooms and/or car park.
Service entrance for staff, goods deliveries and refuse collection.

SITING

The economic appraisal of the site and detailed market research of the particular location requires specialist analysis. This will identify the future of the area, its rate of commercial or social development, or the security of the tourist or leisure amenities. The significance of the site will vary according to the market orientation of the project (i.e. whether it is geared to tourists, leisure activities, overnight guests etc.), and to the relative significance of the component services (restaurant, discotheque, swimming pool, bedroom accommodation).

Furthermore, the restaurant or bar may gain greater importance through proximity to other independent amenities (entertainment, business activity, tourist interests, transport centre) and would require appraisal in this context.

The standard of bedroom accommodation will be directed towards a price level which is related to an evaluation of the site. Furthermore the close proximity of other hotels, or anticipated future hotels, must be studied as competitive or complementary factors. The market analysis of the site should take into account availability of staff and the general costs of establishment and maintenance as affected by location. The cost of housing staff in securing basic services such as fresh water, electricity or drainage could be decisive.

Thus the object of the market analysis in relation to siting is:

1. To define the feasibility criteria of the project.
2. To outline the primary design objectives, category and identity.
3. To establish relative cost limitations relating land costs, loan repayment costs, building costs and running costs.
4. To identify significant related factors; In particular abnormal cost implications.

With this basic appraisal it is possible for the designer to consider the suitability and potential of the site.

Principal items signficant to primary design objectives would be:

(a) Does the site enhance or support the primary marketing aspect e.g. accessibility to tourist interest; suitable surroundings for leisure; appeal to commercial activities etc.
(b) Does the site provide for or is it accessible to transport facilities associated with anticipated customers e.g. provision for private motor car, accessibility to public transport, communication with airport or ferry terminal, accessibility to motorway for motel, etc.
(c) Does the site provide environmental conditions sympathetic to customers' needs e.g. characteristic of

leisure centre, quiet at night time, etc.
(d) Does the site provide conditions in which the image of hotel can be developed e.g. prestige site in commercial centre, beachside setting for leisure hotel, clear visibility to motorists for motel.
(e) Is staff available within the area or will accommodation be provided within the project.

The detailed factors of the site itself would include:

(a) Legislative control, planning, zoning, byelaws, etc.
(b) Size and shape in relation to economic planning of primary components and traffic circulation (Fig. 3.1). Also consideration for expansion.
(c) Orientation and aspect.
(d) Ground bearing capacity and water level.
(e) Relation of surrounding properties, heights, easements and rights of way.
(f) Possibility of flooding or other hazards.
(g) Available services (water, power, drainage) refuse collection.
(h) Land values and long term land use values. Interest in land or financial participation of project e.g. if it is part of a large complex.

PLANNING

The range of hotel buildings can vary from a simple motel consisting of serviced rooms to the vast complexity of a holiday centre or prestige city hotel; each varies in category, length of stay of guests, essential facilities and ancillary services.

The basic planning problem is considered in relation to the principal sections within a hotel complex and the disposition of these in relation to the site, intercommunication and common services (see Fig. 3.2). The sections can be listed as follows:

1. *Public areas.* Arrival area, car parking, entrance hall, enquiry counter, cloakroom, unloading, refuse collection etc.
2. *Function rooms.* Dining room, recreation room, ballroom, etc.
3. Bedroom accommodation including linen store, valet service, etc.
4. Staff and administration, manager's office, staff rooms, staff accommodation, etc.
5. Service rooms, boiler room, ventilation, electrical intake, etc.

Each section has both a significance independent of the functions of the hotel, (e.g. the restaurant would serve more than just residents), and an importance within the circulation pattern and economy of service layouts within the hotel as a whole.

The public areas concerned with large numbers of guests must deal with traffic, unloading, car parking, and the conveyance of luggage in and out of the building. Provision must also be made for the unloading of goods, access by staff, collection of refuse, access for security, clear routes for means of escape and access in case of fire.

The function rooms may require independent access providing for non-residents with traffic circulation to avoid obstruction to access to the hotel. This normally suggests the lower floors, but the particular location of a hotel could benefit by planning the bar, lounge or discotheque on a mezzanine or the top floor.

The bedroom floors will set the basic structural module. The location of individual bathrooms, if provided ensuite with bedrooms, will have a significant effect upon the width of the bedroom floors. The general layout must also take into account easy access and means of escape, location of such service rooms such as linen stores, and utility rooms for preparation of light snacks.

The staff accommodation and administration of a hotel varies in proportion to the size and location of the building. A hotel isolated from the type of accommodation suitable for the hotel staff may have to include staff accommodation on the premises. The administrative offices must be located in relation to security and the cashier. The offices must be accessible to the residents.

Service room, ducts and installation must be planned not only for efficiency, but also to protect residents from noise and inconvenience caused when maintenance operations are carried out.

The clarity of circulation patterns is most important both to the general efficient running of the hotel and the speedy understanding by the residents. A layout that clearly conveys the principal circulation routes is easy to grasp and makes the resident feel familiar with the building and at ease.

From the point of entry by the public, attention should be given to avoiding obstruction either by service traffic or the accumulation of luggage. Where there are several staircases those used only by the public should be clearly defined. Staircases used by staff or escape stairs leading specifically to non-residential parts of the building should be clearly defined. Similar if there are several lifts, allowing specifically for service, luggage and residents, these should be also clearly defined. However, the layout of the lifts should provide a degree of flexibility to allow for maintenance.

The following particular aspects have an important effect on basic planning.

1. Flexibility and change

It is important to consider a form of structure, planning method or module which allows for flexibility and change. During the lifetime of the building demands for different uses will occur and must be allowed for.

2. Hotel organisation

The general administration and organisation of a large hotel is very complex and the work programme for the various types of staff need to be thoroughly understood to allow for efficient working of the hotel. For example, control of incoming and outgoing guests, accounting, catering, daily maintenance and room service.

3. Circulation

It is of prime importance to consider the basic circulation at an early stage in planning. There are three patterns; one route for guests; one for staff; and a general route for deliveries etc.

Guests. Car park/garage—main entrance/subsidiary entrance — reception — lifts/staircases — corridors — bedrooms/public rooms. Guests leaving bedrooms must pass through reception before returning to the car park.

Staff. Staff accommodation—staff entrance—changing rooms—kitchen/service rooms—service lifts.

Deliveries can be subdivided as follows:
(i) Guests luggage—main entrance—luggage lift—bedrooms—luggage rooms.
(ii) Food, drink, stores—deliveries entrance—bulk stores—various departments.
(iii) Rubbish—back entrance—bins/area—chutes for rubbish; linen store—guest room—laundry—linen store.

4. Height and sub-division relating to structure

Open planning and a large area for public rooms (usually on lower floors) will allow for change of functions or priorities. Compact unit-type planning for bedroom/bath units must provide sound insulation and privacy.

5. Services

Ducts for services should be considered in overall planning with ease of access for maintenance. Provision must be made for storage of fuel, method of supplying electrical power, storage or water, discharging refuse and the handling of linen. Lifts and hoists should be accessible to areas served without causing a noise nuisance to guests.

Vertical services from bedroom floors must be related to public areas on lower floors, as they will have a different spatial arrangement.

6. Fire regulations

Fire precautions will be controlled by the Local Authority, Government Recommendations or standards. The necessary escape routes, staircases, lobbies and fire doors are basic to hotel planning.

The length of a bedroom wing is limited by maximum distance that guests must travel to reach a staircase in the event of fire. Recommended Standards are set out under Fire Precautions. Lift and staircases are normally placed together but staircases and landings should be separated from bedroom corridors by self-closing doors to locate smoke. Every part of the building occupied by guests and staff should have two independent escape routes in case of fire except as covered in the Recommended Standards.

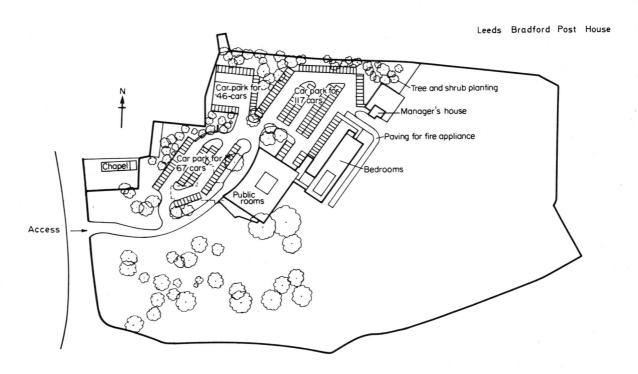

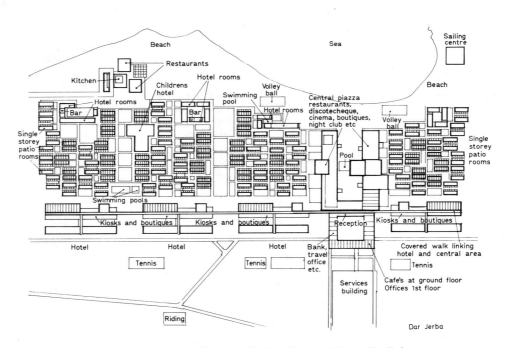

Fig. 3.2   Site layouts of Leeds Bradford Post House and Hotel at Dar Jerba

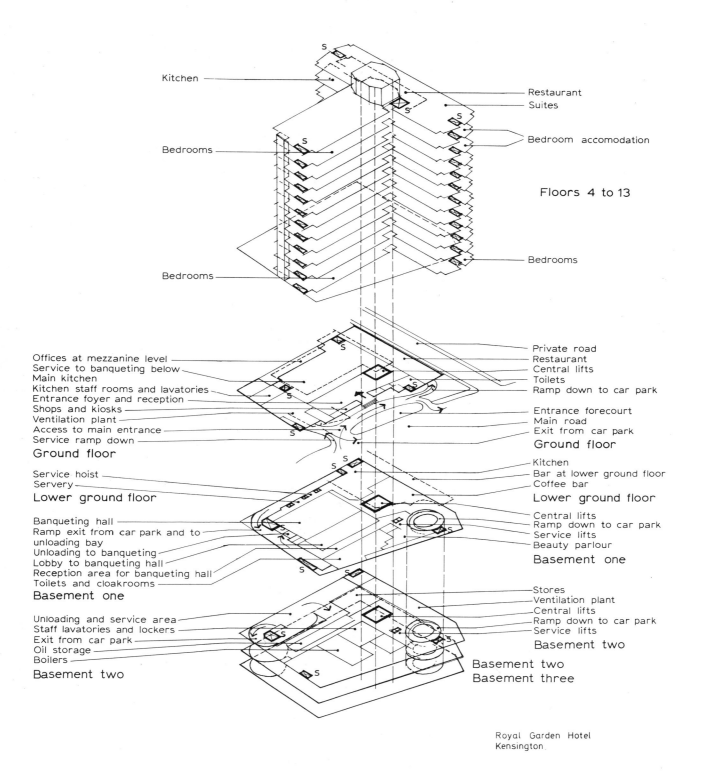

Kitchen

Restaurant
Suites

Bedroom accomodation

Floors 4 to 13

Bedrooms

Bedrooms

Bedrooms

Offices at mezzanine level
Service to banqueting below
Main kitchen
Kitchen staff rooms and lavatories
Entrance foyer and reception
Shops and kiosks
Ventilation plant
Access to main entrance
Service ramp down
Ground floor

Private road
Restaurant
Central lifts
Toilets
Ramp down to car park

Entrance forecourt
Main road
Exit from car park
Ground floor

Service hoist
Servery
Lower ground floor

Kitchen
Bar at lower ground floor
Coffee bar
Lower ground floor

Banqueting hall
Ramp exit from car park and to
unloading bay
Unloading to banqueting
Lobby to banqueting hall
Reception area for banqueting hall
Toilets and cloakrooms
Basement one

Central lifts
Ramp down to car park
Service lifts
Beauty parlour
Basement one

Unloading and service area
Staff lavatories and lockers
Exit from car park
Oil storage
Boilers
Basement two

Stores
Ventilation plant
Central lifts
Ramp down to car park
Service lifts
Basement two

Basement two
Basement three

Royal Garden Hotel
Kensington

Fig. 3.2 (cont.)   Layout of Royal Garden Hotel, Kensington

7. Sound insulation

Sound insulation between rooms is important. It is equally important to identify noise areas immediately below or over-looked by bedrooms.

8. Garages and car parking

Requirements for parking vary according to hotel type and requirements may be imposed by the planning authority. A guide would be one car space for every two bedrooms in residential areas; one car space for every 10 m² in public rooms or one car space for every ten people using public rooms. Adequate space should be provided for moving cars. 32–36 cars can be manoeuvered and parked in an area 27·5 m × 30·5 m.

Separate car parking should be provided for staff and adequate arrangements should be made for delivery vans etc.

SPACE REQUIREMENTS—INTRODUCTION

For all large hotels, there are five main areas to be covered. These together with their sub-divisions are listed below and are described in detail in the following pages.

A. Public areas and function rooms
    1. Entrance and reception, porte-cochere, disabled guests, luggage, doors, porter's and messenger's room, reception area, cashier offices, waiting area, lifts, stairs, miscellaneous.
    2. Cloakrooms and lavatories
    3. Main lounge and television room
    4. Bar and bar lounge
    5. Waiting room
    6. Dining room, restaurants, buffet, bars, coffee shops, breakfast room
    7. Function rooms
    8. Special accommodation, childrens room, miscellaneous.
B. Bedrooms and Bathrooms
    1. Bedroom/bathroom units
    2. Bedrooms
    3. Bathrooms
    4. Corridors
    5. Floor service rooms
C. Staff facilities and Administrative office
D. Kitchen and service rooms
    1. Food service and catering
    2. General service, clean-up and maintenance
E. Staff accommodation

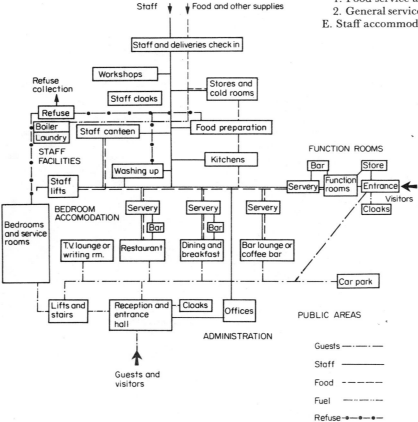

Fig. 3.3 Circulation diagram

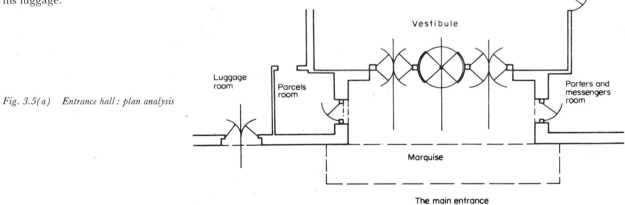

Fig. 3.4   Diagram of entrance and reception area.

A. PUBLIC AREAS

Some typical public areas are shown in Figs. 3.4 to 3.6.

1. ENTRANCE AND RECEPTION

The main entrance of an hotel should be welcoming to the guest. If the hotel is on a first floor level, the Entrance area, lifts and staircases should be solely for the use of the hotel. It should be clear to the guest, where he is to park his car, where to find the reception counter and how to cope with his luggage.

Porte-cochere. It is important to provide a porte-cochere or projecting canopy to protect people from wind and rain. This should cover the whole area allowing for two cars to pass and should be of a height to accommodate buses. Special lighting will help people to find the entrance easily.

Disabled guests. Allow for ramps from the road to entrance doors.

Luggage is usually taken from the guest on arrival by a porter to a special luggage entrance for easy transfer to a luggage room. It is then conveyed by service stairs or a service lift to the bedroom. Barrows are often used to transport luggage and so steps should be avoided. Conveyor belts are sometimes installed.

Doors. If revolving doors are used they should have ordinary sidehung escape doors at each side. A draught lobby may also be necessary. If, as may be the case in the smaller hotel, there is not a separate baggage entrance, doors should have a suitable width to allow for the porter and luggage.

Fig. 3.5(a)   Entrance hall : plan analysis

The main entrance

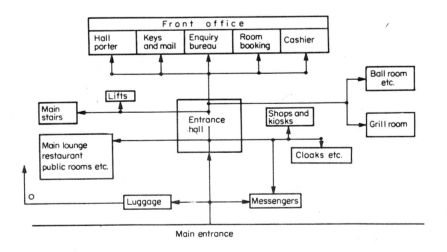

Fig. 3.5(b)   Main Entrance.

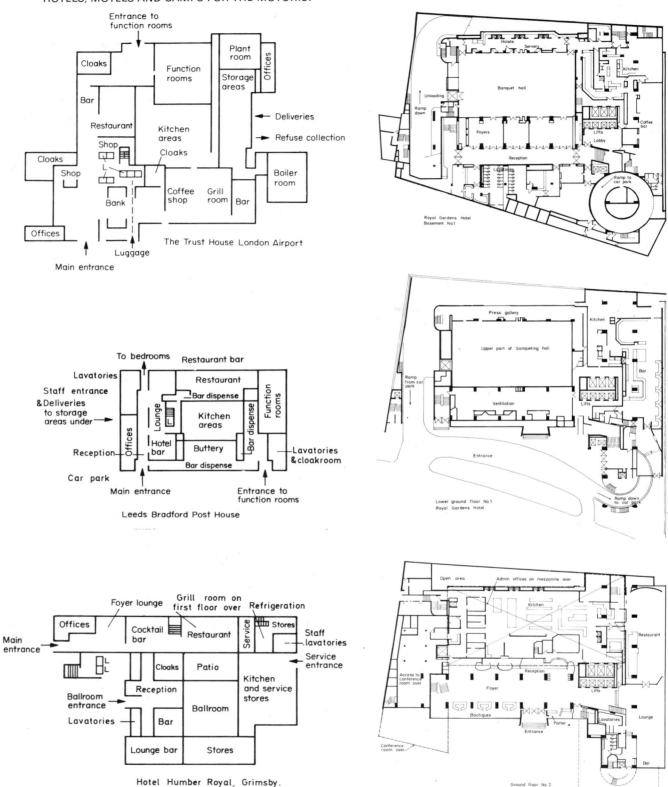

Fig. 3.6 Some typical examples of main public areas (not to same scale).

Porters and messengers room. This room needs to have access to the main entrance for the guidance of guests and handling of luggage. In larger hotels the head porter may have a separate room. In either case, the head porter should be in a position where he has visual control over lifts, stairs and the general reception area. He needs a counter, space for storing small baggage, space for machines, timetables and a cash drawer for small transactions. He should have telephone communications with the garage, luggage room, cashier, receptionist and taxis. Fire alarms and service bells should be positioned in this area.

Reception area. It is important that this area, the core of the working of the hotel, should not be confusing to the guest. As he approaches the area through the entrance the reception desk should be easily seen. This is where the initial checking-in takes place. The desk should be a counter top suitable for writing on and should have a handbag shelf. Room keys are given to guests from here after checking in. Key rails are often combined with letter boxes behind the counter.

A desk unit behind or below the counter is needed for books, records of guests etc. Telephones (internal and external) should be provided for the receptionist. A separate part of the counter may be used for inquiries. The reception clerk should be in a position to see guests entering and leaving the hotel from lifts, stairs etc.

Cashier. In a large hotel, space may be needed for a separate cashier and accounting staff. This may mean a separate counter to the reception area with space for adding or electric accounting machines. Drawers for foreign currency and books should also be provided. Depending on the size of the complex, offices for clerical staff may be needed.

Offices. Office space for general administration and storage of records should be easily available and within easy communication with the Reception area. Space is needed for electronic equipment which is now being used extensively. Offices may include:

Stationery and record store
Control room for main operator for Baby Listening Service and room call system
Manager and assistant
Sales and catering
General manager
General budget and auditing.

These will vary greatly according to the type and size of hotel.

Waiting area. This should be adjacent to the reception desk off the main circulation area and within view of the main entrance and lifts. Furniture should be comfortable and hard wearing. Writing desks should be available.

Circulation area. Allowance must be made for general circulation—guests arriving, leaving, meeting people, making various enquiries. Lifts should be in a prominent position. In hotels catering for groups of people arriving simultaneously (i.e. coach parties), adequate allowance must be made for general circulation.

Lifts are the most important form of access to the bedroom floors and should be sited in a convenient position in relation to the waiting area. At least 2 lifts should be provided to allow for breakdowns and maintenance.

Except for small hotels, separate lifts are supplied for luggage and other freight. At least one should be of sufficient size for the transport of bulky articles such as wardrobes,

mattresses etc. Lifts are usually designed in groups so that only one motor room need be provided.

It is important to allow for a waiting area outside the lift that is not part of the general circulation. In addition to passenger and service lifts other lifts or hoists are often provided in the kitchen and laundry areas.

Staircases. Staircases must be planned in accordance with fire regulations. There may be a main carpeted staircase from the reception area to the first or basement level but, for other floors, the staircase usually acts as a service and staff staircase and an escape staircase. For details of lifts and staircases see *Planning: Architects Technical Reference Data.* The minimum requirements are usually 1 lift for every 100 bedrooms; service lifts: 2 for every 3 passenger lifts.

Miscellaneous. In the main reception area there may be various other amenities:

Public telephones—allow for shelf for writing messages
News teleprinter
Post box stamp machine
Shops or display cabinets
Hairdressers.

2. CLOAKROOMS AND LAVATORIES

These should be easily accessible from main circulation areas and public rooms. The inside of the lavatory area should be screened from any public area when the door is opened. No lavatory should communicate directly with a room used for food. The entrances to mens and womens lavatories should not be adjacent. Women's lavatories should include a separate powder room and cloakroom for leaving coats. Mens cloakrooms are usually separate from their lavatory accommodation.

For further details on cloakrooms and lavatories and the required number of fitments see Table 3.1.

3. MAIN LOUNGE

The lounge as a separate unit is not very profitable and is now usually associated with a bar, coffee bar or tea lounge. It can be an extension of the main reception area or an ante-room to the restaurant. It should be furnished with comfortable chairs, coffee tables and should be informal and relaxing.

The semi-residential or resort type of hotel may require a more cut-off lounge, which becomes a reading and sitting room and has a sense of privacy exclusive to the hotel residents.

4. TELEVISION ROOM

In the smaller hotel where TV sets are not installed in the bedrooms a separate room for those wishing to view should be provided. A television in the main lounge should be avoided.

5. BAR AND BAR LOUNGE

The bar may be incorporated with the main lounge or be a separate unit. The size of the bar will depend on the areas it will have to serve, e.g. lounge, restaurant, coffee shop, banqueting rooms and room service and the number of waiters employed, storage etc.

For details on bars, see Section 5 'Public Houses and Licensed Premises' in *Planning: Buildings for Administration, Entertainment and Recreation.*

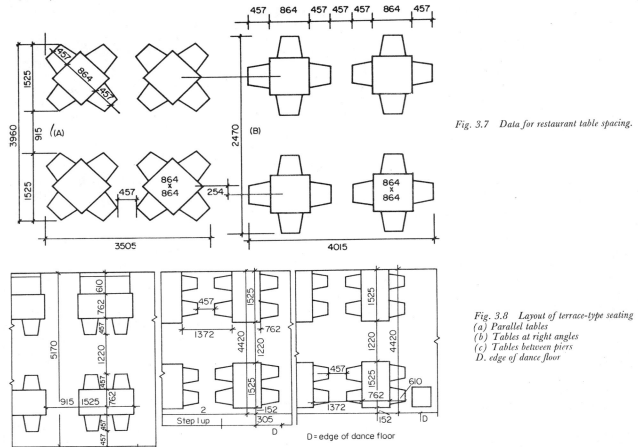

Fig. 3.7   Data for restaurant table spacing.

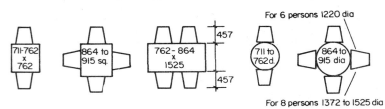

Fig. 3.8   Layout of terrace-type seating
(a) Parallel tables
(b) Tables at right angles
(c) Tables between piers
D. edge of dance floor

D = edge of dance floor

6. WRITING ROOM

In many hotels a writing room is required. This may not be very large, but in hotels catering for commercial travellers and other business men it can be quite important. The room should be designed and finished in a restful manner all with a view to reduction of noise.

Writing tables should be at least 830 × 480 mm exclusive of any fitting for stationery. Writing tables can also be provided in individual bedrooms.

7. DINING ROOM, BUFFET, BARS, COFFEE SHOPS, BREAKFAST ROOM

There is a large range of dining accommodation from just one dining room in the small hotel, to a series of different dining rooms, restaurants, speciality restaurants, grill rooms, coffee shops etc. in the large luxury hotel.

The tastes and fashions for eating change within 5–7 years. It is therefore wise in planning to consider at an early stage a degree of flexibility to allow for different arrangements. Various types of small bar or grill with different characteristics and features can draw in non-residential guests. These as a rule are more informal and cater for about 60–80 people.

Large dining rooms may have a special sprung floor area for dancing. Provision should also be made for a band platform.

Breakfast rooms are sometimes provided as a separate unit. As people do not breakfast at the same time only 50% of the resident guests need be accommodated simultaneously. Usually a part of the main dining room would be used for those not breakfasting in their bedrooms. For a residential or resort hotel, the dining room should have a seating capacity for all the guests at one time. Guests usually keep to the same table for the duration of their stay. For a travelling public it is preferable to have two rooms for meals to cope with different needs simultaneously.

Fig. 3.9   Data for restaurant seating.

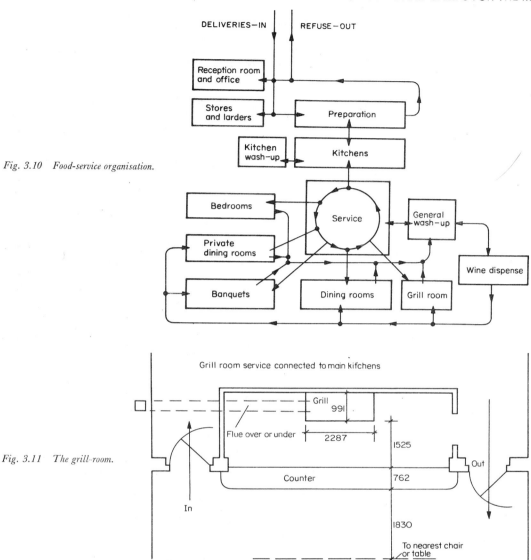

Fig. 3.10   Food-service organisation.

Fig. 3.11   The grill-room.

Most hotels require a small private dining room for hiring out. This should not be less than 4·2 to 4·8 m. Though normally carpeted, it is wise to have hardwood floors to allow the room to be let for small private dances.

Recommended areas are:

Dining Rooms (luxury), 1·7 m²–1·9 m² per seat.

Coffee shop and standard restaurants, 1·3 m² per seat.

Dance floors should not be less than 6·3 m wide in any direction.

8. RESTAURANTS

The layout of restaurants should be related to service access. A long rectangular room with service to kitchen placed on one of the long sides provides economy in table layout and accessibility for waiters. The degree to which food preparation is to be a visual element and the degree of isolation of individual tables are fundamental to the design brief.

The lighting arrangement, alcoves, bays and internal screens can reduce the scale of a large restaurant but attention must be given to service access. The noise and visual effect of food preparation can be reduced by careful screening and lobbies. Where the final stages of the service of food are visible from the restaurant, the wash-up and basic preparation should be kept separate from the restaurant area.

Where terraces or balconies are used in restaurants, protecting rails should be provided at changes of level. Main gangway widths should not be less than 1·200 m. The floor area per person in dining rooms vary from 93 m² to 1·67 m² per seat inclusive of passages, tables, etc depending upon type of restaurant. The average is 1·11 m² to 1·3 m² per seat. Table layouts are shown in Figs. 3.5, 3.6 and 3.7. There should be 914 mm between backs of chairs if the space is required for service, otherwise 450 mm.

B. FUNCTION ROOMS

Owing to high costs, very large rooms are generally used for more than one function. One multipurpose area could be used for ballroom, banqueting room, conferences or exhibitions, wedding receptions. It is important to have a separate entrance (independent of the hotel reception) with its own porte-cochere, waiting area, cloakroom and toilet facilities.

A large amount of storage space is essential to store the furniture, carpets and equipment needed to adapt this room for the various functions.

It is helpful to have large doors at one end for motor exhibitions. Sound insulation must be carefully considered and the acoustics of the hall are important.

A store is needed for the crockery and equipment kept for the sole use of this room. There should be a service room next to this and access to the main kitchen.

Emergency escapes and at least two independent exits are required.

Recommended areas are:

Banqueting room average floor space per person 0·80–1·0 m².

Dancing 0·93–1·45 m²

Banquet storage, 8 % of Banquet area.

Kitchen or pantry, 20 % of banquet area.

CONFERENCE FACILITIES

The provision for conferences which include congress halls, conference rooms, auditoria, exhibition spaces, suites of rooms, with the provision for separate access and separate amenities (toilets, dining room and bar) have become an important feature in certain areas.

It is important to establish a satisfactory relationship with the functioning of the hotel itself. In many cases, this provision has overtaken or developed from the spaces allowed for banqueting and ballrooms. However, the needs are different and particular attention should be given to acoustics, provision and storage of seating, accommodation of ancillary equipment (projectors, display equipment etc) and the relative circulation pattern with other functions within the hotel in particular vehicular access, parking, and the sections in the hotel that should maintain quiet and privacy.

PRIVATE DINING ROOMS

Most hotels require at least one room which can be let as a private dining room for small parties, while in large hotels several rooms may be required. When there are several rooms, it should be possible to put them together to make various sized spaces, to accommodate parties of different numbers. The smallest room should not be less than 4·26 m by 4·87 m. The rooms should be arranged in a group, with convenient access to a service room and located on the ground or first floor of the building. The rooms could be carpeted, but in large spaces, hardwood floors should be provided to allow for private dances.

GRILL ROOMS

The general arrangement and layout of grill rooms is similar to dining-rooms. Many hotels have a grill in the room; the tradition of cooking in the room is still strong, especially in hotels with a large number of male patrons.

Fig. 3.11 shows the approximate area required for the grill itself, the working space for the chef and the counter on which are displayed the various foods and under which plates, etc. are stored. The layout shown, where the grill is placed between the service doors, works well in practice and keeps all service together at one end of the room; it also connects the grill space to the kitchen.

DANCE FLOORS

Consideration would be given to provision of dancing in a restaurant area. Generally, restaurants that are close carpeted over a hard floor would have a removable section of carpet to provide for dancing.

If a permanent dancing area is required, a sprung floor can be provided separate from the dining area. The band area or console can be provided in a recess with the surrounding walls giving sound resonance. The band platform would be raised 0·36 m to 0·45 m and could be 4·26 m wide by 2·43 m deep.

BANQUET ROOMS AND BALLROOMS

Many hotels require a large lettable room for outside use. This room usually has a number of functions as, for example, a banquet room, a ballroom, wedding receptions and temporary exhibitions. It is desirable that the room be placed at ground-floor or street level. If the basement is used, additional ventilation will be required. If the room is to be let for uses apart from the hotel proper, a separate entrance is desirable, together with adequate cloakrooms and lavatories for each sex. The entrance should be accessible to vehicles and the pavement should be protected with a marquise or porte-cochere.

At the entrance there should be a vestibule leading into a hall from which the cloakrooms and lavatories are approached. This hall should be suitable for use as a waiting or reception space. If cloakrooms cannot be accommodated on the same level it is then usual to place men's cloakrooms on a lower floor and the women's rooms on the upper of the two levels. It is often possible to arrange mezzanine floor levels within the space of a hall or banquet room allowing cloakrooms on two levels.

Consideration should be given to providing large doors or even shutters into the banquet room, to provide access for exhibition or display equipment.

The size of a general purpose room cannot be laid down except on a seating capacity basis for banqueting purposes; such seating is generally more cramped than for a normal dining-room as the functions normally preclude individual tables. An average floor space per person in a banquet room is 0·8 to 1·0 m²

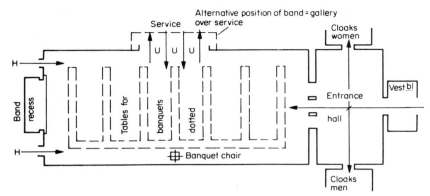

*Fig. 3.12 A typical ballroom layout
H. Approach from hotel*

The general shape should be partially dictated by acoustical requirements so that the distance from top table seats to all parts of the room is equalised. Amplified speech, by means of microphones and loudspeakers, can overcome many difficulties, but good initial planning is of the greatest importance. Banquet rooms are generally square or rectangular, the high table being usually against a long side of the room. A gallery is sometimes required, either for use of spectators or for an orchestra.

When the room is used as a ballroom, it is usual to place the band on a platform slightly raised above the general floor level. Space for dancing can be based on an allowance of 0·93 m² to 1·49 m² for each couple.

Fig. 3.8 shows a basic layout of a ballroom suite. The entrance leads to the hall, giving access to cloakrooms. The ballroom is either entered directly from the hall or via a small ante-room. In large suites a reception or supper room is often added, which may be approached either from the hall or through the ballroom; such a room can be an advantage when the ballroom is regularly let out for dances.

The general layout provides the service entrance opposite the 'top' table. Fig. 3.9 shows alternative positions for the band, and Fig. 3.10 shows alternative table layouts for banquets.

The diagram also shows dimensions for banquet seating; tables are usually about 726 mm and sometimes up to 914 mm. The seats should be placed at about 686 mm centres, which may be increased or decreased by 76 mm according to numbers to be seated. Gangways should be at least 1067 mm to permit two waiters to pass without difficulty but wall or main gangways should be wider.

Ample space should be available adjoining banquet rooms for storage of tables and chairs. The service room may be used for this purpose, if it is only used in conjunction with the banquet room. Collapsible tables are used to economise in storage space. Chairs occupy a large volume when stacked.

The storage room must be accessible as very rapid rearrangement within the banquet room often has to be made.

Good daylight is not essential in the ballrooms of urban hotels, as the majority of functions take place after dark. In resort hotels, especially at the seaside, direct access to terraces, covered lounges and gardens is an attraction which should be planned for whenever possible. Artificial ventilation is virtually essential in all banquet and ballrooms to avoid stuffiness.

SPECIAL ACCOMMODATION

Childrens room. This should be spacious and should be away from quiet areas of the hotel. Sometimes used as a games room for older children in resort hotels. The room should be cheerful and light with hard wearing surfaces. Toilet facilities should be adjacent.

Miscellaneous
Billiards, snooker
Swimming pool (allow for noise element)
Gymnasium
Games room
Turkish and sauna baths
Beauty parlour
Cinema, theatre, TV (protect from noise)
VIP Rooms (protect from noise and routine circulation)
Service flats or suites
Casino or cards room
Discotheque (allow for noise element)
Chapel (protect from noise)
Facilities for conferences

Roof gardens. Obstructions from chimneys, tank room etc. should be avoided. Height limits may be imposed by-laws. Adequate passenger and food lift should be provided if roof garden is to be fully serviced.

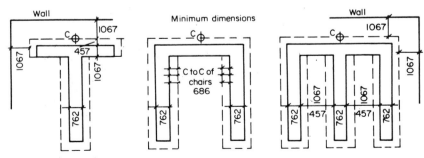

*Fig. 3.13 Banquet seating data
C. Chairman*

C. BEDROOMS AND BATHROOMS

1. GENERAL

Recommended bedroom furniture sizes are shown in Fig. 3.14 and typical bedroom/bathroom units are shown in Fig. 3.15.

Most new hotels provide individual bathrooms with each bedroom. Bedroom/bathroom units are grouped in pairs to share services and ducts. If bathrooms are not planned as part of the bedroom unit they should be grouped together to service a group of rooms. WC's should be separated. Bedrooms should be provided with a washbasin.

The number of bedroom/bathroom units on each floor will depend largely on positioning of lifts and staircases as there is a maximum distance allowed from a bedroom to a means of escape. Bedroom floors are usually repetitive with varia-

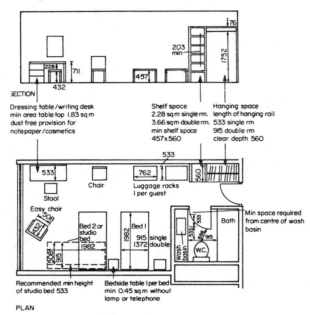

Fig. 3.14 Recommended sizes for bedroom furniture.
The top diagram shows wall arrangements. The illustration depicts an actual suite of single rooms at the Royal Hotel, Grimsby.

tions within each floor.

The bedroom/bathroom unit can be treated in various ways. Bathrooms can be internal or against an external wall. External bathrooms have natural ventilation but take up valuable external wall space and do not make direct access for repairs possible.
The disabled. Allowance should be made for disabled people. Larger bathrooms are necessary to take wheel chairs. The accommodation should be without steps. At least 50% of bedrooms and all public rooms should be accessible to chair-bound disabled people.

2. THE BEDROOM UNIT

This should provide comfort for the guest and efficient storage accommodation. Furniture would include a comfortable chair for relaxing, somewhere to write, telephone, radio and sometimes television (see Fig. 3.14).

Adequate lighting should be provided particularly in relation to the bed, dressing table and writing desk. Provision should be made for hanging clothes. Drawer or shelf space should also be provided especially for the long-term guest. A luggage rack can be constructed that can be folded back when not required.

The room should be designed with a view to easy cleaning and the making of beds. At some hotels the turn-over of guests is very frequent. The three principal causes of damage are: hot liquids and cigarettes, heavy weights and fixtures; knocking of corners by luggage and trolleys.

3. BATHROOMS

There should be one public bathroom for every ten resident guests (other than residents in bedrooms with private bathrooms). Cleanliness and hygiene are of great importance. All fittings should be chosen for good quality and ease of cleaning. It is useful to be able to hose down a bathroom so a floor gulley should be provided. Handgrips should be provided and drip-dry rails for the guests own washing.

Good ventilation and an emergency call button are important. Internal bathrooms require artificial ventilation. The duct which should be accessible from the corridor should have the long side adjacent to the corridor with a removable access panel. It should be designed for good sound insulation. If the bathroom is not beside a corridor the access panel should be in the bathroom.

4. CORRIDORS

It is important to consider ways of breaking up the apparent length of a corridor to make it visually more interesting. When planning the corridor width, it is wise to consider the standard widths of carpets.

Sometimes fanlights over the individual lobby doors are used to help ventilate the corridor, but this tends to reduce some insulation to bedrooms and may contravene the required fire separation.

A lowered ceiling in the corridor can provide a duct for services such as electricity, telephones and ventilation.

The requirements relating to intermediate doors are covered in the Fire Precautions sub-section. Fire regulations have a significant effect upon the detail design of corridors.

ROOM SERVICE

Service to bedrooms will vary according to the type of hotel. Some provide breakfasts which are prepared in the floor service kitchen but most meals are prepared in the main kitchen, brought up in the lifts and just served from the service room. In some new hotels automatic drink and/or cold food dispenser are available either in the corridor or individually in the rooms.

There should be one or more of each of the following service rooms on each bedroom floor.
1. Linen store—storage of baskets etc.
2. Furniture store.
3. Maid's store—with slop sink.
4. Food service room.
5. Small sitting area for maid—with daylight and ventilation (this could be incorporated with one of the other stores).
6. Provision for dirty linen—chutes.
Provision for rubbish and waste—chutes or bins.

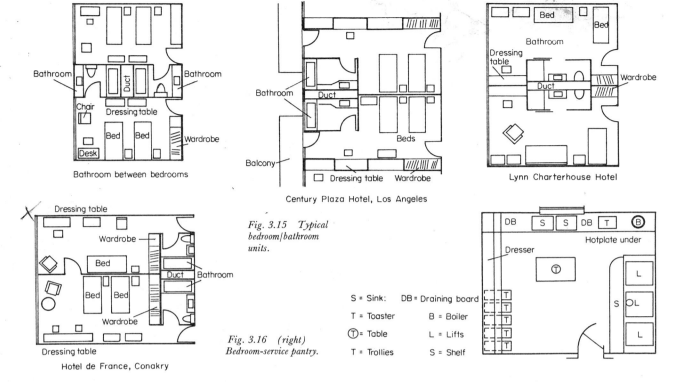

Bathroom between bedrooms

Century Plaza Hotel, Los Angeles

Lynn Charterhouse Hotel

Fig. 3.15 Typical bedroom/bathroom units.

Hotel de France, Conakry

S = Sink: DB = Draining board

T = Toaster B = Boiler

Ⓣ = Table L = Lifts

T = Trollies S = Shelf

Fig. 3.16 (right) Bedroom-service pantry.

Table 3.1 NUMBER OF SANITARY FITMENTS REQUIRED IN HOTELS*

| Fitments | For residential public and staff | For public rooms | | For non-residential staff | |
		For males†	For females†	For male staff	For female staff
W.C.s	1 per 9 persons omitting occupants of rooms with W.C.s *en suite*	1 per 100 up to 400. For over 400, add at the rate of 1 per 250 or part thereof	2 per 100 up to 200. For over 200, add at the rate of 1 per 100 or part thereof	1 for 1–15 persons 2 for 16–35 persons 3 for 36–65 persons 4 for 66–100 persons	1 for 1–12 persons 2 for 13–25 persons 3 for 26–40 persons 4 for 41–57 persons 5 for 58–77 persons 6 for 78–100 persons
Urinals	—	1 per 50 persons	—	Nil up to 6 persons 1 for 7–20 persons 2 for 21–45 persons 3 for 46–70 persons 4 for 71–100 persons	—
Lavatory basins	1 per bedroom and at least 1 per bathroom	In all buildings it is desirable that there should be a lavatory basin (or basins) in the vicinity of each W.C. or range of W.C.s		1 for 1–15 persons 2 for 16–35 persons 3 for 36–65 persons 4 for 66–100 persons	1 for 1–12 persons 2 for 13–25 persons 3 for 26–40 persons 4 for 41–57 persons 5 for 58–77 persons 6 for 78–100 persons
Bathrooms	1 per 9 persons omitting occupants of rooms with baths *en suite*	—	—	—	—
Slop sinks	1 per 30 bedrooms; minimum 1 per floor	—	—	—	—

* (From B.S. Code of Practice, C.P.3—Chapter VII (1950). Engineering and Utility Services.) *See also* Part 1: Sanitation.
† It may be assumed that there will be equal numbers of males and females.

D. SERVICE ROOMS, KITCHEN, ETC.

Guests expect a high standard of service in a hotel, therefore efficient planning at an early stage is important.

Service can be divided into two groups.
1. Food service and catering.
2. General service. Cleaning and maintenance etc.

FOOD SERVICE AND CATERING

Ideally only one kitchen should provide for all the catering in the hotel. This should be on the same level as the dining room and restaurants. If these have to be on separate levels, conveyors as well as hoists should be considered for china etc. If smaller restaurants (i.e. penthouse) they should have their own kitchen and service facilities.

The detailed design of the kitchen and its equipment is very specialised and a consultant should be brought in at an early planning stage. The layout and choice of equipment is of great importance to the efficiency of the kitchen and will reflect the categories of menu to be provided.

Natural light and ventilation are not of primary importance in positioning a kitchen, as some degree of mechanical ventilation and lighting will always be necessary.

The total area required for kitchen and ancillary rooms is likely to be as much as 100% of the total of the dining room areas in first class hotels. It is important to have food preparation areas on the same level as the kitchen but bulk stores, wine cellars, and staff rooms on a different level.

SERVICE OF FOOD

The core of food service is the kitchen and food storage, which will be located adjacent to the rooms requiring the most service, such as restaurant, dining room or grill room. An economic layout would locate the restaurant and other food service rooms next to the kitchen so that waiters enter the kitchen without a service room.

The guests entrance should be kept away from doors leading to service rooms, and would be best on the opposite wall. Consideration must be given to management control of service and the payment of accounts.

The main flow for food service is from a goods entrance through the receiving room to stores and larders, through preparation departments into the kitchen or directly to service rooms as necessary. Garbage and rubbish return to the goods entrance, for removal. Attached to the kitchen is a wash-up for utensils. Prepared food passes from the kitchen through a service space, which may either be part of the kitchen itself, or may consist of one or more separate service rooms attached to the various dining rooms. These service spaces, however arranged, are for prepared food served to dining room, grill-room, bedrooms, banqueting-rooms and private dining-rooms.

In an hotel of this character, service which handles bedroom breakfasts may be used for the remainder of the day to deal with private dining-rooms and banqueting-rooms.

It is now usual to do all washing-up in one general wash-up attached to the main service kitchen. However, in some cases, when special china or glass may be retained a separate wash-up is used.

A wine dispense has to service all the various rooms and is itself fed from the cellars. The wine and spirit dispense is usually attached to the main service, but sometimes a secondary dispense is attached to the banquet or other rooms when they are located far from the main dispense. Bars are stocked from the dispense or cellars before opening hours.

The floor areas required for food service vary according to the type of hotel, the type of catering, patronage, etc. The minimum should be, however, a dining capacity for at least the number of persons for whom sleeping accommodation is provided, while the service space required to deal with dining capacity will vary from about 50% to 100% or the area of the dining-rooms, inclusive of kitchens, stores, staff rooms and other dependencies.

KITCHENS

The detailed planning and equipment of kitchens is a matter too specialised for general planning and it is proposed to confine notes to essential factors only

The best location for the kitchen has already been discussed and, when possible, it should be on the same level as the room to be served. But there are certain other factors which should be considered at the same time. Daylight, although desirable, is not necessary in kitchens, especially if it involves loss of wall space which might be used for subsidiary departments or for apparatus. Daylight can sometimes be provided by placing the kitchen under a light well or open court, but if such a position is chosen, care must be taken to guard against the smell of cooking penetrating to bedrooms, or to rooms used by the hotel guests. It is also important to see that noise does not become a nuisance. Mechanical ventilation is essential to control the supply of air and the smell of cooking; most engineers dislike any likelihood of natural ventilation of kitchens, because, as a rule, it defeats the ventilation system and causes complaints.

The shape and area required for kitchens and the dependent rooms varies according to the type of hotel and its food service. Large spaces clear of columns, piers and supporting walls, aid the kitchen equipment specialist to produce an efficient layout. It is not essential to have all dependent rooms on the same level, but if divisions of floor level have to be made, the main kitchen, service and preparation rooms must go together. Main bulk stores, staff rooms and independent departments such as the bakehouse, linen, wine cellars, etc., may be separated.

The area required for the kitchen proper, for preparation, cooking and service area, exclusive of store rooms, locker and toilet rooms for the staff, varies from 35% to 50% of the aggregate dining-room areas and at least 40% to 45% should be allowed. The smaller figures should only be considered when the meals to be served are mainly table d'hote and to a limited menu, as is the general practice in many smaller and lower-grade types of hotels. For all hotels where the service has a considerable demand for meals a la carte and caters for a large variety of foods, the 50% figure is more likely to be needed. The total area required for the kitchen and all ancillaries is likely to be as much as 100% of the total of the dining-room areas in first-class and luxury hotels.

The arrangement of departments or sections of the kitchen should be planned to avoid as much cross-traffic as possible and the service counter, which is usually divided into sections for differing purposes, should be laid out in a sequence which best suits the service of the most important room. The service counter consists of hot and cold cupboards, bains-marie, etc in which food, plates and dishes are kept hot or cold as required; along the counter front there should be a continuous tray shelf on which waiters may rest trays and push them along.

Storage is an important factor and can be divided into two main groups:

(i) Local storage in and adjoining preparation departments and

(ii) Main bulk storage of goods of all types.

The first type of storage generally consists of shelving, bins and refrigerators, each specially chosen to suit the particular goods to be handled and maintained at varying temperatures to suit each category.

Bulk storage also has to be divided into two main groups; firstly, food which needs either cool storage or refrigeration, such as fish, meat, vegetables and dairy produce, and, secondly, dry, cased or tinned goods which may be placed in large open store rooms fitted with suitable shelving and also with bins.

Shelving should be either of hardwood or metal and the bins of wood, sheet metal or stout wire mesh. Floors should be suitable for moving heavy loads on trucks and should be able to withstand tipping and the dropping of packing cases.

In most hotels the steward's office or goods reception office adjoins the bulk storage, so that all goods are properly weighed and checked on arrival. Large scales are an essential installation. In large hotels an issuing counter is necessary so that only the storekeeper and his assistants enter the actual store rooms, the kitchen porters and cooks collecting from a hatch. The amount of storage space required varies very much with the size of the hotel and its proximity to markets.

In larger hotels the refrigeration section may become very large, requiring as many as six rooms—21·33 m² in area—maintained at different temperatures to suit the type of food kept in each compartment. A central plant is generally used to provide ice requirements and also to cool the various refrigerators throughout the building, with the exception of small independent units in such positions as bedroom-floor service rooms.

Fig. 3.17 illustrates the general basic circulation of food in the kitchen. Food enters and is taken to refrigerators or larders—in the case of perishable food—and to bulk storage for the remainder. It is then passed to preparation and cooking sections, thence to the service counters in kitchen or service rooms adjoining the various dining-rooms.

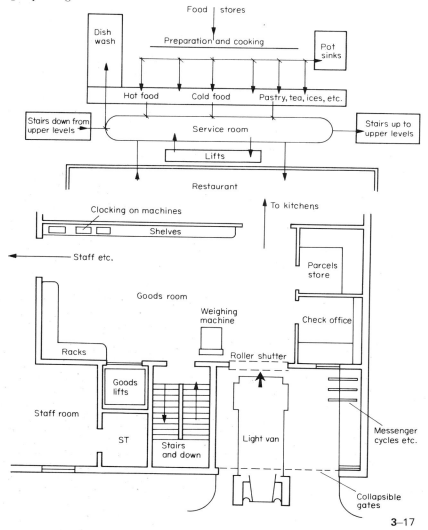

Fig. 3.17   Kitchens: analysis of service circulations.

Fig. 3.18   Service entrance.

If service space is to be provided in the kitchen at least 1·82 m width is necessary, and preferably 3·04 m or 3·65 m where large numbers of waiters are employed. If staircases are required to other levels they should enter and leave from this same service space. Stairs should be at least 0·9 m wide and the traffic in each direction should be either separated by a handrail and balustrade.

SERVICE ENTRANCE

In small hotels, goods and staff use the same entrance, but in larger hotels there should be separate entrances. Each must be controlled so as to check persons and goods entering and leaving the hotel. If store rooms and entrances are at a lower level than the pavement, adequate-sized lifts, hoists or ramps, (the gradients of which are easy) must be installed. Goods lifts must be large enough to carry packing cases, laundry baskets, sides of meat, etc., on a truck or trolley with a man in charge, and should, therefore, be at least 1·82 × 1·21 m. Steps and stairs should be eliminated whenever possible in all service departments, slight changes in level being ramped.

Fig. 3.19 illustrates a typical hotel service entrance in which a backing-in space for vehicles is provided, but not an unloading dock as, in this example, it serves also as a staff entrance. The clerk's office controls the unloading space, the parcels room and time clocks. The weighing machine should be placed between the entrance and the goods lift.

The staircase to the basement is near the lift and is not used to reach the staff rooms, but only the goods stores, boiler room, etc. The staff all have to pass the clocks to reach their locker rooms. A ground-floor receiving department is preferable. The goods entrance should be placed where vans can be within the site boundaries while unloading without interrupting external traffic. The staff entrance, whether combined with goods entrance or not, should lead directly to locker rooms, passing time-recording clocks and a timekeeper's or paymaster's office.

GENERAL SERVICES

Refuse. Refuse will include waste paper, dust, remains of food, tins, jars, bottles, boxes, ashes and trade rubbish from workshops. Space must be provided for storage, sorting and putting into containers for collection. This area should be ventilated, and in hot climates provision should be made for cooling.

Refuse disposal. Refer to local authority to find out frequency of collections. Consideration should be given to waste disposal units and incinerators, water for hosing down and cleaning bins, and the turning circle required by refuse collection vehicles. Refrigerated refuse storage is important in hot climates.

Linen storage. Provision should be made for bulk storage of linen together with dirty linen store and sorting and mending rooms if this is carried out on the premises. It is convenient to have a chute from individual bedroom floors to this area.

Laundry and linen rooms. Linen is either hired or laundered outside the hotel, in which case space must be provided for a three day supply. Storage should be provided on each bedroom floor and should allow for bed linen, tableware, uniforms, towels and trolleys. A space should be set aside for cleaning, pressing and repairing and for storage of baskets.

Some hotels provide a valet service, in which case it would be necessary to provide a special room for this purpose.

The linen store should be adequately ventilated; heating and humidity must be watched. Communication in the form of telephone or speaker should be provided. Chutes for soiled linen should be provided and possibly facilities for home laundry.

Engineer and engineering services

Workshops. One or more spacious workshops are necessary for running repairs. In a large hotel there can be up to 50 employees with a works manager having his own office.

Storage space is necessary for furniture and good workbench areas. Easy access for the delivery of materials should be provided.

Works catered for are: engineers; electricians; glaziers; joiners; upholsterers; curtain makers; mattress repairers; and printing works (for printing of menus, etc).

The security for storage of paints, spares, and electrical equipment is important. These workshops should be kept well away from the guest areas because of noise and smell from paint. A cupboard on each floor for maintenance equipment could be provided.

Telephones. In small hotels the switchboard is in the hotel office of porters' offices, but in a large hotel there may be extensive telephone equipment, with switchboard and many operators. In this case a locker room and toilets and rest room should be provided for the operators. Alternatively it should be near the other office and all office staff can share the same facilities.

Internal communications. The following communications systems should be provided within the building:

    Alarm system and emergency communications
    Housekeeper—maids
    Room service
    Wake-up system
    Messengers desk
    Telex
    TV, radio and taped music.

Service yard and loading bay. An assessment must be made of the number of service vehicles loading or unloading at any one time including supply of provisions, fuel, furniture. Also accommodation for vehicles belonging to the hotel.

Fuel storage. The type and quantity of fuel required for heating, generators, pumps and other mechanical equipment should be considered in relation to reliability of supply and economy of bulk purchase. The fire hazard, dust, colour and appearance of both storage and unloading must be considered when locating fuel storage units.

Garages. Lock-up garages or covered parking bays may be included in the accommodation. Garages are best approached from a side street by ramps if in a portion of the basement. Where there is adequate space at ground floor, lock up garages can be planned around a yard to reduce noise nuisance. Where accommodation for cars is an important element on a restricted site, a multi-storey car park as the centre core of the building can provide close proximity between car and guests bedroom.

Heating. The space and location for boilers and hot water storage whether at basement or roof level will require specialist advice. Attention should be given to the noise and heat from boiler rooms, relation to fuel storage, accessibility for maintenance, degree of control of heat levels and economy in service, ventilation and flue runs.

Ventilation and air-conditioning. Extract from kitchen should be taken up to roof levels—smells must not get back to bedrooms. The space and location for ventilation and air-conditioning plant require specialist advice. Attention should be given to noise, degree of individual control, alternatives in case of failure and economy in service runs.

E. STAFF FACILITIES AND ADMINISTRATION

The staff of a hotel could range from a few to an extensive team of Administrative staff, each requiring offices convenient for the functions under their control. Staff employed in food service and catering, bar and reception and staff employed in the cleaning and maintenance of the rooms all require particular attention.

The number of staff varies according to hotel type. It can range from a staff to guest ratio of 0·8:1·0 in a high class hotel to 0·1:1·0 at an economy class hotel.

The number of rooms serviced by one maid may vary according to plan, type and accessibility but, is usually about 1 maid to 30 guests. Full time staff are employed for everyday cleaning, maintenance and catering work. Due to long hours, shift work is essential. Major repairs and breakdowns are usually dealt with by Contractors who have a planned maintenance programme.

Staff canteen. This is usually to cater for all staff, both residen-

tial and daily. It should have its own service room for storage of china, glass, etc.

Staff locker room. Lockers, changing and toilet rooms are necessary for all staff. These should be near the staff entrance and should be grouped according to type of staff—waiters, porters, kitchen staff, etc.

Staff valet room. This room is where uniforms are stored, cleaned and pressed and should be near the locker rooms.

Bedrooms. For living-in staff. These should be in a separate section of the building.

Manager: The Manager should be in an accessible part of the hotel. The accommodation would consist of a bedroom, sitting room and bathroom.

Managerial staff: Managerial staff require single bedsits, with bathroom facilities.

Housekeeper: The Housekeeper's office accommodation should be accessible to the catering parts of the hotel. In addition a bedsitting room and a bathroom should be provided.

Maids: Maids require bedrooms, with bathroom facilities, a laundry room for private washing and, preferably, two sitting rooms (one quiet for reading and writing and one with television and record player).

Visiting servants: Visiting servants can have a separate 'Stewards' Room for sitting or in which to wait. They would use spare staff bedrooms. Alternatively, there could be a separate annexe of small bedrooms with bathroom and sitting room.

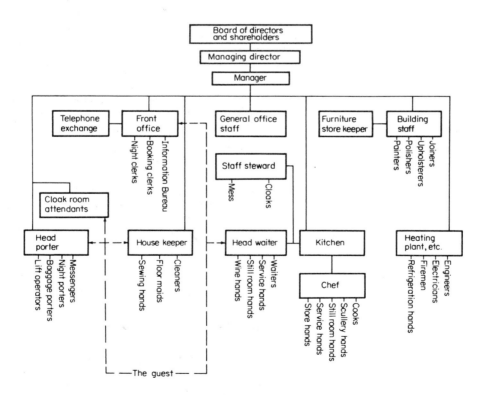

Fig. 3.19 Hotel organisation.

DATA—FIRE PRECAUTIONS

The Fire Precautions Act 1971 makes provision for adequate means of escape and related fire precautions in places of public resort which includes hotels and boarding houses although it is for the fire authority to be satisfied that the means of escape in case of fire and other fire precautions are adequate. In planning the hotel, it is necessary to define 'protected routes' or routes for persons escaping from fire which is separated from the remainder of the building by fire resisting doors and by walls, partitions and floors which are of fire-resisting construction.

TRAVEL WITHIN ROOMS

In rooms with only one exit, no point should be more than 9 m from the exit. In rooms of high fire risk such as kitchens and boiler rooms, this distance should not exceed 6 m. This also applies to compartments within rooms where in addition a clear vision panel should be provided in a suitable position between inner and outer room except where consideration of privacy is paramount.

Where a room has more than one exit leading to an escape route, but which leads to safety in one direction only, the distance from any point in the room to the nearest exit should not exceed 9 m or 6 m in rooms of high fire risk. In large rooms, drawing rooms, ballrooms etc. there should be no less than two exits leading by separate routes to a place of safety.

In a large room, distance from an exit should not exceed 18 m. This can be increased to 30·4 m if there are at least three exits, if the aggregate width complies with the relevant standard and if it is adequate for the notional occupancy of the part of the room it serves.

Alternative exits should be provided so that means of escape in two separate directions from any one point in the room, the angle between the lines drawn from any point in the room to alternative exits is not less than 45°.

TRAVEL FROM ROOMS TO A STAIRWAY OR FINAL EXIT

The maximum distance from an exit from a room to a point of access in a protected route, to an external route, or to a final exit should be:

Rooms with only one or more exits and with alternative routes there from to a separate enclosed staircase, external route, roof exit, final exit or a combination of these 18 m from any exit.

Ground floor rooms into an exit giving immediate access to a place of safety. *No limit* to any internal route.

Room where only one route is available from exit (i.e. cul-de-sac corridors) 7·6 m.

EXITS AND WALL FINISHES

For rooms occupied by more than 5 people, the exit width should not be less than 760 mm. For rooms occupied by more than 100 people, the exit width should not be less than 1 m.

If more than one exit, then with one exit excluded the aggregate width of the remaining exits should be:

For up to 100 people 760 mm
For up to 200 people 1·060 m

An additional 76 mm is required for each additional 15 persons or less.

Exit doors, other than those in ordinary use by guests should be distinctly and conspicuously marked by permanent exit notices.

Surface finishes of walls and ceiling must conform to standards laid down.

STANDARDS OF CONSTRUCTION

Bedroom doors opening onto escape corridors should have the same fire resistance as the walls containing them, up to a modified half-hour's fire resistance. Such doors would not be self closing but fanlights or borrowed lights should have similar fire resistance and be fixed closed. In the case of cul-de-sac corridors, doors should be self closing. Doors to cupboards should be fire-resisting and marked 'THIS DOOR TO BE KEPT LOCKED SHUT'.

STAIRWAYS

Where it is necessary to pass a stairway to reach an alternative escape route, the stairway should be enclosed by fire-resisting construction in such a way that a person need not pass through the enclosure to reach the alternative route. Alternatively, a by-pass must be arranged.

In a building with more than one staircase, doors from rooms other than lavatories should not open directly into the stairway unless the doors are fire-resisting and self-closing. In cases above the 3rd floor a fire resisting screen incorporating fire resisting self-closing doors is provided at every level served. The distance from any such door to the door separating the stairway from the alternative route is to be not more than 4·6 m unless a satisfactory alternative route is available.

CORRIDORS

Main corridors should not be less than 1·2 m wide. Cul-de-sac corridors should be not less than 1·06 m. Finishes to wall and ceilings should be Class 'O'.

Where corridors exceed 18 m in length, fire resisting self-closing doors should be provided at intervals of not more than 18 m.

BASEMENTS

In basements, apart from small basements used for storage only, there should be alternative stairways to ground floor level unless there is a final exit at basement level. The basement should be separated from the ground floor by two half-hour fire-resisting self-closing doors, one at basement level and one at ground level, or by a one-hour fire-resisting self-closing door at basement level.

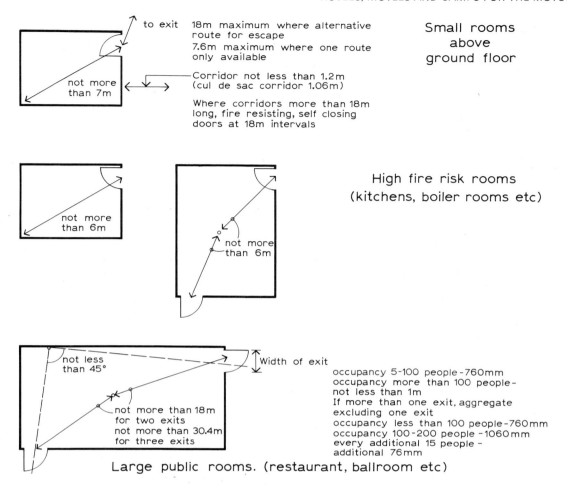

to exit   18m maximum where alternative
route for escape
7.6m maximum where one route
only available

Corridor not less than 1.2m
(cul de sac corridor 1.06m)

Where corridors more than 18m
long, fire resisting, self closing
doors at 18m intervals

not more
than 7m

Small rooms
above
ground floor

not more
than 6m

not more
than 6m

High fire risk rooms
(kitchens, boiler rooms etc)

not less
than 45°

Width of exit

not more than 18m
for two exits
not more than 30.4m
for three exits

occupancy 5-100 people-760mm
occupancy more than 100 people-
not less than 1m
If more than one exit, aggregate
excluding one exit
occupancy less than 100 people-760mm
occupancy 100-200 people -1060mm
every additional 15 people -
additional 76mm

Large public rooms. (restaurant, ballroom etc)

Fig. 3.20   Exitways and means of escape.

TRAVEL WITHIN THE STAIRWAYS AND TO FINAL EXITS

Regarding travel within stairways and to final exits, a single stairway in a building is acceptable if the stairway is enclosed with fire-resisting construction, access to the stairway is through two sets of fire-resisting self-closing doors (except in the case of lavatories) and at ground level, the stairway discharges directly to or via a protected route either a safe place in the open air or to alternative routes to separate final exits.

Where these conditions cannot be achieved, the building having only one floor above ground floor, a single stairway may be acceptable if a roof exit or other external escape route is provided. In addition the single staircase should be screened at the upper floor with fire-resisting construction so that the occupants of the upper floor can reach the alternative exit without having to enter the staircase enclosure. Alternatively the distance from the farthest room door on the upper floor to the final exit should not exceed 18 m and the fire escape route must be protected throughout its length.

In case of two stairways, the individual escape routes must be separated by fire-resisting construction.

GENERAL

Attention should be given to the possible effect on ventilation systems regarding the spread of fire, smoke or hot gases from fire. Also clear instructions must be displayed as to the exit routes. Some form of emergency lighting should be provided to illuminate staircases, routes of exit and directional signs, sufficiently to enable persons to make their way out of the premises. In ballrooms, conference rooms and other rooms where large numbers of people assemble, and in all associated escape routes, the emergency lighting must be kept on when the room is in use and when there is insufficient natural light.

In all premises, means of giving warning in case of fire should be installed, and all premises should be provided with means for fighting fire for use by persons in the building. Except in the case of small premises, hose reels should be provided. Where these are not provided, hand fire extinguishers should be provided in sufficient numbers to give adequate cover to the premises. Appropriate steps should be taken to ensure that information about the action to be taken in the event of fire is readily available to all guests.

HOTELS, MOTELS AND CAMPS FOR THE MOTORIST

EXAMPLES

ROYAL GARDEN HOTEL, LONDON

The hotel is situated on the edge of Kensington Gardens. Town planning imposed a height control of 38 m and thus there are several floors below ground. Of the four basement floors, the lowest two provide space for 300 cars. The third basement floor provides for staff facilities and administrative offices. The fourth basement floor, immediately below ground level, has the staff dining room, Banquet Hall to seat 600 guests and a Coffee House (see Fig. 3.2).

Access from the street is from an elevated drive, serving the upper ground floor level. The ground floor has the foyer, lounge, main restaurant, and kitchen. The lower ground floor has a bar and a smaller restaurant with direct access from the street. The mezzanine level is occupied by conference rooms, private dining rooms and administrative offices. There are are ten bedroom floors, each floor has 28 single and 18 double rooms, and 4 corner suites. There are a total of 500 bedrooms.
Architects: R. Seifert and Partners.

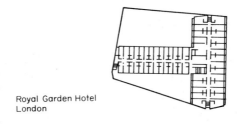

Royal Garden Hotel
London

TRUST HOUSE, LONDON AIRPORT HOTEL

The plan consists of a cruciform tower above first floor with bedroom accommodation, with public rooms at ground floor level. Access to the hotel is separate from the access to the function rooms. The kitchen is centralised, serving grill room, coffee shop, restaurant and two function rooms. The loading bay serves storage areas, refuse compactor and boiler room. The offices are adjacent to the loading bay with the staff facilities separated at first floor. The cruciform multi-storey section has a central lift core. Each wing terminates in an escape staircase.
Architects: Nelson Foley, Chief Architect, Trust Houses Group Ltd.

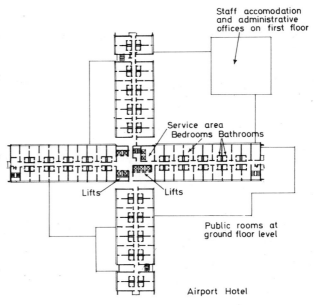

Staff accomodation and administrative offices on first floor

Service area
Bedrooms Bathrooms

Lifts   Lifts

Public rooms at ground floor level

Airport Hotel

ATRIUM HOTEL, BRUNSWICK, GERMANY

The site is in close proximity to a railway line, facing Brunswick's main station, across an open square. Traffic noise was a major consideration and thus an 'atrium' plan was adopted. The corridor layout protects bedrooms from extraneous noise. The hotel consists of 126 beds, 6 double units (one with a sauna), 12 double and 90 single rooms. A few of the rooms can be combined to four suites. There are also 12 long-stay apartments with independent kitchenettes.
Architects: Friedrich Wilhelm Kraemer, Gunter Pfennig, Ernst Sieverts.

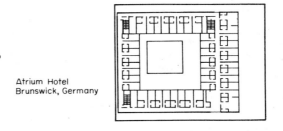

Atrium Hotel
Brunswick, Germany

HUMBER ROYAL HOTEL, GRIMSBY

The general design consists of three main elements; the bedroom block, a separate staircase tower and the single storey section with public rooms. The bedroom block has 49 guest rooms providing 96 beds. The various uses at ground floor level have separate entrances and foyers. It is designed as a commercial hotel, suited to the provincial site.
Architects: Howard V. Lobb and Partners

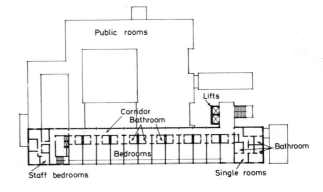

Public rooms

Lifts

Corridor
Bathroom

Bedrooms

Bathroom

Staff bedrooms

Single rooms

Royal Hotel
Grimsby

Fig. 3.21 Typical arrangements.

LONDON CENTRAL YMCA HOTEL AND CLUB REDEVELOPMENT

The building includes 764 bedrooms with residential staff accommodation, offices, shops and a restaurant; also comprehensive sports, recreational, social and cultural facilities, a chapel, a conference centre with a multi-purpose hall and car parking (see Fig. 3.22).

The hotel and residential accommodation is situated above the podium and is designed so that each room has an outlook over London. Bedrooms have private bathrooms and are served by four lifts in the main core. The bedrooms are arranged in groups off the main spine corridor for quietness, security and to give each room an outlook. Each floor is provided with a common room with self catering facilities. Small lounges are provided on each floor for hotel guests. The services and air conditioning equipment for the whole building is situated at podium roof level.

Ground floor accommodation comprises reception, foyers with adjacent bar and lounge, restaurant, travel agency, hotel shops, library and servicing bay. In addition to the multi purpose hall there are sports and practice halls, squash courts, lounges with refreshment areas, access to the galleries overlooking the sports hall and the 25 m swimming pool.

The restaurant can be approached from either the hotel or direct from the street and will be open to hotel residents and the public.

The upper club level includes the swimming pool, linked by a spiral staircase to the solarium and changing rooms below. There is also a chapel, study room, reading room, chess room, television room amongst other areas of activity all linked by glazed screens.

Architects: Elsworth Sykes Partnership.

LEEDS BRADFORD POST HOUSE

The layout separates the principle bedroom accommodation from the public rooms. The hotel entrance is separate from the entrance to the function rooms. The kitchen is centralised serving function rooms, restaurant, restaurant bar, hotel bar and buttery. The staff access and loading area are at a lower level. The bedroom accommodation consists of a rectangular five floor block with central corridor. The sloping site allows access from the hotel lobby to the bedroom accommodation block at floor three.

Architects: Nelson Foley, Chief Architect, Trust Houses Group Ltd.

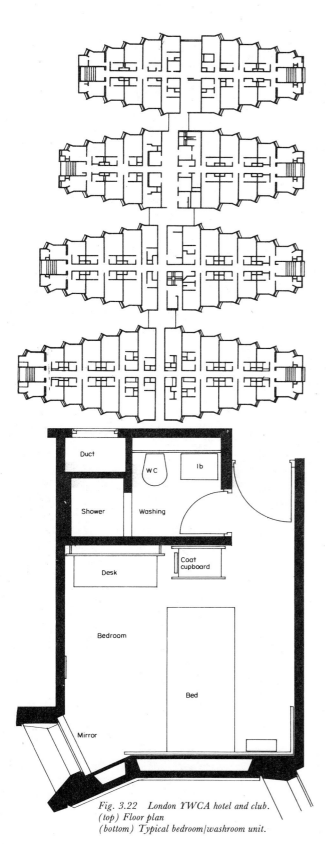

Fig. 3.22 London YWCA hotel and club.
(top) Floor plan
(bottom) Typical bedroom/washroom unit.

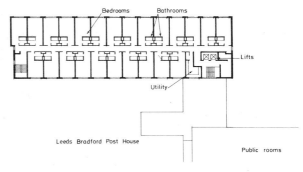

Fig. 3.23 Bedroom accommodation. Leeds Bradford Post House.

3–23

MOTELS etc

This section is concerned with the accommodation for the mobile tourist or traveller en route. It covers Motels, Camps for Motorists and Camping Sites for Tents and Caravans in which provision is made in the most economic form to avoid delays in administration or the expense of unnecessary facilities.

INTRODUCTION

A motel is essential roadside accommodation for the motorist consisting of rooms easily accessible from individual motorcars, and may include catering bar and other facilities otherwise provided in a hotel.

SITING

It is important to consider the visibility and accessibility of the site from the highway. Direct access may be affected by licensing laws which restrict direct access from licensed premises to a motorway. Visibility is important to provide self advertising. In this respect a site rising from the highway has an advantage. A flat site with landscaping may require a two storey section to be visible. A site falling from the highway may protect the motel from noise and the roof form would be particularly evident. A sloping site can gain the advantage of reducing the visual impact of parked cars.

The proportion of the site is important to the basic layout and the relationship of access to outlook. It is better that the outlook is away from highway noise, or where the motel is associated with a particular amenity, that this can be enjoyed without the interference of traffic. The site should be well drained and have all services available.

PLANNING

The main components in a motel complex are:
  1. Access and parking cars.
  2. Accommodation (bedrooms and bathrooms).
  3. Management and control.
  4. Public rooms and amenities.
  5. Landscaping for privacy to reduce effect of parking and traffic.
The basic layout must provide easy access from car to accommodation. Parking at right angles to a footway, angle parking, or parking immediately adjacent to the accommodation unit provide economic layouts. In countries with unreliable weather, it is desirable to have cover to load and unload, which suggests a carport at the side of the accommodation or a continuous canopy on the access side. Car spaces should be numbered as the accommodation units they serve. The bathroom layout should be considered in terms of economy of services, and can be located to act as sound insulation to traffic noise.

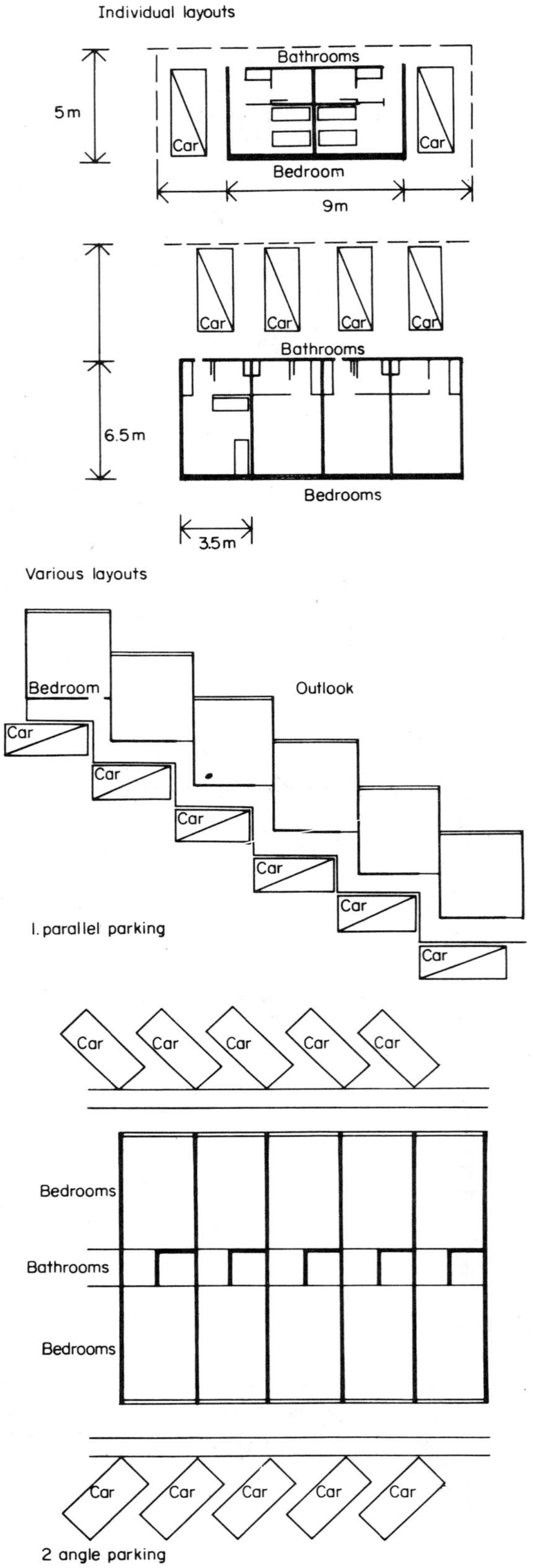

Fig. 3.24   Various layouts for rooms and car parking

Individual layouts

Various layouts

1. parallel parking

2 angle parking

HOTELS, MOTELS AND CAMPS FOR THE MOTORIST

The accommodation units will be planned to the cost level and length of stay anticipated. Each unit should have a private outlook away from access and traffic. The layout of the individual rooms will be similar to hotel rooms with the entrance lobby or area, fitted with cupboard space and will provide sound insulation from traffic noise.

Various layouts are shown in Fig. 3.24 i.e.
1. Linear plan with parallel parking.
2. Linear plan with parking at angles.
3. U plan with parking in centre.
4. U plan with parking on outside.
Individual layouts.

B.	Bed or bunk
Cup.	Cupboard
C.	Chair
ST.	Seat
FS.	Fixed seat (tip up)
CT.	Curtain
D.	Door
W.	Window
L.	Locker
T.	Table
S.	Shelf
M.	Mirror
WR.	Wardrobe
SK.	Sink
DB.	Draining Board
PR.	Plate rack
TT.	Table top
ST.	Cooker
LB.	Lavatory basin
MC.	Motor Car

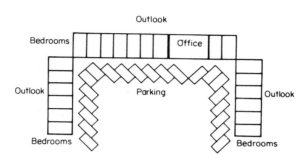

3. U plan with parking in centre

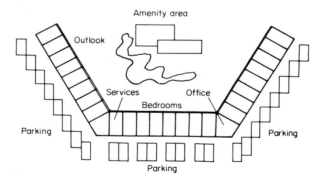

4. U plan with parking on outside

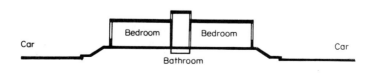

Fig. 3.24 (continued)

CAMPS FOR MOTORISTS

Sites are provided for in transit travellers or holiday, for short stay tourists, providing in some cases only essential facilities for overnight stay. (Toilet, water, and washing facilities) or more elaborate arrangements (cooking, laundry, cafeteria, restaurant, shop, recreational rooms and leisure activities). Accommodation would be provided for a controller.

The two principal functions are:
1. Space for cars, tents and caravans.
2. Amenity buildings.

Landscaping for privacy and to avoid the intrusion of the camp site on the surrounding environment is an important design factor.

LEGISLATION

All permanent and semi-permanent camp developments are subject to planning control and Local Authority Standards. The recommendations of the Camping Working Party are particularly relevant to detail planning requirements.

SITING

The site should provide adequate space for the number of visitors permitted, amenity buildings and landscaping. Well drained, gently sloping ground is an advantage. Terracing can provide additional variety for pitches. Consideration should be given to aspect and prevailing winds. An area already well supplied with trees, also has an advantage. The ground should permit planting sufficient for screening and wind breaks. It is important that the development of the site does not become a visual intrusion upon the landscape. In many cases, the uninterrupted natural landscape will be the principal attraction for visitors.

It should be possible to construct paths and roads which will be usuable when the site is occupied, and services (water, electricity and drainage) should be available or possible to construct within the site itself.

PLANNING

There should be one main entrance with a control point. The general layout could be as Fig. 3.25. Petrol pumps, service stations and repair shops should be separated from the other camp buildings. If a restaurant is provided and it is to cater for passing trade as well as the camp, it should be sited near the entrance and so planned that there is no need for casual users to go near the resident portion of the camp. Separate car parking should also be made available for the restaurant trade.

All traffic entering the camp should pass the main reception office before reaching the sleeping accommodation. Any common rooms should adjoin the reception unit; these should also incorporate general services such as heating, fuel, storage and kitchens. The guests' sleeping accommodation, with the necessary toilet facilities, should be planned away from road traffic and the restaurant to provide maximum quietness.

Some recreation space for use by resident visitors and their children should be planned in association with the sleeping and common-room units. A separate entrance for goods and staff is desirable, leading to an enclosed kitchen yard. There should be garages or parking space for staff vehicles.

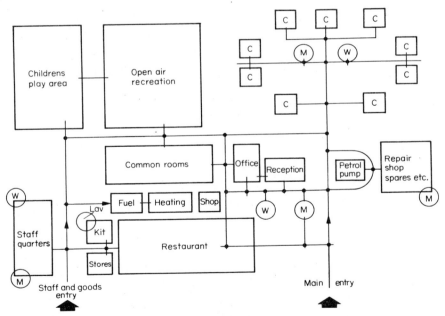

Fig. 3.25   General relationship of a motor camp
C. Cabins
M. Toilets (men)
W. Toilets (women)

PETROL SALES

This may take one of two forms: firstly, a unit associated with the camp and its buildings, or secondly, a separate unit planned on a road at or near the point of juncture of the local road to the camp site. In the second type it is likely to be operated on a lease or concession basis. Full information on the planning of petrol stations is given in Section 10. Great care should be taken to place the petrol station where there is no fire risk to the remainder of the camp, also the coming and going of vehicles. If the pumps are available at all hours, they should be planned to minimise incidental noise or disturbance to the camp residents.

REPAIR FACILITIES

There may be facilities for visitors wishing to carry out their own small repairs and minor overhauls. On the other hand, it may be worth while incorporating a small repair service in charge of a competent mechanic, operated by the camp or let out perhaps with the petrol station, on a concession which will provide services for the vehicles of both camp visitors and passers by. For reference to detailed planning, see Section 10.

NIGHT LIGHTING OF PATHS AND ROADS

It is desirable to provide adequate lighting of all access-paths and roadways within the camp to assist strangers to find the way from cabins to the central building, toilet units, etc. Lamp-posts should be placed well clear of paths; their height and spacing is dependent on the type and power of the lamps installed.

RECREATIONAL FACILITIES

These depend largely on the space available and to a measure on the anticipated duration of a visitor's stay. If the stopping period is mainly to be one, or at the most two, nights little provision need be made, except possibly a small children's playground. If the period is to be longer, it may be desirable to use part of the ground as a play-space, even constructing tennis courts and/or a putting green.

In some larger schemes, where water supplies permit and the climate conditions are suitable, a small swimming-pool might be an added attraction.

ENTRANCES

As camps for motorists may involve a considerable amount of traffic entering and leaving the site, it is important that the planning of the entrance to the site be given careful thought. A simple drive-in with gates on the roadside is likely both to be missed by strangers approaching the site at speed, and to be very dangerous; it is desirable to separate 'in' and 'out' traffic as shown in Fig. 3.26. An arrangement of this type provides a suitable space for a sign, easily visible along the main road. In larger camps any long approach drive should be 6 m to permit two lines of traffic and space for pedestrians; if, however, the approach road is of some considerable length, its width may be reduced to 3 m if 'lay-by's' at least 12 m long are provided every 274 m along the road. Each lay-by should be so placed as to be visible from the next in both directions.

It is desirable to plan camps on land well away from the main roads, to provide quiet and privacy for guest; in such cases adequate direction and instruction signs, preferably illuminated at night, should be placed on the main road near or at the entrance to camp sites.

If camps are to be used by trailer caravans, care must be taken to plan the entrances and road junctions carefully as the combined lengths are great and the radii of curves and roads, if too small, may be difficult to negotiate.

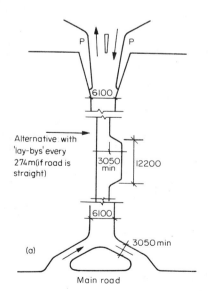

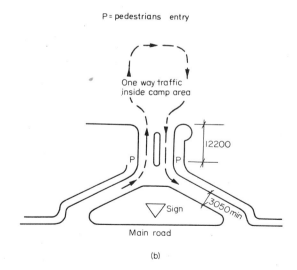

P = pedestrians entry

Fig. 3.26 Camp entrances.

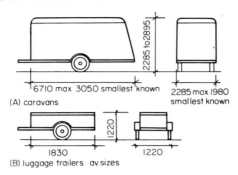

(A) caravans

6710 max 3050 smallest known
2285 max 1980 smallest known
2285 to 2895

(B) luggage trailers av. sizes

1830   1220   1220

Fig. 3.27   Car and trailer data.

EXTERNAL DIMENSIONS AND SPACING

The dimensions of private motor cars are covered in the section on External Circulation in the volume *Planning: Architects' Technical Reference Data*. Fig. 3.27 illustrates the dimensions of trailer caravans and luggage trailers. Sizes of tents vary considerably. A tent for a single person may be 1 m × 700 mm whereas a family tent could be considerably larger. For the purposes of planning, it is useful to assume that they will occupy an area of 3·6 m radius.

TYPES OF CAMP

There are various types of camps for motorists, as shown in Fig. 3.28.

1. CABINS

Camps using permanent or semi-permanent cabins are shown in Figs. 3.28(a) and (b). The accommodation may be detached cabins with an adjoining berth for the user's car, as shown in (a). Grouped cabins are useful for family occupation where single two-bedded cabins do not provide the required sleeping accommodation.

An alternative to car berths adjoining the cabins is shown in (c) and (d). Here all cars are berthed in one or more large Parking spaces, covered areas, or even garages. This layout may be more economic on some sites, as less hard roadway is needed, but it is a solution likely to prove less popular with the users.

2. CARAVANS

Fig. 3.28(e) illustrates the type of trailer caravan camp where the trailers are planned at least 3 m apart with the cars parked adjacent to each caravan. As the trailers are heavy to move by hand, all camps should be planned on the assumption that the car is made readily available by being parked at the side or at the end of the trailer. This may also be necessary if trailers depend on the car batteries for lighting. If camps are to be used constantly for many months of the year, it is desirable to provide concrete or similar hard surface standings for both trailers and cars. Standards for caravan sites are considered later.

3. TENTED CAMPS

Figs. 3.28 (f) and (g) illustrate tented camps which may also be based on parking vehicles adjoining each tent or in central parks or garages. In all camps of a permanent or semi-permanent nature, designed to house more than one group of users, latrines should be placed at least 12 m from sleeping quarters; if, however, water-borne disposal systems or chemical closets are used, the accommodation may be planned nearer to cabins. In the case however, of grouped chemical closets, it may be desirable to adhere to the separation distance of 12 m. Standards for lavatory accommodation are given on page **3**-31.

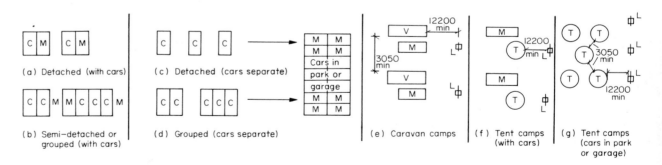

(a) Detached (with cars)

(b) Semi-detached or grouped (with cars)

(c) Detached (cars separate)

(d) Grouped (cars separate)

(e) Caravan camps

(f) Tent camps (with cars)

(g) Tent camps (cars in park or garage)

Fig. 3.28   Some types of permanent and seasonal camps

C. Cabins   M. Car berths   T. Tents   V. Caravans   L. Toilets.

CABINS

There are many possible methods of grouping cabin units within the camp sites, but all should be related to the provision of proper aspect and to avoid long distances from sanitary units to central or communal buildings. Very careful consideration should also be given to economy of road-making, although closely spaced units will involve loss of privacy which is undesirable and must be balanced against cost of layout.

Fig. 3.29 shows the grouping of various types of cabin unit in relation to screened sanitary accommodation. All the cabins shown have individual parking facilities. The diagram shows the effect of combining single storied and double storied cabin units on a staggered plan to attain the the maximum amenities in respect of privacy, air and aspect. The figure also shows desirable minima for road widths, etc. and the use of one-way traffic throughout a single group of units.

In a large camp the type of grouping shown in Figs 3.29 and 3.30 might be repeated a number of times in different parts of the camp and at various distances from the central buildings. Fig. 3.30 shows single and double cabin units arranged around a central car park, at one end of which is sanitary accommodation for each sex.

It is very desirable that all access between the cabins, roadways and central buildings be hard-surfaced and well drained. Roadways in which vehicles may have to turn or reverse must be at least 6 m wide and all roadways for one-way traffic must be at least 3 m wide. Roadways to which two-way traffic has access should be avoided whenever possible, but if they are provided, they should be at least 5·5 m wide. It may frequently be desirable to plan wide access pathways on which a truck may be moved for transport of bedding, furniture and other cabin equipment; such pathways should be at least 3 m wide while normal access paths to cabins should be at least 1·35 m wide, to permit two persons to walk abreast comfortably.

In camps likely to be used in winter, or those sited in areas liable to heavy rainfall at all periods of the year, it may be found desirable to provide covered access from cabins to sanitary units and to a lesser degree to the central building.

Cabins either take the form of small double bedrooms with an individual car shelter attached, or the form of a unit for family use, having several bedrooms with shelter for one vehicle; alternatively, several bedroom units can be grouped

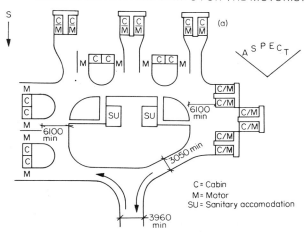

Fig. 3.29   Grouping of cabins. Cars adjacent to cabins
C.   Cabin   M.   Car berth
C/M. Cabin with car under   SU. Sanitary unit

together with shelter for several vehicles. This arrangement can be used either as a family unit or by several separate visitors. In some schemes, the cabins are all grouped together as in a holiday camp and the cars parked or garaged in a separate area. It is probable, however, that motorists will prefer to have their cars adjoining their cabins, if only to simplify loading and unloading luggage.

More elaborate schemes provide not only purely bedroom accommodation but also some sitting- or dining-space. Cooking facilities, when provided for visitors who wish to do their own cooking, are usually grouped with central or communal accommodation. In more expensive schemes, however, in which each unit is completely self-contained, facilities for cooking may be included with those for dining, washing, and sleeping; accommodation of an elaborate type involves heavy capital expenditure, especially in regard to water supplies, drainage and similar services. It is probable that those who could afford such facilities in a camp are likely to prefer the amenities of a hotel and would be prepared to pay any consequent higher charges. When however, central restaurant, cooking and toilet facilities are provided, as would appear preferable in order to reduce capital costs, the cabins may be very simple both as regards accommodation and equipment.

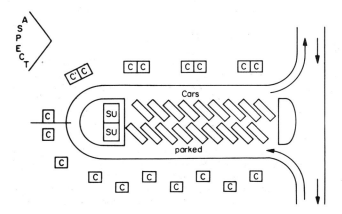

Fig. 3.30   Grouping of cabins. Central car park
C.   Cabin
SU. Sanitary unit

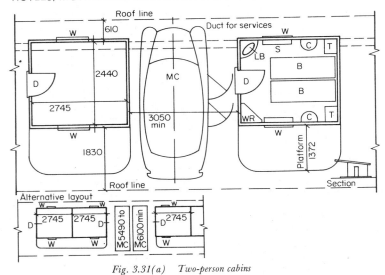

Fig. 3.31(a)   *Two-person cabins*

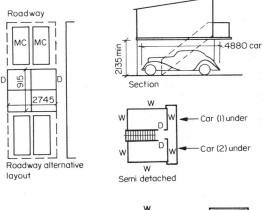

Fig. 3.31(b)   *Two-person cabin with additional space.*

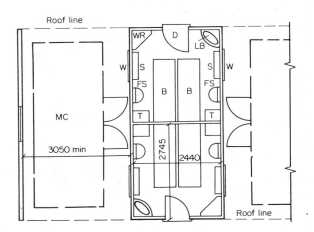

Fig. 3.31(c)   *Back-to-back units.*

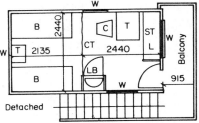

Fig. 3.31(d)   *Two-storey unit.*

Fig. 3.31 illustrates various forms of cabin planning where associated space for vehicle parking is provided. If vehicles are left in central car parks, the planning of the cabins follows closely that given for holiday camps, although in motor camps, small units of only a few cabins each may be preferred. Fig. 3.31(b) illustrates a simple form of cabin and car-berth unit. This may be either, as the larger plan, in form of alternative cabins and berths or, as in the smaller plan, semi-detached with a double car berth between each pair; the first scheme is likely to be more popular with car owners and there is less risk of damage to vehicles. The possible saving in space by grouping the cars is small, although the semi-detached cabins may be more economic to build. Semi-detached units are useful for family occupation and this tends to overcome any objections to two vehicles being parked within a common space.

On exposed sites, or in districts of heavy rainfall, it may be desirable to enclose one end of the car berth to eliminate draught. Car berths should not be less than 3 m wide in the clear, but, even then, cars must be parked close to one wall

to permit the doors to be easily opened. Where two vehicles are parked together, the width may be reduced to 5·5 m for the two cars. Roofs should extend on one or both sides to provide at least 4·9 m of cover, and even greater widths are desirable. The standing spaces must be hard-surfaced and with slight falls to prevent water collecting on them from driving rain or drainage from surrounding ground. The cabins should be raised slightly above the car spaces and should have a small platform or veranda in front of them to prevent vehicles being placed too near to them.

The cabins shown in Fig. 3.31(a) are of minimum size for use by two persons. It is better to equip all cabins with

HOTELS, MOTELS AND CAMPS FOR THE MOTORIST

two beds, even if they are only 762 mm rather than double beds, as this makes the use of the cabins more flexible. In order to economise space in very small cabins, most of the furniture will need to be built-in; it should comprise at least two chairs, a hanging space or wardrobe, some shelving, (which may serve as a dressing-table) and bedside tables. It is better if the cabins are slightly increased from these minimum dimensions to allow for luggage stands, (or at least space for luggage), movable chairs and some drawer-space. If basins are to be placed in cabins, which is preferable but much more costly than the provision of lavatory blocks, they should be planned in such a position that an accessible service duct may be designed for water pipes and wastes.

It is preferable that cabin entrance doors be planned under the cover of the roofs to the car berths so that they allow easy access to the parked vehicles and are sheltered during inclement weather.

Fig. 3.31(b) shows a more elaborate type of cabin unit having not only sleeping space but also dining, cooking and toilet facilities. Such units require considerably more area and the additional depth improves the accommodation of the motor car.

Fig. 3.31(c) shows a method of planning back-to-back units in order to increase the parking depth. The scheme in the larger plan needs a roadway on one side only and an access pathway on the other frontage. If however, cabins are planned in groups of four units, as shown in the small plan, a very economic building may be achieved, although a roadway on both frontages is necessary.

Fig. 3.31(d) shows a two-storey scheme in which the living accommodation is planned over the parking space, and is reached by an open-air stair. Alternatively (as shown in the small plan) two units may be grouped together with a single covered access-stair between them. Units of this type may be very useful on sites with steep falls, as the area to be levelled for each unit of cabin and car park is less.

SERVICES TO CABINS

For the cabins of the simpler types, without any toilet facilities, the only service needed is electricity for lighting, and power if the cabins are likely to be used during colder seasons. If space-heaters are provided, these might be controlled by slot-meters.

For the more elaborate schemes provision of all services may be necessary.

SANITARY ACCOMMODATION

Except in elaborate schemes it is unlikely that WC's will be planned in conjunction with each cabin. Normally they will be planned in blocks associated with groups of sleeping accommodation. The access to the accommodation for each sex should be well separated, although it may be advantageous to plan the whole as a single building. Small blocks near the cabins may be preferable to one large building serving the whole camp, although this is more economic, especially when lavatory basins and baths are grouped with WC's.

WC's should be provided at the rate of one to ten women and one to fifteen men, with one urinal for every ten men. It may be assumed that the visitors will be equally divided between the sexes. If there is a restaurant catering for outside trade, extra accommodation should be provided, preferably separate from that for the resident visitors and in close proximity to the restaurant.

Lavatory basins may be provided in each cabin; generally it is more economic to group them with WC's in sanitary blocks. It is desirable that hot water should be available, this influences the position of lavatory basins as they should not be too far from the central boilers, unless the units are large enough to have their own heating plant, or are equipped with local gas or electric water heating. Basins should be provided at a rate of one basin to every six visitors with a few additional fittings for the restaurant.

Baths are likely to be required in small numbers, especially for the use of children and older persons, but for many visitors, showers are sufficient. An adequate allowance is two baths and one shower to every 20 women and one bath and two showers for every 20 men. In some schemes the baths are likely to be grouped with the basins and WC's and in others they may be planned in the central building, an additional charge being made for their use. In a few elaborate schemes baths or showers may be planned as part of cabin units.

Sanitary accommodation in connection with camp restaurants catering for outside trade should be made on the basis of one WC per 15 women, one WC per 30 men and one urinal per 20 men. The lavatory for female visitors should have ample table and mirror space.

Separate toilet facilities should be provided for each type of staff, e.g. the manager, kitchen, restaurant and general service and should be planned in association with their working accommodation in the central building and/or attached to their sleeping quarters.

As the WC's and urinals are likely to be most used and the baths least used this should be borne in mind in their relationship to the entrance to the block and in the separation of the various types of accommodation into individual blocks placed at varying distances from cabins.

CENTRAL BUILDINGS

The main accommodation to be grouped together in a central building is the restaurant, kitchen and associated storage, visitors' kitchen, if provided, possibly visitors' baths and toilet facilities, manager's office, manager's quarters, staff quarters for unmarried staff, boiler room, fuel and other storage space and possibly a small retail shop. It may also be desirable to provide a lounge for visitors which can also serve for communal activities such as dances and table tennis. Associated with, but separate from, the central building there may also be a petrol station and repair facilities.

The siting of the central buildings should be convenient to the visitors' cabins, especially if cooking facilities for visitors are provided. If there is a restaurant serving outside trade it should be so planned that its customers can be accommodated separately from the resident visitors.

THE RESTAURANT

If the restaurant is to be used for both residents and casual visitors it may be desirable to plan it in two parts; this has the added advantage that if the numbers are, in any way, seasonal and widely varying, one room may be closed, giving a more comfortable appearance.

The restaurant should be planned on the basis of small tables for two and four persons which can be put together for larger parties. The general planning of restaurant and associated kitchens should follow that given under 'Hotels' at the beginning of this section.

KITCHENS AND FOOD STORAGE

The kitchens serving the restaurant and the staff should be separate from the cooking facilities provided for visitors' cooking facilities provided for visitors' own use.

Since these camps are likely to be away from shopping centres, stores may need to be specially large in capacity, particularly in regard to dry storage and refrigerated space. Information on the planning of kitchens is also given under the 'Hotels'.

VISITORS' COOKING FACILITIES

If not provided in each cabin, cooking facilities should be planned as part of the central buildings and should comprise one large room with a series of small larder-lockers attached. Hot water should be available.

A series of units should be planned around the walls, each consisting of some form of simple cooker, preferably electric or gas, with fixed tablespace adjoining. The cookers may, with advantage, be of the table-top type as ovens are not often required. There should be ample cupboard-space for utensils, china and glass. Cookers should be planned at approximately 1200 mm centres and should be provided at a rate of one to each six cabins. Sinks of a normal domestic type about 600 × 450 mm should be provided at a rate of one for every two cookers and should be given at least 160 mm of draining-board space on each side. The sinks should be kept together in one part (or the centre) of the room so that those using them are not in the way of others cooking, and also to simplify plumbing.

Ample daylight should be planned for all kitchens, with good cross-ventilation. Good artificial lighting is also necessary as the kitchens may be used to the maximum during the evening. Ventilated food lockers should be provided at a rate of one to each cabin.

If central cooking facilities are also provided and operated by a staff, or if there is a restaurant where visitors may obtain cooked meals, the visitors' own cooking facilities and food storage may be reduced from the suggested requirements already given.

In the more elaborate types of cabin in which individual cooking facilities are provided, the equipment should comprise a similar small cooker, a small sink with drainboard, a ventilated food locker, and sufficient cupboard space for china, glass and utensils for at least two persons. See under Residential Hostels (Section 2).

Trailer caravan camps do not, as a rule, need to have cooking facilities as the caravans are generally fully equipped for this purpose. Tented camps may need a central kitchen for visitors' own use similar to that for cabin-type camps. Facilities may also be desired for open-air cooking when concrete hearths with dwarf walls to act as wind-breaks are desirable to reduce the fire risk to the tents and surrounding land. If taps, are provided for water supply in the open air, provision for drainage of any overflow water and of dripping taps is essential.

MANAGER'S ACCOMMODATION

The manager's office should be situated in the central building, adjoining the entrance hall and thus immediately obvious on entering the building. It should be a room at least 11·15 m² in area with space for a desk and two or three chairs, filing space and cupboards. An enquiry hatch might communicate with the hall, to act as the reception counter, or an enquiry window should be located in a position accessible to drivers.

The manager may be married and the quarters should be planned on this basis. A private sitting room might adjoin the office and this should have good access to the kitchen. The bedroom accommodation might usefully be placed on an upper floor and should have at least one double bedroom and possibly one additional single room for a child or guest.

STORAGE

It is important to provide ample storage and drying space for linen, blankets, mattresses and spare furniture. If cabins are not heated in offseasons all equipment must be kept dry and aired.

LOUNGE

Whenever a camp has central buildings, the latter should have a lounge or common room for social use in the evening and on wet days. It should be based on providing about 0·93 m² per head (visitors' bed numbers) of the whole camp. A small platform at one end is advantageous. In those camps which do not have a restaurant the room may also be used as the dining room and it must then be planned in close association with the visitors' kitchen and central kitchen if meals prepared by staff are made available.

If camps are to be used in colder weather heating facilities are essential, but if not used in the full winter season a large open fire or openable stove is sufficient. It is preferable if common rooms are rectangular rather than square, facing south-westwards with access to terrace or garden.

BARS, ETC.

If the camps are to act as regular stopping places for long distance bus services a licence for the sale of alcoholic drinks may be required. This will have some influence on the planning, as suitable storage and service accommodation will be needed. It is unlikely that a bar will be provided but, as in many hotels, alcohol will be supplied only in common rooms such as lounges or with meals.

Camps catering entirely for residents, i.e. those spending one or more nights, might occasionally seek a club licence without requiring a normal licence.

SHOP

Facilities attached to or forming part of the manager's office for the purchase of stationery, sweets and tobacco are needed at all camps. When visitors cater for themselves it may also be necessary to sell some food supplies. If the latter is the case, well-ventilated cool cupboards are needed for the storage of dry goods and tinned food and it may also be desirable to provide space for a large refrigerator for keeping the more perishable foods and frozen foods.

STAFF QUARTERS

A number of single rooms, each at least 6·5 m² in area is needed in two groups for male and female staff respectively. The number of staff is likely to be small if visitors do their own catering, but if a restaurant is provided the number of staff will increase considerably.

A factor affecting the amount of staff accommodation is the proximity of the nearest town or village; if this is far away almost all the staff will need to be housed on the site. Some small houses for married staff may also be needed, especially for those who reside on or near the site throughout the year, such as gardeners and service-station staff. If the staff is large a staff common room should be provided. Staff rooms may with advantage be planned on an upper floor of the central building.

CAMPING SITES FOR TENTS

The standards for Camping Sites for Tents are referred to under the Town and Country Planning Act 1963 and the Public Health Act 1936. A licence is issued by the local council which controls density, roads, amenities, safety, etc. The number of days within a year that the land is used for tents is relevant to planning control and whether a licence is required.

As for caravan sites (see below), recreational space should be provided in the camping site, for children to play away from the tents. Roads within the site should permit access for fire engines and fire fighting appliances and first aid equipment should be available. The amenities should be as for camp sites with cabin units.

CARAVAN SITES

The standards for caravan sites are set out in the Control of Development Act 1960. (See Fig 3.32).

Every caravan should be not less than 6 m from any other caravan in separate occupation and not less than 3 m from a carriageway and not less than 75 m from a road. Carriageways should not be less than 3·96 m wide or 2·74 m wide for a one way traffic system. The gross density should not exceed 20 caravans to the acre.

Each standing and toilet block should be connected to a carriageway by a footpath with a hard surface. Footpaths should be not less than 762 mm.

Every caravan should be on a hard standing which should project not less than 914 mm from the entrance of the caravan. Each standing should have a refuse bin. There should be a fire point with water tank, buckets and pump for every two acres.

All sites should be provided with a water supply with stand pipes not more than 18·28 m from a standing or water piped to each standing. Provision should be made for foul drainage whether by connection to a public sewer or by discharge to a properly constructed septic tank or cesspool. Where caravans have their own water supply and water closets, each standing should be provided with a connection to the foul drainage system. Where this is not possible, communal toilet blocks should be provided as follows:

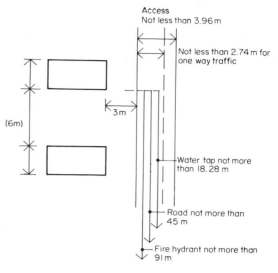

Fig. 3.32   Standards for caravans.

Men: 1 WC and 1 urinal per 15 caravans.

Women: 2 WC's per 15 caravans.
1 washbasin for each WC.
1 shower or bath for each sex per 20 caravans.

Laundry facilities should be provided in a separate room with one deep sink with hot and cold water per 15 caravans. Properly designed disposal points for the contents of chemical closets should be provided with water for cleaning purposes. There should be adequate surface water drainage for carriagewayss and footpaths.

Storage space is recommended to the extent of 2·79 m² of covered storage per standing, not less than 4·57 m² from any other caravan. Storage space should be lockable. Adequate car parking space should be provided. One tenth of the area should be allocated for recreation.

For holiday caravan sites, these standards are amended to a density not more than 25 caravans to the site; water supply and drainage connections to individual standings, paved footpaths and storage space can be dispersed with if caravans are moved in the winter; wash basins would be reduced to 1 for men and 1 for women per 15 caravans, with a laundry suite per 30 caravans; and where caravans are 12 to the acre or less, no caravan should be more than 55 m from a water stand pipe.

TOURING CARAVAN SITES

The standards set out in the 1960 Act are particularly relevant to sites for static caravans. Further recommendations have been made by the Camping Working Party to take into account the increase in tourism. This makes the following recommendations:

1. *Density.* Not more than 30 units per acre (75 units per hectare) calculated on the basis of the usable area rather than the total site area.

2. *Space*. The space between units in separate family accupation should be 6 m.

3. *Flexibility*. For specified peak holiday periods, an additional 10% of the number of units normally permitted would be allowed without provision of additional facilities.

4. *Drinking water*. Each pitch to have a drinking water tap within 90 m. The tap should be provided with a soakaway or gulley.

5. *Waste water disposal*. This should be separate from the drinking tap and should be provided within 45 m of each pitch.

6. *Toilets* (wc's or chemical closets) and washing facilities should be provided as follows:

For the first 30 pitches
   1 WC for men
   1 urinal for men   2 basins for men;
   2 WC's for women   2 basins for women.

Additionally for each 60 pitches
   1 shower for men
   1 shower for women
   Hot water should be provided where showers are included.

Where WC's are not feasible, chemical closets should be provided in proportion twice that for WC's. Whether or not WC's are provided, a properly designed disposal unit for the contents of chemical closets should be provided with a water supply for cleaning containers.

7. *Refuse disposal*. Adequate provision should be made for storage, collection and disposal of refuse.

8. *Parking*. Parking can be arranged in the 6 m space between units. However, 3 m of clear space should be maintained between units in separate occupation to reduce the fire risk.

9. *Fire precautions*. No pitch should be further than 90 m from a fire point at which there should be two 2 gallon water (gas-expelled) extinguishers. The extinguishers should be in an insulated container to protect them from frost. Beaters, as used by the Forestry Commission, should also be provided at each fire point where there is the likelihood of fire spreading due to grass. Fire points should be clearly marked and easily accessible with notices and instructions regarding all emergency action clearly displayed. Where practicable a telephone should be provided.

BIBLIOGRAPHY

Abraben, A., *Resort Hotels, Planning and Management*, Reinhold, New York (1965).

Alio, G., *Alberghi, Motel, Ristoranti*, Hoepli, Milan (1961).

Alio, G., *Hotel, Motel*, Hoepli, Milan (1970).

Architects Journal, *Principles of Hotel Design*, Architectural Press, London (1970).

Architectural Record, *Motels, Hotels, Restaurants and Bars*. F. W. Dodge Corpn, (1960).

Architectural Review, 'Hotels—A Special Issue', *Architectural Press* (1960).

Baker, G., and Funaro, B., *Motels*, Reinhold, New York and Chapman and Hall, London (1965).

Bessho, S., *Japanese Inns*, Hobundo, Tokyo (1958).

Borer, M. C., *The British Hotel through the Ages*, Lutterworth, Guildford, (1972).

Council of Industrial Designs. *Advisory Committee on Hotels and Restaurants*, London (1961).

Doswell, R., *Towards an integrated approach to Hotel Planning*, New Univ Education (Bingley), London (1970).

Elvin, R., 'Motels in Britain', *Industrial Architecture* (August 1968).

End, Henry, *Interiors Book of Hotels and Motor Hotels*, Whitney Library of Design (1963).

Guides to Fire Precautions Act, 1971. *Hotels and Boarding Houses*, HMSO.

Hattrell, W. S., *Hotels, Restaurants and Bars*, Batsford, London (1962).

'Holiday Houses, Holiday Centres and Tourist Hotels', *International Asbestos-Cement Review* (Zurich) No. 50 (1968).

'Hotel Planning: A comparison of vertical and horizontal bedroom blocking' *Architect's Journal* (May 12, 1965).

Koch, Alexander, *Hotelbauten/Motels/Ferienhauser*, Stuttgart (1958 and 1961).

Lapidus, A. H., 'Planning the successful Resort Hotel', *Architectural Record* (July 1968).

Mayer, Otto and Hieri, Fritz, *Hotelbau*, Callway, Munich (1962).

Nagel, S. and Linke, S., *Hotel und Restaurantbauten*, Bertelsmann Fachverlag, Gütersloth (1970).

Peter, P., *Hotels, Feriendorfer (Hotels, Holiday Villages)*, Callway, Munich (1969).

Weisskamp, H., *Hotels: an Internation Survey*, Architectural Press London (1968).

Wenzel, K., *Hotelbauten*, Verlag für Bauwesen, Berlin (1967).

Anthony Wylson, *FRIBA, A.A.Dip.(Hons) is a partner in the firm Anthony Wylson and Munro Waterson and has prepared studies on various hotel projects. These include a motel, a commercial hotel and a Mediterranean tourist complex incorporating hotel, hostel and chalets. The firm has also carried out a variety of residential schemes embracing different aspects of accommodation.*

4 OFFICE BUILDINGS AND BANKS

RONALD GREEN, F.R.I.B.A., A.A. Dip., F.S.I.A.,
Casson Conder & Partners

INTRODUCTION

AIM AND PURPOSE

In order to try to set down standards for the design of buildings which are specifically suited to accommodating business organisations, whether for office use or as bank premises one has to consider the conditions within which commerce customarily finds it most convenient to operate. The way in which buildings can best provide appropriate facilities for such operations must also be taken into account. This section aims to examine these conditions in the abstract, and without specific examples, in order that the principle can be understood without good examples being mistakenly used to produce bad results on wrong sites.

It is perhaps a little too easy when thinking about the design of any building to assume that one is starting from scratch on a brand new site. However, a large percentage of office work is carried out in existing buildings and therefore the section attempts to deal with principles which can be applied to the conversion of existing buildings as well as to the construction of new ones (see Figs 4.1(a) and 4.1(b)).

METHOD

In this section, firstly the subject is looked at in a global context and information is then developed in the order in which one is most likely to encounter the problems: accommodation or briefing; the policy behind the enterprise; and the setting of objectives to meet human needs. The latter can be in an elementary form such as a schedule or briefing list to serve as a memory jogger which a designer and his client can battle with over the course of the first few weeks (or months) or as complex as the setting of performance standards. This section examines the central purpose of this method as an educational period in which both designer and client extricate sufficiently developed attitudes to enable them to select suitable structural forms and to embark on internal planning.

This is followed by a look at the logic behind the planning of various departments in a building; the point at which the work is done, whether by an individual at a desk, a man with his secretary or with a working group, and the way these relate with other working groups (see Fig 4.2). Following this, limitations are dealt with by introducing the designer to certain obligations which are the legal or desirable equivalents of, and complementary with, the human needs considered earlier in the section.

Any attempt to give digests which encourage short cuts has been avoided. There are no short cuts to meeting statutory obligations; minimum escape stair widths and handrail heights, thermal insulation standards, structural wind resistance or depths of foundations, will all differ from one country to another. Reference to the appropriate planning or building laws and regulations is the only route to complying with them. While the broad scope of the information refers to UK practice, a great deal of the source material is found outside the UK and therefore references should not be regarded as 'gospel' and certainly not to the detriment of innovation or original design which might serve to take things further forward. It is not impossible that proposals under consideration may be being practised elsewhere without question. Illustrations are used to support points made in the text and deliberately avoid saying more. A person wishing to investigate a completed building must visit it and not draw conclusions from paper.

Progress can only be made in any subject where the boundaries are not too tightly drawn. Dimensions, or recommended criteria are given in this section only as a guide to approaching the specific design subject and by which some sort of assessment can be made in the first instance. Beyond this anyone engaged in the design of any building must develop it from the demands of the brief he has worked out with his client.

CHARACTERISTICS OF BUILDINGS

'STRUCTURE'

Office buildings have long and short term characteristics, not unlike those of a ship. They have a structure, or hull; and an interior which has to be fitted out. The fitting out can change as much as is necessary to meet different conditions while the hull remains substantially the same throughout the life of the structure.

Fig. 4.1(a)   Offices have to be accommodated in existing as well as new buildings

Fig. 4.1(b)   Offices for Willis, Faber Architects: Foster Associates. Glass and suspended assembly design by Pilkington Bros Ltd.
(Photographer: Jocelyne van den Bossche)

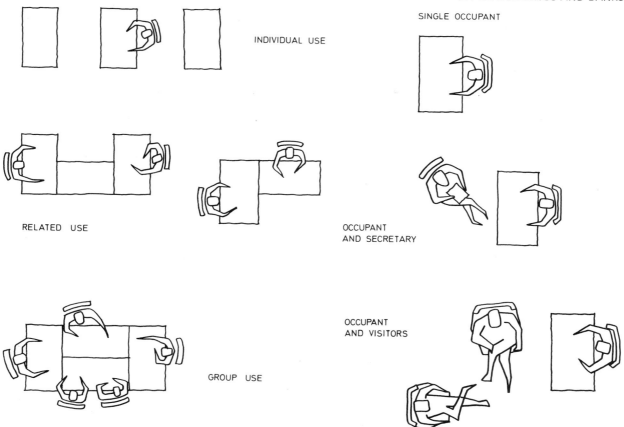

Fig. 4.2   Type of occupancy

The changes in the interior can be either superficial or fundamental, but it can be seen that while it is perfectly possible to strip out such items as the entire mechanical and electrical servicing which is creating the internal environment of the building, clearly it would be irresponsible to do so. There are elements of the servicing arrangements as fundamental to providing these facilities inside the building, as the structure is to the stability of the building. Main vertical ducts serving the full height of the building as part of a lift and staircase core are examples and are as much a part of the structure as the structural elements of the building. The main horizontal ducts could be said to be the same but the outlets for the air conditioning system, and possibly the electrical underfloor grid; though preferably not, might be regarded as superficial and therefore perfectly changeable.

'FITTING OUT'

It would be wrong however to assume too early that major changes can be made in the interior layout of a building without creating very considerable difficulties or presenting high costs and which might in certain circumstances make other alternatives more attractive. But it is in the nature of the subject that the range of options open to providing premises suitable for commercial use is very wide—either in the conversion of existing buildings or the design of new ones.

DIMENSIONAL CONFLICT

New projects often include the need for mixed types of accommodation and to incorporate shops, residential apartments, showrooms and parking spaces as well as offices. Different types of accommodation suggest different forms of construction or structural dimensions best suited to the economics or use of that particular type of building, and this factor naturally introduces complications in the determination of structural form suited to all uses.

PLANNING LIMITATIONS

Different forms of building each have their own characteristics and perform their functions in very different ways. A 'tower' form of building with a central core of stairs, lifts and lavatory accommodation but with relatively shallow space between the core and the outer wall is not well suited to the provision of large office areas. It provides no simple means of surrounding one working group with a whole series of other groups.

The large open plan office on the other hand has characteristics which lend themselves to large group use but cannot be multi-storey; is probably best kept to one single level and is limited in the extent to which it can be divided to provide smaller enclosed spaces.

The large standard 'off the peg' office block has been built without tenants in most countries for many years to meet most of the conditions required by an average office user, but because of this, it is a compromise that does not specifically provide the best conditions for any particular user.

Many of the existing town buildings, of almost any age, will have sprung from their early use as large scale houses. For office use, it is almost inevitable that they are best suited to providing individual offices or suites on a cellular type of plan, although it is not impossible within the existing character to release the space a little to provide slightly more generous areas in which small groups can work.

However, in considering the use of an existing building, a building of any age has to be taken into account and it is fair to say that the problems probably increase with the age of the building. Where traditional detailing simply does not deal with increased traffic noise—or where lack of insulation encourages high running costs or where an open window fills a room with exhaust fumes, these additional problems have to be met. Other problems may involve the introduction of air conditioning in a room in which there is insufficient height to take ceiling ducting or an historically significant façade through which it is impossible to insert grilles; the formation of adequate fire division of one section from another, or the problems of a route for escape.

IDENTITY

In a 'speculative' office block, which, for the purposes of this section is seen as an existing, though new building, the accommodation provided will by its nature be 'safe' accommodation. It meets all these needs but there will be no sense of owner identity or perhaps architectural distinction.

The depth of office area will have been planned to be safe enough for the space to be leased to anyone, running any kind of business. It follows therefore, that although a tenant company will need to subject its needs to scrutiny and prepare its brief very carefully, the answers that come from it will have to be those which fit the mould of the speculative space provision.

BUILDING PURPOSE

The commissioning of a new office building however, naturally falls into one of two categories; the building which is to be built for letting or resale to any client who may wish to occupy it, and the one which is purpose designed for a specific client. Many of the basic requirements of a purpose designed owner occupied building will apply equally to a building which is to be occupied by the unknown tenant. From the tenant's point of view, the decision to go into an existing building carries with it the need to follow the same process of analysis of use but working within the confines of the structure that exists. The real advantage to the client who decides to commission a purpose-designed building is that it gives him the unique opportunity to rethink the company structure and to commission a building which will be designed to accommodate it. A building which has been put up speculatively and then sold to an office user removes that option and has clearly taken a number of major decisions on behalf of the tenant company in the adoption and organisation of the plan form of the building.

BACKGROUND TO BRIEFING

MULTIPLE OCCUPANCY

Surveys have provided certain pointers to the use of space occupied by companies which give useful background to the subject of suitability. These indicate that it is the smaller firms of anything between ten and fifty people who tend to require individual offices for employees and so far as the London area is concerned where it has been said that only about 5% of firms have more than 100 staff, it follows that the accommodation these companies utilise is considerably less than the total area afforded by a multi-storey building. Therefore, the existing or proposed multi-storey building is in many cases inevitably committed to accommodating more than one firm each requiring quite separate and self contained space though perhaps enjoying the option of using certain communal facilities. The implications of shared catering or maintenance of the premises and the need for continuity in house management must be recognised however, whether the client is the building's owner or the lessee.

It seems that open plan offices have proved to be well suited to the work of insurance offices, large banks or accounts or similar departments of large commercial organisations.

SINGLE USE SPACE

This must be weighed against the fact that despite the advantages claimed for large open plan offices, a typical London office is still made up of rooms holding only a few people. One of the problems with office buildings which have been built in recent years, is that of an inability to divide the larger spaces against the relative ease of 'opening' smaller spaces.

However, the snag with surveys is that the results almost inevitably lead to the adoption of over-logical conclusions in cases which sometimes require very special solutions. Surveys have to have a starting point and while statisticians may need to assume that a small office is below 40 m² and that a large office is something above 150 m² with a medium one of anything between, these items are statistically interesting and valuable background but are essentially 'averages'. The designer must take the space for what it really offers and see it in relationship to the function it is to perform and those functions to which it is itself related. A statistical solution bears no comparison with first hand knowledge of the work to be carried out in the space and it is this that must be obtained from the briefing and the closest observation.

HEIGHT VERSUS AREA

If the client is starting from scratch it can be seen that there are certain forms of building which will be better suited than others to the type of conditions he is hoping to provide. In a multi-storey block, it is perfectly possible to provide completely independent lettable suites of offices at each level and on the basis of the suggested figures typical of company sizes, might be well suited both to the number of occupants and to 'cellular' division; but beyond a certain number of storeys it is thought inadvisable to open windows for ventilation—or perhaps even for cleaning due to wind velocity. In this case the outside wall becomes, in effect, a 'sealed skin' to the building and in turn offers no alternative but to introduce air conditioning to provide ventilation to the building (though systems exist for obtaining ventilation without opening windows). Due to high running costs, this raises questions of high costs to a small company and may change the entire basic requirements on which the project started.

The basic plan dimensions of the tower block took as its starting point the maximum acceptable depth of penetration of natural light and ventilation into a room from the perimeter of the building. This room was served by an inner corridor surrounding a central service core of lifts and lavatories. The adoption of mechanical ventilation or air conditioning, provided the option of increasing this depth with the aid of both perimeter and inner area ventilation systems, but there are still limits to the amount of space available on any one floor as a result (see Fig 4.3).

COSTS AND CONDITIONS OF TENURE

The true cost of a building over its life span, comprises capital and cost in use and a client may not recognise the potential savings over the economic life of the building when balancing these initially. Neither are the cost in use and the cost of building necessarily true reflections of actual cost in the case of a leasehold or tenancy occupation unless the cost of re-instatement on termination of the lease is included in the initial balance of costs. The brief must pay regard to the status of the client. He may be the freeholder or a lease-holder. He may be a sub-tenant, and the freeholders or head lessee may require him to comply with specific construction conditions. These are in themselves as important as the accommodation outlined in the brief or indeed the requirements of the statutory authorities.

Equally important are the Contract terms and their cost implications. A client must recognise the problems introduced where the building's owner and several tenants are working with different architects and contractors in one building. The subdivision of tenancy liabilities must be very clearly defined.

COMPANY IDENTITY

It has been said that a new building provides the company with the opportunity to express the personality of the company or the characteristics of its management. Perhaps this is where the architect may need to become the conscience of the company. Chairmen tend to come and go and Company policies alter but buildings stay on forever. Staff changes can mean that even in the owner occupied building the people responsible for briefing never actually occupy the building at all.

PERSONALITIES

An over-accommodating attitude of mind on the part of management can lead to the invitation and incorporation of too many individual or perhaps even personal requirements at the briefing stage at the expense of the whole scheme. Potential monuments to the occupants can only be a liability.

The options are unlimited and in the event of a room or department changing hands frequently have to be modified drastically. This subsequent 'remedial' work is undertaken

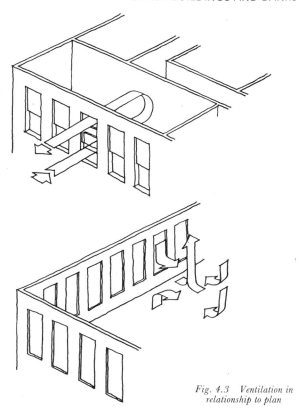

Fig. 4.3 Ventilation in relationship to plan

later, and therefore with lack of knowledge of, attention to, or sympathy with, the overall planning and design policy originally determined for the building.

FACILITIES

Office buildings can be large, and, in the USA, frequently accommodate up to 7000 people. Once inside their building, they use all its facilities for working, eating and relaxing. They use its vending machines or shops for their daily requirements. The buildings are well finished and a pleasure to use, so unless people wish to, they need not go out into extreme temperature changes.

It follows that the interiors of such buildings are very carefully designed. The obligations to such a large number of people—let alone those additional people who visit it during the course of a working day—are enormous.

PERPETUATING PROBLEMS

An inherent problem of moving office is that of carrying forward arrangements which were dictated by a previous building, or systems which are no longer necessary.

Continuity of habit can produce planning arrangements which are adopted without question and actively prevent the company from taking up the opportunity to exploit the space or to adopt new methods provided by the new building. This has the effect of confusing the occupants themselves, and often the visitor, whom the company must provide with the clearest possible conception of departmental activity and position.

LEVEL OF DECISION TAKING

Whatever the size of building, and no matter whether it is existing or new, decisions must never be allowed to be made arbitrarily. It is essential that this is recognised for the opportunity that it really is. Everyday events must not be allowed to just happen. Everything must be questioned and the right answers incorporated in the schemes; such points as whether the building is to accommodate its own maintenance staff, and if so, what provision is to be made for workshops, what will happen to post, what filing system will be adopted? These decisions must not be allowed to be taken on anything but the highest levels, and only by people whose decisions will not be questioned.

The results have to be lived with, and where the decision is taken at the wrong level, it always produces one of two results; either a disgruntled management who face it for the first time in the completed building, or by constant changes throughout the contract which incur very heavy additional expense and make a nonsense of the briefing period and planning opportunities.

ARCHITECT'S CONTRIBUTION TO BRIEFING

The architect can never hope to become fully acquainted with all aspects of his client's business. Nevertheless he is a consultant and it is a mistake not to get as closely involved as possible. He should be able to bring to the client's team a reasonably clear view of how he sees the organisation from outside and must extract from the company as much information as possible to make whatever contribution he can. His view will be free of the natural prejudices which arise from their internal pressures or obligations.

It is essential that the client has full confidence in his handling this sort of situation. If there is a reluctance to regard the architect's views as sound, the company should not employ him, but if they do regard them as sound, he must have authority equivalent to that of a board member if he is to be allowed to do his job properly. It is then obviously in the interest of both the client and the architect to investigate all aspects of the business together in testing the terms of the brief against possible architectural solutions. There is never another opportunity without incurring heavy expenditure.

OCCUPANTS

The occupants also have obligations to the arrangement of their building whether an open or enclosed office system, but must naturally know what these are. Some people live in their buildings beautifully, and obviously enjoy them or conversely, some buildings accommodate their occupants beautifully.

Companies must play their part in assessing this correctly. Interiors must be 'right' for the company and the occupants —they spend a third of their life in them.

COMPILING A BRIEF

FEASIBILITY

The feasibility of producing a building which can fulfil the intended brief is a joint effort that is undertaken between

architect and his client; it aims to establish the suitability of the site and the adequacy of the cash available for the building. It is of value to the formulation of a good brief that the client should see his own needs clearly enough to state the objectives for building and the way in which he intends to carry them out.

The brief for a building of any complexity emerges from a continuous exchange of information and reaction over some period of time. The outline statement will usually come from the occupying company, though this is not invariably the case as some International companies determine the central nature of all their buildings from this parent organisation and require the occupying company to discuss local details of the brief only as agents.

STAFF INFLUENCES

In either case, the statement will set out particular accommodation requirements for their staff and an hierarchical system will emerge. Whether for convenience of organisational recognition or as a means of determining the way in which a person is progressing through the structure of the company, the difference in either space allowance or in the type of furniture which he is entitled to enjoy at different levels in the company is present in most organisations.

The civil service is the usual example of the establishment of the 'identifiable' means by which these levels of attainment are recognisable to the outsider or indeed to anyone within the structure, though all companies have similar ways of showing this to a greater or lesser degree. The extent to which this attainment and entitlement is demonstrated by the company reflects itself in the interiors and the architecture.

INFLUENCE BY CUSTOM

There is no doubt therefore that when contemplating commissioning an office building a company must be prepared to be particularly honest with itself. The 'form' or 'nature' of the building will spring from the way the company sees itself, and if the company is deceiving itself it will be the wrong building. There are facts that must be faced squarely: the degree to which housing itself is also an investment, the likelihood of the company staying there for ever, the possibility of its splitting into smaller groups, the importance of the geographical relationship of department to department.

It must solve its own self imposed issues—whether a proposed building in the centre of a city need carry forward its custom of providing staff catering facilities where its new neighbouring buildings include restaurants and sandwich bars; or where particular characteristics of the previous building are perhaps sentimentally, misguidedly or even deliberately being taken to a new building to the detriment of its future use. It is not inconceivable that a firm regards it as essential to build safes into a number of rooms in the new building because several senior members of staff had them as part of their equipment in the previous one. These safes were built into their routines and it may not be recognised that their introduction had been the result years ago of poor security in a 'fringe' location combined with rather more elementary accountancy methods.

A bankers problem however is the opposite. There has always been the need for strong rooms usually, for convenience, in a basement, but future tenants may have no possible use for such immovable accommodation and may want to turn the space into a staff training theatre.

A company may have a clear view of its present policy and may have no intention of selling out or going elsewhere but, over the years, its methods or ideas may change to the extent that it will have space to spare and will need to let. This is borne out by many examples. To this extent therefore, space may need to be flexible enough to be of value to someone who wants it. It must also be capable of subdivision with security and with access to all facilities. There are certain types of company who expand and contract frequently enough during the course of their activities to enable this requirement to be calculatedly built into their building.

It is important, however, that prejudices or limitations are not permitted to deflect the client from the real purposes and opportunities of building. 'Limitations' can always be considered afterwards but it is not quite so easy to define the problem when all these limitations have been ranged against a good brief too early and are determining those things which are difficult to do before the client has even started.

TYPES OF ACCOMMODATION

Historically, offices have tended to provide two different types of accommodation; single offices, occupied by management staff and large areas devoted to clerical or similar high population activities. Neither have proved wholly satisfactory in that the first is the most expensive way of utilising the space available to a company occupying a building and the second up to now has been the least acceptable by implied social stigma. Watch a secretary's face when you say 'typing pool' or an accounts clerk when you say 'general office'.

The 'open plan' office was the means by which these characteristics have been minimised and the benefits brought together. It was based upon the analysis of the work being done by all people in the company and brought together those who have related tasks and designed the interior of the space so that desk and storage relationships took advantage of and exploited the actual working relationships one to another. This, almost accidentally, gave the most economic use of space and equally accidentally provided the widest opportunity for design within a given volume. There are however, disadvantages related to acoustics, daylight and different social problems with larger numbers of people in one volume and anonimity of activity in any one space.

The resolution of the problem really revolves around the need for actual privacy for specific reasons. Perhaps the smaller organisations where all aspects of the business are known to everyone, needs its single office accommodation only for people who conduct matters which are confidential between those who run it and those who work in it e.g. the invoice clerk who wishes to discuss a private matter with the manager.

In the larger organisation a second line of confidentiality

is introduced in protecting the nature of one client's business from another e.g. the advertising campaign being prepared for a client.

When a company considers flexibility it will be thinking of policy and staffing and will naturally tend to ask for the ability to change in any direction, but a designer must anticipate physical change in the most difficult direction. From the evidence available, it seems that this is that of converting space provided by an open planned office into small rooms to accommodate single or double occupants to give oral or visual privacy dictated by their jobs. Complications are introduced in the modification of the air conditioning, the lighting, the tapping of general services, or in acoustic insulation where noise can be defeated by the construction of a partition only to become vulnerable in the void of the suspended ceiling through which the services are running and where continuity is essential. To anticipate this flexibility needs the provision of all the appropriate individual controls for the air conditioning in the 'optional' offices to provide appropriate means of separation should such changes be required. It is almost impossible to build into the open plan type of building in the first instance without a totally disproportionate budget to the benefits offered.

It appears that the decision will relate entirely to the type of business. One should not consider designing for both.

While it has been said, in German publications, that the usable area in a landscaped office ranges between 72% and 83% against a usable 58% to 67% in a conventional corridor layout, the sophistication of correct analysis methods used for setting up open office layouts confirms that more traditional ways of solving these problems does not make equally good use of the space. If open office planning is suggested by the nature of the organisation for which the design is being prepared, then appropriate analysis methods must be adopted as provided by specialist consultancy related to the specific business of the company.

The further advanced a building design gets, the more attention the people who will occupy it will be prepared to devote to its detail. They can 'see' it more clearly and then will discuss every aspect. It is slightly more difficult to achieve at the beginning, as the points are by their nature more abstract. They are however vital in the influence they exert or fail to exert on the results.

Many things influence a building for the better when properly considered at the beginning, but probably among the most important are the following:

1. The appointment of consultants whose expertise will ensure the establishment of objectives intelligently related to the requirements and those who have the ability to achieve them.
2. Not to jump too many guns. There is no point in trying to anticipate the kind of conditions in which companies will run their business in twenty years' time at the expense of the way in which they can operate well at the moment.

3. The need to start with a clear idea of the relative importance of cost in use; the anticipated life of the building, the appropriate quality standards for the building and the need to 'buy the article' from the right shop in terms of the selection of a suitable contractor. A realistic design period and building programme and completion date which recognises removals and furnishing time, and the type of construction contract which is best suited to the project.

4. The ability to take full advantage of the option to learn from other people's experience by discussion and investigation at first hand. These people would have discovered that their greatest asset was the allocation of more time than was sensibly needed to construct the building and had the opportunity to resolve planning problems rather than being forced into decisions by legal guillotines. Some companies would have anticipated the need to allocate money in the budget for the provision of full size mock-ups of typical office space to permit theories to be tested under controlled expenditure conditions and avoid multiple errors in their building.

CLIENT LIAISON

A company will not necessarily appreciate that it is essential in a large building project for one particular person to act on its behalf in dealing with the day to day matters which concern the architect and the consultants. It is even more important that the client recognises that this cannot be a member of his staff with another job to do, but must be someone in the organisation with sufficient authority to take very responsible decisions on behalf of the Board of Directors or a building committee and not be hampered by his own every day job.

He will be involved from the beginning for a period of never less than two years and probably nearer to five—taking the work through on behalf of the company from briefing to the settlement of final account long after they have moved into the building.

THE ORGANISATION OF ACCOMMODATION

SCHEDULE OF ACCOMMODATION

A basic schedule of accommodation prepared by the client should be used to calculate approximate areas but should be reviewed in relationship to existing conditions or parallel conditions in other companies. It is not unusual for a client to describe what he has got rather than what he needs. The total number of staff occupying, and of visitors likely to use the building must be included in the brief.

SPACE PER PERSON

There is some evidence to suggest that in the provision of space in existing buildings the area per person decreases as the number of room occupants increases up to about five people. After this there is little change in the average provision and people tend to use between 4 and 5 m² of gross area per person. Where a single occupant needs a room of his own he can very rarely do with less than twice this amount to make a useful room. In other cases, surveys suggest that the average area allocated per person varies from 8 m² to about 13 m² with the optimum between 9·5 and 10·5 m².

A test as to the amount of space required of a building from the known number of occupants is the figure required, of the means of escape regulations in case of fire, of 9·2 m² per person but excluding stairs, lifts and sanitary accommodation.

SPECIAL ACCOMMODATION

Establish any special requirements, for example:

The need for computer room which has specific constructional and thermal control problems;

Will the public as well as the occupants use parts of the building with a need for separation of circulation for cloakroom facilities?

Will the building be available outside normal working hours perhaps in connection with staff 'clubs' or similar functions affecting security and access and are showers or other facilities needed in connection with the areas?

Will the building have its own maintenance staff with the need for workshops?

Will it operate contract or hire service for maintaining the building with a need for stores access?

PLANT SPACE

Plant space must in no way be confused with the concept of 'boiler' rooms. They are spotless, tidy and efficient. They are also colourful, frequently using 'tracer' colours for identification purposes on the different service routes.

In a sophisticated building the plant engineer will probably operate the installation from a control room by console which is designed to spot check the correct functioning of any piece of equipment in the entire building. From the control room the temperature and humidity readings in all rooms and areas could be monitored throughout 24 hours. The percentage of space devoted to plant is usually thought to be in the region of 7% of the gross area of the building with vertical duct area accommodation 3% of the area.

KITCHEN AND RESTAURANT POSITION

Analyse the possible arrangements very carefully for kitchen position and deliveries. In city areas in the USA where parking hours are heavily restricted, it has been found necessary to adopt overnight deliveries, and this can conflict with the security system of the building itself.

A low level kitchen and restaurant arrangement, though complicating the ventilation as the area of ducting becomes greater, provides the opportunity to form a completely separate section of building and offers operation quite independently of access and circulation to the main building which is particularly important in a bank building.

RESTAURANT ARRANGEMENTS

The restuarant arrangements can be required to form an 'executive' part of a company's business. Banks, in particular, frequently utilise their smaller dining-rooms as a part of their meeting/business arrangements which give privacy and comfort for discussions, and they often approach the provision of these facilities in very different ways.

Depending on the company, there seem to be several combinations of executive eating arrangements in use; some favour one large open restaurant, containing a large table for bank officers without guests, combined with a series of small tables for about four, where people can entertain to lunch in the same room. Some firms partition a large dining area to form smaller areas for officers with guests, but these tend to be fairly restrictive in use possibly as a result of the approach to planning for division and introduce circulation problems with difficulty in service. Other companies operate best with a series of small executive dining rooms where luncheon meetings can be held; but where this arrangement is adopted, small service rooms are also provided.

THEATRE

Many buildings find it necessary to include a small theatre or auditorium. This is an important area for a company to consider as it has been found that where these are not included in the planning stage, it is frequently found necessary or desirable to add later in some part of the building whether for staff training, talks, conferences, staff clubs use or similar purposes. It has to be seen as outside the possibility of 'doubling' with the restaurant area as these functions conflict sufficiently badly as to make it a highly undesirable match.

When planning an auditorium, it is necessary to provide space which is totally flexible and to include such things as built-in vertical battens for shelving or 'display' presentation of any kind. This invariably leads to the need for seats which have the option of 'writing' arms, and to many other aspects which might spring out of a close look and the ultimate use of a building of this type.

RECEPTION

Office reception facilities have always been an important function of the organisation and an essential part of the discipline of the building's staff and visitor control and circulation patterns. There are several movement patterns going on in a building at the same time, permanent staff, invited visitors, casual visitors, service delivery and/or maintenance and emergency routes. All must be very clearly identifiable and controlled from an entrance, circulation and exit point of view.

Banking practice tends also to provide a reception area and small offices or conference and discussion rooms in the safe deposit vaults area. These reception lobbies are regarded as rather special public areas, fully carpeted and are given a very high standard of finish and furnishing. An early decision must be taken on this principle in order that lift lobbies and circulation spaces in the vicinity of these vaults—and indeed the finishes of the vaults themselves—can be designed to play their full part in providing this accommodation and be maintained as a security route; a visitor usually is escorted through it.

VAULTS

It is fatal to the life of the building to under-assess vault space requirements. Careful forecasting of possible future banking methods may be of value to help to anticipate future needs as it is not possible to add or amend later with anything like the same degree of security provision.

As the most elementary form of security, vault structures are usually constructed independently of any existing build-ing structure apart from the floor itself. A gap of some 50 cm is maintained between the vault and the outside wall and is frequently visually monitored by means of mirrors at each angle to give clear vision round the vaults back to the viewer. The security 'layers' extending beyond this may be extensive both within and outside the vault area and will depend upon the bank's policy on the type of building and security risk involved.

LAVATORY ACCOMMODATION

The key to this part of the accommodation is that the decision to adopt central lavatory accommodation, or floor by floor lavatories and cloakrooms will determine the whole character of the building, including lifts, provision and security arrangements. The means by which staff enter the building in the morning, circulate during the day and at lunchtime, or disperse in the evening is the starting point in deciding the discipline requirement for the building and from this the provision of lockers/storage/lavatory or other welfare facilities will begin to take their pattern.

Equally, it must be recognised that in an open plan office, 'domestic' storage accommodation must be provided for lunchtime shopping, carrier bags and personal items, and where anyone wishes to retain these in their own work space with security it must be accommodated without detriment to the space in general.

SECRETARIES OR SECRETARIAL SERVICES

The decision on secretarial/typing service to the company is very far reaching. An early decision to adopt audio typing services for example will change the entire planning concept and space allocation and place strong emphasis on document circulation.

FILING

Filing in open plan offices is normally confined to central filing and most offices have found it convenient to place central filing systems in areas which have no natural light, each floor is served by a document hoist or similar mail distribution system.

The adoption or otherwise of central filing, however, is the decision of the company and will largely be determined by the nature of the business. To say the least, it does a considerable amount to eliminate the problems created by individual filing—often by junior or inexperienced staff. The decision will also need to be related to document circulation in the building generally, the resolution of post distribution and mail despatch.

LIFTS

It seems to be generally agreed that firms who skimp on the numbers of lifts in their original planning live to regret it. People tend to become impatient beyond a set time and it is suggested that 30 seconds is the maximum waiting time.

It can be seen how important the initial assessment for movement between floors becomes in the initial briefing—an additional lift is exceedingly difficult to fit in at a later date.

MATERIALS

Difficulties can arise from the use of the best and well-tried materials in 'standard' situations where they are adopted as the result of pure analysis of function only. In walking from an executive or similar 'soft furnished' area into a clerical area in which there are vinyl tiles, metal partitions and metal ceilings, there is a distinct rise in noise level.

It is in these very areas that the quieter materials are needed to combat the naturally higher noise level and the logic of using totally 'functional' materials is lost and becomes a positive disadvantage. This is a common and very noticeable fault in many buildings. It is as well to note that it can as easily accidentally arise from an imbalance of cash allocation for the finishes in executive and clerical areas when setting the first budget.

FURNISHING AND OFFICE EQUIPMENT

In furnishing terms, particular groups in the company will be using particular types of equipment. The means by which these can be reduced to a fairly simple schedule of requirements is in the form of brochures which bring together the types of equipment best suited to the particular groups. But this pre-supposes that the designer will be invited to extend his services to include furnishings and equipment and this in itself may take several forms. A company may have its own purchasing department and simply require a view on items selected for consideration, but most, having got this far will see the services as being complementary with the design of the interiors and the equipment and a natural extension of the general design work.

A well developed interior will have natural design continuity from the air-conditioning grille to the filing tray or the desk drawer handle.

CARS

The designer cannot disregard the implications of the accommodation of cars related to the occupants or visitors to the building. But these will be determined by the conditions prevailing locally, the characteristics of the management, site or the local authorities.

STRUCTURAL/PLANNING

STRUCTURAL FORM

The principal dimensions of a building's structural system can be influenced by many things. It is possible in the case of a building whose function is to remain almost totally flexible that a very large structural grid, determined only by the maximum sensible spans of the structural components would be the most suitable form. But where the function to be performed is known in detail and the building is to be essentially tailor-made to a particular operational use, the grid can be tailored to the function and may even adopt a much smaller grid related entirely to planning requirements.

There is every possibility in between these two, but in the end the governing factor in the determination of an appropriate structure for any office building will be the consideration at the one end of a suitable constructional grid which will provide the spaces best suited to the likely uses of the building, and at the other a planning grid which will be best suited to the nature of the operation to be conducted within the building. Both need to be considered and the structure determined which establishes a satisfactory relationship between the two.

It will be understood that, however precisely standards for planning or structural grids may be set or recommended for particular types of accommodation, the brief, the site and local conditions will always influence these in one way or another and the eventual solution must pay regard to these influences.

While large office structures require a structural 'grid', the designer must not lose sight of the simple solution for smaller structures of 'traditional' load bearing walls which has the economic advantage of providing natural sound and thermal insulation.

Fig. 4.4 Depth of building and office space

PLAN SHAPE

It need hardly be said that the longer and narrower a building, the easier it is to provide natural light and ventilation to the office spaces formed within it. Though in cost of structure it is extremely uneconomical as the nearer the plan form is to square (or circular) the shorter is its perimeter and therefore its enclosing element. A width of about 15 m is thought to be a reasonable maximum and anything beyond this requires mechanical means of introducing fresh air and removing stale air from the middle of the building which cannot effectively be ventilated by windows on the external walls. From the planning point of view however, this dimension is over-wide and 12 m is thought to serve rather better a conventional central spine corridor with offices either side (Fig 4.4).

The more concentrated forms for providing accommodation such as towers have to be considered carefully in respect of their ratio of office space to circulation space as this is normally a little disproportionate unless it is a fairly generously sized tower plan. The area per floor tends to be limiting where flexibility is required to accommodate different departments of different sizes. With small yield areas such as those in tower floors, the overflow of one department on to another floor can introduce difficult circulation problems when balanced against the ability to spread a little further along a larger floor on the same level in a rectangular plan.

In any event it is necessary to consider ancillary accommodation as well and to think of such problems as those related to lift and circulation space. With lifts for example, it is comparatively easy to leave spare space for the lift shaft without the expense of installing the car and motors.

GRID DIMENSIONS

Materials naturally have a strong effect on the basic planning or structural dimensions. Principal constructional or even interior components will influence the development of a structural grid and it is not entirely out of the question that even the tube lengths of fluorescent lighting can be a determining factor in the basic dimensional set up of the building at the planning stage. It is generally found that basic dimensions for most office buildings vary between 1·32 and 1·34 m and provide the most usable single or dual occupant office of say two of these modules by three modules deep giving a room of approximately 3 × 4·5 m. This coincides with an air conditioning output effectiveness to an easy depth of about 4·5 m from perimeter units.

It is normally thought that an office space of these dimensions offers a good relationship with structural demands and that on the assumption that partitions are likely to follow this kind of grid the structure begins to determine itself (Fig. 4.5).

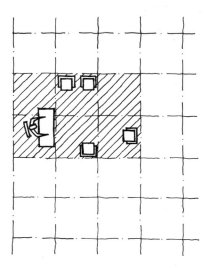

Fig. 4.5 Grid dimensions

The kind of dimensions that are likely to emerge from the consideration of a third type of space, deep or open office planning, are frequently arrived at by considering the area required by an individual and all his equipment, or more safely is probably best related to the space occupied by two individuals plus the access corridor or circulation space related to the occupants. This as a basic dimension is thought to work out at something in the region of 5 m. In structural dimension terms however, the span between columns is thought to be better at not less than 6 m.

It is thought that for acoustic reasons the lowest limit for the dimensions of an open plan office are 20 × 20 m. This area could be expected to accommodate 40–50 people. But the suggestion that only a small percentage of firms can utilise such large areas implies that a multi-storey office block providing such large area on all floors, would inevitably face the impossible problem of subdivision on any one floor to provide a certain amount of cellular office space. It seems therefore, that the firms requiring the larger dimensions are those which must be confined to single-storey development only.

For group use with spaces occupied by about 5–15 people, it is thought that a building is well suited at some 15–20 m deep. If a number of small companies occupy a building, possibly floor by floor, each floor must be a separate entity with its own access and service point. The ideal area per floor has been indicated at some 450–540 m² without incurring the problem of doubling the number of lifts, escape routes, lavatories etc.

Because the need to subdivide rather than open up space is an occupational hazard of the management process, it may be that a floor width within the limits suggested by daylighting conditions is accidentally the most convenient for its inherent ability to provide the type of accommodation that best suits most firms.

TYPES OF STRUCTURE

In the design of all buildings of any significant size, the problem has to be solved of ensuring that the structure causes the least inconvenience to the function. The way in which the main structural parts; the columns and the enclosing skin, are related to each other are normally the means by which a reasonable solution is achieved.

Where there is incompatability between the structure and the planning requirements of the building, an answer to accepting the difference between these two is to remove the columns from the space that they are likely to disturb.

A structural form which will do this is one in which the columns around the perimeter of the building stand outside the enclosing skin so that the skin is continuous and can accommodate internal partitioning at any point along its face.

An alternative form of structure is to reverse this by cantilevering the floors beyond the perimeter columns and to place the enclosing skin of the building outside the columns at the edge of the floor slab. This provides clear window space outside the principal structural column grid and the same flexibility for the accommodation of partitions as in the previous form, if the floors cantilever beyond the external

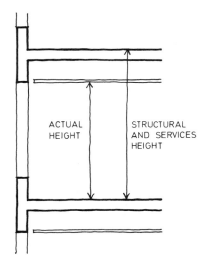

Fig. 4.6 Heights of ceilings

row of columns and deep enough not to interfere with say a possible small cellular office depth.

The structural mullion external wall system provides mullions at frequent enough intervals to accommodate partitions at almost any point.

A further system of construction takes the core as its central support unit and the floors are designed to span one way between the inner core and an outer load bearing structure. A characteristic of this type of structure is that the outer form is inevitably exposed to the weather and temperature change and that the enclosing structure and inner core tend to move differently. It is claimed however, that the benefit of this 'hull core' structural form is in the economy afforded by the symmetry of its shape.

HEIGHT

In internal planning terms columns are naturally more inhibiting than the depths of beams and though it is true to say that excessive beam depth makes servicing difficult, it is slightly more manageable as a problem than trying to 'lose' columns. In the USA a clear space of 700–800 mm between ceiling and structure is thought to be the most realistic to accommodate all the services required for this type of building. This is usually combined with a floor deck distribution system which allows electrical and telephone services to run in the floor and serve the offices on a service grid. This hollow floor system combined with a service grid has proved to be most universally employed in practice.

Floor to floor height might be in the region of 3·50 m which will include the clear service space and leaving a room height, depending upon particular needs, of no less than 2·4 m and preferably 2·5 m (Fig. 4.6). In an open office plan or a deep office, the ceiling height becomes oppressive if kept to the minimum and with the need for noise baffles usually requires an increased floor to floor height than would be used in a cellular system of planning.

FURNISHING

The working area is, however, the focus of the office function and many furnishing manufacturers base the design of their office systems on the economics of office space use. They make certain that all their equipment relates so that there is no space loss and by the relationship of one piece of furniture to another, can form either open work spaces or furnish a perfectly traditional cellular office. With the same articles they aim to give flexibility of use for a furnishing system in an office building which provides different types of working situation.

SYSTEMS

It almost goes without saying therefore, that a good deal of research has been carried out by the manufacturers of furnishing systems for offices. Several have carried out independent studies with universities or similar research institutions to discover the best conditions under which to work in offices and have designed entire furnishing systems around the results. Some of their observations are given below:

(a) Ten minutes watching any secretary will tell you that one desk to be used for both typing and writing means frequently sliding the typewriter along the top of the desk to provide writing space. A side table is almost essential for a secretary.

(b) Stationery items available to a secretary's desk must be openly accessible and not in drawers. Stationery storage units in desks are not sufficient as the type of stationery and equipment which are used even in a small company vary sufficiently for it to be impossible to accommodate in the desk itself. A separate storage unit is required.

(c) There are certain key needs that most people look for: adequate desk top space, which should be smooth and on which they can write without aids like blotters. The ability to seat three or four people around the desk without built in drawers or storage units preventing them from getting their knees under. Ability to open a drawer fairly easily from a sitting position and easy accessibility for the storage units used in conjunction with the desk. Most people prefer telephones off the desk but within easy reach of the desk.

(d) A manager/executive or anyone conducting interviews or meetings in his room may well be better served by a table with independent storage units rather than a desk in which he has pedestals of storage space. (While it has been said that there is very little reason for a desk being wider than 900 mm, bankers have traditionally had very wide desks. It is a characteristic which is built into the whole banking procedure and probably had its origins in the need for visual privacy for documents although supporting an attitude to the need for 'customer' relationship between themselves and a visitor).

(e) It must be remembered when considering a flexible office system, that the furniture must also be flexible in its own use. There is no point in designing what is imagined to be a 'flexible' open plan landscape to fill the volume of an office, if it is the only arrangement which can be made with that particular type of furniture. Similarly if the system changes, and one section of the office is to be replanned, the management must be capable of storing the articles not used or alternatively to use them in another type of accommodation. The units must therefore be fairly light in construction as well as flexible enough in their form to be used in several ways.

(f) Desk or working tops should not be in a colour which contrasts badly with the materials being used. A strong contrast produces optical distortion which is unpleasant and unacceptable. The top should be capable of withstanding coffee cup rings, spilled ash and preferably be non-shiny to prevent papers slipping or being blown off.

In considering the various furnishing systems available for office use, a certain amount of caution must be exercised in the claims made on saving circulation space. Very high percentages are sometimes claimed but in practice these benefits cannot always be exploited as it is obvious that fire escape routes must be left through all spaces and in any event, circulation space is frequently as important environmentally as is the working space.

SERVICES

In the case of a fully air conditioned building services may represent about 33% of the cost of the building and take up to about 10% of the plan area. Their function is to control the internal environment of the enclosed volume in terms of light and air, plumbing and sanitation, the provision of vertical transport and the power installation for all the office machinery.

In specific terms the building will include the following items and therefore there is the need to anticipate their integration into the planning and structural solution through proper accommodation of duct ways for pipes and cables and all the accessories that are associated with the proper servicing of the building.

INCOMING SERVICES

Water. The area devoted to water storage will be determined by the calculation of the water storage requirements for the total building, normally based on a 24 hour storage system. If this is at low level in the building it will require pumping so storage tanks are generally placed at a high level to take advantage of gravity feed for internal distribution.

Electricity. This service will probably need a sub-station to accommodate transformers and high tension switchgear and this in turn will need appropriate precautionary measures to protect high voltage cables and provide specialist fire protection. It must be accessible day and night for maintenance purposes. An intake room will be required adjacent to the sub-station for medium voltage distribution.

Gas. The gas service needs a gas meter room and from this a mains distribution system round the building; this is frequently in the form of separate structural duct enclosures to terminal outlets. Again, this installation will need to be constructed within stringent ventilation and fire proofing conditions.

These three principal incoming services will usually be controlled by local public service installation conditions and the type of supply. Storage where appropriate and distribution within the building will be closely controlled by the Public Service authority concerned.

Heating. There are two basic forms of heating service to a building of this nature. The first is a waterborne system and provides heating throughout the building in pipes from a central boiler which is gas, oil or solid fuel fired and which serves conventional radiators normally sited in the area of greatest heat loss—either windows or perimeter walls. In certain cases, the system might serve a heated ceiling or heated floor installation.

A second type of system is airborne. It is served by a central boiler, but instead of pipes to radiant heating forms, it is carried as fresh air through ducting—perhaps even builders work, and supplies warm air to the building spaces. With this, is frequently incorporated a ducted extract return air system. The system as a whole works to a predetermined number of air changes per hour to different types of accommodation in the building and in this system it would be usual for the fresh air intake to incorporate filtering.

AIR CONDITIONING

The object of air conditioning is to control automatically and continuously the condition of the air within the building to a comfort level for all the occupants.

A number of systems are employed for bringing effective air conditioning into a building and these are best assessed by a services consultant bearing in mind the characteristics of the building and the type of accommodation, its location and all factors related to the control of the environment in a given set of conditions. It is important however that the alternatives need to be investigated by a competent advisor as the balance of capital versus running costs and indeed the effect of the different types of system on the concept of the building itself are vastly different and must be assessed for their true value.

It is therefore incumbent upon the designer to recognise that the starting point in considering the whole problem of heating and cooling in buildings is that he should have provided a structure that minimises the heat losses from the building and the heat gains to the building within the form of the building itself. This will either be through thermal insulation to counteract heat loss, or by shading or reflective devices to reject heat gain. Since windows are the cause of the greatest thermal loss and solar gain, the reduction in their area directly reduces the capital and running cost of any heat or cooling system employed in the building.

ELECTRICAL SERVICES

These will normally require sub-mains, handling the distribution at each level in the building with its own switching and therefore will require a vertical duct space for a rising main throughout the height of the building.

Lighting installations for this type of building will vary to meet differing local standards and the types of occupant. Generally they should be glare free and will usually take the form of discharge light resources rather than incandescent because of the greater efficiency of the system and the longer lamp life. In a building of this type it is also usual to have either a perimeter or under-floor network system to provide flexibility in the distribution of circuit cables and communications systems cables. This feeds socket outlets at almost anywhere in the building. Electrical services also include the need for an audible fire alarm system normally set into operation from manually operated contacts or alternatively with automatic heat or smoke detector heads which trigger the alarms.

LIGHTNING PROTECTION

The tallest structures in 'high strike' lightning zones and frequently an office building of this type normally carries lightning protection in the form of metallic tape around the roof perimeter and down the structure where it is grounded to earth.

VERTICAL TRANSPORT

This will need to be considered under three headings, the first being a conventional lift of the traction or hydraulic category. The traction lift has its motor room above the shaft with the problems of over-ride and roof projection, and the hydraulic lift which has its motor room remote from the shaft at low level.

The second category is the paternoster which is a continuous moving string of lift cars providing both upwards and downwards service and by its nature is best restricted to a limited number of floors.

The third is the escalator service serving two or more floors between which there is a known consistently high rate of traffic flow.

Each of these systems has its own particular characteristics which are well suited to some conditions while not so beneficial to others. They should therefore be adopted only after careful analysis by a services consultant in direct relationship to an analysis of the known requirements of the building.

DRAINAGE

This covers both the soil and rain water from a building and which is cleared by one of two different systems, combined or separate. It is the more usual to separate soil from surface water so that the clean water can be discharged without pollution or the need for costly treatment through a sewage system. All drainage from a building must however be run at a self-cleansing velocity and rain-water pipe sizing should be based on local conditions and will naturally be supported by appropriate falls in roof structure and drainage systems as well as external gulleys for paved areas.

In dealing with soil waste, there are two principal systems. The one-pipe system which assumes that all traps are individually ventilated with its anti-syphon system and therefore fully protected against a loss of seal. This is the system most commonly used in buildings where it is difficult to group sanitary fittings. The second, the single stack system, is used where sanitary fittings can be grouped and permits connections to a single ventilated stack. In both conditions, the installation is controlled by local regulations regarding sizes, distances and falls.

PLANNING

INTERIOR LAYOUT

In detail it should be recognised that air-conditioning makes a fundamental change to the whole interior planning of a building. The moment that a building is 'sealed' it becomes a different piece of architecture, and the biggest problem for the newcomer is that of realising the extent to which all the devices which are incorporated in the average building to combat noise, dust and draughts can be discarded.

In planning terms, executive rooms and board rooms frequently find their way to the top of a building, not so much for the possible grandeur that such a position might be assumed to offer so much as the fact that this is the place that is least likely to get tied up with the general circulation problem or other activity patterns of the rest of the building.

For the same sort of reasons staff restaurants, libraries and similar types of accommodation tend to sink to the bottom of a building; the staff restaurant because it has daily delivery problems and short term occupational needs, and following the argument that the space with natural light is best reserved for the more important office working requirements; the library because it has weight problems and frequently is embarrassed by the presence of windows and that the shelving for libraries, storage and archives, central filing systems or whatever utilises as much external wall space as interior space.

If this argument is not supported by the circumstances of the company, an alternative is to provide flexibility for the accommodation of this type of use by overdesigning floors to carry 'live' loads. This allows the use of any part of the building for any purposes and provides for any type of tenancy in the future.

CIRCULATION

In parallel with the question of the provision of large or small spaces it is necessary to consider the nature of the organisation. Whether it is built up of large working groups perhaps with essentially a 'paper passing' function, or a smallish group that operates closely within itself although perhaps for working convenience, with the need for fairly close proximity to another small group. Alternatively there may be a managerial condition in which individual spaces are designed to be appropriate to the work being done by a single occupant.

In considering physical proximity it has to be realised that there are certain conditions in which vertical 'circulation' provides a more convenient link between departments than vast long corridors on the same level. However, it must also be remembered that communication is just not simply a pedestrian walking from one place to another but trolleys full of files, bouncing coffee cups or messengers carrying parcels. Lifts, stairs, and escalators are therefore inevitably more of a hazard and the matter is a question of balance of advantages versus disadvantages.

In densely populated buildings the analysis of vertical circulation needs is crucial, and an investigation is very important to determine which groups of people will move between which floors.

It has been found that an escalator serving two floors can be better than additional lifts, particularly in the case of a low building with principally horizontal circulation. It is as well to pay particular attention to the traffic between particular areas where this may give considerable advantages such as a restaurant and general office area.

In many of the tallest buildings in the USA, principal circulation spaces outside lift lobbies or serving general office areas averages about 3 m in width. This is considerably in excess of the allocation normally provided in the UK but is related to the larger population encountered in high buildings. A building owner must consider the proportions of population to given areas to determine whether there will be a need to accommodate large numbers for short periods during a working day in specific circulation areas. Owners might, at the same time, give consideration to the installation of vending machines for staff use as these will need to be associated with circulation lobbies or at least non-working areas and they will therefore have a bearing on the circulation space dimensions to be built into the building; this applies to both cellular and open plan offices where in any event it is necessary to assume 'imaginary' corridors representing principle circulation patterns with secondary gangways to support them; these gangways usually have a width of 1·8 m and 0·9 m respectively.

SPACE DIVISION

The need for division between working areas falls into two categories; either that of providing visual privacy between the person working and a visitor passing through the space, or that of acoustic privacy where the space is devoted to interviewing or discussion which has enough privacy in its content to require some form of barrier. It has to be recognised that certain functions cannot possibly be conducted in open spaces and there is frequently a strong case for cellular subdivision for activities requiring specific visual or sound security.

A partition is not the only way of creating a wall, and has the disadvantage of being difficult to maintain continuity of surface with floor carpeting, wall plastering or ceiling finish, if it is decided to move partitions. It is even more difficult to provide switches or electrical runs within the partitioning.

Dividing screens serve many purposes but can naturally become pin boards or 'vehicles' on which to hang shelf units or storage cabinets. One of their main uses however is to introduce additional absorbent elements into a large volume where absorbency is an important requirement for sound reduction.

Depending on types, screens in large open areas do not always so much reduce the sound as deflect its path. This means that reflections or bounce within closely grouped screens can equally well behave in the same reflective manner as walls in a small cellular office. This naturally suggests that screens should be soft in nature to absorb as much noise as possible and 'screens' made up of banks of filing cabinets for example should not be formed into bays where the reflection would give a high level of reverberation.

In open-plan offices, it has been found that furniture should be arranged so that people do not face on to each other's work, but also that acoustic screens should never be permitted to be used to create cubicles or cells as such. The rest areas should accommodate something like 10–15% of the staff in lounge-like conditions and be available throughout the day.

The division between 'interior finish' and 'furnishing' is almost impossible to make in open plan offices. Depending upon the layout of furniture and the degree of privacy or the related tasks, furniture may be grouped to provide continuous spaces where people are moving documents from one desk to another, or as a series of isolated work areas; either open or closed, depending upon the nature of the business.

If the essence of open office planning is the option to use the space in a flexible manner the implication is that the furnishing should all be self-contained. A unit should not depend upon another unit to support the other end.

As the nature of open planning is flexibility in the use of the space and therefore an implied need for visual restraint, it follows that materials used in the interior should preferably be nondirectional in form. This assumes that they are ideal conditions without need of correction and must not discount, in the case of existing buildings, the need to visually correct in interior design terms, an over narrow space or perhaps reduce the length visually of an over-long one.

In considering materials, it is necessary to repeat that there are dangers in adopting methods or materials without critical analysis and it is too easy to get the wrong answer for your own building from the right reasons on everyone elses. It is the *reason* for the selection of materials which must be appreciated and the results of their combined use in various parts of the building which must be anticipated before materials can be accepted or rejected.

The dangers of advising on materials or methods have always been as great as the benefits, but it may be useful to recognise that in the bulk of the major buildings built over the past twenty years in the USA, consideration of conditions seems to have led to constants being used to meet certain circumstances of performance. Vinyl fabrics used on circulation space walls show a major saving over painting maintenance. Black vinyl or plastic, flush or recessed skirtings at the base of panelling or facings, guards against damage by dirt or cleaning machines. Vinyl asbestos tiles have shown themselves to be the most appropriate for service rooms and circulation spaces, and in some cases general office areas, as this is thought to be the tile form that reduces scuffing and cigarette burns to a minimum.

Many office buildings adopt a high quality hard surface for reception and lift lobby flooring of the travertine, marble or terrazzo variety. Sizes vary but for scale and handling are of 'paving' rather than 'tiling' sizes.

In other cases it has been regarded as more economical to fully carpet reception areas or a banking hall where a regular cleaning and replacement cycle will balance the initial cost and maintenance of terrazzo or a similar surface. The policy of totally carpeting office space, first arrived out of an analysis of material versus labour and maintenance costs and it still needs to be considered for each case.

Ceilings are generally of suspended 'manufacture-finished' white perforated metal pans and offer the flexibility to meet the daily demands of services engineers for access to the service runs in any part of the ceiling. Other ceiling finishes often run into the problems involved in maintenance. For convenience the major service runs are normally confined to corridor ceilings and corridor lighting should therefore avoid cutting across them, though the installation of lights on the corridor walls introduces the problem that switch drops cannot readily be brought down where using demountable partitions.

The finish on service or escape stairs depends on the company's use of the building. It is possible to encourage secondary stair circulation by adopting a high standard of finish between two allied floors, though more frequently for economy reasons, it is more general to adopt a strictly 'service' finish for these stairs with a fairly steep rise.

Lavatories, cloakrooms etc, are probably best fully tiled or similarly wall surfaced to their full height. Partition systems which cantilever clear of the floor surfaces are important. In existing buildings, a laminated plastic facing envelope inside the 'broken' profiles of lavatory accommodation will probably be a better way of providing cleaner surfaces.

Ironmongery is in most cases heavy duty aluminium or stainless steel. There is some question as to whether a bank, or indeed some office buildings, needs to fit its building from top to bottom with locks on door ironmongery when a main security system is being used.

The ancillary equipment used in support of general services should where appropriate, incorporate automatic disposal by pulping of kitchen waste. Pulping machines take little space, and are said to reduce refuse storage needs by 90%. It is important that large kitchen refuse storage areas are refrigerated.

Incinerators are also used for general refuse, but where an incineration system is to be adopted, it is important that the refuse arrangements includes collection bags which are also totally disposable. All aspects of the building's refuse system must be carefully geared to incineration. In high buildings, where practicable, it helps to plan the incinerator arrangement at high level in the building to eliminate excessive flue lengths.

Loading bays serving the buildings for both kitchen and general deliveries, might be well served by incorporating electrically-operated ramps to accommodate the varying loading heights of trucks or vans.

Security systems vary but most banks adopt planning arrangements where portions of the building can be approached through 'main' doors. These main doors, few in number, are regarded as security doors on which some form of scanner or TV control registers at a point which can be supervised by one guard only. In some cases the door detectors can be associated with a camera to record any disturbance.

A firm design and furnishing discipline which restricts the range of choice to an adequate but limited number of selected items, colours or materials gives visual clarity and a 'considered' quality to the building. If the maximum is to be gained in setting the correct character for the building, as well as benefits from stock maintenance items, all work must be done within this framework. It is essential that the policy is understood by the people responsible for the future furnishing and maintenance work in order that changes or modifications are an extension and not a dilution of the policy.

The most successful buildings and interiors are without exception those in which the furnishings, floor and general finishes are not only restricted in range and colour but of consistent quality throughout the whole building, including reception areas, offices, board rooms or circulation space. This simplicity does a great deal to underwrite and complement the directness and sense of location in the building, and gives considerable advantage to its sense of purpose.

Concerning the maintenance of materials in general in buildings with high density populations there is a tendency to adopt the view that the maintenance work, cleaning and mechanical services are best done as a specially contracted operation.

EXAMPLES AND FURTHER SOURCES OF INFORMATION

In the light of the major changes which are taking place both in the method of conducting business and the requirements of the buildings for commerce and banking, it is unwise and deceptive to be specific in recommendations. It is the author's intention that the section is seen as a backcloth against which design work can take place and buildings inspected to assess the suitability of approach or the solution of particular problems.

There are sufficient examples of recently built office and bank buildings to act as their own source of reference, and the examination of a large number of these buildings concurrently with undertaking the design of such a building is of immense value.

In general terms, it goes without saying that the natural centres for the comparative study of high buildings which perform similar functions but in very different ways and degrees of success, are cities like New York or Chicago, Toronto or Montreal and it is valuable to study these on a comparative basis. For the open planned offices, the natural place for the consideration of a number of the same types of building is Germany, and perhaps particularly Hamburg.

In specific terms the 'House' manager of any large office building or the 'Premises' manager of any banking group are the most appropriate source of information for their complete working knowledge of the failures and successes of the buildings for which they are responsible.

For selection of examples which are in the first instance and for general reference material, the information published by the Architectural Press is recommended as giving good coverage of all current developments in its technical journals. Most aspects of the subject from the requirements of legislation to environmental standards are dealt with in some depth by the various books on the subject.

ACKNOWLEDGEMENTS

The author wishes to acknowledge a number of items for this section which include background and supporting sources of reference in published material of the Architectural Press, the Building Research Establishment, clients whose specialist departments have contributed to the information. Thanks are also due to various furniture manufacturers whose researches are freely given in advisory technical literature and also to specialist consultants on the assembly of information related to their subjects.

Ronald Green *qualified at the Architectural Association, London in 1953; is a partner in the firm of Casson Conder & Partners and has been closely associated with a great deal of the banking and commercial work of the practice. He is the author of two books on architectural practice and is involved with architectural and design education.*

5 DEPARTMENT STORES, SUPERMARKETS AND SHOPS

NADINE BEDDINGTON, F.R.I.B.A., F.S.I.A.

INTRODUCTION

FUNCTION

The primary function of a shop is to sell goods or services to the public at an acceptable profit to the retailer. Retailing methods and shopping patterns have to change rapidly to meet new social conditions. Recent causes of change have been:

1. Increase in population.
2. Increased car ownership and increased car traffic.
3. Greater share of market held by larger undertakings and decline in number of independent traders.
4. The increased ownership of deep freezes and refrigerators.
5. Abolition of resale price maintenance.
6. Full-time employment of married women.

All of these are causing major changes of emphasis in shop planning and selling methods, and any designer of this building type must keep abreast of new developments and their impact on design. (For instance, the energy crisis is bound to affect retailing techniques).

MERCHANDISE

Merchandise sold in shops can be classified as:

1. Convenience goods, i.e. daily shopping needs.
2. Comparison goods, or consumer durables, where customers compare quality, variety and price, service offered, etc.

SHOP TYPES

The main types of goods and services are:
Food (perishable and non-perishable)
Clothing (Men's, women's, children's)
Hardware
Furniture and Home Furnishings
Services
Miscellaneous
Institutional
Refreshment facilities

Any of these may be sold individually in specialist shops, or as part of a larger composite enterprise. Main composite shop building types are:

(i) Department Store
(ii) Hypermarket or discount store (5000 m² sales area min.)
(iii) Variety Store
(iv) Supermarket or Superstore

These are classed as 'large space users' in Shopping Centre terms.

SHOP BUILDINGS

These may be erected in two ways:

1. Purpose designed individual units. This will be either:

(a) Piecemeal redevelopment or modernisation and extension of one unit (of whatever size) on an urban site for tenant or owner;

(b) Department store or large variety store or supermarket forming part of new complex, on lease agreement and subject to landlord control;

(c) 'One-stop-out-of-town' hypermarket or discount store.

2. Speculative development of shopping complex for letting. This may be either:

(a) Row of shops forming 'infill' in existing street;

(b) New or redeveloped shopping complex or shopping centre. This may comprise, depending on size and location, some or all of the following: Department Store; Variety Store; Supermarket; Standard Units.

The developer will provide the shells of the standard units for letting, the tenant being responsible for shop front, finishes and shop layouts. If known in time the larger units may be tailored to the needs of the larger space user (see 1b above).

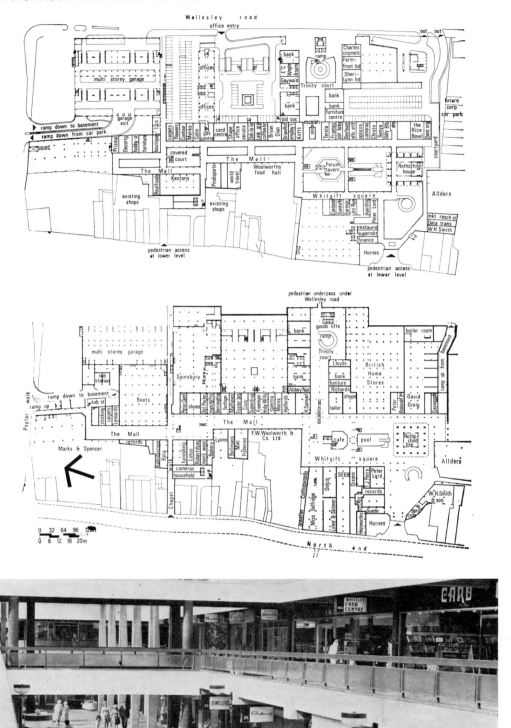

Fig. 5.1   Whitgift Shopping Centre, Croydon (Designed by Fitzroy, Robinson & Partners) (above) Upper ground floor plan (centre) Ground floor plan (below) 'Open Mall' (From article on 'Shopping Centres' by Nadine Beddington; Building 30/4/71)

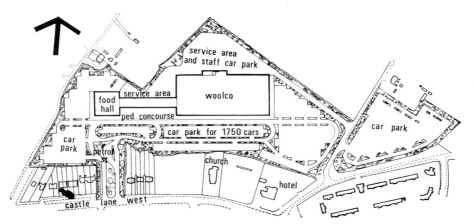

Fig. 5.2   The Hampshire centre (above Pedestrian concourse (below) Plan (Designed by Lionel E. Gregory & Partners for Second Covent Garden Property Co. Ltd., Part of Star (GB) Holdings Ltd.)

THE CENTRE

The shopping centre may be either a redevelopment or extension of an existing central or district urban area, or may be a one-stop complex in a 'greenfield' or suburban location, to which customers travel in order to shop.

It is becoming a prerequisite that the shop frontages are served by a traffic-free pedestrian precinct known as a 'Mall'. This may be open-air (with or without canopy protection to the shops), or enclosed, with partly or fully controlled environmental conditions.

Adequate and convenient transport and car parking facilities are essential, and pedestrian and vehicular traffic will be separated as far as possible.

Most shopping centre and hypermarket developers, as well as the large multiple retailers, have their own standard briefing guides on design and planning of shopping com-

plexes and shop units, frequently up-dated to meet changing trends and their own specialised requirements and policies, and these should be carefully studied.

Fig. 5.1 shows the Whitgift Shopping Centre, Croydon, which is an example of urban expansion with a new 'Open Mall'. The shopping centre is grafted onto existing shopping and covers a 4·8 ha site. There are two multiple storey car parks for 1100 and 900 cars. There is provision for 200 letting units. A 3·9 m difference in level between front and rear allows two-level shopping with lifts, stairs and moving ramps. It also includes banks, cafe, restaurant and public house.

The Hampshire Centre (Fig. 5.2) covers 8 ha. Two are occupied by Woolco with 9290 m² of totally enclosed air-conditioned individual selling space. Woolco is connected by twelve smaller units to a 2230 m² supermarket. Car parking is provided for 1750 cars.

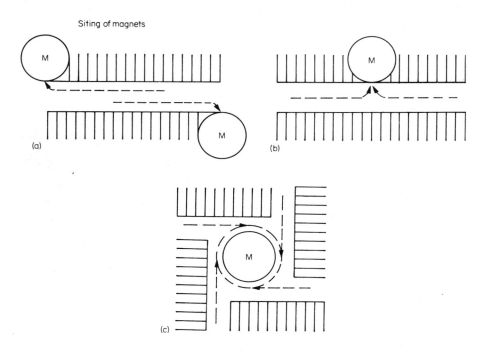

Siting of magnets

Fig. 5.3   Siting of magnets (a) 2 magnets at opposite ends. Good pedestrian flow between magnets (b) Single magnet centrally placed. Good pedestrian flow (c) Central magnet in pedestrian mall. Good pedestrian flow in all directions between specialist shops and magnet

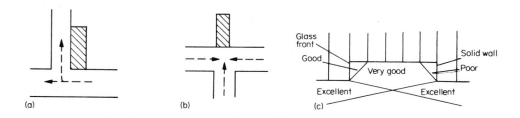

Fig. 5.4   Siting for impact (a) Maximum shop frontage with external display but reduced wall space (b) Good impact siting (c) Example of the effect of siting

SITING

Main considerations in siting of an individual shop are:
1. To attract trade.
2. To provide convenient customer access.
3. To provide efficient servicing.

1. ATTRACTING TRADE

The siting of any shop will directly affect its trading potential. The greater the foot traffic past a shop, the greater the potential trade. Department stores, variety stores and supermarkets are 'magnets' and will affect the trade of their neighbours. For success of the whole centre they should be sited to draw shoppers past as many units as possible. Pedestrian routes from car parks must be carefully planned to avoid by-passing key shops.

The minimum catchment area for a 'large space user' is a population of 70 000–80 000 (see Fig. 5.3).

A shop needs maximum impact for its shopfront and should be seen from as many angles as possible and should be related to car parks, bus stops, street junctions, in convenient positions to attract the maximum flow of customers (see Fig. 5.4).

2. CUSTOMER ACCESS

Correct relation between shop and car parks (and public transport) is essential. Shoppers car parking should not be shared with commuters' long-term parking. For Supermarkets and Hypermarkets standards are stipulated by developers (see sub-section on 'Planning'). Minimum standards of car parking are stated by Multiple Shops Federation to meet the normal weekly peak shopping demand (per 100 m² gross of retail area).

1975

In an area of low regional car ownership	3·50 car spaces
In an area of high regional car ownership	5·50 car spaces
In an area of average car ownership	4·50 car spaces

1980

In an area of low regional car ownership	4·00 car spaces
In an area of high regional car ownership	6·50 car spaces
In an area of average car ownership	5·25 car spaces

(This information is taken from Multiple Shops Federation Publication 'Car Parking for Shoppers').

The maximum distance between shoppers' car (or bus stop) and principal shops should be 201 m and should be within the inner distribution road system. Access to car parks must be easy, without congestion or delay. As an example, given one hour shopping time per customer, 1000 cars will enter and leave a car park serving a 9,300 m² Hypermarket every hour.

Car parking serving supermarkets and hypermarkets must allow for easy trolley access from check-out points to car boot. (Trolleys will normally be collected, returned to check-out points by shop staff.) Multi-storey car parks should discharge onto as many shop levels as possible if serving shops on different levels. Lifts must be adequate to take trolleys, and collection bays will be needed on each deck.

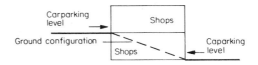

Fig. 5.5 Entry at two levels of shops

Shop units on upper levels are seldom satisfactory unless contours allow entry at 'ground' level to each shop, Fig. 5.5. (See also section on External Circulation in the volume *Planning*: Architects Technical Reference Data.)

3. SERVICING

Efficient rear servicing is a prime factor in goods handling. Service vehicle access must be separated from customer vehicles (see Fig. 5.6). Servicing includes:
(i) *Deliveries*. These may be either: controlled delivery, from retailers own warehouses or manufacturer; random delivery from numerous suppliers, or a mixture of both.
(ii) *Dispatch*. This may vary from returnable empties or unused stock by small unit to full customer delivery services from department stores.
(iii) *Refuse disposal*. Collection may be by commercial firm as well as local council (See sub-section 'Accommodation' and also section 8 'Warehouses').

4. SITING OF OUT-OF-TOWN CENTRES AND HYPERMARKETS

The catchment area may be 25 minutes driving time for the outer zone and 10 to 15 minutes for the inner zone. The road patterns must be right, with sufficient major roads to allow the population to do the journey in this time.

Roads in the immediate vicinity must be adequate to allow easy access to the site. This must be clearly visible with good signposting and free-flow two-way entry and exits for cars.

PLANNING—LAYOUT AND ARRANGEMENT

LAY-OUT RELATED TO METHODS OF SELLING

Selling methods control shop and department layout and fittings, and are basic to the internal shop design. The methods can be classified as follows: personal service, self-selection and self service.

1. Personal service

Customers are served by an assistant, sometimes from behind a counter. At completion of sale the assistant takes the cash to cash point and may give a receipt and pack goods. This method suits high value or technical goods, such as jewellery or cameras and exclusive salons or small specialist boutiques, as well as some types of food shop (delicatessen, cooked meats, etc).

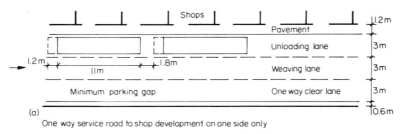

(a)
One way service road to shop development on one side only

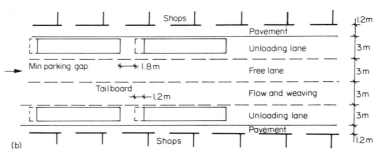

(b)
One way service road to shops development on both sides

Service entries

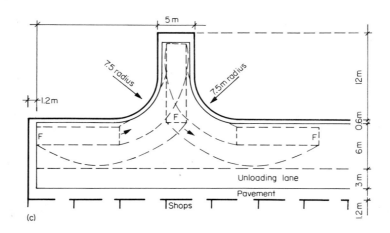

(c)

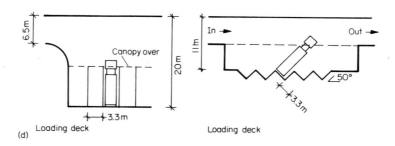

(d)

Fig. 5.6 Service entries (a) One-way service road to shops development on one side only (b) One-way service roads to shops development on one side only (d) Access to loading bays (from 'Standards for Service Areas in Shopping Centres' published by Multiple Shops Federation)

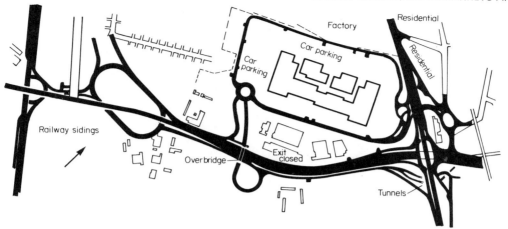

Fig. 5.7   Location plan for one shop shopping centre at Brent Cross (From 'Shopping Centres' by Nadine Beddington in Building *30/4/71)*

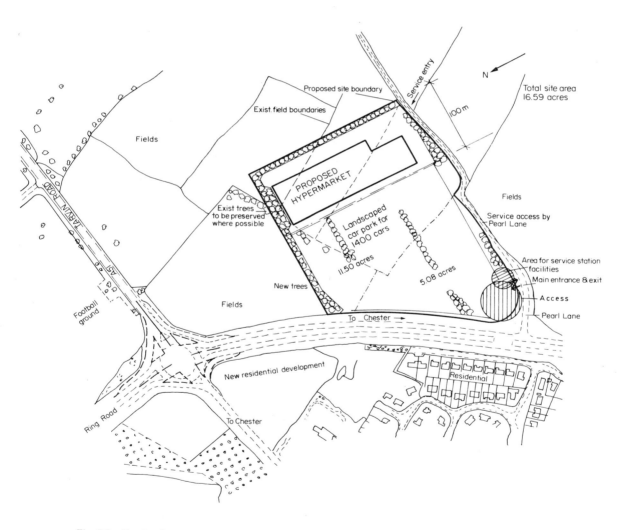

Fig. 5.8   Site plan for proposed Hypermarket at Vicars Cross; Scale 1 : 2,500 (Designed by Triad for Carrefours)

2. Self-selection

Customer may handle and select goods and take them to cash point for payment or wrapping. There is some staff assistance available. This system is general in variety stores and many departments in department stores, as well as specialist shops.

3. Self-Service

Customer walks round store, filling a basket or trolley and takes goods to check-out point for payment, wrapping. 'In' and 'Out' entrances being separated. This is the principle of supermarket and hypermarket trading and is basically suited to convenience goods.

In personal service shops the customer is influenced by the advice and sales technique of the assistant and, although display is necessary, all available merchandise need not be on display. In self-selection and self-service shops sales talk is replaced by display technique. In self-selection shops customers must be able to identify and handle the available merchandise (and can often try on clothing in fitting rooms) so merchandise must be grouped and laid out for this purpose, flexibility being of maximum importance.

In self-service shops (and, also in self-selection) the internal shop layout and arrangement of entrances and exits must encourage customers to follow as continuous a route as possible from entrance to exit, exposed to the maximum amount of display. This must be achieved without monotony or congestion and with an impression of spaciousness, which will depend on design and disposition of circulation aisles and of sectional planning.

Merchandise can be classified as 'demand', 'semi-demand' and 'impulse' goods, which are placed at eye-catching level. 'Demand' goods need not be so conveniently or so obviously sited.

Layout of self service and self selection areas must provide for general surveillance, from offices, check-out points, service desks, preparation areas, etc.

The amount of shelf or display space to be allotted to various products is of key importance. The relation of floor area, shelf display area, commodity location and turnover is delicately balanced and part of the trader's expertise. Standards cannot therefore be laid down and maximum flexibility in design of interior fittings and layout is needed.

STORAGE

The amount and disposition of storage for support stock is a key factor in shop layout. It will be related to 'stock Turn' or the length of time an article can profitably remain in the shop before being sold, as well as to weekly turnover, delivery frequencies and methods of stock control.

The present trend is to bring as much stock as possible direct to the selling area and present it on display. This is known as 'forward' stock. Supporting or 'reserve' stock is held in stockrooms, ready to replenish sales areas as required. See typical layouts shown in Figs 5.12 to 5.14 later in this section.

PLANNING OF SHOP TYPES—DEPARTMENT STORES

A department store usually requires a space of 20 000 m² gross, or over, though there are also 'Junior' department stores. This is the most complex shop type which provides full service throughout full range of specialist merchandise and services and is, of necessity, multi-storey.

Main planning considerations are:
(i) Disposition of areas required for departments and ancillary accommodation (see Fig. 5.9).
(ii) Number of storeys and structural grid dimensions.
(iii) Vertical and horizontal circulation and means of escape requirements.

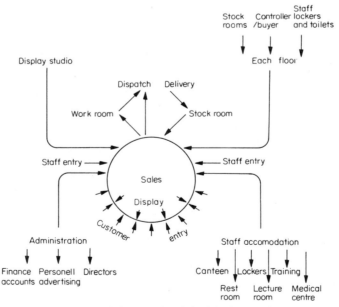

Fig. 5.9 Disposition of elements and analysis of circulation in department store

(iv) Siting of customer entrances and service access.

Building Regulations require the division of a multi-storey shop into compartments of maximum size 2000 m² or 7000 m² which may be doubled if sprinklers are provided. This division may be horizontal or vertical. Basement areas also require smoke extraction provisions. (See sub-section on Legislation.)

DISPOSITION OF DEPARTMENTS

Ancillary accommodation

Unit selling time will affect placing of departments. Quick sales of small items will be on ground floor near entrances to attract customers into the shop, with 'demand' goods on upper floors. A typical layout of floors might be as follows:

Ground Floor. Quick sales or small items, e.g. cosmetics, hosiery, scarves, haberdashery, handkerchiefs, stationery and books, handbags, gloves, silverware, jewellery and watches, cameras, chemist.

Basement. Glass, china, electrical and household goods, "Do-It-Yourself" items.

First Floor. Clothing—men's, women's and children's.

Upper Floor(s). Radio, television, furniture, floor covering and textiles, exhibition area, restaurant, hairdressing.

Top Floor. Staff, administration and finance.

Each floor demands maximum uninterrupted sales area to allow flexibility of department planning, which may be subject to frequent rearrangement. Irregular shapes may not necessarily be a disadvantage, as they may suit 'shop within a shop' solutions. (For planning of individual departments see appropriate specialist sections.) Ancillary accommodation is complex and must be related to service access and to appropriate departments.

Subsidiary accommodation will be needed on each floor to service individual departments but main elements of servicing, stockrooms and staff accommodation should be at the rear or on upper floors or basement (see sub-section Accommodation). For plant rooms see under heading 'Large space users' and sub-section 'Accommodation'.

Customer lavatories should not be readily accessible from street. They may be dispersed, say, on alternate floors, or central, adjoining Restaurant, but preferably entered through departments and not off stairs (see Section 3 'Hotels').

Internal circulation

Vertical and horizontal circulation is a crucial planning factor and concerns both customers and goods.

Customer circulation is fundamentally affected by Means of Escape Regulations. The numbers, siting and dimensions of escape staircases will be governed by Means of Escape Regulations and are related to travel distance, 'occupancy load' and minimum number of exits, which must discharge direct into the street. Maximum uninterrupted counter lengths on escape routes is also limited (see sub-section Legislation).

Vertical circulation, in addition to escape routes, may be by a combination of the following:

1. *Accommodation staircase(s)* within sales areas, i.e. staircase not forming part of escape route.

2. *Lifts* (essential to accommodate elderly, infirm, and handicapped (see volume on *Planning: Architects Technical Reference Data*).

3. *Escalators.* These are essential for large department stores. If within compartment they need not be enclosed (see sub-section Legislation).

For further information see section "data" and volume on *Planning: Architects Technical Reference Data*).

Horizontal circulation will be through aisles within the departments towards vertical circulation points. Escalator and lift positions should be well within the shop, so placed as to draw customers through as many points of sale as possible and to make ascent as inviting as possible.

SITING OF CUSTOMER ACCESS AND SERVICE

Entrances

A Main Carriage entrance strategically placed in relation to external traffic should be supplemented by walking entrances at convenient intervals related to street pattern and car parks and separated by display windows with as continuous a flow of display as possible (see under Shop Fronts in sub-section Data).

Circulation of goods must be considered as between point of entry (service delivery), through receiving room, sometimes via stockrooms, to selling position. Goods may then pass back via packing, to dispatch (point of exit) or be taken out by customer. Refuse and waste also has to be handled from departments back to dispatch, via waste disposal area.

Staff entrances must be separate and provide for signing in and checking out, with convenient access to staff locker rooms and lavatories (see sub-section 'Accommodation'). Staff and administrative accommodation can be remote from departments as long as there is adequate connection to departments (see sub-section 'Accommodation').

Grid

The structural grid (Fig. 5.10) should be between 6 and 9 m, bearing in mind relative beam depths. Floor to floor height should be a minimum of 4 m with a maximum of 5 m, dependent on servicing, ducting, etc (see also 'Large space users' below).

PLANNING OF SHOP TYPES—LARGE SPACE USERS

The difference between the Variety Store, Supermarket, Hypermarket and Discount Store is getting increasingly blurred as they expand in size and variety of merchandising. Much planning information is common to all these types, i.e. ancillary accommodation, goods handling, preparation areas, staff accommodation, type of sales equipment, layout.

For planning of individual departments and shop types, see under specialist shop types, later in this Section. The following information applies generally to shops having say 1200 m² or over, of sales area.

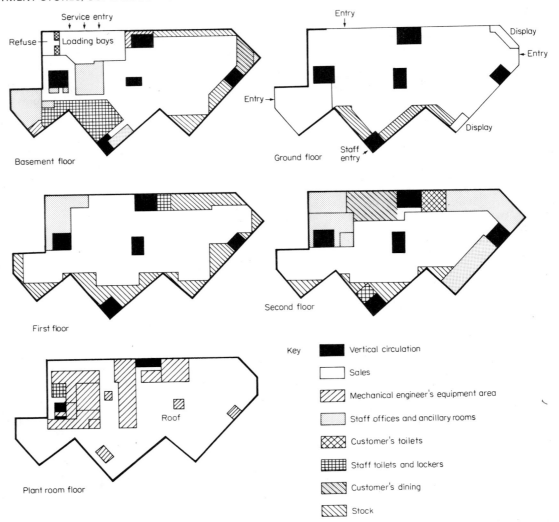

Fig. 5.10   Circulation plan of department store relating essential ancillary areas to sales area (Designed by T. P. Bennett & Son for Selfridges (Oxford) Ltd)

(i) *Allocation of space.* Proportion of ancillary accommodation may vary between:

60% sales	40% ancillary
48% sales	52% ancillary

Some ancillary accommodation may be on upper floors or basement. (See sub-section on Accommodation.)

(ii) *Goods handling.* Unloading should be within site curtilage onto loading platform with a minimum of 2 bays (though more may be required in individual cases). (See sub-sections on Siting and Accommodation.)

(iii) *Number of staff.* This is related to selling methods, takings and size of sales area. As an example, 3000 m² sales area might require up to 200 staff (see sub-sections Department Store and Accommodation).

(iv) *Customer toilets.* These are not usually provided except where cafe or restaurant facilities require them (see sub-section on Legislation).

(v) *Car parking.* The amount of car parking is critical—1 car parking space to 9·300 m² of sales area should be the aim, within 183 m of store. (See sub-section on Siting).

(vi) It is not satisfactory to use the standard shop structural grid for the large space user. 7·315 m to 9·150 m grid on the frontage is satisfactory. 9·150 m in depth is preferable. Heights floor to floor should also not have to be aligned with the standard shop—3·660 m clear height is preferred, with depth of between 0·3–1·2 m between ceiling level and structural slab, to accommodate services dependent on service requirements.

(vii) *Compartmentation.* Building Regulations require the division of all multi-storey shops into compartments of 2000 m² or 4000 m² if sprinklered. (See sub-section on Legislation.)

(viii) *Plant.* A large uninterrupted area is needed for plant rooms—up to 10% of sales area, if air conditioning is included—in which case it may best be sited at roof level, though the basement may be an alternative. (See sub-section on Accommodation.)

INDIVIDUAL SHOP TYPES AMONGST LARGE SPACE USERS

A variety store should have 1200 m²–3000 m² of sales area. This description covers the large multiple chain store, such as Marks & Spencer, Littlewoods, British Home Stores, Woolworths, etc. Other multiples, previously providing more specialised merchandise, are moving into this category. Traditionally the chain store sold non-food convenience goods, but in recent years they have expanded to cover food, clothing and other consumer durables using self-service and self-selection methods. Food sections may be fully self-service with check-out points (see sub-section on Supermarkets).

A catchment area of approximately 70 000 to 80 000 population is needed to support the larger units.

Main planning requirements are:

(i) One-level trading is preferred; but larger units may need two-level trading for adequate area.

(ii) A rectangular shape is preferable, as each floor will be laid out as one sales area of open space. Irregular shaped units can give interest, where 'shop within a shop' areas are intended. Selling will normally be by self-selection, with conveniently spaced service desks incorporating cash registers and wrapping counters.

(iii) Vertical circulation of customers will be by escalators and staircases, also acting as escape stairs. These are preferably sited on the perimeter to allow maximum flexibility of layout and uninterrupted space for counter planning. Perimeter walls should whenever possible follow the same lines from floor to floor throughout sales areas to facilitate planning of Escape Routes. (See sub-section on Building Legislation).

(iv) Ancillary accommodation will depend on size of store and merchandising (see under Department Store and Supermarket and sub-section on Accommodation).

(v) Entrances should discharge in direction of counters and main aisles (see sub-sections on Accommodation and Data Shop Fronts).

(vi) Staff employed may be 200–300 and staff entrances, adequate staff rooms, lavatories, lockers and cloakroom must be provided, at rear or on upper floors (see under Department Store and sub-section on Accommodation).

(vii) A customer cafe or restaurant may be required (see Section 3 'Hotels, Motels and Camps for the Motorist'.

A Supermarket should have 400–1500 m² of sales area and a Superstore 1500–2500 m² of sales area. Sales areas are preferably planned on one floor (if two floors, see earlier comment on Variety Stores).

Commodities sold in food shops can be classified under general headings as follows (Fig. 5.11):

Grocery foods (dry goods)
Meat and poultry
Fish
Greengrocery
Dairy and provisions
Bakery
Frozen foods
Non-foods

Planning considerations are dealt with in the following paragraphs and typical examples are shown in Figs 5.12, 5.13 and 5.14.

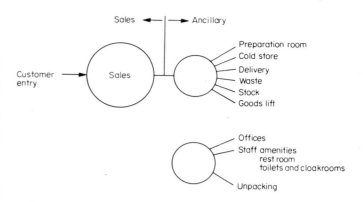

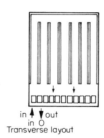

Fig. 5.11 Disposition of elements and analysis of circulation in supermarket

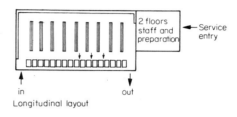

Longitudinal layout

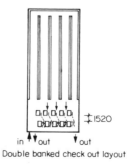

Fig. 5.12 Three methods of layouts for check-out points. Layouts are determined by size and shape of site. Generally, double-banked check-outs are used for very narrow frontages to allow for faster customer through-put. A bar runs centrally between check-outs in outer lane to determine direction of thoroughfare

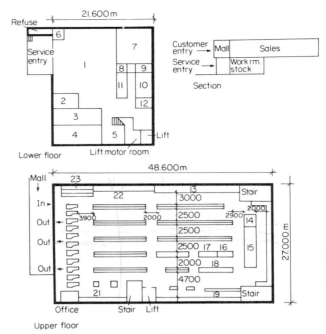

Fig. 5.13   Typical layout of supermarket
1. Grocery store room. 2. Frozen foods store. 3. Service provisions store. 4. Meat preparation. 5. Fruit/vegetable preparation. 6. Security cage. 7. Toilet/cloak-rooms. 8. Managers office. 9. Kitchen. 10. Staff room. 11. Wine store. 12. General office. 13. Cooked meats/dairy. 14. Frozen meat. 15. Poultry. 16. Fish. 17. Home freezer. 18. Ice cream. 19. Serviced provisions. 20. Fruit/vegetables. 21. Self service wine/spirits. 22. Promotions. 23. Trolleys

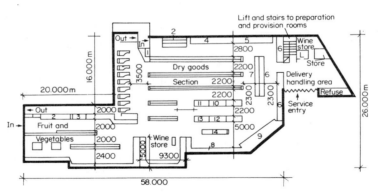

Fig. 5.14   Supermarket layout. Use of space on irregular site. 1. Basket stackers. 2. Trolleys. 3. Cigarette kiosk. 4. Diary. 5. Cooked meat. 6. Fresh meat. 7. Poultry. 8. Bakery. 9. Delicatessen. 10. Home freezer packs. 11. Ice cream. 12. Frozen foods. 13. Fish. 14. Sugar and eggs

Sales areas

The method of selling will be self service, with layout, entrance and exit all governed by arrangement of check-out points, the design and layout of which are a key to successful super-market trading (see sub-sections on Accommodation and Data). Minimum frontage should be, say, 18 m. Ideally a sales area of 2000 m² would prefer a frontage of 58–60 m. Narrower frontages demand double-banked check-out points which are less satisfactory.

Food items are sited together, separately from non-food items which are increasingly being stocked by supermarkets; perhaps on a different floor in a two-floor arrangement.

Customer service for delicatessen and provisions will adjoin the preparation area, and an off-licence will need special security measures (see sub-section on Security).

Chilled and deep freeze cabinets for counter-selling will be grouped in permanent positions (see sub-sections on Accommodation and Data). Space must be provided for trolleys and baskets at entrances and exits; as these must be used by customers for security reasons (see sub-section on Data). Pram parks may be needed.

Ancillary accommodation

The proportions of perishable to non-perishable goods (average 55% non-perishable to 45% perishable) will affect layout of storage and preparation areas. Cold stores are needed for fish, meat, provisions and poultry.

Refrigeration plant for cold stores may also serve chilled and refrigerated cabinets, or these may have plant integral in the cabinets (see under Department Store and sub-section Data).

Perishables, e.g. meat, cheese, and bacon will be prepared on the premises in preparation areas, preferably immediately behind the sales areas, but related to delivery positions, cold stores, etc (see sub-section Accommodation).

The Hypermarket type needs a minimum of 4644 m² gross sales area to make it viable. Success depends on a high volume of sales, permitting low cost bulk buying and minimum distribution costs and quick turnover of goods, resulting in discount selling at highly competitive prices.

Hypermarkets sell similar merchandise to the superstore and variety store, but with greater coverage of non-food goods and consumer durables (see previous comments on Supermarkets).

Because of the wide-reaching effect on the environment and on existing trading centres all Town Planning Applications for shops of 4644 m² or over must be referred to the Department of the Environment, who will either call in the application to be dealt with by the Department, or pass it back to the Local Authority for decision.

Under the Building Regulations, a single-storey building, if without galleries and far enough from the boundary, needs no fire resistance and is not restricted in size by compartmentation, though it must comply with Means of Escape requirements. Any two-storey part comes under the fire resistance and compartmentation provisions of the Building Regulations (see sub-section on Legislation). Air conditioning will be an essential requirement.

Planning considerations which distinguish this type from the Superstore are chiefly those of scale, i.e. car parking and external services, goods handling, and extent of administration, which approximate to that of a department store.

External planning

Customer entry and exits will be directly related to car parks. There may be no shop front display or shop windows, though a canopy is desirable at access points. Good visibility from feeder roads is essential. Filling stations and tyre bay must be accessible to customers, but not to passing motorists.

The car park area must be softened by landscaping and the service area must be screened. (For car parking and service access see sub-section on Sitings and Fig. 5.8.) The latter shows a landscaped car park for 1400 cars which is proposed for a Hypermarket at Vicars Cross, nr Chester. This shows a typical desirable arrangement where adequate space is available.

Internal Planning

The sales areas will be divided into:
Fresh Food (Perishables)
Dry Food (Non-Perishables)
Clothes
Household Goods (see under Supermarket and Department Store).
Customer Restaurant (see section 3).

The selling method will be self-service, with check-out points related to entrances, exits, the customer circulation system being similar to that for the supermarket (see under Supermarket). The arrangement of selling spaces must indicate different areas without physical barriers (by colour, signing, etc.).

Ancillary Accommodation

Areas for the sale of food have already been specified under Supermarkets but areas will be increased proportionately (Fig. 5.15). Storage areas will be arranged on Warehouse lines (see Section 8 Warehouses).

The method of restocking shelves in the Sales Area may be by forklift truck, carried out at night, with a 24-hour occupation of the building (see sub-section Accommodation).

Staff accommodation and administration offices can be on upper floor or at rear. There may be up to say 300 staff occupying the building at one time.

PLANNING—SPECIALIST SHOPS

SHELL OF STANDARD UNIT

Maximum Ground Floor sales area is required and a single sales floor is preferable if of adequate area. A Basement sales area is preferable to 1st Floor, with easier access for customers, and less obstruction of floor area by the staircase. The staircase position is vital and must entice up or down, and not appear as a deterrent.

The design of the stairs will be controlled by Means of Escape regulations. Under the Building Regulations 1st Amendment Means of Escape excludes shops with sales area of less than 280 m² or not more than three storeys (one of which may be a basement storey). These shops are defined in Code of Practice Chapter IV as 'small shops' and are dealt with separately as regards Means of Escape. They are covered by the Shops, Offices and Railway Premises Act—though a Fire Certificate is not needed for shops employing less than 20 people or 10 people above the ground floor (see sub-section on Legislation).

Standard unit dimensions (Fig. 5.16) are:
Width on frontage: between 5·3 m and 6 m.
Depth, front to back, ground floor: 18 m to 36 m.
Floor to floor height: 3 m, dependent on services. Unnecessary floor to floor heights deter customers and are tiring for staff.

The area of upper floors needs to be related to the ground floor depth to give adequate area for stock and staff rooms, related to the sales potential and catchment area.

Minimum staff accommodation of one toilet for each sex is usually provided with space at rear or on upper floor for staff room and food preparation facilities.

The amount of stock room area required varies with the type of retailer and some 'standard unit' tenants may prefer a reduced first floor area if the ground floor area is adequate.

There is a demand from small specialised trades needing narrow frontages and minimum storage and some should be provided in each speculation development (4 m frontage by 12 m depth).

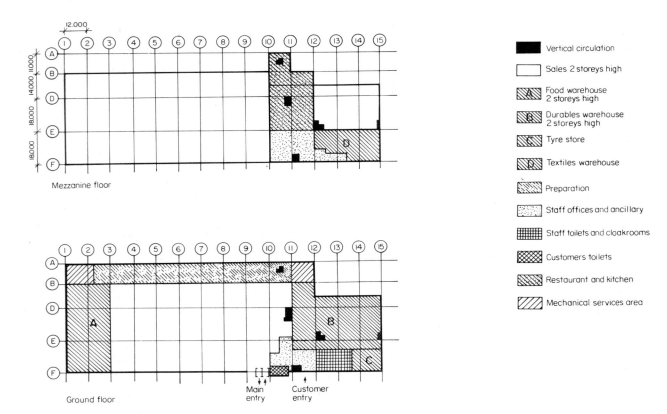

Fig. 5.15 Circulation plan of Hypermarket. Relating essential ancillary areas to sales area. (Designed by Triad for Carrefours at Eastleigh)

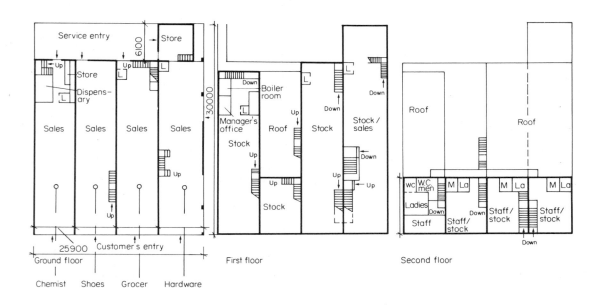

Fig. 5.16 Circulation layout showing adaptation of standard units for specialist shops. (Designed by Nadine Beddington for Bedworth Consortium)

INTERNAL PLANNING OF SPECIALIST SHOPS AND
'SMALL SHOPS'

It is not practicable to lay down planning requirements for
every type of specialist shop. Not only will this depend on
shopkeepers' retailing policy, but there are a vast number
of possible permutations of selling within this category.

Staff accommodation is in all cases related to number of
staff required. Staff accommodation is controlled by the
Shops, Offices and Railway Premises Act, which stipulates
toilet accommodation, etc. Clothes lockers and means for
drying clothes must be provided. Wash basins must be provided in preparation areas of food shops (see sub-section on
Legislation).

A small Manager's office is usually required with safe or
strong room, sometimes supplemented by clerk's or cashier's
office. Stock areas will be needed to retailer's requirements
and other ancillary accommodation must be ascertained in
each case. For typical layouts within main categories see sub-
section on Accommodation.

Some general rules on specialist planning requirements
are given below (see sub-sections Accommodation and Data
for illustration and details). These are also applicable to
appropriate departments within Department Stores, Supermarkets and Hypermarkets (see Fig. 5.17).

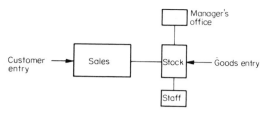

*Fig. 5.17 Disposition of elements and analysis of circulation
in specialists shops*

FOOD SHOPS

These may comprise the following types:
Fishmonger
Butcher
Provisions
Fruit and Vegetables
Baker

In all these the shop front will be glazed (see also sub-
sections Legislation, Accommodation and Data).

Sales in personal service shops will be mainly over counter,
which may contain refrigerated display, and equipment.
There may be a central pay desk, or cash till or cash register
on or behind counter. Window display varies with each trade
(see sub-section on Data). Fruit and vegetables are displayed
within shop (or outside) in bins, groceries on shelves, fish on
slabs, fresh meat on racks and hung on rails in addition to
refrigerated cabinets.
Ancillary accommodation may comprise:
(i) *Cold Rooms*, connected to delivery bay by lift or conveyor
if necessary, directly accessible to preparation areas.
(ii) *Preparation Areas*, are best sited adjacent to sales area;
in some cases visible to customer.
(iii) *Cooking area or cook room*, where required.

WOMEN'S AND MEN'S FASHION SHOPS

Shop windows need to be flexible to take promotional and
seasonal displays. The size and design will depend on type of
trading. Design of windows and 'Shop Front' will identify
the character of a specialist fashion shop and may be the main
challenge to the designer, together with the design and finishes
of the interior.

Clothes are displayed on free standing or wall racks in
self-selection shops, arranged with adequate circulation space;
in *personal service* shops they will be in glass-fronted counters
and hanging cabinets, with specially arranged displays in
windows and at promotion points.

Counters for *personal service* may have cash till or register or
there may be centralised service desks with cash till/register
and wrapping counters, as for self-selection. Fitting rooms
must be provided. In all fashion shops the ideal is to provide
a flexible plan with moveable equipment, the correct
atmosphere being generated by the design elements (for
illustrations see sub-sections on Accommodation and Data).

SHOE SHOPS

Shop windows may either be designed to show full range or
for small individual displays (see comments on Fashion
Shops above).

Due to range of merchandise related to sizes, correct
planning of stock areas is the essential key to successful
trading and fast efficient service in personal service shops
depends upon allocation of area between 'forward' stock,
i.e. immediately available to sales staff, and number of
customers who can be served at one time. The situation of
stock areas controls the time taken to serve a customer. The
extent of stock areas depends on trading policy and delivery
periods and 'stock turn' and the amount of 'stock holding'
must be determined at start of project.

In self-service shoe shops gondola fittings and wall shelving
take the place of chairs, all 'lines' being on display, divided
into sizes (see sub-sections Accommodation and Data).

JEWELLERY SHOPS

The articles on display are small and valuable and need
special security precautions, e.g. window grilles, burglar
alarm systems, safes and special display techniques.

Sales are usually personal service from behind glass-fronted
display counters.

WOMEN'S HAIRDRESSING

The shop front should identify the image and type of service.
The interior will have three basic service positions:
(i) Dressing table for cutting, styling and setting;
(ii) Shampoo basin (these will control the number of
positions for (i) and (iii);
(iii) Drier.
Also some cubicles for privacy for special treatments,
colouring, etc. There must be a reception or waiting area for

5–15

appointments and cash desk and cloakroom for customers' coats.

There may also be:
  Treatment clinic.
  Beauty room.
  Display points.
  Ancillary accommodation may consist of:
  Dispensary.
  Customer lavatory.
  Storage for customer record cards.
  Cash office.
  Staff accommodation.
  Small galley kitchen for serving customers snacks.
  Adequate provision for hot and cold water services to basins.

ACCOMMODATION AND SPACE REQUIREMENTS—DEPARTMENT STORES, VARIETY STORES, SUPERMARKETS AND HYPERMARKETS

NUMBER OF CUSTOMERS

The throughput of customers in a big store is very fast and results in intensive use of the building, particularly at peak trading times. Thus, selection of materials, space standards, etc., and accommodation must be considered with this in mind for all large stores.

The maximum number of customers in a store at any one time cannot be accurately estimated, though a useful guide is given in the Code of Practice, Chapter IV, Part 2 (1968), as follows:

1. For shops trading in the common type of consumer goods (food, hardware, clothes, cosmetics, fabrics, etc), 1·9 m² of gross sales floor area per person.
2. For specialised shops in more expensive or exclusive trades (bespoke tailoring, furs, furniture, jewellery, carpets, etc.), 7 m² of gross sales floor area per person.

On the basis, taking an average visit of one hour, and an occupancy load of, say, 2000, the daily throughput might be 16 000.

DEPARTMENT STORE

The main elements of accommodation are as follows (see Figs. 5.18(a) to (e) for examples):

(a) Sales areas

Areas allotted to departments can only be determined by trading policy of store in relation to total Sales area available, so flexibility is essential. (For classification of departments see previous sub-section on Planning.) For accommodation in individual departments see Specialist Shops, Supermarket, Variety Store, Restaurants and kitchens.

(b) Exhibition area

An Exhibition area incorporating a stage, is needed for promotions and fashion shows, etc.

(c) Stock Rooms. (For food see under Supermarkets below)

Main stock rooms may be laid out with racking and/or cages and work benches, served by gangway. (See Section 8 Warehouses). First Reserve Stock on Sales Floor will be in similar racking. 'Controlled delivery' goods from own warehouse may go straight onto Sales Floor. These are often computer-controlled.

(d) Work rooms

Work rooms for the following services may need to be provided:
  (i) Fashion. For alterations may adjoin fashion departments.
  (ii) Furniture repairs and upholstery; curtain and carpeting workroom.
  (iii) Curtain cutting.
  (iv) Curtain making up.
  (v) Carpentry.
  (vi) Carpet workroom.
  (vii) Radio, television and electrical appliances.
Items (ii) to (vi) should be adjoining or near service lifts.

(e) Display studio

A display studio may be needed for preparation and construction of window displays, backdrops, models, ticketing, showcards, etc. It should be accessible to shop windows and to the main sales areas.
  Equipment needed:
  Drawing tables
  Designers' benches
  Carpenter's bench
  Shelves
  Storage (min. 9 m by 6 m)

(f) Staff Accommodation

Staff entry	Space for clocking-in cards, racks for shopping bags and parcels, porter's desk (with fire checkpoint officer) display of staff regulations, stations and duties.
Cloakroom and lavatory accommodation	Lavatories to minimum standard of Shops, Offices and Railway Premises Act (see Legislation). Lavatory with supply of drinking water must be readily accessible to staff and not unduly centralised. Separate lavatories required for senior staff and general staff. Clothes locker room may be centralised on main staff floor with provision for drying clothes (see Legislation). Handbag lockers, or small personal lockers, should be provided for all staff within their department.

Staff accommodation may also include the following. These are all related in size to staff numbers which may vary from, say, 500 to 5000 for major stores.

Staff canteen
Senior staff restaurants
Rest room
Medical centre: first aid; doctor; dentist
Staff lecture room
Staff training rooms.

(g) Administration

Offices will include:
(i) Executive offices (Director and Management)
(ii) Finance. Hire purchase and credit accounts (accessible to customers, with private office). Sales accounts, bought ledger office (buyers orders and payments) wages and cashier, staff wages, expenses and petty cash, statistics, audits, accounts, strong room.
(iii) Advertising.
(iv) Personnel (accessible to applicants).

Serving the above are: computer; correspondence control; stationery store; communications (telephone exchange).

A buyer's or floor controller's office is needed on each floor. The minimum requirement would be an office with desk, telephone and visitor's chair; outer waiting reception area with shelves to take buyers samples and table, chairs, etc.

(h) Goods handling and delivery area. (Within site curtilage)

These may include:
Loading bays and platform (see sub-section on Siting).
Drivers' lavatory.
Goods lifts.
Food hoist.
Book hoist.
Conveyor.
Waste disposal (say 3·6 × 3·6 m including baler or compacter).
Transport superintendent's office.
Service staircase.
Receiving room, for unpacking, checking and ticketing of random delivery goods.
Garage for servicing, and repainting delivery vans and company cars.
(For information on staircases, lifts and hoists, see *Planning: Architects Technical Reference Data*).

(i) Plant rooms

All or part of the store may be air conditioned and in cases of a food hall, refrigerator plant will be needed. Plant rooms must accommodate:
Electrical switch gear with stand-by generators.
Refrigeration and air condition plant.
Space for water heating installation (see under Supermarkets).

VARIETY STORE

Sales areas will be fitted out flexibly to comprise some counter sales with assistant service for:
Pharmaceutical.
Specialist cosmetics.
Men's and women's knitwear, etc.
Self-selection will be from standardised fittings i.e.
Wall shelving.
Island or 'gondola' fittings.
all served by gangway minimum 2 m width and with service service desks containing cash registers (see sub-section on Data).

For food sales, staff accommodation, administration, goods handling and storage, see under Supermarkets and Superstores below.

SUPERMARKETS AND SUPERSTORES (see Figs 5.21a and b)

The number of check-out points will be related to turnover. This varies with unit sale but as a rough guide:
5 check-out points for £8000 per week turnover
16 check-out points for £30 000 per week turnover
or 16–21 check-out points for 1860 m² floor area.

Turnover per square metre varies in accordance with trading policy but averages are:
below 200 m² £1·80
200–800 m² £1·60
800 m² £2·50
a unit sale for weekly customers might be approx. £10·00.

These statistics are from the Institute of Grocery Distributors and, in view of inflation, will need continual upward adjustment.

Allocation of sales area may be, say, 45% perishable, sold from refrigerated or chilled display cabinets (see sub-section on Data) to 55% non-perishables (dry goods) sold from 'gondola' fittings and high wall shelving—laid out in aisles with gangways, minimum 2·2 m (or 2·3–2·4 m for larger stores.

Preparation areas and cold stores are needed for:
Fresh meat (butchery).
Cooked meat.
Dairy and provisions.
Fish.
Fruit and vegetables (see under Specialist Shops later in this section).
Stock rooms. For information on these see sub-sections on Planning and Data.
Goods handling. This has been covered under Department stores.
Waste disposal. Storage capacities can be based as follows:
300 m² gross area, average capacity required is 35 m³ per week
160 m² gross area, average capacity required is 2·3 m³ per week
Types of refuse are as follows:
1. Wet and semi-wet (for greengrocers, fishmongers, butchers).
2. Dry; non-crushable (e.g. crates, containers, metal, glass and plastic).

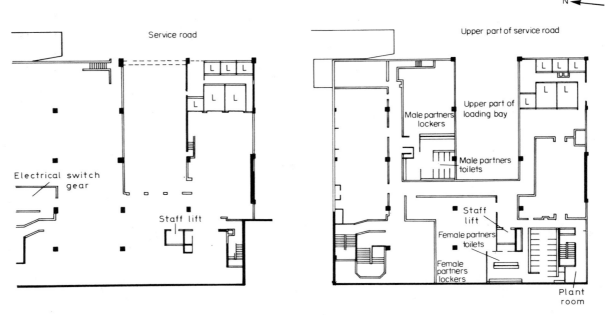

Fig. 5.18(a)   *Department store for Jessops at Nottingham. Basement floor plan (Designed by Arthur Swift & Partners)*

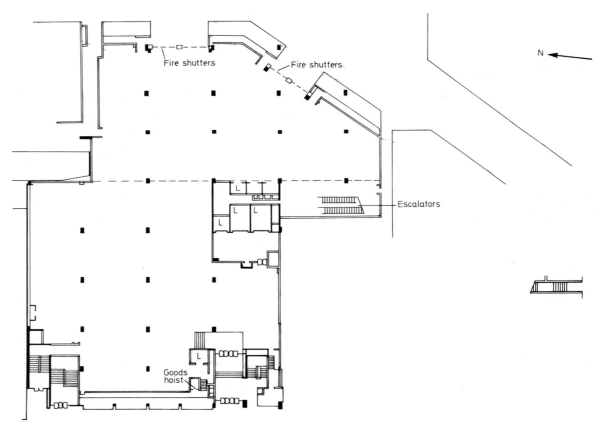

Fig. 5.18(b)   *Department store for Jessops at Nottingham. Ground floor plan*

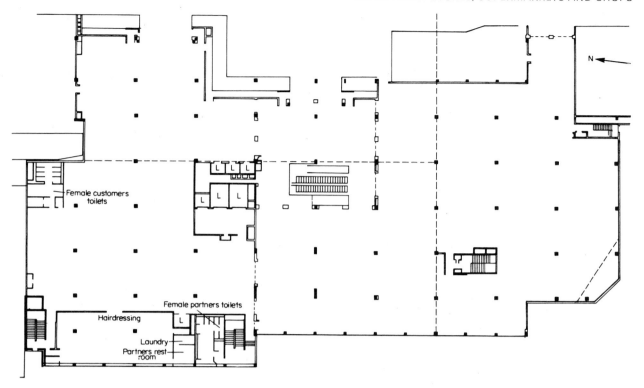

Fig. 5.18(c)   Department store for Jessops at Nottingham. First floor plan

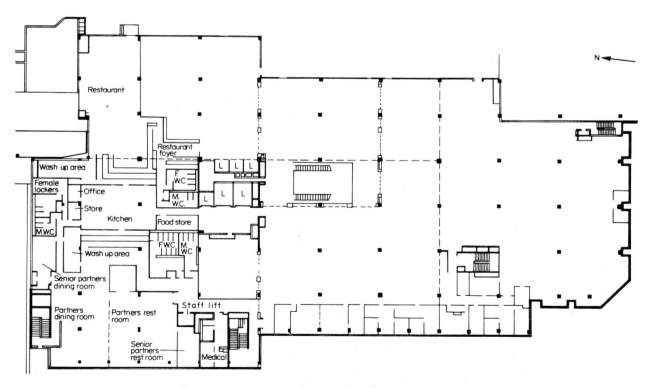

Fig. 5.18(d)   Department store for Jessops Nottingham. Second floor plan

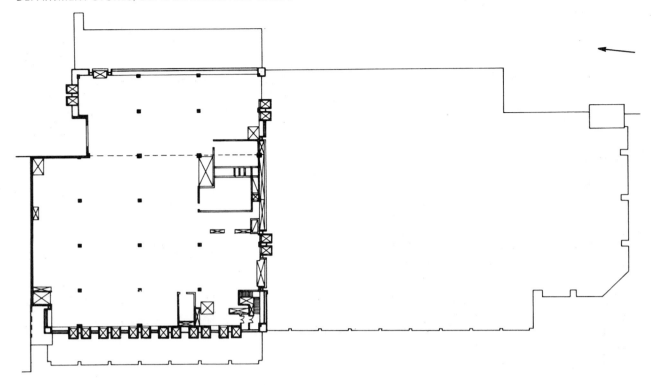

Fig. 5.18(e)   Department store for Jessops, Nottingham. Plant room floor

3. Dry; crushable (e.g. cartons, wrappings, etc.).

Refuse listed in 1 and 2 should be kept separate for disposal; refuse covered in 3 can be compacted and baled.

There are three types of refuse disposal:

1. Bins or paladins (see volume on *Planning: Architects Technical Reference Data*).
2. Incineration.
3. Compaction machines.

Collection may be made by the local council or a refuse contractor (for foodstuffs, paper waste, etc).

Staff accommodation will be related directly to estimated staff population and to trading policy. Lavatory accommodation must comply with the Shops, Offices and Railway Premises Act (see under Legislation). Also needed are:

Locker rooms with clothes drying facilities.

Rest room for both sexes.

Canteen and kitchen or food preparation facilities.

First-aid room.

Administration varies but should include:

Cash office.

Manager's office.

Clerk's office.

Safe or strong room.

Offices may be of minimum size (see S.O. and R.P. Act on Legislation).

The plant room will depend on whether the store is air-conditioned and whether a central refrigeration plant serves refrigerated cabinets. The area may be up to 10% of sales area (see also under Department Store and sub-section on Planning).

HYPERMARKET

A typical accommodation layout for a Hypermarket is shown in Figs. 5.21 and 5.22.

ACCOMMODATION—SPECIALISTS AND NON-SPECIALIST FOOD SHOPS

TRADITIONAL FOOD SHOPS

Main categories of food shops and their produce are:

Greengrocer. Fresh vegetables, fruit, flowers, frozen vegetables.

Fishmonger. Fresh and frozen fish, cured fish, shellfish, poultry and game.

Butcher. Fresh and frozen meat, meat products, poultry and game, fats.

Grocer. Bacon, eggs, cheese, fat, packaged, frozen and tinned foods, cereals, biscuits, beverages, dried fruits and preserves, sauces, spices, dry goods, soaps, detergents, cleaning materials, pet foods, paper products, chemist's sundries, toilet and hygiene requisites.

Dairy. Milk, cream, eggs, butter, cheeses.

Baker. Bread, cakes, biscuits, flour, pies.

Confectioner. Chocolates, sweets, cigarettes, tobacco, newspapers.

Most of the above are now combined into compound shops, comprising several trades.

Traditional and Self-service food shops will need:

Safe (with daily banking).

Lavatory basins adjoining food preparation (see Food Hygiene Act in sub-section on legislation).

Scales in view of customer (see Weights and Measures Act in sub-section on Legislation).

Preparation area, immediately behind sales area.

Food shops, needing lower temperatures, require a Staff Room with localised heating (see S.O. & R.P. Act in sub-section on Legislation).

Staff accommodation in accordance with Shops, Offices and Railway Premises Act (see sub-section on Legislation).

Some basic requirements for certain trades are given below though these are changing rapidly with new techniques, equipment and packaging. Typical layouts (shown in Figs 5.23 and 5.24) are given as a guide.

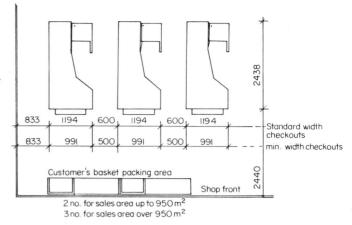

Fig. 5.19   Critical dimensions between checkout points

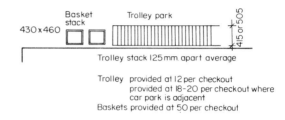

Fig. 5.20   Space requirements for trolleys and baskets

GREENGROCER

Arrangement of Sales Area	Open front being replaced by windows (see "Legislation"—(Food Hygiene Act in sub-section on Legislation). Open bins for root vegetables and fruit. Slab or mesh shelves for green vegetables. Cash desk with cash till or register. Scales and wrapping counter (in customer view). Frozen food display in cabinets (see sub-section on Data).
Preparation	Preparation table. Sink. Shelving. Cold Store or refrigerated cabinets. Lavatory basin.

FISHMONGER

Arrangement of Sales Area	Closed shop front with refrigerated display on marble slab behind glass (see Food Hygiene Act in sub-section on Legislation). Water connection for spraying slab. Service counter. Refrigerated and chilled cabinets.
Preparation	Cold rooms. Cleaning tank, with preparation counter. Ice box. Ice maker. Preparation table. Sink and lavatory basin. Cooking room or cooking shelf.

BUTCHER

Arrangement of Sales Area	Refrigerated display in wondow (or racks and counter) with meat rails over. Service counter with cutting blocks. Service counter with glass riser for provisions as separate unit to avoid cross contamination (see Food Hygiene Act in sub-section on Legislation) slicing machine. Pay desk and cash register.
Preparation	Cold Stores. Cutting room. Boning table. Meat blocks. Sink and lavatory basin.

NON-FOOD SHOPS

There is an immense variety of specialist non-food shops and a list is given below:

Antiques	Moped, cycle and motor accessories
Bank	Motor trade
Betting shop	Newsagent
Bookseller	Off-licence
Chemist	Optician
Dry cleaner, launderette	Pet shop
Electrical goods	Photographic
Florist, garden shop	Post Office
Funeral director	Radio, music, records
Furniture, home and office	Shoe repairs
Gas, electricity showrooms	Shoes
General, corner shop, etc.	Sports equipment, toys, games
Hairdresser: women's, men's	Stationer, printer
Hardware, ironmongery, decorating, D-I-Y	Sweets, tobacco
Jeweller	Travel agent
Leather and fancy goods	Women's and children's wear
Men's wear	
Miscellaneous repairers	

5–21

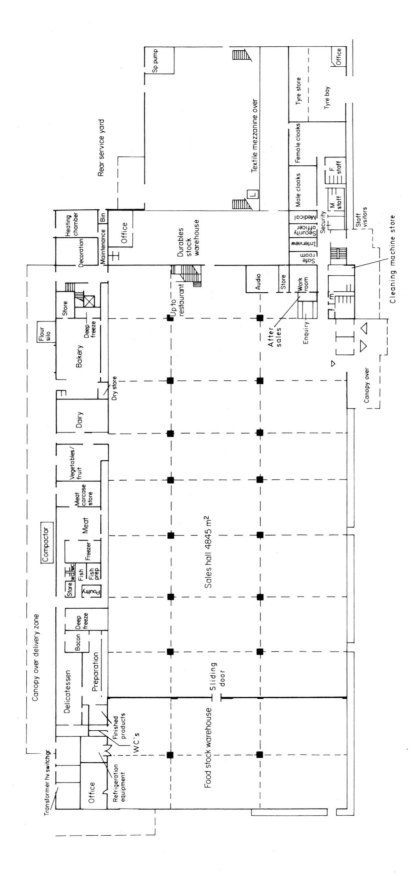

Fig. 5.21 Hypermarket at Eastleigh. Ground floor plan (Designed by Triad for Carrefours)

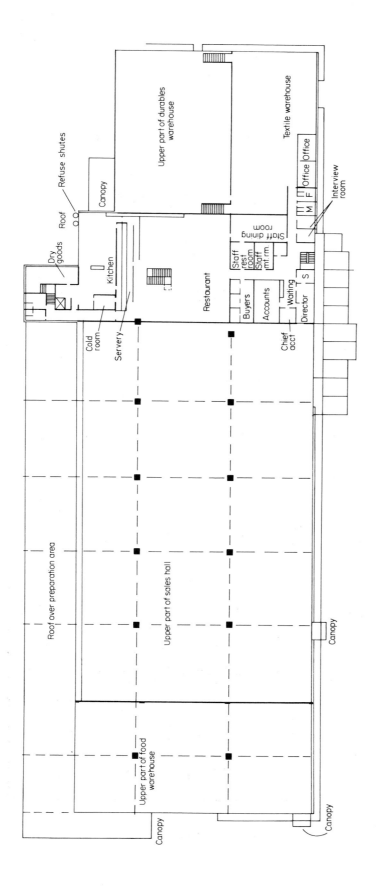

Fig. 5.22 Hypermarket at Eastleigh. Mezzanine floor plan

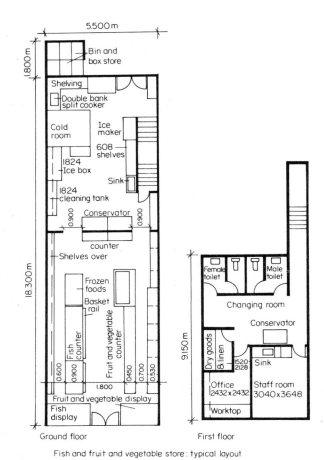

Fig. 5.23   Typical layout of fish and fruit and vegetable store

Fish and fruit and vegetable store: typical layout

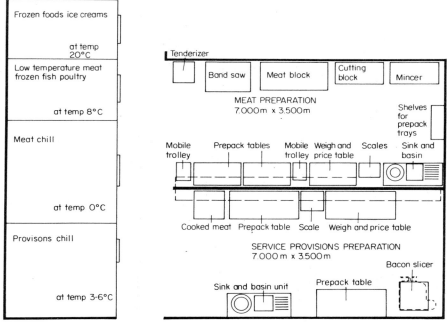

Fig. 5.24   Typical layout for meat and service provisions; preparation rooms.
Cold room storage related to temperature :
higher temperature : smaller area
lower temperature : bigger area

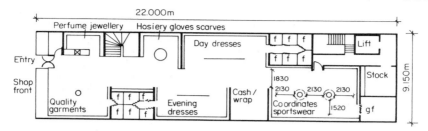
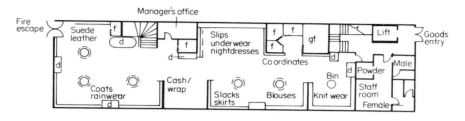

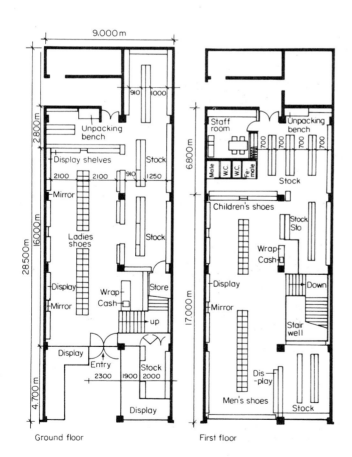

Fig. 5.25   Typical layout for women's fashion store
    f. Fitting room, min size 1200 × 900 (with staff assistance 1200 × 1200)
    g.f. Group fitting room
    d. display

Fig. 5.26   Typical layout to shoe store

Ground floor

First floor

It is not possible to identify all these in detail. With a general appreciation of retail needs, information can be gathered from 'on the spot' observation and research, from Trade Associations and from the client's brief, but some key types illustrated in Figs 5.25 and 5.26 and some notes given of special requirements for certain trades (see also sub-section on Data).

DATA

SHOP FRONTS

Shop fronts are needed for all shops except:
(i) Where giving on to enclosed mall;
(ii) One-stop unit such as hypermarket.
The function of a shop front is to attract attention, identify the shop, provide for display of merchandise (if this is a requirement) and entice customer into shop. Considerations which will govern the design are:
(i) Number and position of entrances, to be related to frontage, internal planning, and external siting (see also sub-section Means of Escape);
(ii) Relation of shop front floor area to total floor area;
(iii) Character and density of display.
Supermarkets and variety stores may have only flat glazed fronts with batteries of entrance doors, through which to see shop interior, with no display, or open backed windows with minimal display.
Specialist shops rely on their shop fronts to display their merchandise to the greatest possible number of potential customers. Shop windows may have either glazing to full height or independent show case windows (see Fig. 5.27). They may be glazed to the floor, or have window beds and stall risers. (Glazing should be ventilated at the base to avoid steaming up.)

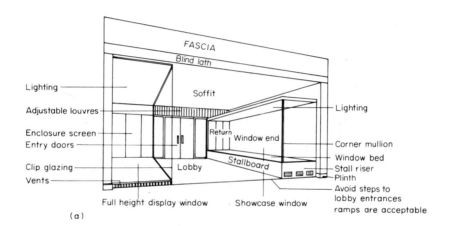

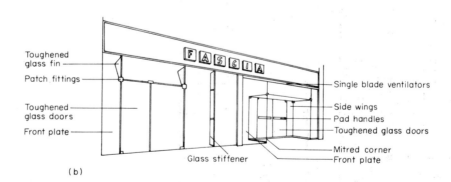

Fig. 5.27 Shop fronts
(a) Perspective showing components of typical shop front
(b) All-glass construction to shop front

WINDOWS

Windows may be open to the shop or be enclosed, with solid or glazed window backs, in which case, access is required for window dressing, and must be quick and easy if goods are to be sold from window. Dimensions will vary, being related to type of merchandise and trading policy.

Furniture may need 2·8–3·1 m depth with maximum height (and adequate space for handling). Jewellery may need only, say 300 mm depth and small individual glazed openings. Provision must be made in soffites for window lighting.

ENTRANCE DOORS AND FASCIA

Entrance doors may be either hinged, folding, sliding/ folding, revolving and automatic, or fold-away to leave un-

obstructed opening with or without warm air curtain.

The fascia takes the shop sign and masks the structure and blind box. The shop sign, illuminated or not, is the identification of the shop.

A blind is usually required to protect the merchandise from solar gain (and sometimes the window shopper from the rain), when no canopy is provided, unless the shop faces north.

SECURITY

Shop-lifting or 'Shrinkage' is a major problem in retail stores and is increasing with the popularity of self service. Many of the necessary precautions are a matter of 'housekeeping', but there are important design considerations to be taken into account in planning.

In Supermarkets it is dealt with by such measures as the

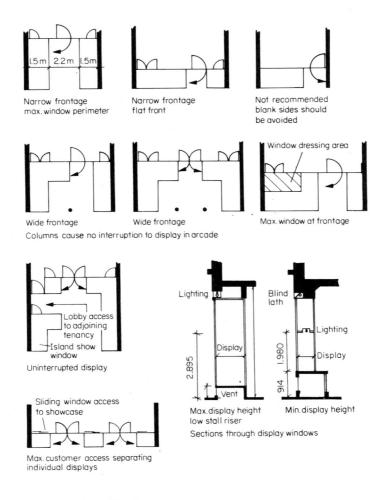

Fig. 5.28 Types of shop front
Maximum perimeter display is suitable for fashions; shoes; and furniture
Shallow window display is suitable for jewellery; books, stationery and music

use of check-out points and compulsory use of trolleys and baskets. Where possible an additional help can be adequate provision for shoppers to deposit their own baskets at entrance while shopping.

In all shops certain precautions can be taken, e.g. strategic planning of cash desks and supervisory offices on long axis of self-service counter runs, to improve supervision. No 'cul de sac' bays, adequate lighting in all parts, control of entrances to fitting rooms, etc. Many stores now use closed circuit television. Cash desks must not be readily accessible to customers or passers-by and protected adequately by positioning of counters, etc.

Special high value merchandise, such as jewellery, furs, cameras, need specific security measures such as shop windows fitted with grilles and alarm systems. Counters, cabinets and display windows containing high value merchandise must be fitted with locks.

Special racks which fit both stockroom, display area and trolley, can be kept locked continuously from delivery to sale. For security in stockrooms see section 8 'Warehouses'.

Parcels and register lockers and arrival and departure control points for staff are a necessary part of security precautions.

Wines, spirits and tobacco need special precautions. Licensed premises must be planned to allow isolation and shutting off when shop is closed.

LEGISLATION

Principal provisions specifically governing planning of shop buildings are listed below.
Building Regulations 1972 (with 1st, 2nd and 3rd amendments)
Shops in the Building Regulations are classified as purpose Group V in Part E (Structural Fire Precautions). Part EE (Means of Escape in case of fire) was introduced in the Building (1st Amendment) Regulations on 31st August, 1973.

Office, Shops & Railway Premises Act 1963. Under which are also: *Sanitary Amenities Regulations 1964; Washing Facilities Regulations 1964.*

Food Hygiene Regulations 1970. Made under the Food & Drugs Act 1955.

Weights & Measures Act 1963.

Licensing Act 1964.

Fire Precautions Act 1972—For Inner London only.

London Building (amendment) Act 1939, Part VI. Under which are made: Constructional Byelaws—For Inner London only.

Building Standards (Scotland Consolidated) Regulations—For Scotland only.

Clean Air Acts, 1956 and 1968.

Highways Acts 1959, 1961–1971.

Note: The Health & Safety at Work Act 1974 will radically alter Building Legislation and the application and extent of the present Building Regulations, as well as of the relevant Acts quoted above.

BS CODES OF PRACTICE

Many deemed to satisfy and statutory requirement clauses in the Building Regulations refer to British Standard Codes of Practice (e.g. floor loading, means of escape, fitness of materials, etc). Specifically relevant British Standard Codes of Practice are:
CP3 Chap. V Part 1 1967 Superimposed floor loads.
CP3 Chap. IV Part 2 1968 Fire precautions in shops and stores.
This code is used as guidance by Fire Authorities under the Shops, Offices and Railway Premises Act as well as 'deemed to satisfy' under 1st Amendment of Buildings Regulations and forms the framework of Fire Precautions and Means of Escape standards in all shop buildings.

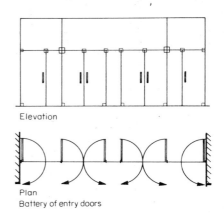

Elevation

Plan
Battery of entry doors

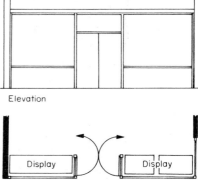

Elevation

Plan
Open back window with free-standing display fittings

Fig. 5.29   Types of entrance

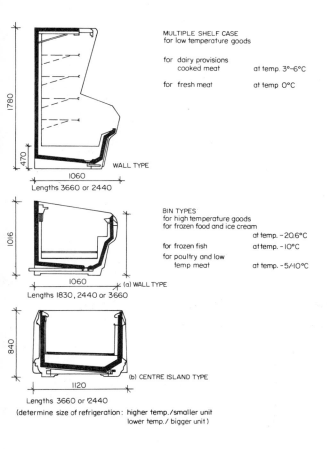

MULTIPLE SHELF CASE
for low temperature goods

for dairy provisions
cooked meat   at temp. 3°–6°C

for fresh meat   at temp. 0°C

1780

470

WALL TYPE
1060
Lengths 3660 or 2440

BIN TYPES
for high temperature goods
for frozen food and ice cream
                     at temp. –20.6°C
for frozen fish   at temp. –10°C
for poultry and low
temp meat   at temp. –5/–10°C

1016

1060   (a) WALL TYPE
Lengths 1830, 2440 or 3660

840

1120   (b) CENTRE ISLAND TYPE
Lengths 3660 or 2440
(determine size of refrigeration: higher temp./smaller unit
                                    lower temp./ bigger unit)

Fig. 5.30   Refrigerated display units

Fig. 5.31   Moving belt checkout (Showrax Ltd.)

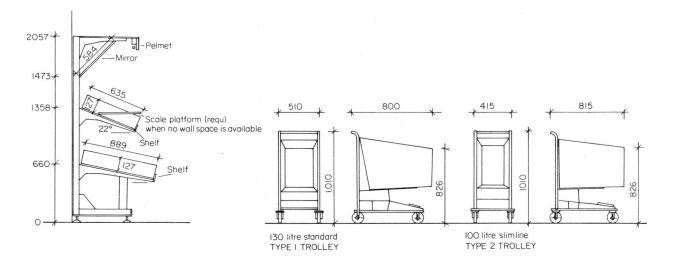

2057

584   Pelmet
           Mirror

1473

635
127
1358
22°   Scale platform (requ)
           when no wall space is available
889   Shelf

660
127   Shelf

0

Fig. 5.32   Section of typical wall shelving for
fruit and vegetables

510   800   415   815

1.010   826   1010   826

130 litre standard   100 litre slimline
TYPE 1 TROLLEY   TYPE 2 TROLLEY

Fig. 5.33   Types of trolley
1. 130 litre standard
2. 100 litre min-size used in high density stores with narrow checkouts

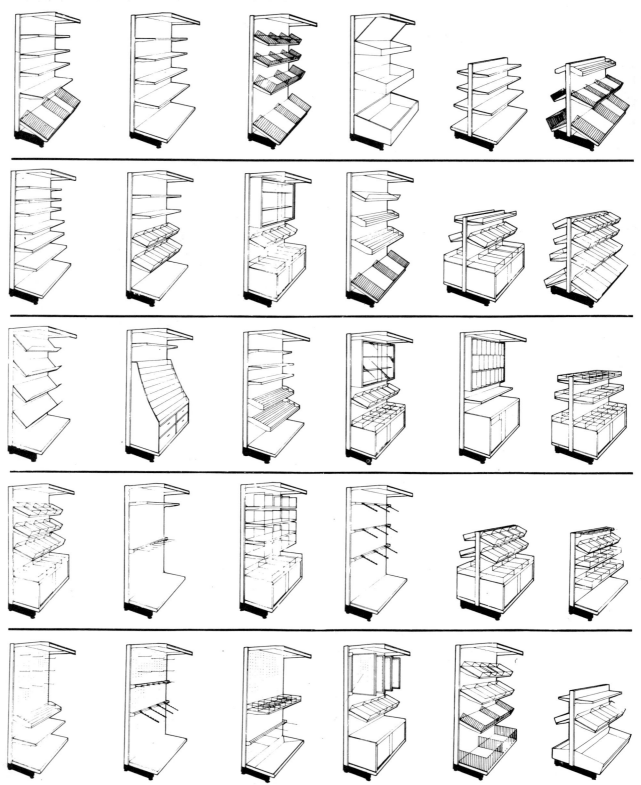

Fig. 5.34   Wall fitted and Gondola display fittings (Showrax Ltd.)

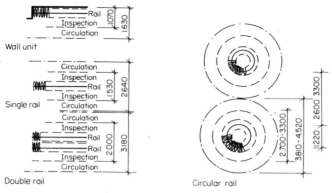

Wall unit

Single rail

Double rail

Circular rail

SPACE REQUIREMENTS FOR RACKS AND CIRCULATION AROUND
GARMENTS HUNG FROM CIRCULAR AND STRAIGHT RAILS

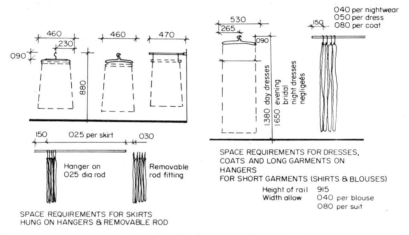

Hanger on
025 dia rod

Removable
rod fitting

SPACE REQUIREMENTS FOR SKIRTS
HUNG ON HANGERS & REMOVABLE ROD

SPACE REQUIREMENTS FOR DRESSES,
COATS AND LONG GARMENTS ON
HANGERS
FOR SHORT GARMENTS (SHIRTS & BLOUSES)

Height of rail 915
Width allow   040 per blouse
               080 per suit

040 per nightwear
050 per dress
080 per coat

Fig. 5.35   Space requirements in women's fashion store

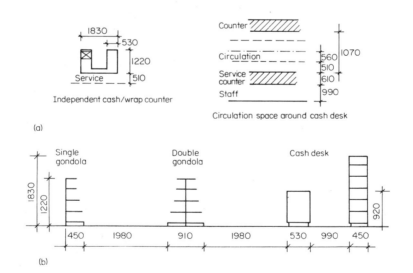

Independent cash/wrap counter

Circulation space around cash desk

(a)

(b)

Fig. 5.36   Cash desk
(a) Counter layouts
(b) Gangway clearances

Single criss cross   Double criss cross

Fig. 5.37 Escalator types suitable for department store
Escalator capacities:
5000–5700 person/hour. Internal width 805 mm
8000–10700 persons/hour. Internal width 915 mm
Angle of pitch 30° and 35°

EXAMPLES

* Runcorn New Town Centre, Cheshire
Architects Department, Runcorn Development Corporation
AJ 5/1/72

* Brent Cross Shopping Centre
Architects: Bernard Engle Partnership
BD 5/3/76

* Blackburn Centre
Architects: BDP
Arch. Review February 1970

* Victoria Centre, Nottingham
Architects: Arthur Swift & Partners
Building 2/5/69

Arndale Centre, Poole
Architects: Leslie Jones & Partners
Building 30/4/71

Carrefour, Caerphilly
Architects: Peter Black & Partners

Carrefour, Eastleigh
Architects: Triad

Hampshire Centre
Architects: Lionel E. Gregory & Partners
Building 30/4/71

John Lewis, Nottingham
Architects: Arthur Swift & Partners
Arch. Review 30/3/73

Selfridges, Oxford
Architects: T. P. Bennett & Sons

* Contain examples of most shopping types.

BIBLIOGRAPHY

A.J. Handbook, *Mechanised Storage*, Architectural Press
Architects' Journal, *Shop Buildings Design Guide*, Architectural Press (1966)
Board of Trade, *Report on the Census of Distribution and Other Services 1966 (Main Tables on Retail trade, Service trade)* HMSO

Beddington, Nadine, 'Shopping Centres', *Building* (3/4/71)
Darlow, Clive, 'Enclosed Shopping Centres', *Architectural Press* (1972)
Distributive Trades, *The Cowley Shopping Centre*, EDC 1968, HMSO
Distributive Trades, *The Future Pattern of Shopping*, EDC 1971, HMSO
Distributive Trades, *Urban Models in Shopping*, EDC 1970, HMSO
Fairweather, Leslie and Silwa, Jan A., *A.J. Metric Handbook*, Architectural Press
Gill, William H., *Building & Planning Legislation*, Architects Standard Catalogues (1973/74)
Gruehn, V. & Smiths, L., *Shopping Towns, USA*, Reinhold (1960)
Hadfield, W., *Designing for Deliveries Research Report No. 1*, Freight Transport Association
Jennings, A., Sharp, G. H. and Whibley, D., *Delivering the Goods (a study of the Walfield Service—only precinct)* Research Report No. 2, Freight Transport Association
Jones, Colin S., *Regional Shopping Centres*, Business Books (1969)
Car Parking for Shoppers, Multiple Shops Federation
The Planning of Shopping Centres, Multiple Shops Federation (1963)

ACKNOWLEDGEMENTS

The author would like to acknowledge the following organisations for their help in providing illustrations and information used in this section.

Andrew Grima Ltd.
Arthur Swift and Partners
T. P. Bennett & Sons
'Building'
Mr. Fairclough of Carrefours
Institute of Grocery Distribution
John Lewis Partnership
Mr. Keeble of Triad
Mac Fisheries Ltd.
Multiple Shops Federation
J. Sainsbury Ltd.
Selfridges
Showrax Ltd.
Arthur Swift & Partners

Nadine Beddington, *FRIBA, FSIA, FRSA, Trained at Regent polytechnic, qualified in 1940. Became interested in retail store design while working as an assistant architect in private practice. Joined Freeman Hardy Willis as advisory architect 1955, and from 1957–1967 was Chief Architect to Freeman Hardy Willis, True Form and Character Shoes (three shoe retailing companies, part of British Shoe Corporation), heading an Architectural department responsible for modernising, extending and providing new shops and shop buildings. In 1967 she started in private practice. Was Member of the RIBA Council 1970–73; Vice President RIBA 1972–73; Member Architects Registration Council, 1969–75; and Chairman of the Camberwell Society 1970–75. Publications include articles in the technical press on shops, shopping centres and building maintenance.*

6 FARM AND AGRICULTURAL BUILDINGS

JOHN WELLER, A.R.I.B.A.

INTRODUCTION

THE INDUSTRY

Agriculture is a major industry, and in a world of food short-ages and political instability, it is a vital industry. The UK produces 55% of our food requirements; this could be in-creased. Though four-fifths of our land is non-urban, only about one-half is reasonable farmland and, of this, about 20 000 ha is taken each year for urban needs.

The agricultural workforce, which has declined at an average rate of 20 000 a year for the last decade, now repre-sents but 2% of the national workforce, but food production has increased substantially, and the industry now has an annual turnover of nearly £5000M. With intensive produc-tion, farm buildings become increasingly important and investment in these is nearly £200M p.a. With fewer skilled men, buildings need to be more mechanised, specialised and of higher performance specification.

INTENSIVE AND EXTENSIVE PRODUCTION

Intensive food production, supported by high output per hectare and per worker, depends on high levels of capital investment. Some farmers, in suitable circumstances, can show that extensive systems, which require little capital but low output, can be profitable. These will need only a few, simple buildings.

In contrast, factory farming based on purchased feed con-version via livestock can be carried out without much land but require specialist buildings. The spectrum of building design is broad; this leads to a profusion of acceptable designs for each enterprise.

THE ENTERPRISES

Traditionally, farmers think in terms of farm enterprises and will specify a building brief on this basis. In simple terms, this may be termed corn, cows, beef, pigs, etc. In reality, the issue is more complex (paragraph on 'Enterprise Planning'). Buildings for corn storage may be coupled to drying facilities

and/or to milling/mixing requirements if fed on-farm to stock. In the latter case, barley may be stored dried (14% moisture content) or wet (from the field and up to 28% moisture content). The former requires floor storage or bin storage, and the latter hermetically sealed towers.

The matter can be further confused by the farm producing more than one species (wheat, barley, oats, etc), of several varieties (different seeds) and for harvesting at different times (June to September). These crops may have to be handled and stored separately. In the same way, livestock buildings can be also complex. Not only is there a division between rearing, fattening and dry stock requirements but there are many different techniques for the management, feeding and bedding of stock. Though the farmer may con-sider his enterprises, building layouts can be confused further as storage and service buildings may be used in relation to more than one enterprise and as spaces may be used in rela-tion to more than one enterprise and also for more than one function. For these reasons, as well as for architectural pur-poses, it may be best to define a brief in terms of 'functions'.

THE FUNCTIONS

In principle, all farm buildings are for one of three functions, i.e. storage, processing (which may be combined with stor-age), and production (basically, livestock). These are grouped as follows (see *Farm Buildings, Vol I*, (J. B. Weller published by Crosby Lockwood):

(a) Storage	*(b) Processing*	*(c) Production*
Straw	Grass drying	Milk
Hay	Hay drying	Beef
Haylage and Maize	Ensilage	Calves
Grain and Seed	Grain drying	Veal
Feedingstuffs	Milling and Mixing	Pork and Bacon
Fertilizers	Milking	Weaners
Manure and Slurry	Dipping and	Mutton
Potatoes and Roots	Shearing	Lamb
Implements	Potato chitting	Poultry
Records and	Workshops	Eggs
Office	Packing	

There are other enterprises, including horticulture, cheese, rabbits, etc. which either rarely require on-farm buildings or are not normally termed 'agriculture'. Any of the production functions may be supported by a number of storage and processing functions, some of which may take place within the same building structure or even within the same air space.

DESIGN REQUIREMENTS

When the function(s) for the building and enterprise have been defined, the brief for the design should include certain data:

(a) *Management*. The overall farming system, including the relation of the buildings to fieldwork, to labour, to finance etc. (see Fig. 6.5).

(b) *Production techniques*. Specific requirements which will control building layout, e.g. nutrition policy, farm waste policy etc.

(c) *Labour force*. Personnel available, skilled or unskilled, full-time or part-time (e.g. a fieldworker helping at the buildings), working week etc.

(d) *Work routines*. Frequency of operation, method of performance, together with available mechanization (see paragraph on 'The man/machine Ratio').

(e) *Circulation*. Flow-line or circulation routes for materials, men, machines and stock, together with spatial requirements.

(f) *Volume*. Critical space dimensions, including by-products etc.

(g) *Equipment*. Data for equipment, including both fixed and mobile.

(h) *Environmental control*. Physical environment required, degree of controlled environment, production of by-products and their physical attributes.

(i) *Services*. Electrical, water, ventilation, drainage, etc. Data.

(j) *Siting*. Relation of building to other functions and enterprises, site selection and constraints, both physical and legal.

(k) *Costs*. Investment criteria and constraints.

BUILDING FORM

There are four main building structural types:

(a) *The vertical storage container*. Either cylinder or rectangular bin, sometimes elevated on supports for gravity emptying.

(b) *The barn*. Normally portal framed (more rarely with segmented roof, i.e. the Dutch Barn) used for floor crop storage, cattle, sometimes pigs, implements, etc.

(c) *The kennel*. Monopitch structures for cattle and for simple construction. Sometimes placed close together like a barn with open ridge.

(d) *The insulated box*. Long, low buildings, normally of timber frame and wall cladding, providing minimum volume, with insulated roof and walls and, often, with fan control of environment; used for poultry, sometimes pigs and calves. The only structure, within this simplified analysis, comparable with building types for other industries, is the portal framed enclosure. For the small to medium span frames, perhaps up to about 15 m, in some farm situations, a lower level of requirement and safety factor than for other industry may be permissible, especially in terms of wind loading (see BS 2053: 1972, *General purpose farm buildings of framed construction*). In other respects, that is from managerial requirement, farm buildings are basically factories in the same way as any other industry.

SITING

Traditionally, most farmsteads had courtyard plans. Barns were sited to protect stockyards from prevailing winds, with farmhouse adjacent for security and control (Fig. 6.1). Most steadings were sited to take advantage of local topography.

In contrast, the modern need is for flow-line production based on linear layouts for materials handling. New farm buildings tend to be detached and set alongside a service road (Fig. 6.2). The workforce being mobile, dwellings may

Fig. 6.1   Traditional arrangement of farmhouse and barns

Fig. 6.2 Modern arrangement of farm buildings having access to service road

not be essential. A linear layout, when modernising a steading, superimposed over a courtyard form may have disadvantages.

There are eight main factors to consider when siting a new farm building: logistics; access; services; security; soil mechanics; climate; expansion; appearance.

LOGISTICS

Food production concerns the conversion via photosynthesis of raw materials (seed, fertilisers etc) into primary produce (grain, vegetables, fruit etc) or into secondary produce via the conversion of grass, grain etc (meat, milk, eggs, etc), together with their byproducts (leather, bonemeal, methane etc).

The conversion process requires buildings for storage, processing and production together with associated materials handling. Handling and double handling of materials is the interface between managerial requirements and building layout. It is an important cost factor in food production. However, tonnage of materials handled to produce units of bacon, milk, potatoes, etc, within different managerial systems and building layouts has not been studied. Similarly, energy consumption for such handling methods and using different prime movers (tractor, electrical motor, man etc) also remains unknown.

However, the above two factors should determine whether a new building should be sited near the primary production land (the fields), or within a farmstead (with its centralised sources of power and equipment), or ex-farm (near secondary processing, packaging and distribution). For example, a grain store may be best sited near the cornfields to reduce trailer-turn-round time and distances when grain is sold ex-store. If grain is converted into livestock feed for on-farm consumption, the store might be near the mill-mix unit, in turn near the stock buildings. Alternatively, co-operative storage for 20 000 t will prove cheaper per tonne than 20 smaller units on individual farms.

With cattle, the relationship between grass production, conservation and consumption may be critical to siting new buildings. Even within a farmstead, logistics may control the best choice of site for a new building. Flow-lines should be drawn.

ACCESS

Siting buildings must be related to vehicular access between and into them, to livestock handling routes (especially dairy cattle), and to farm access from the highway. Critical dimensions for turning circle and turning radius for tractors, tractors + attachments, harvesters and bulk tankers vary with make and size of vehicle (Fig. 6.3). The following are approximate guides (mm):

	max. ht.	length	circle	radius
Small tractor + cab	2400	3000	1800	6400
Medium tractor + loader/rake	3300	5800	7000	10 000
Medium tractor + rake	2500	7900	4900	12 500
Medium harvester	2500	3300	2000	6700
Grain tanker	3750	8000	7000	10 000

Wet, dirty surfaces will cause wheel slip, increasing the circle and radius required. Tractor + attachment data or bulk tanker data will prove critical to building access and siting as well as to farm road layout and highway access. Rear attachments based on pick-up hooks on the tractor may double the latter's turning circle, whereas a pin-hitch may only add 50 % (see Fig. 6.4). Cattle buildings, in particular, may be designed to permit feed and cleaning vehicle access. Most crop and livestock buildings are designed with gable access.

SERVICES

Most buildings require an electrical supply and livestock housing both water and, possibly, foul drainage. Access and services are expensive to provide and may prove critical to site selection. Electrical supply, if overhead, should clear

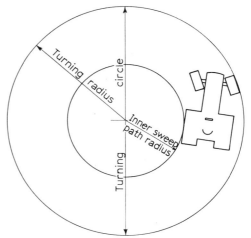

Fig. 6.3 Turning definitions: maximum tractor lock

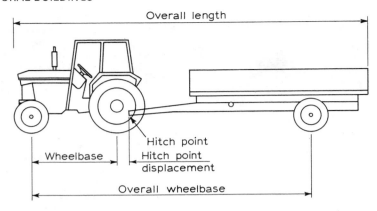

Fig. 6.4 Tractor and trailer: Critical dimensions which control the turning circle

farm vehicles; a height of 6 m is normally required and this may be greater than building apex height. With low loadings, underground cables may be more suitable. Buildings with high loadings, such as milling machinery, should be close to the meter position.

Drainage can be assisted when site falls of 1:40 to 1:80 are in a suitable direction. Storm drainage, nearly always, should be piped separately from effluent so that it can discharge direct to ditch or ground.

SECURITY

Vandalism and theft should be considered. The former can be serious near urban areas or public access. Stock, fuel and even crops are valuable and, particularly, have proved at risk near motorways. Isolated storage should be locked and without fire hazard. Isolated stock buildings should have internal farm access only.

Most buildings should be under supervision though not necessarily adjacent to farm dwellings. Stockmen usually live close to rearing and breeding units. Farmsteads should have a fire control plan and equipment, clearly marked, preferably with hydrants. Inflammables and poisons should be set apart and marked; poisons should be stored and locked.

SOIL MECHANICS

Most farm buildings, except silos, have relatively low loadings compared with other building types. However, foundations can be a higher proportion of total costs since most superstructures are relatively low cost. Well drained soils or gravel/sands are preferable; roof drainage discharge can prove critical. Foundations for crop retaining walls can be difficult within plastic soils.

Larger stock and storage buildings, especially with gable access at both ends, need careful siting in relation to contours. Most buildings prove to be cheaper on flat sites, but some livestock layouts are best with 1:60 longitudinal falls to assist effluent drainage.

CLIMATE

Minor variations in siting can influence microclimate. Topography, aspect and local features, such as trees and buildings, will be critical for wind and temperature.

Semi-open or part-open stock buildings must be sited with care to reduce wind tunnel effects or draughts. They should be considered only when site conditions and building layout provide reasonable shelter. Totally enclosed livestock buildings may be best sited on a N-S axis so both flanks receive sunlight, either a.m. or p.m. Partly enclosed livestock buildings, particularly for adult cattle or pigs, usually are best with solid dwarf perimeter walls with space boarding above to eaves level. The dwarf wall can be as follows:

Pigs	1200 mm high.
Cattle	1800 mm high.
Cattle on straw bedding	2500 mm high.

Eaves height will vary due to other factors, but can be:

Pigs, kennels, no man-access	1200 mm high.
Cattle, normal allowance	2500 mm high.
average allowance	3000 mm high.
Cattle on straw bedding	3750 mm high.
Tractor access areas	2750 mm high.

Space boarding, also known as hit-and-miss and (incorrectly) as Yorkshire boarding, is formed from vertical pressure-treated boards nailed to rails. The boards can be 100–150 mm wide with spaces between of 6–20 mm. Most boards shrink and should be spaced to allow some increase in space dimension. The ratio of solid:void depends on building layout, site conditions and livestock age. Wider spaces should be used for adult cattle in sheltered sites. Normally, a space of 10 mm width is adequate per 100 mm board.

Buildings which include fan control such as some poultry, pig and calf houses, need fans and buildings to be sited in relation to micro-climate conditions. This may determine whether fans are used to extract from or to intake air to the building.

EXPANSION

Siting and layout should permit each enterprise to have room to expand. Most storage and livestock buildings are a rectangle with gable access from one or both ends (Fig. 6.2). Linear expansion is easy when open space and levels at the end of a building are considered in the design.

Increased unit size after a few years becomes possible with improved management confidence or better mechanical aids. Equally, changes in field area or practice may increase the building size required to service the enterprise. However, provision for expansion, as well as external circulation, fragments the grouping of buildings and extends the areas of road and services. This can be costly and ugly.

APPEARANCE

This is not a reference book of visual design, but it can be mentioned that most farm buildings are visually very prominent and often situated in attractive landscape. Linear requirements disrupt the traditional courtyard groupings. Most farm buildings have a precise form reflecting specific requirements, however, many requirements are not so critical there is no margin for manipulation of siting and of mass. In addition, proportion, materials and colours usually permit a considerable degree of design permutation.

There are several points to consider, relevant to all rural buildings but more pertinent to farm buildings because of their lack of fenestration and use of factory-made claddings. These are as follows:

(a) Colour relationship (as well as profile and texture) both of roof to wall and of new building to vernacular materials and soil is critical.
(b) Buildings often are seen from distant viewpoints and from above depending on topography.
(c) Size of modern farm buildings tend to break tradition either by being much bulkier or by being long, low 'sheds'.
(d) Services tend to be prominent, whether electrical supply, or extract fans and ducts, or feed hoppers and conveyors etc.
(e) External circulation areas and effluent holding areas tend to dominate views towards the buildings.
(f) Loss of hedgerows and trees has increased viewpoints across countryside.

PLANNING

Farm buildings have a complex relationship between management, production and layout systems. As 'fixed equipment', buildings are an aid to management, in the same way as is 'mobile equipment' (machinery). Sometimes, as in a milking bail, building and machinery are integrated. The distinction mainly is one of capital depreciation, often taken as 20, 10 and 5 years respectively for general purpose buildings, for specialised structures and for machinery. Landlords, normally, like to provide the former, leaving the tenant to buy the specialist fittings and machinery. Owner occupiers frequently wish to recover their capital in 10 years or less. This is a fundamental distinction.

The building designer needs to be basically a 'systems engineer', with knowledge of farm management, economics, mechanisation and environmental control. There must be skill also in building technology and in social issues, such as appearance and landscape.

BASIC ECONOMICS

The annual cost of capital invested in a farm building must be amortised; this data will be required early in the planning/design brief i.e.

Table 6.1 ANNUAL COST ($£$) PER $£1000$ INVESTED AT VARIOUS INTEREST RATES

Years	6%	9%	12%	15%	20%
5	238	258	278	299	334
10	136	156	177	200	239
15	87	110	134	160	205

Thus, a G.P. building costing £10 000 with machinery at £5000, at 12% interest, would have an annual charge against the enterprise of £1340 + £1390, plus an allowance for maintenance costs, say £3000 in total. This charge would have to be recovered either by increased output or by reduced use of resources or by both. For example, output in a dairy unit could be increased by more cows or by more milk/cow. Similarly, resources could be conserved by reducing labour or feed wastage, the latter perhaps by building a hay drying barn. Table 6.2 gives most of the main types of farm building.

Table 6.2 BUILDING TYPE USAGE (EXAMPLES)

SPECIALIST	SEMI-SPECIALIST
Bull yards	Silobarn
Cow kennels	Pig yards
Cow cubicles	Sheep yards
Slatted yards	Battery houses
Cowshed/shippon	Boxes
Milking parlour	
Dairy	
Weaner houses	
Pig houses	
Broiler houses	
Deep litter houses	FLEXIBLE
Sheephouses	Cattleyards
Grain bins	Portal frame barns
Grain silo	Dutch barns
Grass tower silo	Grain store
Workshops	Potato store
Chitting houses	Implement shed
Glasshouses	
Cold stores	
Hay drying barn	

Many farmers wish to have flexible layouts which permit changes of management, even to the extent of a complete change in output. In practice, many requirements are either specialist or perform best within specialist buildings.

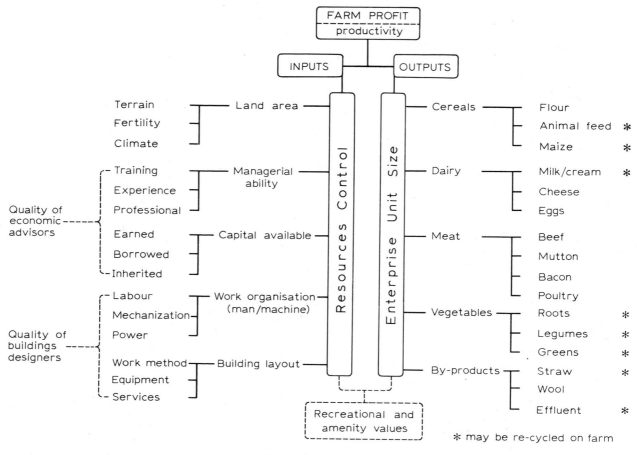

Fig. 6.5   Economic Planning

ECONOMIC PLANNING

Every farm building relates inputs to outputs, thereby influencing productivity. Fig. 6.5 outlines basic considerations in planning each enterprise. In most cases, all the inputs shown must be assessed though the enterprise, and the buildings for it, may have only one output, though others may be recycled on farm.

THE MAN/MACHINE RATIO

Labour should be organised on a 5 day/week basis. Livestock require labour for a 7 day/week. Thus, a 3-man unit will permit 2-men on duty at any day. This becomes an efficient unit of labour. Stock numbers will depend on the level of mechanisation provided. The numbers given in Table 6.3 are an approximate guide.

FARMSTEAD PLANNING

Most new farm layouts are simple being no more than a small group of buildings around a service road for a single enter-prise. A farm with two enterprises, such as corn + baconers, with supporting service buildings, will need careful planning especially if the units are large. A mixed farm, say of around 400 ha (1000 acres) could support several enterprises, such as might require buildings for about 700 t of grain, 240 cows + 180 calves and heifers, 120 sows + 1500 baconers, 1000 t of potatoes, plus service buildings.

Fig. 6.6 illustrates how complex a new farmstead can be to serve such requirements. Careful design is required to relate function, circulation and possible expansion to any site; layout is likely to be linear to a main access farm road. No ideal layout can be given since each farm will need its specific assessment and planning.

Table 6.3 3-MAN UNIT: NUMBER OF LIVESTOCK PER UNIT

Mechanisation:	limited	moderate	considerable
Dairy cows	120	180	240
Beef	300	500	800
Baconers	600	900	1200
Sows	80	150	500
Broilers	5000	7500	10000

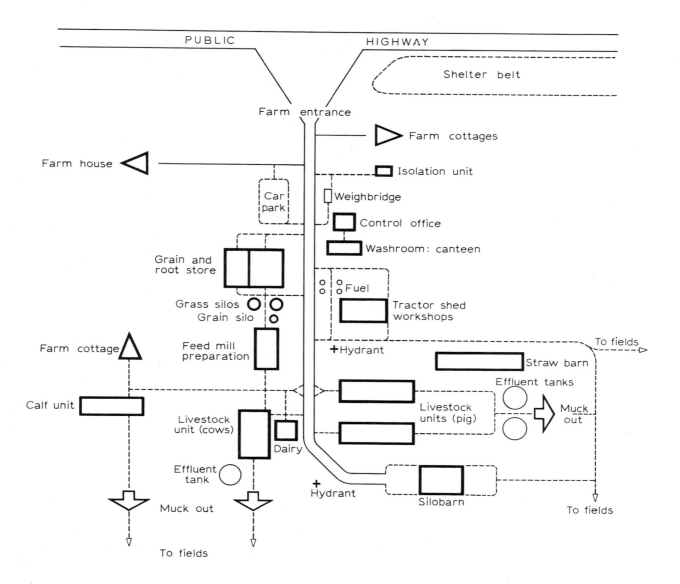

Fig. 6.6   Farmstead Planning A large mixed farm

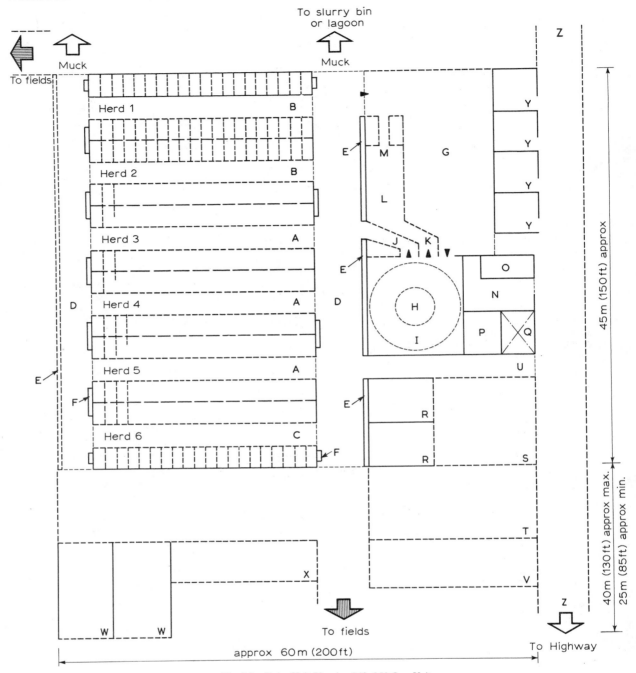

Fig. 6.7   Dairy Unit Planning 240–250 Cow Unit

A   *Three herds × 40 cows low yielders* = *120 cows* ⎫
B   *Two herds × 40 cows high yielders* = *80 cows*   ⎬ *kennels*
C   *Dry herd* = *40 cows* ⎭

—

max: 240 cows

D   *Exercise/Feed Yards*
E   *Manger Troughs*
F   *Water troughs*
G   *Collecting yard*
H   *Milking parlour pit*
I   *Rotary milking platform*
J   *Parlour exit to yards*
K   *Parlour exit to Hold Yard*
L   *Hold Yard*

M   *Inspection yoke*
N   *Dairy with bulk tanks*
O   *Office*
P   *Messroom*
Q   *Bulk feed tower over w.c. and shower and store*
R   *Loose housing yard*
S   *Open yard*
T   *Spare open yard*
U   *Access passage*
V   *Implement shed*
W   *Silobarn*
X   *Dutch barn*
Y   *Isolation box*
Z   *Farm road*

ENTERPRISE PLANNING

Each enterprise requires its own set of buildings, though sharing common storage and service facilities. For example, a large dairy enterprise for around 250 cows (excluding followers) will require a complex of buildings, possibly as shown in Fig. 6.7.

Circulation of stock, feed and muck, together with that for milking, needs careful planning and controls. Layout will be conditioned by management policy for feeding, effluent and milking as well as basic stockmanship. The latter will include items such as the number of cows milked and housed as one batch or 'herd' within the unit. Similarly, a decision to handle effluent as a liquid or as farmyard manure would alter the layout shown. Any other type of enterprise will need the same detailed consideration.

ENVIRONMENTAL PLANNING

Environment (appearance) has already been considered under 'Appearance'.

Environmental control (atmosphere) must be discussed early within the planning process. All buildings control the environment. The degree of control required increases capital cost sharply as standards are increased. In the case of crops, control should retain their quality over longer periods. Processing crops may enhance quality or, in the case of animal feed, improve palatability.

Control, in the case of livestock, is to improve health or to reduce feed required for 'maintenance' (i.e. to maintain health without liveweight gain in fatstock or without milk production in dairy cows). For example, bacon pigs in uninsulated buildings may have a feed conversion ratio of 1:4 to 1:5, i.e. 1 unit of liveweight increase to 4 or 5 units of feed consumed. Most reasonably controlled buildings will reduce the ratio to 1:3 and good control and management to 1:2·3.

The capital cost of higher standards of buildings can be offset against reduced feed costs. However, not every farmer accepts the need for environmental control, particularly in the case of cattle. In the case of Fig. 6.7, the 'economy' design would include an uninsulated roof over areas:

A, B, C: cubicle kennels only and not passageways and over H, I, N, O, P, Q, R, V, X, Y

The 'quality' design would include, probably in three stages of priority:

1. J, K, L, M, W
2. A, B, C: passageways
3. D (including E and F), G, S, U

In the same manner, the degree of wall enclosure will be taken in stages of priority. Similarly, only the quality design would include roof insulation firstly to the isolation boxes (Y) then to the milking area (H, I, N, O, P, Q) and possibly to the spare housing (R).

A few units have been designed where housing and feeding areas also have insulated roofs, even though internal spaces are well ventilated, to improve air flow without turbulence. Some beef producers have 'topless cubicles', that is they have no roof over the winter cattle yard.

It is clear that environmental control, and its cost implications, both capital and production, should be agreed in the design process.

SYSTEM PLANNING

The various planning processes, economic, mechanical, farmstead, enterprise, etc, have to be brought together into a 'system' for the enterprise and its buildings. Alternative solutions between different possible systems need to be considered on a comparative basis. In all solutions, there must be an acknowledged 'risk factor'.

The basis for building system selection is shown in Fig. 6.8. This needs to be considered against the previous assessment made in Fig. 6.5.

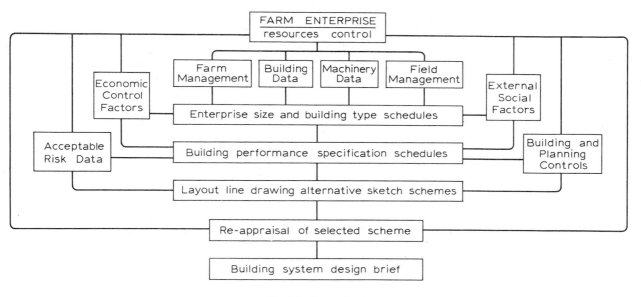

Fig. 6.8 System planning

SPACE REQUIREMENTS

STORAGE BUILDINGS

Storage of crops and materials may be in specialised containers or, in many cases, in bulk on the floor or loft floor of a building. In principle, storage should maintain the commodity's original condition. There are exceptions, silage, for example, is grass from which effluent drains and in which some fermentation takes place.

Storage may be combined with processing machinery as in the case of a corn bin which includes drying facilities. Thus, space requirements, may have to be based on other factors than minimum cubic capacity. Storage may be required prior to the material being used either in the buildings or in the fields or prior to its sale from the farm. Siting should be related to this factor.

Double handling of materials is undesirable and bulk handling into and out of storage is important. With some materials, unloading may be by gravity or by suction: others may need mechanical choppers, conveyors or tractor attachments.

LIVESTOCK BUILDINGS

Space requirements for livestock of all species and ages are complex. In some cases, space will be divided into lying, dunging, feeding and circulation areas; in others, some of these areas (or all of them) may be combined. Type of bedding and feeding will be relevant, as will the degree of environmental control required.

The physiology of the animal and recommendations made by the Brambell Committee (see under 'Legislation') must be considered.

SPACE REQUIREMENTS

These are given as follows:

Table 6.4 Crops and Solids.
Tables 6.5 to 6.7 Liquids.
Table 6.8 Livestock.

Table 6.4 SPACE REQUIREMENTS: CROPS AND SOLIDS

Material	Bushel weight (lb)	Quarter weight (cwt)	Quarters per ton	kg per m³	m³ per tonne	Notes
Wheat	63	4·50	4·50	785	1·30	Density for grains taken at 14% moisture
Barley	56	4·00	5·00	705	1·44	content with angle of repose at 28° to 30°:
Oats	42	3·00	6·60	513	1·98	allow 45° for self-emptying.
Rye	57	4·00	5·00	705	1·44	
Peas	63	4·50	4·50	785	1·30	
Beans	66	4·75	4·20	833	1·22	
Linseed	54	4·00	5·00	705	1·44	
Maize	59	4·25	4·75	737	1·36	
Meal				513	1·98	Allow up to 60° for self-emptying.
Pellets				609	1·70	
Nuts				688	1·47	
Roots				640	1·60	Potatoes, average density: angle of repose 30°
Fertilizer				993	1·02	to 40°, most roots.
Wheat straw				64	17·60	Loose.
Barley straw				48	22·70	Loose.
Baled straw				112	9·20	Medium density bale.
Loose hay				112	9·20	Wilted to 65% moisture content.
Baled hay				160	6·10	
Wilted grass				481	2·15	Wilted to 55% moisture content.
Grass silage				800	1·27	Long cut.
Chopped grass				881	1·16	Cut, lacerated for silage.
Pea haulm				769	1·33	Silage.

Table 6.5 LIVESTOCK WATER INTAKE *(Nominal requirements for normal conditions i.e. environment, feed, etc)*

	Nominal consumption per head per day (litres)
Cows in milk (including cleaning and milk cooling)	150
Cattle or Horses	50
Calves	25
Pigs, dry fed	15
Sheep	5
Poultry, per 100 birds	25
Domestic (farm cottage)	120

Table 6.6 LIVESTOCK EFFLUENT OUTPUT: DAILY AVERAGE 1*

	Animal Weight kg	Total Quantity		Dry Matter Content kg	BOD kg	COD kg	Organic Carbon kg	Total Nitrogen kg
		Urine litres	Faeces litres					
Cow	500	90·5	44·3	4·72	0·50	7·46	1·87	0·22
Calf	160	7·2	20·4	2·72	0·35	3·00	0·63	0·11
Pig, dry fed	68	1·7	2·7	0·50	0·14	—	—	0·02
Sheep	—	1·7	2·9	0·55	0·12	0·58	0·14	0·022
Hen	2	—	0·11	0·04	0·01	—	—	0·002

DAILY AVERAGE 2*

	Litres/day	day matter
Pigs		
fatteners on barley wheatmeal: dry	4·5	9·5%
fatteners on barley wheatmeal: wet	7·0	9
fatteners on whey: liquid	14	2
sow on barley wheatmeal: wet	11	4·5
Cattle: Friesian		
225 kg beef on silage + barley	12	13
450 kg beef on silage + barley	27	13
cow on silage + concentrates	36	13
Poultry: 1000 head		
light-medium layers	140	25
layers (deep litter)	64	75
broilers (to 9 weeks)	7	70

*Data varies due to natural variations of environment, stock & feed

Table 6.7 LIQUID STORAGE

(a) Storage of milk, whey, skim milk, liquid fertilizer, liquid effluent is based on the same space requirements as water:

Weight	Capacity
10·1 lb/gal	6·25 cu.ft./gal

(b) The volume of slurry depends on the solids present between semi-liquid and semi-solid: normal allowances are 40–50 cu.ft./ton

(c) Petrol and diesel fuels are as normal, i.e. 8 lb/gal

Table 6.8 SPACE REQUIREMENTS: LIVESTOCK

Type of Stock	Age or Weight	Type of Housing	Area/Head Lying or Pen	Area/Head Dunging or Loafing or Feeding (unless restricted)
CATTLE: Dairy cows	Large (Friesian)	Loose yards	3·75–4·75 m²	1·80–2·30 m²
		Cubicles/kennels	1200 × 2150 mm	2·80–5·60 m²
	Small (Jersey)	Loose yards	3·25–3·75 m²	1·40–1·80 m²
		Cubicles/kennels	1050 × 2000 mm	2·50–3·75 m²
Beef cattle	12–18 month finishing	Slatted yard	1·00–1·40 m²	Normally combined with lying area, but strawed yards may have a feed passage of about 1·60–2·60 m² in addition
		Strawed yard	1·80–2·80 m²	
	18–24 month finishing	Slatted yard	1·80–2·40 m²	
		Strawed yard	3·25–3·75 m²	
Calves	Up to 14 days	Controlled environment	0·90–1·45 m²	—
	14 days to 3 months		0·90–2·40 m²	—
	3 months to 6 months	Semi-controlled	1·80–2·40 m²	—
	6 months	Semi-open yards	1·80–2·80 m²	—
Yearlings/heifers	9–15 months	Semi-open yards	2·80–3·75 m²	Part may be open unstrawed yard
Bull	Individual mature	Pen + run/yard	4·50 × 3·60 m	4·50 × 6·00 m
SHEEP: Sheep	Lowland ewe + lamb	Straw or slat yard	0·90–1·20 m²	—
	Upland ewe + lamb	Ventilated yards	0·90–1·45 m²	—
	Welsh mountain lamb	Ventilated yards	0·40 m²	—
	Scotch Blackface lamb	Ventilated yards	0·50 m³	—
PIGS: Sows	Adult: dry or in-pig	Open yards	1·20 m²	1·5–2·4 m²
	Adult: dry or in-pig	Stalls	600 × 2100 mm	—
	Farrowing + litter	Solari pen	2·700 × 1·500 m	2·700 × 1·500 m
	Farrowing + litter	Pen with creep	2·400 × 3·000 m	—
		Crates + creeps	2·400 × 2·000 m	—
Piglets (rearing)	Up to 6 weeks 100 lb:45 kg	Controlled environment	0·35 m²	0·20 m²
Porkers	Up to 72 kg		0·45 m²	0·24 m²
Cutters	70–80 kg		0·50 m²	0·26 m²
Baconers	70–100 kg		0·55 m²	0·30 m²
Heavy hog	100–120 kg		0·75 m²	0·35 m²
Baconers	45–100 kg	Suffolk type yards	0·55 m²	0·55 m²
Boars	Adult		1·800 × 2·400 m	7·00–9·50 m²
POULTRY: Broilers/rearing	Day old–4 weeks	Controlled environment	0·025 m²	—
	4 weeks–8 weeks		0·09 m²	—
	8 weeks–16 weeks		0·27 m²	—
Turkeys	As above + 25% space		+ 25%	—
Deep litter layers	1 to 3 years maximum		0·27–0·36 m²	—
Battery layers	1 year normal		300–430 m	—
Turkeys	Adult	Pole barn	0·50–0·90 m²	—
Ducks	Up to 4 weeks	Simple shelter	0·07–0·09 m²	—

Table 6.8 SPACE REQUIREMENTS: LIVESTOCK—*continued*

Height to Eaves m*	Feed Trough Length/Head	Bedding Requirements	Notes
3·000	600–700 mm	15–30 cwt/cow/winter/straw	
2·200	600–700 mm	3–7 kg/cow/week/sawdust	
3·000	550–600 mm	(generally as above: winters	Free and feeding space depends on
2·200	550–600 mm	4–6 months normal for cows)	overall layout and materials handling.
3·000 min	450–525 mm	—	Intensive systems may have totally
3·000 min	450–525 mm	15–30 cwt/head/helaf year max:	slatted yards & permanent housing.
3·000 min	525–700 mm	—	
3·000 min	525–700 mm	750–1500 kg/head/half year max:	
2·200	bucket } clipped to	3–7 kg/calf/week chopped	Usually individual pens +
2·400	bucket } rail	straw	feed passage
2·400	300–450 mm	3–7 kg/calf/week straw	3–5 head per pen
2·500	trough + hay rack usual		8–15 head per yard
3·000	450–525 mm	1500–3000 kg/head/winter straw	20–30 head per yard
2·500	600–750 mm	1500–3000 kg/bull/year	service pen optional extra
2·400	300–400 mm	5–8 kg/ewe/week straw	Can be open shelter
2·400	300–400 mm	ewe/week straw	Probably slatted yard
2·200	225–300 mm	as above	
2·200	400 mm	as above	
2·000	300 mm	3–7 kg/sow/week straw	Wide variety of layouts
2·000	600 mm	—	Individual attention
at rear 1·500	2400 mm	minimal: insulated pen floor: heat	Can be used for fattening
2·400	1800 mm	minimal: insulated pen floor: heat	Portable crate optional
2·000	600 mm	minimal: insulated pen floor: heat	Part may be slatted
2·000	200–250 mm	minimal: insulated pen floor	Batch of 20 per pen
2·000 to 2·400	250 mm / 300 mm / 300–350 mm / 400 mm	minimal: insulated pen floor	Many different layouts with 10 to 20 per pen: may have part or totally slatted floors
kennel 1·250	floor feeding possible	minimal or up to 10 lb/head/week	Kennel + covered yard
2·000	450 mm	minimal or up to 10 lb/head/week	Pen + open yard
1·500	pen 2·400 m		
1·500	100 3·600 m		
1·500	birds 5·400 m	200–250 mm wood chippings on floor during life cycle	Deep litter
1·500	+ 25%		
1·500	per 100 birds 6·000 m		
2·200	300 m	individual cage: mesh floor	Normally tiers of 3 high
1·500		250 mm shavings, chopped straw	fox proof mesh sides
1·500		250 mm shavings, chopped straw	On range after 4 weeks

* Depends on access heights required e.g. Stock height—varies
 Man height—2000 mm
 Tractor height—2500 mm (min)

6–13

DATA

ENERGY

Intensive farming systems, including modern farm buildings, are based on the use of energy inputs. These may be made more effective, and therefore more economic, by good building design. Energy consumption in relation to building layout and construction has seldom been emphasised as of priority amongst other management factors.

The revolution in the cost of energy could make farmers conscious of the need to plan energy consumption as critically as other inputs. Data tends to be sparse but some tentative information is available (see also sub-section on 'Siting').

ENERGETIC EFFICIENCIES

Table 6.9 shows the relationship between the gross energy (nutritional value) and the support energy (input) of various farm products. It is clear that a diet based on corn and vegetables is considerably more efficient in the use of natural energy than on livestock where they convert solar energy based products (see Introduction).

ELECTRICAL ENERGY CONSUMPTION

Electrical requirements for various products or enterprises will have wide differences in relation to management and building efficiency. Table 6.10 gives data on average consumption rates established by the Electrical Development Association in terms of power, ventilation and heating. These provide a working basis for comparison but are not absolute figures for all situations.

ILLUMINATION: NATURAL AND ARTIFICIAL

The data given below outlines some basic lighting require-ments both for livestock and for crops. Nevertheless, there is considerable latitude for interpretation depending on other requirements and on building layout.

A. LIVESTOCK (n.b. waterproof fittings will be required in areas of humidity)

(a) Cattle yards and cubicle houses
Natural. Translucent roof sheets to equal about 2% of covered floor area; particularly above feeding positions, plus for enclosed buildings diffused light from space boarding under eaves.
Artificial. Fluorescent strip over 150–200 m², preferably above feeding positions but also providing general background light of 20 lx. An extra night-light circuit is desirable for inspections and cattle movement, say, at one per 300 m². Vehicular approach and external yards to have inverted shovel reflector shade with 200 W lamp set 6 m above ground, lighting generally an area of 500 m².

(b) Milking parlours
Natural. Windows helpful for circulation and amenity reasons (but can be omitted), thus designed in relation to fenestration and ventilation.
Artificial. Work areas to have minimum 160 lx, at udder working plane, evenly distributed to provide shadowless illumination at each milking and recording position, probably from banked fluorescent strips (but underfloor lighting and low level bulkhead fittings can be used). Recording board position may need spotlight. Background illumination over cow and circulation areas should ensue from above but ensure cow exit door and passage is well lit.

(c) Dairies
Natural. As for parlours, but windows considered 'desirable'.
Artificial. Bulk tank and work areas to have 160 lx, plus background lighting around.

(d) Boxes (Calving, loose, isolation)
Natural. Optional, but normally included.
Artificial. Inspection positions (when required) to be 100 lux or more, plus half this allowance per box for background or general illumination.

(e) Calf Houses
Natural. Excluded for veal, otherwise intermittent windows under eaves and 500–800 mm high and up to 1:2 (void: solid) ratio is 'normal' practice.
Artificial. Uniform low level illumination along access/feed passage of around 50 lx should be adequate, but heat-lamps above pens may be included additionally or alternatively.

(f) Pig yards (Miscellaneous semi-intensive layouts)
Natural. No particular need: most layouts have no windows except when lying and dunging areas are separated when the latter will have some windows or rooflights (say 0·10 m²/4 pigs) since this attracts dunging to the right place. Semi-open yards can be well lit provided kennels are dark.
Artificial. Uniform low level illumination along manger/feed passage area of around 50 lx, preferably with dimmer switches and some independent night light (say one per 10 m run). Dung areas when separate can have bulkhead fittings (say one per 2 or 3 pens).

Table 6.9 ENERGETIC EFFICIENCIES: AGRICULTURAL PRODUCTS AT THE FARM GATE*

Product	Gross energy in produce / Support energy in product
Maize	2·8
Wheat	2·2
Cereals (general range)	1·4 to 2·1
Oats	2·0
Sugar Beet	1·8
Barley	1·8
Potato	1·1
Milk + cull cows	0·62
Lamb + wool	0·39
Broiler hen carcase	0·11
Battery hen eggs + culls	0·16

*Work based on University of Reading + Grassland Research Institute: Span. Vol. 18 No. 1 1975
Total energy input exceeds that contained in products based on livestock: thus animal energy uses solar energy less efficiently than crops.

Table 6.10 ELECTRICAL ENERGY CONSUMPTION*

Enterprise	Function	Units consumed	Per
Dairying	Bulk milk cooling	79	
	Acid circulation cleaning	155	
	Udder waisting	78	
	Milk pumping in parlour	1	Cow per year
	Vacuum pumping	50	
	Frost protection	7	
	Lighting	36	
		406	
Food preparation	Crushing + conveying	15·4	Ton (cereal)
	Milling + mixing	27·4	Ton (cereal)
	Crushing + milling + mixing	20·5	Ton (mixed feed)
	Wet feed mixing	2·9	Ton (dry feed)
	Pumping wet feed	7·5	Ton (dry feed)
Pig rearing	Infra-red heating (winter)	12	Piglet
Pig fattening	Automatic fan vent (8 weeks winter)	2·5	Baconer
	Automatic fan vent (8 weeks summer)	6	Baconer
Chitting	Lighting	55	Ton
Hay	Contioning	60	Ton
Workshop	General use	4	Week

*Based on data from the Farm Electric Centre, Stoneleigh

(g) Farrowing and Dry Sow Yards (Stall layouts and pen systems)
Natural. Not essential, but some insulated windows acceptable provided direct sun avoided.
Artificial. Good illumination to all farrowing areas of up to 160 1x and not less than 100 1x to circulation and cleaning areas. Creeps can be kennels but may have infra-red heaters.

(h) Poultry houses
Natural. Most broiler, battery and deep litter houses exclude all windows, but some battery and deep litter units include minor, shaded natural light.
Artificial. Light and heat tend to be specialised and integrated within specialised buildings, together with ventilation. Advice should be taken, but a bulkhead fitting per 3–4 m bay is probable plus some night light. Lighting may be coupled to specific time schedules.

B. CROPS AND STORAGE

(Note. humidity and dust can be serious in some locations especially for crop drying or feed preparation)

(a) General areas
Including bulk storage, granaries, and other non-work situations:
Natural. Should be excluded from most storage areas especially grain since light attracts birds. General areas will be based on other design requirements.
Artificial. 50 1x general lighting.

(b) Work areas
Including riddling, sorting, milling, mixing, workshops, machinery circulation and other specific tasks:

Natural. Optional and based on other design considerations.
Artificial. At least 160 1x. Intensive tasks such as work benches, welding, mixing controls are likely to be flood-lit or under fluorescent strip lighting.

(c) Offices
Including control room, secretarial, mess-room, cloakroom etc:
Natural. To normal design standards.
Artificial. To normal design standards.

Note. Electrical requirements, including lighting and power, are covered in the series of booklets, 'Farm Electrical Handbooks'. In the case of power requirements, all prime movers for equipment must have their own, adjacent cut-off switch. All services are required to conform to standard regulations. Within farm buildings, due to humidity and dust, as well as inflammable materials, such as straw, fire is a particular hazard aggravated by distances from emergency services. There should be a fire control plan. In livestock buildings, emergency escape doors need particular consideration and tend to be difficult to include.

VENTILATION PRINCIPLES

Livestock housing can be designed on climatic or on controlled environmental principles (see also under 'Climate' in sub-section on 'Siting'). The basic difference is shown in Fig. 6.9 by SFBIU. Climatic housing is suitable for adult cattle, sheep and, in some cases, pigs, but rather less so for young stock.
The principle is to obtain the maximum rate of high level cross-ventilation, drawn by convection currents generated

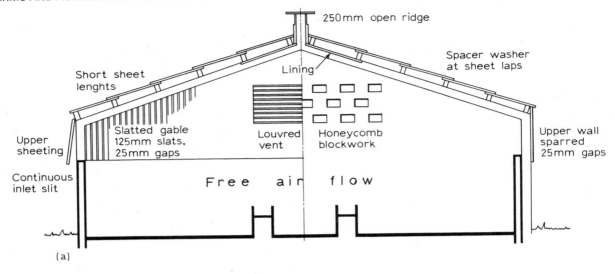

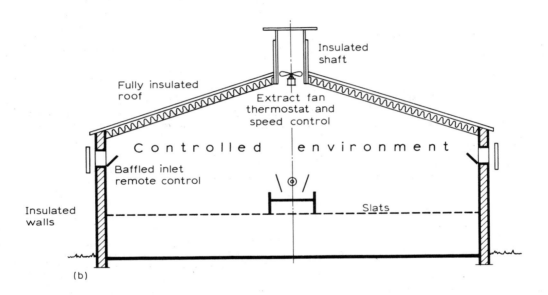

Fig. 6.9 Ventilation Principles (a) Climatic Housing (b) Controlled Housing
(Based on data from Scottish Farms Buildings Investigation Unit)

by the stock up to a chimney vent ridge, but without internal air turbulence creating draughts. Since there will be condensation at the cold chimney outlet some precaution is desirable by having timber purlins and a lined upper slope. Perforated ridge corrugated sheets can be used or short sheets may have spacer gaps and this will improve air movement.

In contrast, controlled environment houses need to be well insulated with an internal vapour seal and smooth roof slopes for preference. The internal volume should be kept low. Air movement will need fan assistance. This can be from eaves baffled air inlets combined with chimney ridge shaft plus extract fan.

Fig. 6.10 shows basic construction with the shaft extended to a flat ceiling. The shaft must be insulated and sealed. In some circumstances, if volumes are correct, no fan will be required. If the chimney is too small in relation to stock numbers, a fan should be introduced. Alternatively, other systems are possible. Air can be fan assisted into the building and extracted at the eaves or through a slatted floor to a vent. A horizontal perforated plastic tube from gable to gable can be linked to a gable intake fan to distribute air more evenly than from chimneys.

Table 6.11 LIVESTOCK: BASIC SIZES

	Length* mm	Width mm	Height mm	Weight kg
Calf (3 months)	1900	380	1150	100
Small cow (Jersey)	2150	560	1350	400
Large cow (Friesian)	2400	610	1500	500
Friesian cow-in-calf	2400	1000	1500	600
Bull or large steer	2600	500	1800	1000
Small ewe (upland)	1000	350	650	60
Large ewe (downland)	1150	450	750	75
Sow or baconer (adult)	1400	300	650	100
Sow + suckling litter	2500	1000	450	250
Hen	400	200	350	2

*Lying spaces may be less, i.e. a Friesian requires only 1750 mm length

Table 6.12 PIG PRODUCTION (AGE DIFFERENTIALS)

Product Type	Approx. Weight kg	Approx. Age days
Early weaners	6·50	18–24
Normal weaners	20	50–56
Porkers:		
young	55	130
medium	63	148
mature	73	165
Cutters	82	175
Baconers:		
(rationed feed)	100	186
(ad-lib feed)	100	170
Heavy hog	120	210

Table 6.13 DAIRY: BULK TANK STORAGE
(APPROXIMATE TANK DIMENSIONS)

Capacity	Length m	Breadth m	Height m
FIBREGLASS			
454	1·100	1·000	1·600
910	1·800	1·250	1·650
1364	2·550	1·250	1·650
1820	2·400	1·650	1·750
2270	2·850	1·650	1·750
2730	3·050	1·800	1·750
4550	3·073	2·050	2·100
STAINLESS STEEL			
454	1·500	1·000	1·400
910	2·050	1·650	1·600
1364	2·650	1·650	1·600
1820	3·200	1·650	1·650
2270	3·850	1·650	1·750

Allow minimum 900 mm clear space around the tank. Working height for tank calibration approx. 2600 mm.

Table 6.14 ANNUAL PRODUCTION AND DISPOSAL OF CEREAL
STRAW IN ENGLAND AND WALES (1973)

Total Produced t × 10⁶	Disposal method	Disposal %
3·42	Burned	36·6
3·40	Bedding and crop storage	36·4
1·40	Feeding	15·0
0·86	Inter-farm sales	9·3
0·15	Ploughed in	1·6
0·10	Non-agricultural use	1·1
9·33		100·0

Table 6.15 CROP STORAGE BARN CAPACITY: EXAMPLES

1. BARN TYPE: portal frame or dutch barn
   - width of storage   6000 mm
   - height of storage   4500 mm
   - capacity/metre run   27 m³ (1000 cu.ft.)

Storage capacity of barn per metre run in t (approximate)

Loose straw	55–60 kg/m³	1·5 t minimum
Baled straw (medium)	105–110 kg/m³	2·8 t
Loose bay	120–130 kg/m³	3·3 t
Baled hay (medium)	190–200 kg/m³	5·2 t

2. BARN TYPE: portal frame
   - width of clamp   1200 mm
   - settled depth   2500 mm
   - capacity/metre run   30 m³

Storage capacity of barn per metre run in t (approximate)

Ware potatoes		1·60 m³/t	18 t	
Dry wheat	(14% m.c.)	1·30 m³/t	23 t	
Dry barley	(14% m.c.)	1·45 m³/t	20 t	
Unwilted grass	(78% m.c.)	1·56 m³/t	19 t	(3·6 t d.m.)
Wilted grass	(70% m.c.)	1·40 m³/t	21 t	(6·3 t d.m.)
Wilted chopped grass	(70% m.c.)	1·27 m³/t	24 t	(7·0 t d.m.)
High-wilt-chop grass	(60% m.c.)	1·23 m³/t	24 t	(7·2 t d.m.)

3. TOWER SILO: specialist cylindrical silo for high-wilt-chopped
   grass as above

Silo diameter	6000 mm	6700 mm	7300 mm
storage height			
12 m	280 t	340 t	400 t
15 m	350 t	420 t	500 t
18 m	340 t	500 t	600 t

Table 6.16 TOWER SILAGE: LOADING AND UNLOADING RATES

LOADING

Tower diameter m	Dry matter at settled height of 18·3 m t	Dry matter to be ensiled per hour (*) t	Gross weight at 40% dry matter ensiled per hour t
6·1	149	2·87	7·2
6·7	181	3·47	8·7
7·3	215	4·14	10·4
7·9	252	4·84	12·1

UNLOADING

Settled silage depth m	Total feeding days at 75 mm depth/day cow/days	Daily unloading rate over 180-day winter housing* mm
15 (50)	200	85
17 (55)	220	95
18 (60)	240	100
20 (65)	260	110
21 (70)	280	120

*Loading should be based on a minimum rate of fill of 3 m per day. Unloading rates should be not less than 75 mm per day.

BASIC SIZES: IMPLEMENTS

Mechanical handling is an important part of building design. Most transport equipment will be used in or around buildings, whereas field equipment may require implement storage. Some of the basic sizes are given in Table 6.11 but different manufacturers' equipment may vary these dimensions.

BASIC SIZES: LIVESTOCK

Data concerning stock and their requirements are given in Table 6.8. The basic dimensions for livestock are given in Table 6.12.

BASIC SIZES: BULK TANKS

Details of milking parlours are given later in this chapter under 'Accommodation'. Milk production per cow varies due to breed, individuality, feeding policy and lactation cycle. The normal range for Friesians is 4000–5500 litres per lactation of around 305 days with a peak yield during the first 100 days.

The peak yield can be taken as 1/200th of the lactation. Channel Island breeds are more likely to yield 3000–4000 litres. The herd peak yield will vary due to calving policy. If this is concentrated in the spring or autumn, it will be an aggregate of individual peak yields; with all-year round calving it will be less. This calculation will determine the size of bulk tank storage required (Table 6.13) since collection usually is daily. Some areas still have to store in churns, there being no bulk collection.

STRAW PRODUCTION AND DISPOSAL

Table 6.14 gives data on straw usage (see also Tables 6.4 and 6.15).

CROP STORAGE: BARN CAPACITY

From Table 6.4, the size of barns or towers for crop storage can be calculated. Some examples are given in Table 6.15. Normally, capacity requirements are related to stock numbers and their rations. Deep litter straw for bedding is likely to be about 4–8 kg/cow/day, depending whether it is restricted or ad-lib. Cubicles will have around the same allowance over 10 to 20 days, unless sawdust or other bedding is used.

Hay rations will depend whether hay is used to supplement other bulk foods or is the main component of the feed. It is important to allow for hay over-heating and stack widths between free air flow should be kept to 5–6 m. Silage and hay may be conserved from 2 to 4 cuts per annum from each ley. The average ration per cow is likely to be around 9 kg of *dry matter* per day (allow for moisture content to assess volume requirements).

Tower silo diameters will be limited to a minimum depth to be emptied per day. For preference, this should not be less than 75–150 mm per day (see Table 6.16). Clamp silage will have a settled depth of 2·000–2·500 m for self-feeding to cows, but can be double this for cut-and-cart feeding. Clamp

widths, for practical purposes, will be not more than 9–12 m but, with self-feeding on an ad-lib basis will be based on about 150 mm width/cow. Wheat and barley storage may be based on harvesting at about 5000 kg/ha at about 20–25% moisture content. For long term storage, unless in hermetically sealed towers, this must be reduced to 14%.

Bulk floor storage is normally limited to 2 m if there are no air ducts or up to twice this if the grain can be conditioned after drying by forced air. Alternatively, grain can be stored in rectangular or circular bins (Fig. 6.14). Drying can be by forced air, sometimes warmed, sometimes refrigerated, via a perforated floor, horizontal/lateral ducts or, in circular bins, by vertical perforated drums.

CONCENTRATE FEEDS

Nearly all livestock depends on some concentrate feeds based on barley plus additives. Poultry and pigs, unless using skim milk or whey, will have all concentrate rations fed as meal, pellets or cubes. Basic rations are given in Table 6.18.

In the case of cattle, the policy will vary; most cows will be fed concentrates related to yield whilst being milked. Beef may be fed from around 2 kg/head/day up to nearly an all concentrate diet. All feeding is based on maintenance (to keep natural health) plus production (milk yield or live-weight gain).

Table 6.17 shows the basic different flow diagrams, based on the Electrical Development Association, to take concentrates to cattle.

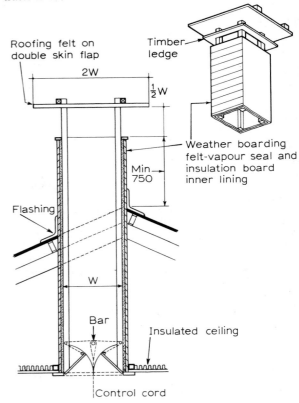

Fig. 6.10   Chimney ventilation shaft
(Based on Scottish Farm Buildings Investigation Unit)

Table 6.17 CONCENTRATE FEED DISTRIBUTION TO CATTLE

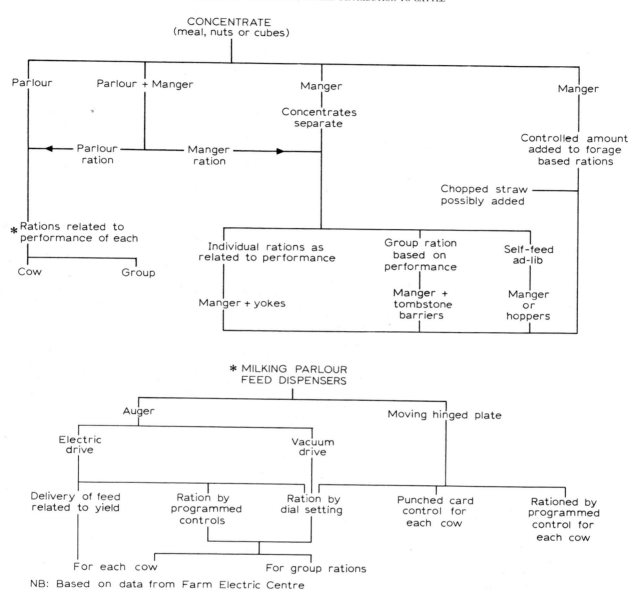

NB: Based on data from Farm Electric Centre

Table 6.18 CONCENTRATE FEED: SHORT TERM STORAGE

Short Term Storage = Stock numbers × daily ration ×
storage refill period

Daily rations		
Poultry	Layers, depending on breed	85–145 gm
	Table chicken, depending on age	120–180 gm
Pigs	Sows or gilts (maximum)	3·6 kg
	Porkers	1·9 kg
	Cutters	2·6 kg
	Baconers	2·6 kg
	Heavy hogs	2·9 kg

ACCOMMODATION

INTRODUCTION

The information previously given in the sub-section on 'Planning' should be considered when considering alternative types of accommodation. There are few absolutes in terms of management policy but, in terms of building design, there can be fairly precise requirements to satisfy a specific policy. It is impossible to give full guidance.

EFFLUENT

With livestock, effluent storage and disposal must be a priority in any layout and design of buildings. Basic data is given in Table 6.8. The aim is likely to be to keep the effluent in one of several main types:

(a) Liquids. Up to 10% dry matter, bedding being excluded (except sawdust), storage being in a cheap lagoon or via a tank direct onto land through organic irrigation pipes. Lagoons, to permit bacterial action plus evaporation should be 600–1000 mm deep.

(b) Semi-liquids. Up to 20% dry matter, including some bedding, stored in above ground slurry bins (constructed from metal sheets also used for tower silos) of any diameter and up to about 3 m high, and handled either via pipelines or slurry tanker spreaders.

(c) Semi-solids. Up to 30% dry matter, including straw bedding waste, handled by tractor-plus-blade or scoop since it only flows when pushed, often stored in middens or compounds (Fig. 6.12), and disposed onto land by muck spreader.

(d) Solids and farmyard manures. Up to 50% dry matter, handled as deep litter with tractor + fork or grab, stored *in-situ* or on concrete slabs and disposed onto land by muck spreader.

(e) Treatment. The usual aim of treatment processes, and several systems are under trial, is to separate solids from liquids, so that a fibrous manure can be handled as a solid and so that the liquid can have further treatment to make it acceptable for disposal into water courses without pollution. Seperation processes by tower filtration, centrifuge, etc, are possible. Complete treatment of liquids tends to be expensive. A basic flow diagram is shown in Fig. 6.13.

(f) Effluent System. The production and disposal of effluent, as well as the bedding method, should be considered as a system. A proprietary system is shown in Fig. 6.14, where cattle on a perforated (slats or mesh) floor have their effluent sluiced down channels to an external pit, from which it is augered or pumped to a holding tank which also allows it to be re-circulated or filled into a tanker. Since effluent gases can return to the cattle in cold weather, a trap (as shown) is desirable even though this can create a point for blockages to occur. Similar techniques are possible for pigs. Poultry and sheep effluent is too stiff.

GRAIN

An in-bin drying and storage system is shown in Fig. 6.15. Grain is tipped from the combine trailer into the intake pit from which it can be cleaned and dried and circulated to any bin or to the discharge spout for off-loading to sacks or to a tanker. Such systems are flexible, efficient and high in capital cost.

The nest of bins can be of any size, but usually each bin is up to 5 m square maximum or 4 m normal and 6 m high. They can have self-unloading bases. The elevator top is likely to be up to 5 m higher than the bins. The pre-dryer (8) can be omitted and a drier installed to force air through ventilated bins. Circular bins are cheaper but waste space. The machinery can be placed in a standard barn with pent for elevator tops. Alternatively, bins can support their own roof.

A different system is to have a radial layout of circular bins, each with conical roof, arranged around a central auger and pit. Grain can be dried and stored in bulk on a damp-proof floor and between retaining walls, generally as shown in Fig. 6.11. This is a cheap system but becomes complicated if there are more than two varieties of grain.

MILLING AND MIXING

The conversion of grain into concentrate feed on any large corn + livestock farm can require sophisticated equipment which extends the principles of grain storage. A proprietary system is illustrated in Fig. 6.16 which shows the complexity. Such equipment can be housed in a portal framed barn.

However, much smaller layouts that that illustrated are possible. The smallest become economic when about 1 t/week of meal is required. The layout shown could produce at least 20 t/week.

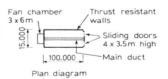

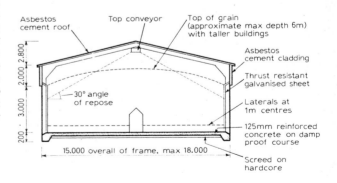

Fig. 6.11   Grain storage and drying

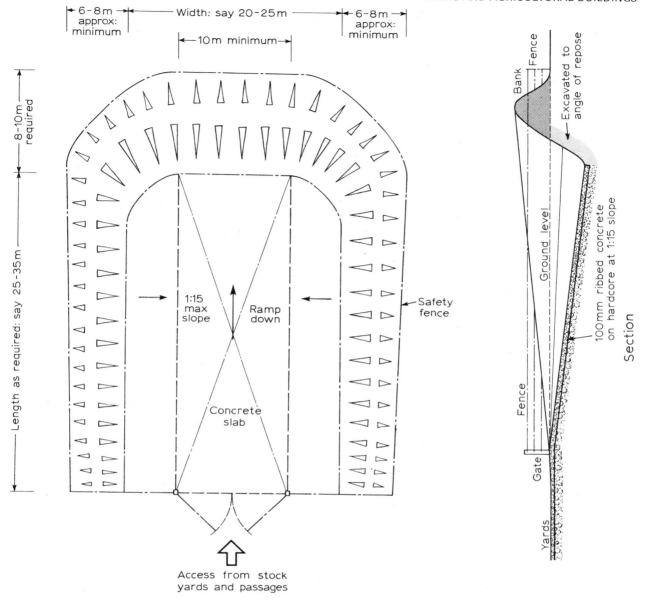

Fig. 6.12   Slurry storage compound
(Based on data supplied by the Ministry of Agriculture, Fisheries and Food)

FEED DISTRIBUTION

The principles of concentrate feed distribution to cattle are shown in Fig. 6.17. The storage of wilted grass in a tower and its mixing with a concentrate and its distribution to cattle mangers in a building is shown in Fig. 6.17.

If silage is stored in a clamp or in a tower, it can be cut and placed in a self-unloading trailer, which is powered by tractor p.t.o. drive, and which can distribute the feed evenly in mangers provided there is an adjacent roadway (see Figs. 6.18 and 6.20). A decision whether to have automatic conveyors or self-unloading trailers is fundamental to the layout and design.

CATTLE HOUSING YARDS

There are many different types of cattle housing within yards, some of which are shown in Fig. 6.18.

(a) A sophisticated, part insulated and fan ventilated slatted yard for beef in which feed is distributed by conveyor to a centre bank of mangers. Totally slatted yards are not suitable for dairy cows.

(b) Covered, strawed yards can be combined with manger feeding, filled from a self-unloading trailer along its central feed access road.

(c) As alternative to (b), space can be saved by having a conveyor rather than the feed road (see also Fig. 6.17).

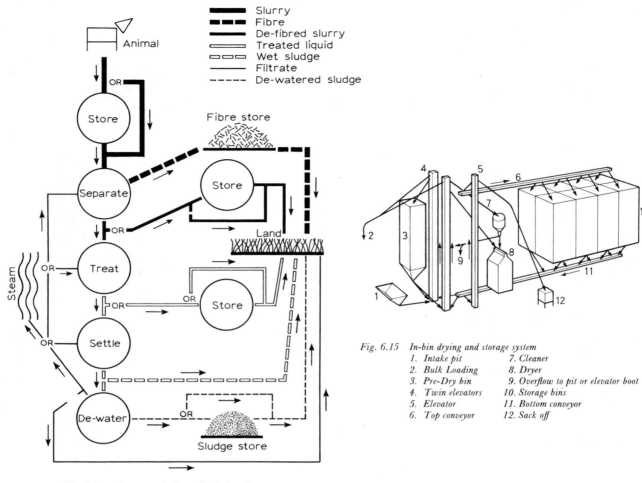

Fig. 6.13 Treatment of effluent. Basic flow diagram
(Based on data from the National Institute of Agricultural Engineering)

Fig. 6.15 In-bin drying and storage system
1. Intake pit   7. Cleaner
2. Bulk Loading   8. Dryer
3. Pre-Dry bin   9. Overflow to pit or elevator boot
4. Twin elevators   10. Storage bins
5. Elevator   11. Bottom conveyor
6. Top conveyor   12. Sack off

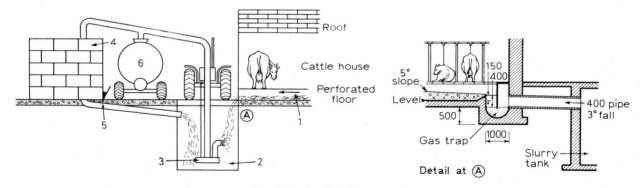

Fig. 6.14 A typical effluent system

1. Removal of manure from cattle stall
2. Manure enters mixing pit
3. Breaking-up and mixing manure with cutter and nozzle agitator
4. Transfer of manure to storage tank

5. Recirculation of manure from surface tank to mixing pit
6. Removal of manure to tanker for spreading
(Based on proprietary equipment (Alfa-Laval); other techniques are possible; trap data as recommended by Scottish Farm Buildings Investigation Unit)

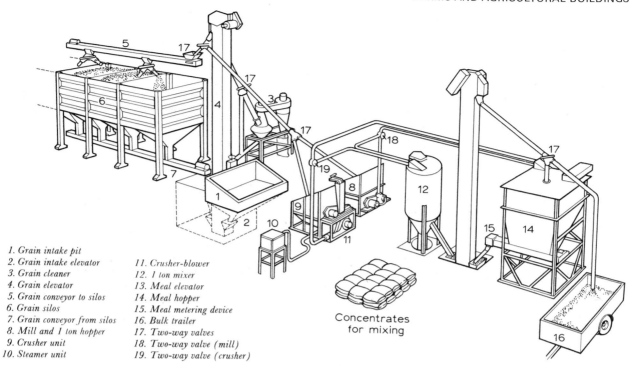

1. Grain intake pit
2. Grain intake elevator
3. Grain cleaner
4. Grain elevator
5. Grain conveyor to silos
6. Grain silos
7. Grain conveyor from silos
8. Mill and 1 ton hopper
9. Crusher unit
10. Steamer unit

11. Crusher-blower
12. 1 ton mixer
13. Meal elevator
14. Meal hopper
15. Meal metering device
16. Bulk trailer
17. Two-way valves
18. Two-way valve (mill)
19. Two-way valve (crusher)

Concentrates
for mixing

Fig. 6.16   A typical system for the conversion of grain into concentrated feed (Copyright: E.H. Bentall & Co. Ltd. Maldon: Essex)

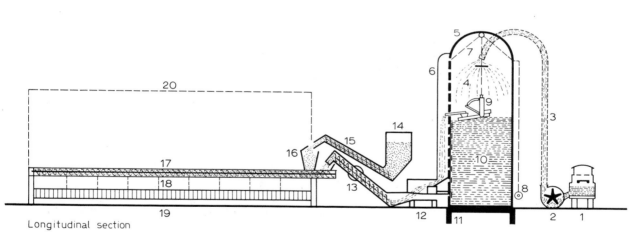

Longitudinal section

Fig. 6.17   Store tower for wilted grass

1. Self-unloading field silage trailer for wilted chopped grass
2. Electrical paddle blower (removeable)
3. Filler pipe: 225 mm dia (9 in)
4. Grass spread evenly by deflector plate (when No. 9 raised
5. Top-unloading tower silo
6. External outlet chute with access hatches into tower
7. Top-hung winch cable to unloader
8. Electric winch control
9. Suspended rotating cutter and auger
10. Settled silage
11. R.C. ring beam and floor (with sump drain)

12. Silage weigh hopper with auger
13. Auger elevator with beater to even out silage
14. External rolled barley hopper: Self-unloading
15. Auger
16. Barley weigh hopper
17. Horizontal conveyor auger with controlled outlets and deflector boards
18. Manger (yokes optional) at 600 mm run (2 ft) per head (yokes 750 mm/head)
19. Concrete feed passage floor
20. Cattle house enclosure

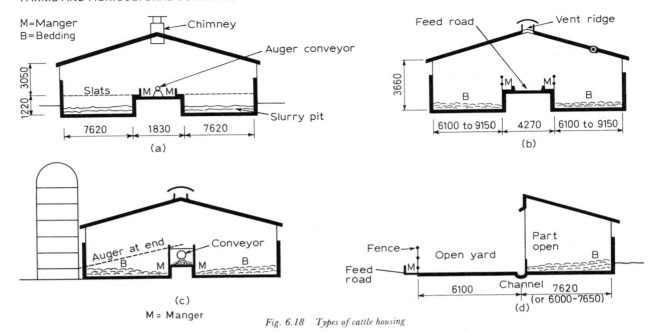

Fig. 6.18 *Types of cattle housing*

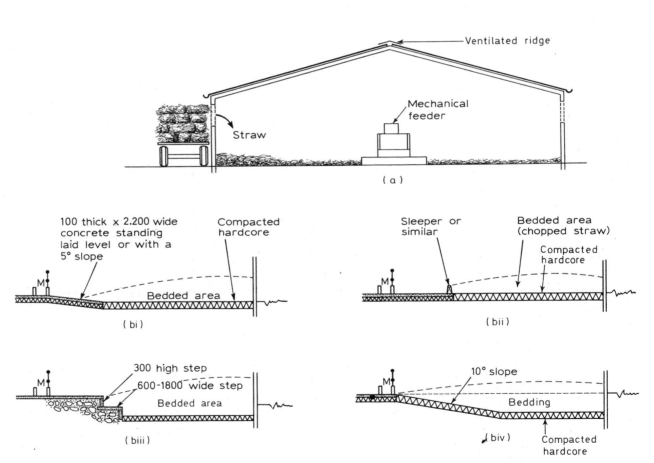

Fig. 6.19 *(a) Straw delivery to cattleyard (b) Suggested pen floor layouts to save bedding*

(d) Simple cattle shelters, part open to one side to external yarding which is flanked by a feed fence and manger are economic and, on sheltered sites, reasonably effective. However, open yards increase the problem of effluent.

The delivery of straw to yards and the profile of the yard or pen floor needs to be considered, examples being shown in Fig. 6.19. Straw may be delivered by trailer, bales being dropped into the yards, the twine being cut and the straw tossed out by fork. If there is no central feed road, access panels in the space boarding along the perimeter will be required. Herds of 60 cows per yard are satisfactory, but beef may be better penned in groups of 15 to 30 to give more control over feeding. Floor profiles are indicated Fig. 6.19(b) as follows:

(bi) The almost level hardcore base with a concrete feed strip alongside the manger is economic, but bedding builds up and is scuffed towards the feed area where it becomes fouled. Feed areas should be scraped out daily.

(bii) With low bedding allowances, using chopped straw, the feed area is easy to clean and less straw is wasted.

(biii) A recessed floor with steps up to the feed area is efficient but more expensive to construct.

(biv) Cheaper but less efficient than *(biii)* is a recessed floor and with no concrete area so all dunging is onto the deep litter.

A single width of yard + feed area, to form a building with well ventilated cross-section and with external feed road access (which saves the need for the feed trailer to enter the building) is shown in Fig. 6.20. The cattle feed area is scraped out daily and the cattle can be held back by dropping the electric fence gate.

In a different type of American beef yard the cattle tread their effluent into flume channels and which are flushed out into a lagoon.

CATTLE HOUSING CUBICLES

The principle of the cubicle is that each cow has a lying space between light divisions and with minimum bedding, approximately 2200 × 1200 mm each, and set in rows between circulation passageways. The cows are free to select their own cubicle and to move into the passages, unlike the traditional cowshed where they were tied to their stall.

Figs. 6.21 gives some basic dimensions for different types of cubicle division, each tending to have their own proponent. At the simplest, cubicle rows are simple shelters with open ridge, usually known as kennels. Fig. 6.22 shows a central feed area for self-unloading trailers with kennel units to each side. The kennel roofs can become leanto's to the central barn and the frame then would be a portal type, as in Fig. 6.23, which shows a portal with a layout to permit perimeter or central feed road access.

MILKING PARLOURS

Milking a cow, based on yard or cubicle layouts, requires a milking parlour supported by diary and other offices, including a cow collecting yard and, sometimes, exit yard. Some typical modern parlours are shown in Fig. 6.24 with approximate dimensions overall. The diagrams show six types as follows:

A. *Abreast.* This is the first parlour type and still popular with some cowmen. The cows cross the work area and step up 250 mm to a stall, then exit via a gate and passage.

B. *Herringbone.* Batches of cows to each side of a pit 750 mm deep and set at an angle to the milking position, each side being milked and let out as a group. Work routine is easier than A. Modern herringbones can have low level jars set under the cows which stand on a cantilevered floor.

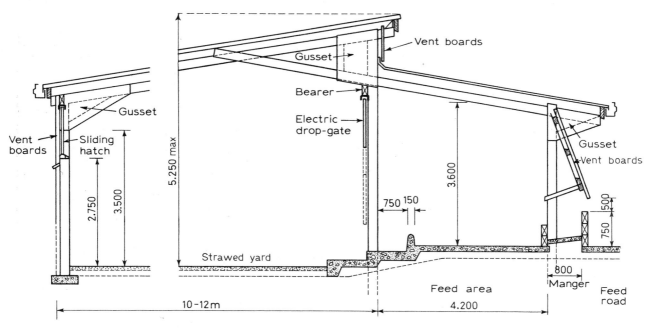

Fig. 6.20   A typical arrangement of yard and feed area
(Strutt and Parker Farms Ltd. Architect: John B. Weller)

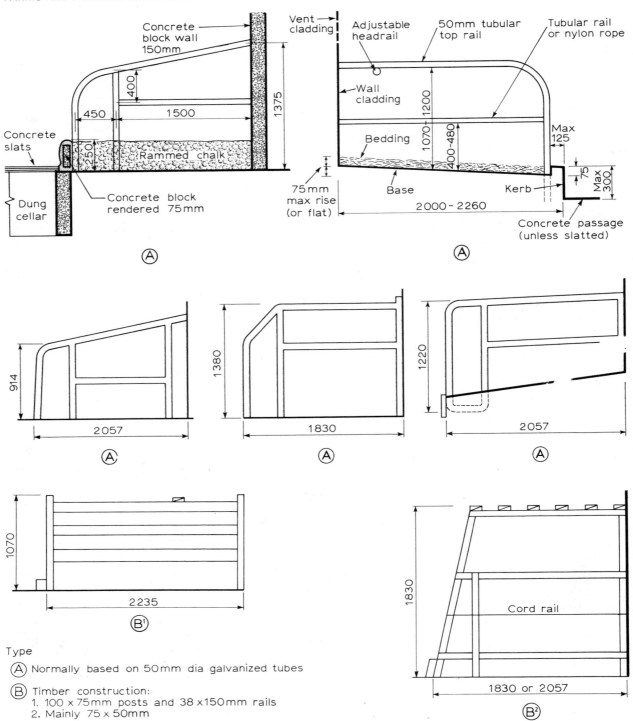

Type

Ⓐ Normally based on 50mm dia galvanized tubes

Ⓑ Timber construction:
   1. 100 × 75mm posts and 38 × 150mm rails
   2. Mainly 75 × 50mm

Basic dimensions for cubicle division
Type A Normally based on 50 mm and galvanised tubes
Type B Timber construction:
   1. 100 × 75 mm post and 38 × 150 mm rail
   2. Mainly 75 × 50 mm

Fig. 6.21 Basic dimensions for various types of cubicle (based on Farm Buildings Information Centre report)

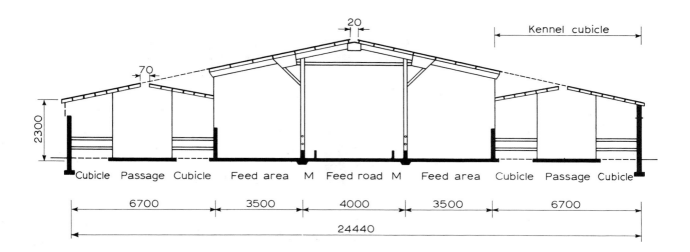

Fig. 6.22   Central feed area for unloading trailers

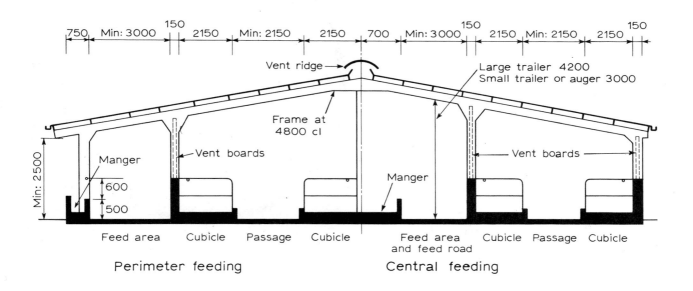

Fig. 6.23   Alternative arrangement of cubicles

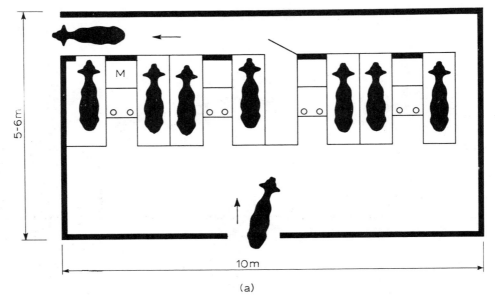

5-6 m

10m

(a)

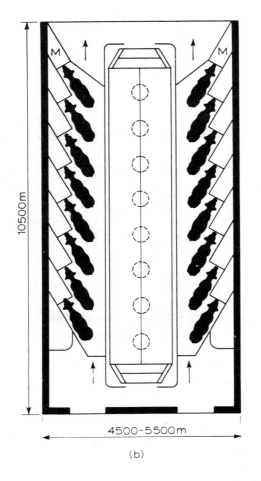

10500m

4500-5500m

(b)

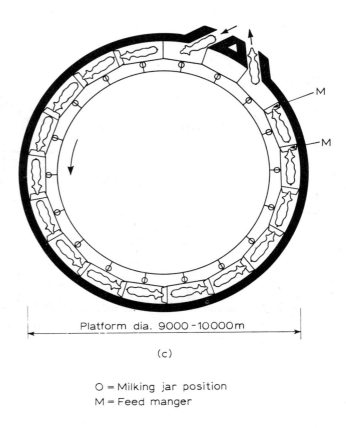

Platform dia. 9000-10000m

(c)

O = Milking jar position
M = Feed manger

Fig. 6.24   Some typical milking parlours

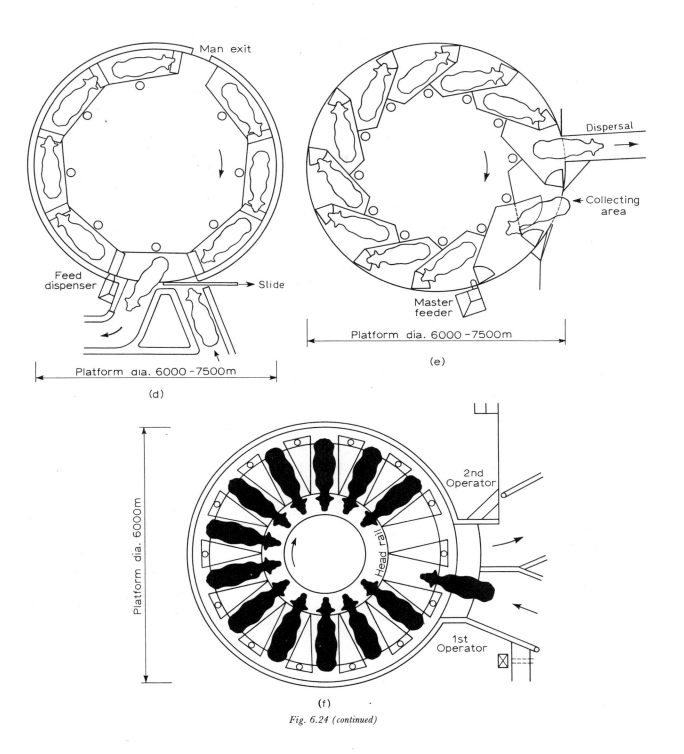

Fig. 6.24 (continued)

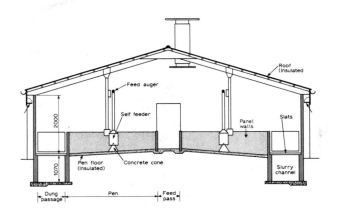

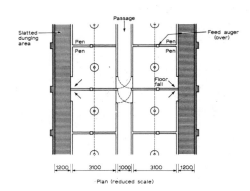

Fig. 6.25   Plan and section of pens for pig fattening

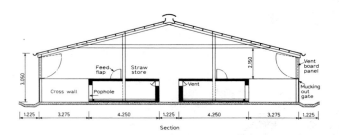

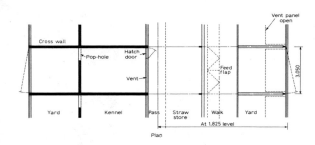

Fig. 6.26   Alternative layout to that shown in Fig. 6.25

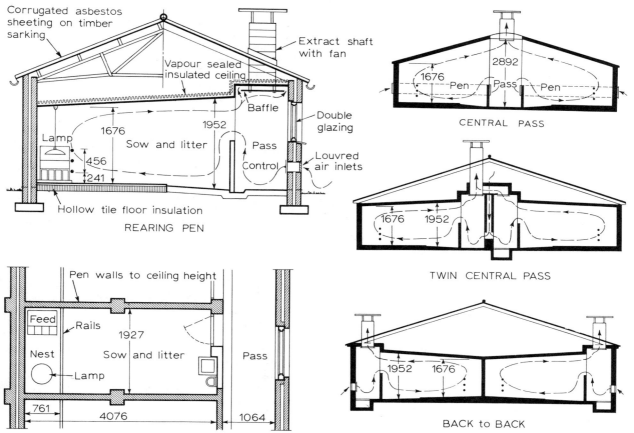

Corrugated asbestos sheeting on timber sarking

Extract shaft with fan

Vapour sealed insulated ceiling

Baffle

Double glazing

Louvred air inlets

Lamp

1676

1952

Sow and litter

Pass

Control

456

241

Hollow tile floor insulation

REARING PEN

2892

1676

Pen

Pass

Pen

CENTRAL PASS

1676

1952

TWIN CENTRAL PASS

1952

1676

BACK to BACK

Pen walls to ceiling height

Feed

Rails

1927

Nest

Sow and litter

Pass

Lamp

761

4076

1064

Fig. 6.27   Typical sow and litter pen (Scottish Farm Buildings Investigation Unit)

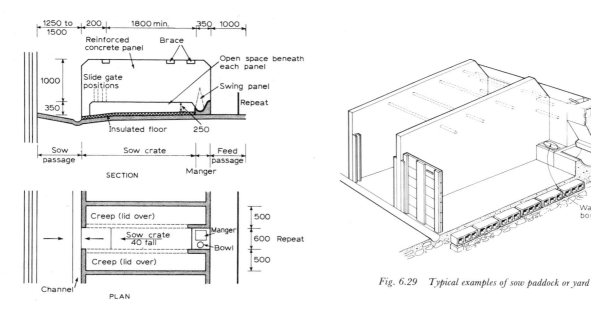

1250 to 1500

200

1800 min.

350

1000

Reinforced concrete panel

Brace

Open space beneath each panel

Slide gate positions

Swing panel

1000

Repeat

350

Insulated floor

250

Sow passage

Sow crate

Feed passage

Manger

SECTION

Creep (lid over)

500

Sow crate
40 fall

Manger

600

Repeat

Bowl

Creep (lid over)

500

Channel

PLAN

Fig. 6.28   Sow crate and creep layout

Water bowl

Fig. 6.29   Typical examples of sow paddock or yard

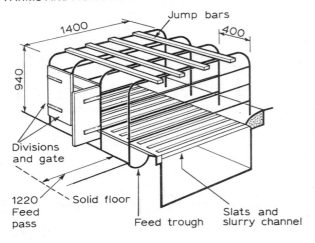

Fig. 6.30 Details of individual sow stalls

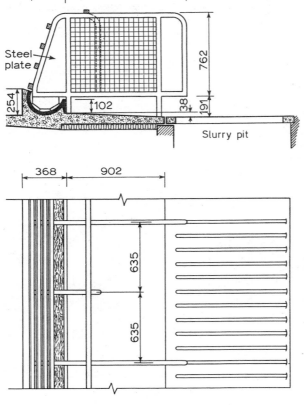

Fig. 6.31 Details of tether sow stalls

C. *Rotary tandem.* Cows enter a revolving platform and stand in stalls head-to-tail, being milked within one circuit. The cowman stands in one place to place the milking machines as cows go past.

D. *Rotary tandem.* As above, but smaller parlour type.

E. *Rotary herringbone.* As above, but cows set at an angle and building smaller per cow.

F. *Rotary turnstyle.* Cows side by side on platform, facing inwards but having to back out after milking.

Note that all the above parlours can have more or less cow places but most are designed to permit either one or two men to cope with the milking routine, and with either one milking point per cow or, sometimes, per two cows.

PIG FATTENING (BACONERS)

Most fattening houses are based on a central feed walkway flanked by pens, holding 10 to 20 baconers, with perimeter dung passages. The latter can be slatted over a slurry channel or pit (see Fig. 6.25). Sometimes, this layout is inserted with central dung passages, usually slatted. The buildings are well insulated with controlled ventilation.

Feeding can be by conveyor direct to self-feeder or to floor, as shown. Alternatively, each pen will have a manger flanking the central feed passage at an allowance of 300 mm per pig. A different type of layout, semi-open and without controlled ventilation, is shown in Fig. 6.26.

The pigs have insulated kennels and covered, but open, dung yards. The latter will be strawed, bales being kept above the kennels which also include a walkway with flaps for floor feeding in the kennels. However, many types of housing are also acceptable depending on management.

PIG FARROWING AND WEANERS

Traditionally, the sow farrows and weans her 8 to 12 piglets for 8 weeks when she is taken away and the litter is fattened in the same pen either to cutter or bacon weight (Table 6.12). A simple sow and litter pen is shown in Fig. 6.27, which also shows alternative arrangements for double-banking the pens with combined or segregated air spaces. Some layouts, single-banked, are designed on a semi-open basis.

A more sophisticated and better controlled system is the sow crate and creep layout (Fig. 6.28). Construction is similar, but with the creep spaces, to Fig. 6.29. The piglets can be early weaned (3 weeks) or normally weaned (8 weeks) and are then moved to a fattening house.

DRY SOWS

When sows are not in-pig or farrowing, they may be kept in paddocks or in simple yards. However, they can be held in special stalls for part or all of the time. An example is shown in Fig. 6.30 and an alternative, with slatted floor, in Fig. 6.30. A further example, part slatted, with the sows tethered to their stall is given in Fig. 6.31.

SHEEP HANDLING

Flocks of sheep need to be inspected, dipped and sorted. This is easiest within special facilities which can be portable or fixed. A typical race, which is likely to lead to a sheep dip, is shown in Fig. 6.32. A complete layout of handling pens, race and dip is shown in Fig. 6.33.

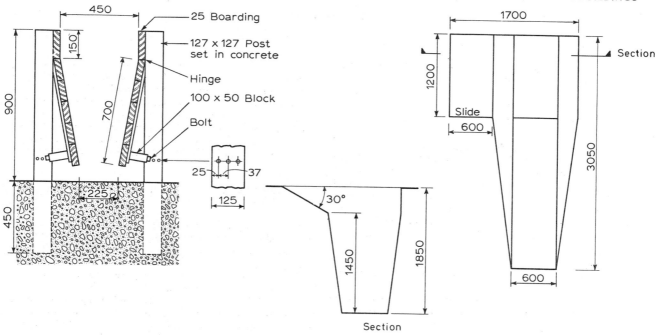

Fig. 6.32 Sheep handling (a) section through drafting race. (b) Plan of sheep dip bath. (c) Section through sheep dip bath

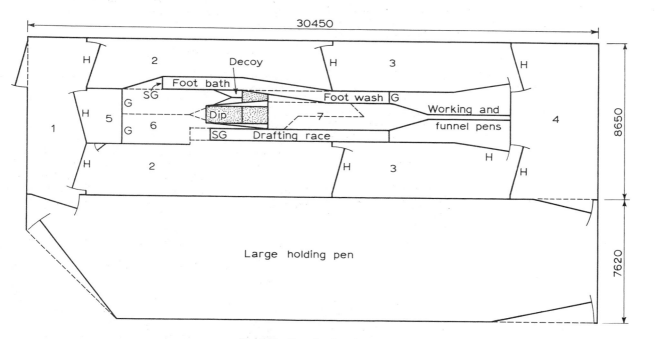

Fig. 6.33 General outlay of handling pen

SG Stop gate
H   Hosking gate
G   Guillotine gate
1   Loading pen   5   Drawing pen
2   Drafting pen   6   Draining pens
3   Forcing pen   7   Electricity and water supply
4   Holding pen

LEGISLATION

Farm buildings are controlled by legislation dealing with planning, construction, safety, health and pollution. There are exemptions, partial exemptions and variations to legislation normal for other building types.

TOWN AND COUNTRY PLANNING ACT, 1971

This act consolidated previous legislation. The subsequent Act of 1972 dealt mainly with Development Plans. Statutory powers for Planning Control are contained within Part III. Section 22(i) defines the meaning of development for which permission is required including all 'building, engineering, mining or other operations in, on, over or under land'. Subsection 2 defines permitted development not requiring permission as 'use of land for agriculture or forestry and use of any building occupied together with land so used'.

Under Section 24(5)(a), a General Development Order can be made for specific areas in which permitted development is withdrawn. In all cases where development consent has to be obtained, applications, together with their method of consent, refusal and appeal, conform to normal procedure.

THE BUILDING REGULATIONS, 1972

Agricultural buildings are classed mainly as 'Buildings partially exempted from the provisions of these regulations' and are defined within Schedule 1 Part A Class 6 as 'A single storey building (not being within Class 7 or Class 8)* which:

(i) is used exclusively for the storage of materials or products, for the accommodation of plant or machinery, or for the housing of livestock; and
(ii) is a building wherein the only persons habitually employed are engaged solely in the general care, supervision, regulation, maintenance, storage or removal of the materials, products, plant, machinery or livestock in the building; and
(iii) is wholly detached from any other building.'

It is important to stress farm buildings attached to a farmhouse or other building type and two-storied farm buildings are not exempt. (Future legislation is expected to redefine the the requirements for agricultural buildings in relation to regulations specific to their function).

AGRICULTURE ACT, 1947

This Act defines 'Agriculture' to include: 'Horticulture, fruit growing, seed growing, dairy farming and livestock breeding and keeping, and the use of land as grazing land, meadow land, osier land, market gardens and nursery grounds and the use of land for woodlands, where that use is ancillary to the farming of land for other agricultural purposes, and 'Agriculture' shall be construed accordingly'.

---

* Class 7 governs glasshouses and Class 8 plant storage buildings other than farm machinery.

AGRICULTURAL HOLDING ACT, 1948

Section I defines 'Agricultural Land' and 'Agricultural Holding' respectively as 'land used for agriculture which is so used for the purpose of a trade or business'.

In this Act the expression agricultural holding means the aggregate of the agricultural land comprised in a contract of tenancy, being a contract under which the said land is let to a tenant during his continuance of any office, appointment or employment from that held under the landlord.

AGRICULTURAL (SAFETY, HEALTH AND WELFARE) ACT, 1956

Powers are granted to the Ministry of Agriculture, Fisheries and Food and to the Secretary of State for Scotland to make regulations for the safety of farm workers including the guarding of stairs, openings and pits and the provision of sanitary facilities. The majority of the requirements are commonsense, such as the requirements for guard rails.

Most of the Regulations created following the enabling Act of 1956 are related to machinery. All prime movers, including electric motors, must have an accessible, marked cut-off switch and adequate lighting facilities must be provided. All moving parts must be guarded. All buildings in which operations create dust injurious to health should be ventilated or fitted with extraction equipment. Grain bins and silos should have ladders and rails.

PETROLEUM (CONSOLIDATION) ACT, 1928

Farm storage of petrol is governed by the same regulations as on other premises. A licence must be obtained.

THE FACTORIES ACT, 1961

If a property is subject to rating as industrial use, it needs to comply with the Factories Act. This could include the larger packing premises and broiler units, etc, considered excessive in size in relation to the agricultural land on which they are erected.

THE SHOP, OFFICES AND RAILWAY PREMISES ACT, 1971

Larger farm offices will be governed by this Act as for any other office.

FOOD AND DRUGS ACT, 1955
THE MILK AND DAIRIES (GENERAL) REGULATIONS, 1959

Dairy farms have to be registered. Part V of the Regulations contain provisions relating to buildings and water supplies with the three main clauses stating:

13. No occupier of any building, part of a building or shed shall use it as a milking house unless

(a) those parts of the surface of the floor liable to soiling by cows are impervious and constructed of such material and in such manner as render it practical to remove any liquid matter which may fall thereon and to prevent, as far as is reasonably practical, the soiling of the cows;
(b) the floor is so sloped and provided with gutters or channels or some impervious material as to ensure that any liquid matter which falls on the floor, or in the gutters or channels, is thereby conveyed to a suitable drain outside the building and thence to a suitable place of disposal, but nothing in this regulation shall be deemed to prohibit the practice of providing for the absorption of such liquid matter into some removable material which is afterwards disposed of outside the building;
(c) those parts of the surface of any walls liable to soiling or infection by cows are impervious and capable of being readily cleansed.

14. The occupier of any milk room or building or part of a building in which milk is handled, processed or stored, or is kept or used for the purpose of sale or manufacture into any milk product for sale, shall

(a) cause the interior thereof and any furniture and fittings therein to be cleansed as often as may be necessary to maintain them at all times in a state of thorough cleanliness;
(b) except in the case of a building or part of a building in which milk is solely or mainly dealt with by way of retail sale:
(i) cause the floor thereof to be constructed of such material and in such a manner as to render the surface impervious so that it is practical to remove any liquid matter which may fall thereon, and cause such floor to be sloped as to convey such liquid matter to a suitable and properly trapped drain;
(ii) cause the surface of any wall or part of a wall liable to splashing by milk or otherwise to be smooth and impervious; and
(iii) cause such floor and any such wall or part thereof to be cleansed with water at least once in every day.'

Pt VI. 17(1). Every farmer after milking:

'shall, without any delay other than that caused by any process of straining or centrifugalisation to which the milk may be subjected, cause the milk to be cooled either (i) to a temperature not exceeding 50°F, or (ii) if the temperature of the water supply available for cooling is 45°F or above to a temperature not more than 5°F above the temperature of that supply.'

AGRICULTURAL (MISCELLANEOUS PROVISIONS) ACT, 1968: PT. 1 LIVESTOCK

A number of standards are prescribed for the manner and conditions to be used for stock keeping, especially in relation to areas, based on the recommendations of the Brambell Committee. These standards are part of recommended space requirements.

RIVERS (PREVENTION OF POLLUTION) ACTS, 1951 AND 1961
WATER RESOURCES ACT, 1963
CONTROL OF POLLUTION ACT, 1975

The Rivers Acts made it unlawful to discharge trade or sewage effluent into a watercourse without the consent of the Water Authority. Farm drainage was classified as a trade effluent under the Public Health Act 1961 Part V. Standards are not rigid, but concern:
1. The nature and composition of the effluent.
2. The temperature of the effluent.
3. The maximum quantity to be discharged in any one day.
4. The maximum rate of discharge.

Seldom will a discharge be permitted above 20 mg/l BOD and 30 mg/l suspended solids. The Water Resources Act Section 72 prohibits liquid waste discharge to an underground strata via any well, borehole or pipe. The Control of Pollution Act introduce Codes of Practice for farm wastes.

CODE OF PRACTICE FOR FARM AND HORTICULTURAL BUILDINGS

A draft code is in preparation. It covers a wide range of data including materials, construction and loading, fire protection, insulation, all services, human and animal welfare, and infestation, plus reference data on associated matters. When introduced, it should exert considerable influence on farm building design and future legislation.

BS 5061: 1974. CYLINDRICAL FORAGE TOWER SILOS AND RECOMMENDATIONS FOR THEIR USE

This specification, though without statutory powers, sets a standard unlikely to be broken by reputable manufacturers and may be essential in any grant aided scheme. It gives data for foundation loading and design.

BS 2053: 1972 GENERAL PURPOSE FARM BUILDINGS OF FRAMED CONSTRUCTION

This specification, though without statutory powers, sets a standard for farm building frames which is used widely by manufacturers as a basis for design. It gives data for foundation loading and design.

GENERAL BRITISH STANDARDS AND CODES OF PRACTICE

The following BS and CP are specific to farm buildings:
BS.3854: 1965. Farm stock fences
BS.2505: Pt. 2: 1972. Fixed equipment for cowhouses
BS.4008: 1973. Cattle grids on private roads
CP.3007: 1968. Milking installations

DIMENSIONAL CO-ORDINATION AND SPATIAL RECOMMENDATIONS

The following recommendations are specific to farm buildings:

(a) Dimensional co-ordination in agricultural building, MAFF, 1972.
(b) Supplement No. 1 (1974) to PD 6444: Part 2: 1971, Recommendations for the co-ordination of dimensions in building: co-ordinating sizes for fixtures, furniture and equipment: agricultural items, BSI.
(c) Animal welfare codes, MAFF. No. 1 Cattle; No. 2 Pigs; No. 3 Domestic fowls; No. 4 Turkeys.

FARMS AND AGRICULTURAL BUILDINGS

REGULATIONS OF THE INSTITUTE OF ELECTRICAL ENGINEERS

The Regulations, which are revised from time to time, concern the installation, inspection and maintenance of circuits. Section K gives requirements related to agricultural and horticultural installations. Though non-statutory, the Boards will not connect up to a lower standard.

IMPROVEMENT GRANTS

Farm buildings, whether converted, extended or new, can attract a capital cost grant based on either actual costs or on a fixed standard cost. Improvements have to be of a specified standard. Grants are administered by the Ministry of Agriculture, Fisheries and Food.

AUTHORITIES

Ministry of Agriculture, Fisheries and Food; Whitehall Place, London SW1A 2HH;

Development and Advisory Service, Great Westminster House, Horseferry Road, London SW1P 2AE;

Regional Offices

	Government Buildings, Brookland Avenue, Cambridge.
East Midland	Shardlow Hall, Shardlow, Derby.
Northern	Government Buildings, Kenton Bar, Newcastle-upon-Tyne.
South Eastern	Government Offices, Coley Park, Reading.
South Western	Government Buildings, Burghill Road, Westbury, Bristol.
West Midland	Woodthorne, Wolverhampton.
Yorks & Lancs	Government Buildings, Lownswood, Leeds.
Wales	Trawscoed, Aberystwyth.

Department of Agriculture and Fisheries for Scotland, St. Andrews House, Edinburgh.

Ministry of Agriculture, Northern Ireland, Dundonald House, Belfast, N.1.

Agricultural Research Council, 160 Great Portland Street, London W1N 6DT.

Farm Buildings Centre, National Agricultural Centre, Kenilworth, Warwickshire CV8 2LG.

Farm Buildings Association, Secretary—Roseleigh, Deddington, Oxford OX5 4SP (or at Farm Buildings Centre).

Scottish Farm Buildings Investigation Unit, Craibstone, Bucksburn, Aberdeen AB2 9TR.

National Farmers Union, Agriculture House, Knightsbridge, London.

Country Landowners Association, 7 Swallow Street, London.

Architects in Agriculture Group, c/o RIBA West Midland Regional Office, Birmingham Building Centre, Broad Street, Birmingham.

The following organisations have a particular interest in farm buildings:

Design Council (Farm Buildings Committee)

Electricity Council (Electrical Development Association)

Cement and Concrete Association

Timber Research and Development Association

National Institute of Agricultural Engineering, Silsoe, Bedfordshire

Foreign

US Department of Agriculture, 12th and Constitution Avenue, Washington DC. 20250, USA.

Institut voor Landbouwbedrijfsgebouwen, SL Mansholt-laan, 12 Wageningen, Holland.

Department of Agricultural Structures, Agricultural University of Norway, N1432 AS-NLH, Norway.

Institut for Bygningsteknikk, Norges, Landbrukshagskole, Vollebekk, Norway.

Landsbygdens Byggnadsforening, Kindstugatan 1, Stockholm, Sweden.

Statens Byggeforskningsinstitut, Forskningscentret, 2970 Horsholm, Denmark.

Rijksfaculteit de Landbouwwetenschappen, Coupure Links 235, Ghent, Belgium.

Director Instituto di Topograffia e Construzioni Rurali, Via de Nicola, Sassari, Italy.

Lehrstuhl Landliche Siedlungsplanung und Entwerfen, 7 Stuttgart 1, Postfach 560, Germany.

Institute National de la Recherche Agronomique, BP1, 37 Nouzilly, France.

Rural Building Authority, Landbunadarins, Reyjavik, Iceland.

School of Agricultural Engineering, Guelph, Ontario, Canada.

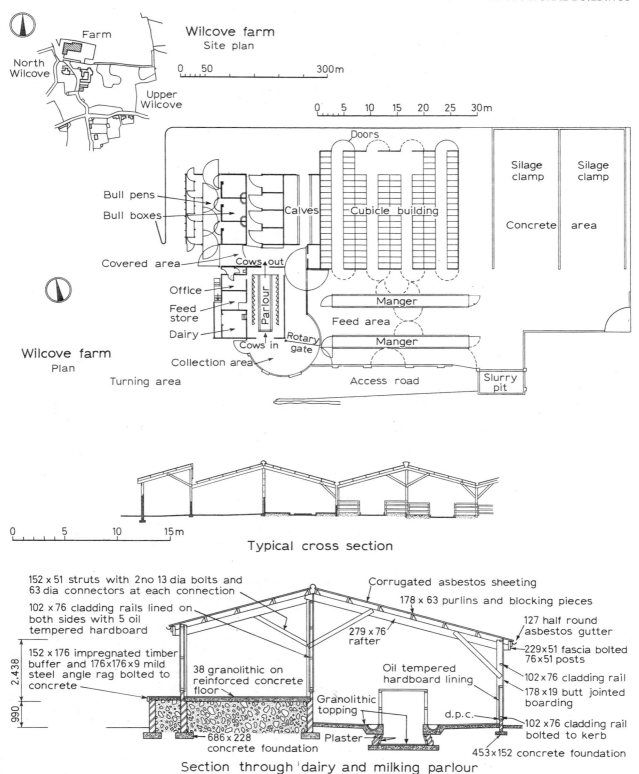

Wilcove farm
Site plan

0   50   300m

Farm

North
Wilcove

Upper
Wilcove

0   5   10   15   20   25   30m

Doors

Bull pens

Bull boxes

Calves

Cubicle building

Silage
clamp

Silage
clamp

Concrete

area

Covered area

Cows out

Office

Feed
store

Dairy

Parlour

Manger

Feed area

Manger

Wilcove farm
Plan

Cows in

Rotary
gate

Collection area

Turning area

Access road

Slurry
pit

0   5   10   15m

Typical cross section

152 x 51 struts with 2no 13 dia bolts and
63 dia connectors at each connection

Corrugated asbestos sheeting

178 x 63 purlins and blocking pieces

102 x 76 cladding rails lined on
both sides with 5 oil
tempered hardboard

279 x 76
rafter

127 half round
asbestos gutter

229 x 51 fascia bolted
76 x 51 posts

152 x 176 impregnated timber
buffer and 176 x 176 x 9 mild
steel angle rag bolted to
concrete

38 granolithic on
reinforced concrete
floor

Oil tempered
hardboard lining

102 x 76 cladding rail

178 x 19 butt jointed
boarding

Granolithic
topping

d.p.c.

102 x 76 cladding rail
bolted to kerb

2.438

990

686 x 228
concrete foundation

Plaster

453 x 152 concrete foundation

Section through dairy and milking parlour

*Fig. 6.34   Details of Wilcore Farm. Site plan, Plan, Typical cross section, Section through dairy and milking parlour
(Surveyors: Stratton and Halborow)*

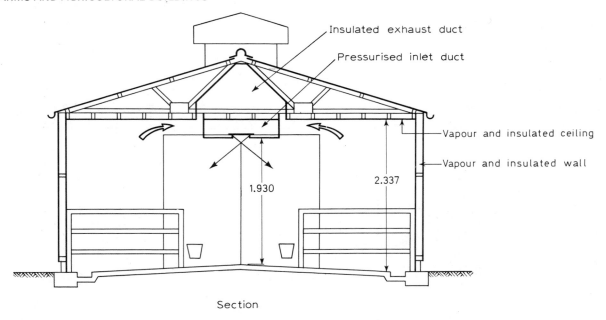

Insulated exhaust duct

Pressurised inlet duct

Vapour and insulated ceiling

Vapour and insulated wall

1.930

2.337

Section

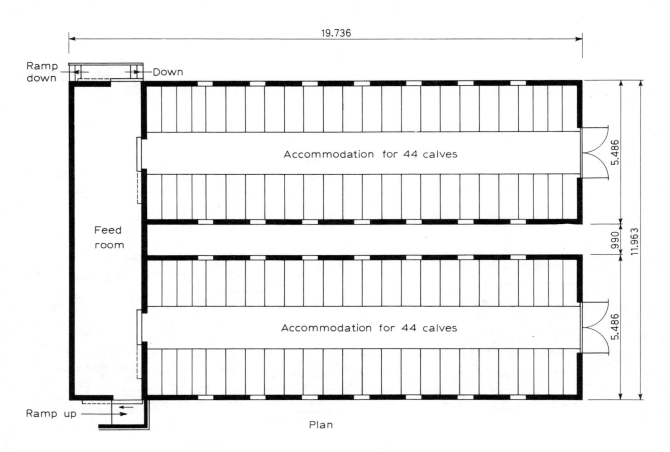

19.736

Ramp down

Down

Accommodation for 44 calves

5.486

Feed room

990

11.963

Accommodation for 44 calves

5.486

Ramp up

Plan

Fig. 6.35 Controlled environment calf house for 88 calves at the National Agricultural Centre

Fig. 6.36 A 200 Sow and progency layout at Colsterworth, Grantham, Lincs. A maximum security and minimum disease policy, within genetrically controlled pedigree stock units, is essential for large breeding companies— hence a perimeter fence and, once delivered, pigs do not leave the covered buildings (Farmers Weekly, pp vii and x (20/6/75))

1   Midden
2   Isolation pens
3   Finishing house
4   Weaner house
5   Covered midden
6   Farrowing house
7   Amenity area
8   Dry sow and boar house
9   Despatch ramp
10   Shaving store
11   M/C shed
12   Stockman's house
13   Manager's house
14   Inner security fence

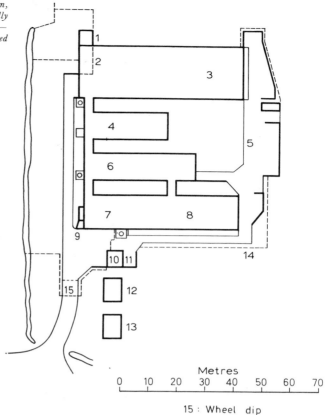

Metres
0   10   20   30   40   50   60   70

15 : Wheel dip

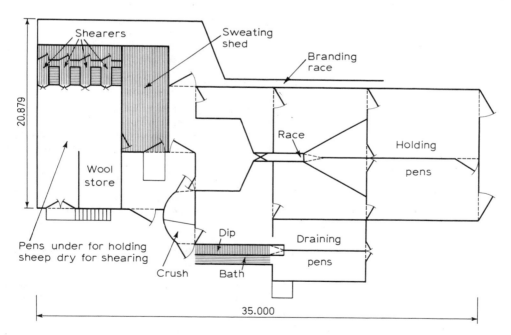

Fig. 6.37   Layout plan for sheep handling and shearing unit Cwmhasgyn Farm, Frongoch, Merioneth (Farm Buildings Information Centre Report 39, pp 15–27 (December 1973) 2000 mountain ewes and lambs: sheep handling and shearing unit 1964

6–39

EXAMPLES

SOURCES

Case studies and examples of farm buildings, which give full coverage of building design, are rare within agricultural journals. Most reports are concerned primarily with farm management and, though of interest, make the interpolation of data from one layout to another both difficult and dangerous. The two main sources for examples which contain a reasonable, though seldom comprehensive, range of design data are to be found within the quarterly's Farm Buildings Centre 'Digest' and Scottish Farm Buildings Investigation Unit 'Farm Building Progress'. Few of the studies give elemental cost breakdown of the building works. The few examples published within the Architects' Journal do give elemental costs. Overseas examples are rarely available in this country though some reports made by the Farm Buildings Association do include European farm buildings.

ARCHITECTS' JOURNAL INFORMATION LIBRARY

1.3.72   pp. 435–439   Cattle & Horticultural & Estate Building, Lee Abbey, N. Devon.
1.3.72   pp. 440–448   160-cows and followers: Wilcove, Torpoint, Cornwall.
12.3.69   pp. 440–448   Milk Marketing Board beef progeny testing station: Lambourn, Berkshire.

Farm Building Progress   Examples are given in Project Sheets, published by Farm Buildings Information Centre and '*Farm Buildings Progress*' published by the Scottish Farm Buildings Investigations Unit.

Examples (Cattle)
Lee Abbey building from Architects' Journal (see 8.2) for mixed farm of 105 ha (260 acres) for 40 cows and followers, forestry and estate yard, and horticultural packing room.
Fig. 6.34   Plan and section of Wilcove Farm from Architects' Journal (see 8.2) for a specialist farm unit of 80 ha intensive grassland supporting 160 cows plus 3 bulls and 30 calves.
Plan and section of Park Farm, Chidcock for 200 cows under one roof as described (briefly) in Power Farming.
Fig. 6.35   Plan and section of controlled environment calf house at the National Agricultural Centre for 88 calves (see Digest 77).

Examples (Pigs)
Fig. 6.36   Layout plan for an intensive pig farrowing and fattening unit as described (briefly) in Farmers Weekly. (See Figs. 6.25 and 6.26) layout plan and section for intensive fattening unit with floor feeding and slatted dung area as described in Progress No 34 (Oct 73).

Examples (Sheep)
Fig. 6.37   Layout plan for sheep handling and shearing unit as described in Digest Report 39.

BIBLIOGRAPHY

Agriculture

ARC, *Studies on Farm Livestock Wastes,* HMSO (1976).
Leach, G. *Energy and Food Production,* International Institute for Environment and Development (1975).
Nix J., *Farm Management Pocket Book* (6th ed), Wye College (1974).
Moore I., (ed) *The Agricultural Notebook (16th ed),* Newnes-Butterworths (1976).

Farm Buildings

Bibliography of farm building research (miscellaneous reports), HMSO.
Culpin, C., *Farm mechanisation management,* Crosby-Lockwood.
Farm electrification handbook (series), The Electricity Council.
Harvey, N., *History of farm buildings,* David & Charles (1971).
MAFF, *Farm building bulletins (sundry subjects),* HMSO.
MAFF, *Farm buildings pocket book,* HMSO.
MAFF, *Fixed equipment on the farm (series of leaflets),* HMSO.
Potato storage (miscellaneous reports), Potato Marketing Board.
Report of the technical committee to enquire into the welfare of animals kept under intensive livestock husbandry systems, HMSO (1965).
Sainsbury, D., *Pig housing,* Farming Press (1971).
Smith, P. C., *Stables,* W. H. Allen (1967).

Journals and Reports

'Farm Buildings Digest' (Quarterly). Published by Farm Buildings Centre.
'Farm Building Progress' (Quarterly). Published by Scottish Farms Building Investigation Unit.
Journal of the Farm Buildings Association (Annual).
Farm Buildings Information Centre: Building Reports (see Table 6.19).
Farm Buildings Information: Project Sheets (see Table 6.20).
Scottish Farm Buildings Investigation Unit: Farm Building Progress (see Table 6.21).
Farm Building Cost Guide. SFBIU (Annual).

John B. Weller, *A.R.I.B.A., Dip. Arch. (Birmingham School of Architecture). National Farmers Union Research Fellow for Farm Buildings 1958/59. Has been in private practice since 1960, specialising in agricultural, rural and conservation work. Part-time lecturer at the Department of Planning, Chelmer Institute. Member of the Design Council Farm Buildings Committee; the BSI Farm and Horticultural Buildings Committee and Vice-Chairman of 'Architects in Agriculture' Group. Council member of the Suffolk Building Preservation Trust and member of the Society for the Protection of Rural England, the Vernacular Architecture Group and Landscape Research Group. John Weller has written many papers and articles and is the author of* Farm Buildings—Vols 1 and 2 *(Crosby Lockwood) and* Modern Agriculture and Rural Planning *(Architectural Press).*

7 FACTORIES

PAUL DARRINGTON, A.R.I.B.A., A.I.Arb

INTRODUCTION

DEFINITIONS

Factory

Almost all formal definitions include reference to 'Trade' and 'Manufacture'. The Factories Act, 1961, includes both terms, and specifically includes external and ancilliary spaces. From the designer's view, a more functional definition is helpful. This could be:

A Factory comprises a defined set of spaces in which materials, energy and men are brought together for the purpose of producing a given set of end products.

It is important to realise that the three introduced elements are each necessary; even in a fully automated workshop, for example, men are an implied element, even if only for supervision or maintenance. Further it should be realised that waste is an implied by-product of any such process.

Workshop

This term is virtually synonymous with 'factory', although it is frequently used in reference to a particular part of a factory building. There is no legal or functional distinction.

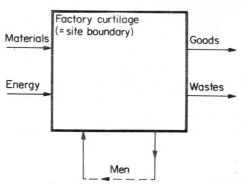

Fig. 7.1   Fundamental requirements of industry

Flatted factories

Again, there is no legal or functional distinction, except the implied problem of transportation due to differences of level. It is usually applied to a group of tenement premises in one structure. The 2nd Schedule and 55, 120–122 of the Factories Act, 1961, in these cases, transfers some of the obligations from the occupier to the owner(s. 157 of the Act). The general implication is that the flatted factory is a speculative *building* which here is referred to as 'Unit Factories'.

Unit factories

These are those that are built for sale or lease, and as such, the fabric may be designed without knowledge of the process or purpose to which it may be put. Thus the designer may act only on quite generalised information. The implications of this, and the result that definite physical restrictions (by reason of the structure) are created in advance of the use, tend to restrict the use of such buildings to a limited class of industry, which may generally be referred to as 'light'.

CLASSIFICATION OF INDUSTRY

The first classification has already been given above, i.e. that of known or unknown purpose. A word of warning about the use of the term 'light industry' should be added, as it is not strictly defined, referring variously to the amount of manual work involved, the amount of energy required in the process, or the size and specialisation of the plant or machinery employed. A further classification is given in the Use Classes Order, 1963 (see sub-section on Legislation) which is concerned with the general environmental effects of siting.

For the designer's purpose the following classification is suggested:

Primary industry. Those processes which require plant, machinery and transportation facilities of such scale that these parts must be built in-situ; e.g. steelworks, mines, etc.

Secondary industry. Processes requiring special or fixed facilities of building, plant, services or environmental conditions, arranged in a given production sequence or sequences.

Tertiary industry. Those processes which require only general facilities not necessarily permanently fixed.

Thus, while it will be seen that these three definitions correspond roughly to the concepts of 'heavy', 'medium' and 'light', they are given in functional terms, meaningful to the designer.

PRIMARY ANALYSIS

The ideal of any factory production manager is to obtain the smoothest and optimum continual flow of materials though the system which his factory represents. This is why flow diagrams are so much used by production engineers. They are, of course closely analogous to architects' circulation diagrams. Hence the problems of design are simplified in principle by reason of an overriding aim, but may be complex in solution by reasons of many necessary

subsidiary functions and restrictions (see Fig. 7.2).

FLOW AND STORAGE OF MATERIALS

Certain methods of production and transportation provide batch movement, others continuous flow (e.g. delivery by vehicle compared with delivery by conveyor belt). It is thus almost always necessary to provide holding stores at the start and finish and at various points during the process, within the curtilage of the factory (see Fig. 7.3).

The storage facilities for solid materials (not services) are exactly analogous in most cases to warehouses and reference to Section 8 should be made for the design of these. For raw materials in liquid or gaseous (or finely divided solids analogous to fluids) states special silos or tanks etc., must be provided. Since the transport of raw materials and finished goods to and from the site is frequently by the same system, loading and unloading may be considered in some cases the same basic function. This has advantages for control and supervision, and amends the basic analysis diagram as given in the following paragraphs.

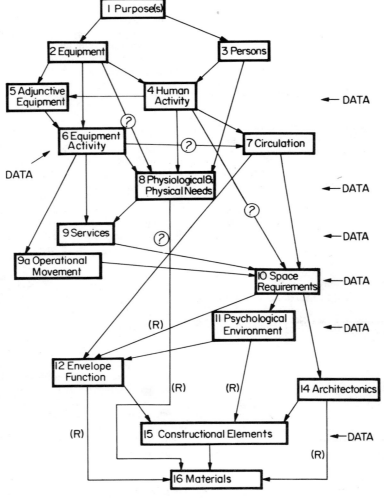

Fig. 7.2   Design process information flow

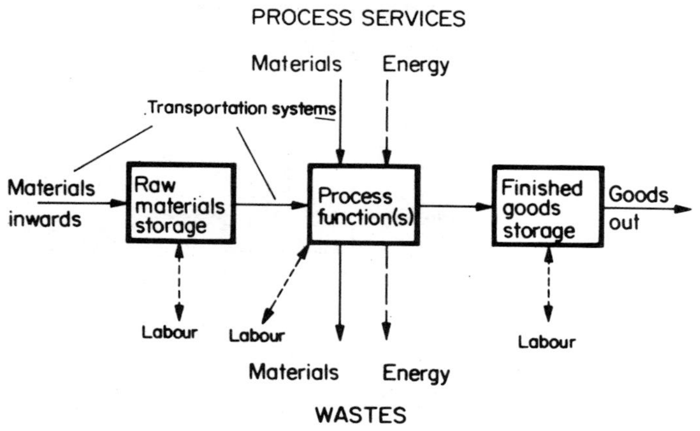

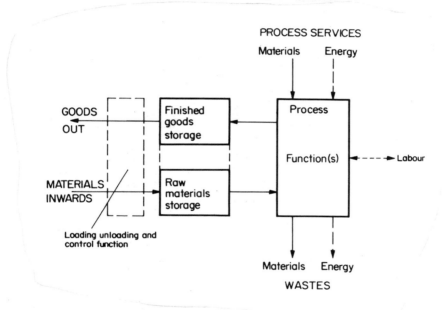

Fig. 7.3 *Basic materials flow. It should be noted that work is frequently carried out in the storage area which then come under the Factories Act, and also may require materials and produce waste (e.g. packaging materials)*

Fig. 7.4 *Basic materials flow showing unified loading and unloading*

PROCESS FLOW

Process flows may be broken down into operations or work-elements. These may be automatic machine tools linked to the next by conveyors, or they could be work-stations for manual or man-controlled operations on the embrionic product. At each such operation the introduction of the three requirements, materials, energy and manpower, will be necessary in principle. It should be noted that the work throughput at each operation may be either flow or batch.

Frequently the production flow may be branched and parallel flows exist simultaneously, either by reason of, say, assembly and manufacture of components of the product carried out in the same factory, or by the need to deal with by-products. In the first case correlation of flow rates and the design of holding storage is critical.

BY-PRODUCTS

In all processes there are by-products, even if they are all known as 'waste'. Where they are valuable or saleable the holding storage and subsequent processing (forming a sub-sidiary process) or transportation becomes part of the basic design problem. Where they form a nuisance or a local or public health hazard, the existence of this factor should be determined at the earliest possible stage (see sub-section on Planning).

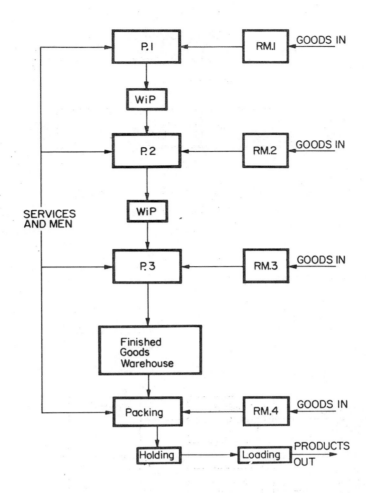

Fig. 7.5   Process flow sequential operations

PROVISION OF ENERGY

Apart from the normal building services (the requirements for which follow from the manpower requirements) the provision of energy is the second primary need. It will be closely related to the process and technology available and in many primary and secondary industries will represent a major part of the capital investment needed. The scale, siting and servicing of these important subsidiaries must be considered at the outset.

Combined Energy Centres are often considered, being economic in maintenance, but this notion should be balanced against the capital costs of extended services mains, the security and integrity of the whole (or a critical part of the) factory, and the likely costs, in the event of a central breakdown. Clearly the best theoretical site for the energy source is at the centroid of the points of consumption, weighted by their individual consumption rates. Considerations of access,

maintenance and safety may well modify this. Where energy is provided by boiler plant and the like the problem of fuel storage and supply should be first established, (see Fig. 7.7).

PROVISION OF OTHER PROCESS SERVICES

Process services requirements should be checked against the process flow schematic and every input and output should be accounted for, (including waste disposal services). The CI/SfB schedules (50) to (69) may also serve as a useful secondary check. An amplified list is shown in Table 7.1. The form and rate of supply of water and other consumable or disposable materials also come under this heading, and whether movement is continuous or batch, the rate of supply required will determine the buffer storage requirements and hence the space requirements. Supply, maintenance and access needs should again be considered at this stage.

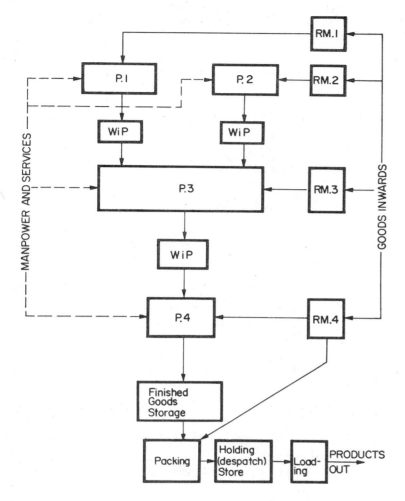

Fig 7.6   Process flow parallel and branched operations

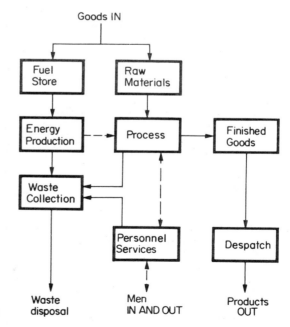

Fig. 7.7   Provision of energy to the process

Table 7.1 CHECKLIST OF SERVICES REQUIREMENTS
Based upon SfB table 3 (50) to (79)

(50) SITE SERVICES
All external services requirements outside building not associated directly with building function:

50.1 Site Refuse Centre

50.2 Site Drainage
    50.2.1 Land drainage and water run-off control, soakaways, etc.
    50.2.2 Surface water drainage from paved areas, roads and paths.
    50.2.3 Petrol interception and contamination control and pre-treatment.

50.3 Site Water Services
    Water supplies for site use, decoration, etc.

50.4 Site Gas Services

50.5 Site Refrigeration

50.6 Site Heating
    50.6.1 Frost prevention services to roads, paths, sports grounds etc.
    50.6.2 Heating to external areas.

50.7 Site Ventilation

50.8 Site Process Services

(51) REFUSE DISPOSAL
Handling, storage, treatment and disposal of discrete solid wastes.

51.1 Incineration

51.2 Refuse Chutes and Collection Areas

51.3 Crushing and Baling Equipment

51.4 Treatment and Sorting Equipment

51.5 Decontamination and Isolation Equipment for Noxious or Dangerous Wastes

51.6 Sanitary Incinerators

(52) DRAINAGE
Collection and disposal above and below ground of liquid and water-borne wastes originating in the buildings, or working and storage areas.

52.1 Surface Water
    52.1.1 Rainwater goods and rainwater pipes.
    52.1.2 Rainwater drains.
    52.1.3 Yard drainage, petrol interceptors.
    52.1.4 Disposal of rainwater to drains, soakaways, natural watercourses, etc.

52.2 Foul Wastes Collection
    52.2.1 Human soil and wastes.
    52.2.2 Contaminated wastes, e.g. laboratory and process wastes.
    52.2.3 Waste oils.
    52.2.4 Sediment-bearing wastes.

52.3 Waste Treatment
    Pre-disposal treatment for contaminated or valuable wastes. (e.g. ion-exchange, sedimentation, dilution, chemical neutralisation or precipitation).

52.4 Outfalls and Disposal
    52.4.1 Mains connections.
    52.4.2 Cesspits.
    52.4.3 Septic plants.

(53) HOT AND COLD WATER SERVICES
All water pumping and water distribution services excluding water consumed in process installations and fire-fighting water and hydraulic mains.

53.1 Cold Water Services
    53.1.1 Gravity CWS.
    53.1.2 Pressure CWS.
    53.1.3 Drinking water services.
    53.1.4 Constant pressure services.
    53.1.5 Chilled water supply.

53.2 Treated CV Services
    53.2.1 Distilled.
    53.2.2 Demineralised.
    53.2.3 Deionised.
    53.2.4 Asceptic e.g. chlorinated.
    53.2.5 Other treated waters.

53.3 Hot Water Services
    53.3.1 Gravity.
    53.3.2 Pressurised.
    53.3.3 Constant pressure.
    53.3.4 Constant temperature.

53.4 Water Heating Equipment
    53.4.1 Centralised.
    53.4.2 Local.
    53.4.3 Valves and control gear.
    53.4.4 Insulation and protection.

(54) GAS SERVICES
All gaseous distribution including steam and vacuum services.

54.1 Fuel Gases
    54.1.1 Town's gas, normal pressure.

    54.1.2 Town's gas, boosted pressure.
    54.1.3 Cylinder and explosive gases (e.g. hydro-carbons).

54.2 Power Gases
    54.2.1 H.P. Steam.
    54.2.2 L.P. Steam.
    54.2.3 Compressed air.
    54.2.4 Vacuum.

54.3 Process Gases
    54.3.1 Compressed air supply, including compressor plant.
    54.3.2 Oxygen.
    54.3.3 Inert gases.
    54.3.4 Poisonous gases.

54.4 Medical Gases

(55) REFRIGERATION SERVICES
All cooling requirements and media excluding air conditioning (56) and chilled water (53.1.6)

55.1 Cooling water

55.2 Cooling Liquids (other than water).

55.3 Cooling Air
    Local units (e.g. cold rooms) including refrigerants, compressors, etc.

(56) SPACE HEATING SERVICES
Heating and temperature control for environmental (but not process) purposes.

Table 7.1 – *continued*

FACTORIES

56.1 Primary Equipment
56.1.1 Boiler equipment.
56.1.2 Heating fuel equipment, including fuel storage and delivery equipment.
56.1.3 Fume and smoke removal, flues, etc.
56.1.4 Energy conversation and control equipment, calorifiers.
56.1.5 Energy circulation equipment, pumps, fans, etc, as applicable.

56.2 Energy Distribution Services
56.2.1 H.P. Steam.
56.2.2 L.P. Steam.
56.2.3 HPHW.
56.2.4 LPHW.
56.2.5 Oils.
56.2.6 Salt Solutions.
56.2.7 Electrical.
56.2.8 Cooling water.
56.2.9 Air ducts (plenum and A/C systems).

56.3 Equipment and Fittings
56.3.1 Radiation.
56.3.2 Convection.
56.3.3 Air conditioning units (local).

56.4 Control System
56.4.1 Thermostatic circuits.
56.4.2 Humidistat circuits.
56.4.3 Timing controls.

(57) VENTILATION SERVICES
Atmospheric environmental control, excluding process ventilation (58) and ventilation air used as space heating distribution medium (56).

57.1 Supply
57.1.1 Natural controlled.
57.1.2 Controlled tempered (warmed) temperature controlled.
57.1.3 Filtration and contamination control.
57.1.4 Humidification control (conditioned air).

57.2 Extract
57.2.1 Dirty.
57.2.2 Dusty.
57.2.3 Dangerous (explosive, oil, paint, etc).

(58) PROCESS SERVICES:

Sports and Recreational Centres
58.1 Fuel oil storage and pumping:
Petrol
Diesel.
Vapourising.
Two-strokes.
Any others.
58.2 Lubrication oil storage
58.3 Pool water services:
Pumping.
Filtration.
Chlorination.
Heating.
Refrigeration (ice visitors).
58.4 Ground floodlighting.
58.5 Timekeeping installations:
Auto recording.
Starting gates and signals.
58.6 Automatic Scoring, Scoreboard Equipment and services.

58.7 Mechanical Services for adjustable or mobile sports equipment.
58.8 Sun and Lighting Control.
58.9 BBC/ITV Broadcasting facilities:
Studios.
Commentating boxes.
Aerials.
Vehicle parking spaces.
Temporary cableways.

(60) SITE INSTALLATIONS
Electrical and security installations on site not directly required by building or process.

60.1 Site Power

60.2 Site Electricity, Sub-stations and primary distribution installations.

60.3 Site Illumination
60.3.1 Road lighting.
60.3.2 Footpath lighting.
60.3.3 Floodlighting.
60.3.4 Decorative lighting.
60.3.5 Illuminated advertising signs.

60.4 Site Communications

60.6 Site Transportation
60.6.1 Lifts.
60.6.2 Hoists.
60.6.3 Gantries.
60.6.4 Cranes.
60.6.5 Escalators.
60.6.6 Travelators, etc.

60.8 Site Security Installations (can include illumination, see 60.3, above).

(61) PRIMARY POWER AND ENGINE INSTALLATIONS

61.1 Heat pumps and exchangers

61.2 Transformers

61.3 Generators, primary and standby.

61.4 Engines (mechanical transmission).

61.5 Compressors and air pumps

61.6 Hydraulic power mains and equipment

(62) ELECTRICAL POWER DISTRIBUTION INSTALLATIONS
Building electrical power distribution and control excluding illumination (63) and communications (64).

62.1 MV AC Supplies
62.1.1 Distribution switch and protection equipment.
62.1.2 Sub-main and sub-transformation equipment.
62.1.3 Power socket outlets, fittings and equipment connections.

62.2 Constant Voltage Supplies

62.3 HV Distribution

62.4 MV Distribution

62.5 LV Distribution

62.6 ELV Distribution

62.7 DC Distribution

62.8 Rectified Current Distribution

62.9 Special Supplies Distribution

Table 7.1 – *continued*

(63) ILLUMINATION INSTALLATIONS
Provision for artificial illumination.

63.1 Distribution and Control Equipment

63.2 Inter-connection Switching

63.3 Lighting fittings
    63.3.1 Tungsten.
    63.3.2 Fluorescent.
    63.3.3 Cold cathode.
    63.3.4 Mixed.

63.4 Pilot and Police Lighting

63.5 Display Lighting

63.6 Decorative Lighting

63.9 Special Purpose Lighting
    63.9.1 Theatrical.
    63.9.2 Operating theatres.
    63.9.3 Inspection.
    63.9.4 High acuity illumination.

(64) COMMUNICATIONS INSTALLATIONS
E.L.V. electrical and other installations for conveyance of visual, audio and coded information.

64.1 Clocks
    64.1.1 Time clocks.
    64.1.2 Master and slave systems.
    64.1.3 Synchronous clocks.

64.2 Staff Location, Personnel call systems (including radio)

64.3 TV, Radio Distribution and Aerials

64.4 Bells, Buzzers and Alarms (not security)

64.5 Audio-call, public address

64.6 Cinema Sound

64.7 Speech Reinforcement

64.8 Central Dictation

64.9 Telephones
    64.9.1 G.P.O.
    64.9.2 Internal.
    64.9.3 Intercommunication.

64.10 Teleprinters

64.11 Monitoring Systems

64.12 Pneumatic Tube

64.13 Closed Circuit Television

64.14 Illuminated Signs and Advertisements

(65) ADMINISTRATION AND CONTROL SYSTEMS
Systems and methods of performance control not necessarily relying on physical services or installations, but which often have fundamental influences on planning.

65.1 Activity Data Analysis

65.2 Plant Layout and Operational Methods

65.3 Pollution and Waste Disposal

65.4 Industrial Physics

65.5 Environmental Analysis

65.6 Legislation and Insurance

65.7 Operational Safety
    65.7.1 Personnel.
    65.7.2 Industrial Hazards.
    65.7.3 Fire and Explosion Risks.

65.8 Energy Analysis
    65.8.1 Fuel economics.
    65.8.2 Fuel tariffs.
    65.8.3 Total heat concepts.

65.9 Stock Control
    65.9.1 Movement.
    65.9.2 Storage.
    65.9.3 Identification and coding.

65.10 Transportation and Distribution Analysis

(66) TRANSPORTATION
Installations for the conveyance of people.

66.1 Travelators

66.2 Escalators

66.3 Passenger lifts
    66.3.1 Electric.
    66.3.2 Hydraulic.
    66.3.3 Electro-hydraulic.
    66.3.4 Paternoster.

66.4 Bed Lifts

66.5 Passenger/Goods Lifts

66.6 Special Lifts

(68) SECURITY SYSTEMS
Services and installations concerned with the control and warning of hazards.

68.1 Fire
    68.1.1 Auto-fire control:
    Gas.
    Steam.
    Pneumatic-powder.
    Sprinklers and drenchers.
    Foam.
    Ventilation.
    68.1.2 Manual Equipment
    68.1.3 Dry risers, foam inlets.
    68.1.4 Fire Alarms:
    Auto-head detection.
    Auto-smoke detection.
    Manual local.
    Public and fire station warning.

68.2 Watchman's Call

68.3 Burglar, Intrusion and Bandit Alarms

68.4 Safety, control Warning Beams

68.5 Safety and Control Automatic Barriers

68.6 Closed Circuit TV Monitoring

68.7 Electrical Protection
    68.7.1 Lightning protection.
    68.7.2 Static earthing.

68.8 Pressure Warning Installations

68.9 Vermin Protection and Control

Table 7.1 – *continued*

(73) CULINARY FIXTURES
Catering, Cooking and Bar Equipment, excluding chilled water services (53.1.6).

73.1 Storage Equipment

73.2 Refrigerators

73.3 Sinks, Waste-disposal Units, Preparation Equipment

73.4 Cooking Equipment

73.5 Serving Equipment (including Hot Closets)

73.6 Washing-Up Equipment

73.7 Bar Equipment

(74) SANITARY FIXTURES

74.1 Soil
    74.1.1 WCs and Closets.
    74.1.2 Urinals.

74.2 Bathing
    74.2.1 Baths.
    74.2.2 Showers, Fittings and cabinets.

74.3 Washing
    74.3.1 Bidets.
    74.3.2 Footbaths.
    74.3.3 Lavatory basins, washing troughs.

74.5 Cleansing Media
    74.5.1 Soap dispensers, liquid soap services.
    74.5.3 Special cleansing liquids.

74.6 Drying
    Towel rails, dispensers, hand dryers.

74.7 Mirrors

74.8 Drinking Fountains

(75) CLEANING FIXTURES
Fixtures and services directly required by cleaning operations.

75.1 Window Cleaning Equipment, cradles, etc.

75.2 Laundry, clothes washing equipment.

75.3 Clothes Drying Equipment

75.4 Cleaners Fittings, cleaners sinks, slop sinks etc.

75.5 Dry Cleaning Equipment

75.6 Vacuum Cleaning, installation and fixtures.

PERSONNEL REQUIREMENTS

The Factories Act, 1961, and the Health and Safety at Work, etc. Act, 1974, are essentially concerned with the safety, health and welfare of personnel, and cover such subjects as the requirements for workers in noxious industries (such as asbestos works) to more general topics as the numbers and design of lavatory accommodation. Having determined the process and its manpower needs, a check should be made on the substances and processes to which special regulations are applicable (see Bibliography). These may demand special safety and environmental services closely allied to the process, and must be defined.

Secondly, the general welfare requirements, such as canteens, rest and recreation spaces, should be considered. This would include staff car parking and other external facilities, which may well influence the external circulation requirements.

The problems arising from shift-working may also modify the requirements, by reason of additional numbers and the unusual hours, affecting most aspects of ancilliary accommodation.

CIRCULATION

This means the circulation of staff. The movement of goods and materials has been defined, and one now needs to design the access of all staff in connection with the process within the entire factory system. Staff here includes *all within the factory gates*, including workpeople, supervisory staff and maintenance men, as well as those working in subsidiary functions such as offices, canteens, first-aid, quality control etc, and possibly visitors.

A good circulation with few crossing paths as possible will provide for optimum control and security of staff and visitors (both casual and regular) the safety of all personnel, the efficient movement of people and goods, as well as contributing to the total integrity of the process in the event of a partial failure. Where crossed circulation cannot be avoided, such points should be confined to paths of intermittent traffic, and be examined and designed with a view to the physical detailing ameliorating the disadvantages of the crossing.

Tables 7.1 and 7.2 show checklists for factory functions and departments and energy services requirements. A checklist for personnel services is given in the following sub-section.

Table 7.2 CHECKLIST OF FUNCTIONS AND DEPARTMENTS OF A FACTORY

1. Gatehouse:
      security; barriers + gates; checking; weighbridge; timeclocks,
      gatehouse staff, lavs, mess; telephone
2. Unloading Bays:
      road; rail
3. Raw Materials Warehouse (Goods inwards):
      Materials used, classified by phase (solid, finely divided solid, liquid, gas); classified by mode of delivery, bulk quantity,
      handling unit; security risks
4. Manufacturing Areas (workplaces):
      Holding stores for work-in-process
5. Finished Goods Warehouse:
      Variety of manufactures (classified as Raw Materials)
6. Packing Department—preparation for shipment:
      packing materials store (classified as Warehouse);
      packed goods holding store
7. Loading Bay:
      vehicles used; type and size of unit handled; checking; offices
8. Quality Control Laboratory:
      offices
9. Administration Offices
10. Design Offices
11. Maintenance:
      Offices;
      Stores;
      Staff facilities
12. Vehicle Parking:
      internal transport;
      staff;
      visitors;
      contractors/suppliers vehicles;
      maintenance and service;
      fuelling

Table 7.3 CHECK-LIST OF ENERGY SERVICES REQUIREMENTS

1. Energy
   1.1 Transformers, electrical supply
   1.2 Stand-by generation
   1.3 Boiler plant, fuel storage
   1.4 Refrigeration plant (provides heat as waste)
   1.5 Mechanical power transmition source
   1.6 Pneumatic power plant;
       Compressed air/vacuum plant
       (usually localised)
   1.7 Hydraulic power plant
2. Waste
   2.1 Storage
   2.2 Disposal

Table 7.4 FUNDAMENTAL CLASSIFICATION OF MATERIALS

| Solids | | | | Fluids | | |
				Liquids		Gases
large units	small units	finely divided	with solids in suspension	viscous	non-viscous	gases

SPACIAL REQUIREMENTS

QUANTIFICATION OF FLOWS

Having established the flow process with the production engineers, it is necessary to quantify the flows related to the total design throughputs. Where the process changes from batch working to continuous flow (which may be frequent, occurring at many points in the process) the holding storage requirements to maintain the continuity of the process can be determined. Statistical methods may have to be used, especially where variable flows or working conditions will be experienced, and in such cases specialist advise should be obtained.

It is very important that work to this stage should be done in close collaboration with the production engineers and the Works Manager, as the spacial requirements of the process areas will closely follow the decisions made, and the economy of the whole factory may be closely entailed.

UNIT WORKING

The current tendency to modify mass-production techniques in the interests of workers' 'job-satisfaction' is interesting in that it may well change the typical production flow process and hence the process flow and personnel circulation requirements. More space may have to be allocated to transportation and to staff facilities, and more attention to the analysis of the work station required. Where this is not fully understood, Activity Data Analysis can be useful technique.

ACTIVITY DATA ANALYSIS

In principle this technique may be applied to all processes in which work on goods or materials is performed. With modern machine-tools and automatic processes the analysis has been done in the design of the plant, and the space and services requirements and other design data required by the architect is or should be available from the manufacturer.

Where skilled labour or a number of operations is carried out at the same work-station, activity data analysis was devised to determine the logical and necessary design requirements for the efficient execution of the tasks.

WORK IN PROGRESS

This implies a space requirement in the process being considered, in which partially manufactured goods are temporarily stored while awaiting the subsequent work operation. For efficient use of machine tools the amount of work stored must be adequate to permit maximum working throughput, the space being considered as a holding or buffer-store.

Its capacity will be determined by the rates and frequency of both input and output in *relation to the store*. In some processes, notably those which are predominant batch movement, work in progress can take up a large proportion of floor space, and so should be reduced to a minimum consistant with the maximum economic idle time of the machines and workers. The concept is of the greatest importance when considering the dimensions to transcribe the agreed circulation or flow-diagram into a plan.

BULK OF MATERIALS, COMPONENTS AND PRODUCTS

This idea is central to the solution of storage space, transportation, the production flow, as well as process services. See Table 7.4 for the basic classification.

The flow routes of each constituent in the process has to be integrated into the system, providing the basic requirements of transportation and holding storage. Large bulk solids offer particular problems in space allocation, e.g. where they are long and thin or particularly heavy. Finely-divided solids and the fluids have to be checked for safety requirements, e.g. fire and explosion, leakage, and environmental hazards (see sub-section on 'Planning').

Where storage and handling of goods uses pallets or stillages (see Section 8 'Warehouses'), the pallet should be considered the physical unit (module) of work-in-progress in production areas where it is introduced. It thus becomes a large discrete unit solid for the purposes of transportation and space requirements. Note also that questions of stock rotation may influence the disposition, plan shape or access requirements of work-in-progress areas.

INSURANCE REQUIREMENTS

It is as well to check any particular insurance requirements which would influence the form or construction of the building, especially where the factory is to contain a new process. A common example is the reduction in fire insurance premiums for processes and materials (e.g. timber) where sprinklers are installed. The necessary equipment, such as pressure tanks, can take up appreciable space.

CHECK LIST: UNLOADING

Facilities required for unloading clearly depend upon:
Transport and method of delivery.
Form of material (see Table 7.3).
Unit bulk of material.
Quantity of single delivery.
Packaging materials to be discarded.
Handling method from unloading to storage.
Frequency of deliveries.
Checking and security measures necessary (see Fig. 7.8).

CHECK LIST: PACKING

Facilities required for packing depend upon:
Size and function of Finished Goods Store, whether it is a holding store or main warehouse.
Form of transport after despatch.
Destination of goods.
Fragility or risk of breakages.
Through-put of department.
Security and accounting requirements.
Labelling.
Number of lines of finished goods.
Bulk and form of finished goods.

FINISHED GOODS STORAGE

The requirements for packing also bear upon those for the Finished Goods Store, to which should be added:
Storage life, and stock rotation.
Handling and transportation within Finished Goods Area. (For design of stores see Section 8 'Warehouses).

SORTING

This is a space-consuming activity which is often very necessary. In effect it is the problem of a holding store spread out onto a single level, increasing the areal extent, together with the requirements of transportation and working space. It may simply be a corner of a warehouse; but its size is a function of the number of product lines proposed (see Fig. 7.9).

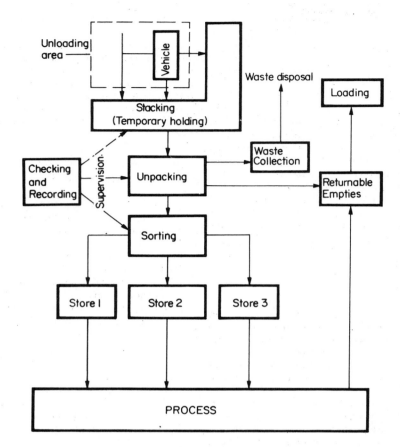

Fig. 7.8 Form of unloading area

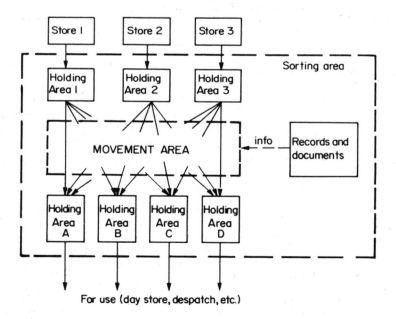

Fig. 7.9 Sorting

CHECK LIST: ANCILLARY AND STAFF ACCOMMODATION

Ancillary and staff accommodation will probably include most of the following units:

Visitors' reception and waiting.
Administrative office.
Quality control laboratories.
Production supervision and shop floor offices.
Design offices.
Production maintenance stores and workshops.
Building maintenance stores.
Gatehouse and vehicle control.
Car park.
Lorry parking.
Weighbridge.
Locker/changing rooms.
Clothing storage (protective clothing).
Laundry.
Lavatories/showers/baths.
Rest rooms/smoking areas.
Recreational facilities.
Canteens and mess rooms.
Printing shop.
Emergency showers/personnel safety equipment.
Building and process service accommodation (see Table 7.2).

PLANNING GENERALLY

This phase clearly follows from the Process and circulation Flow Diagram, taking into account the operational space required for:

Plant.
Plant operation and personnel activity.
Maintenance.
Work in progress.
Transportation.
Personnel circulation, access and safety (including Means of Escape).
Visual control.
Process services.
Personnel ancillaries.

Add to this the assessed need for flexibility, future alterations in process, and possible expansion. The plan may well be influenced by process *time* and conveyor speeds, e.g. glass-fibre parts fabrication, where the rate of drying in the process and conveyor speeds determine the space requirement. Fig. 7.10 shows low process space requirements influenced by production process rates/time factor.

EXAMPLE 1:

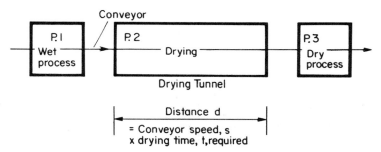

NB: This is also work in progress

Example 1: Where conveyors and process time are parameters

EXAMPLE 2:

If P2 is duplicated, WiP = 0 (theoretically)
If P2 is not duplicated, WiP = (2x−x)(difference in operating hours)
Units of storage

In this case down-time on P2 is half operating time on P1

Example 2: Where process activities have varying production rates

Fig. 7.10   Flow process space requirements

BUILDING CONSIDERATIONS: HEIGHT AND SECTION

These can be influenced by:

Transportation (clear height of overhead conveyors, cranage etc.)

Working height of process.

Access and maintenance.

Gravity-feed systems.

Crossed circulations.

High level supervision.

High level services distribution (aid to flexibility).

A clear height of 5·2–5·5 m allows 2-storey planning within the building space. This is advantageous, the additional inherent flexibility enhancing its capital value in event of later sale or adaptation of production process.

Fig. 7.11 shows a typical section showing 2-storey ancilliary spaces within production height.

Table 7.5 TYPICAL FACTORY CLEAR INTERNAL HEIGHTS

Light craft workshops* c. 2·9 m to service zone	Medium craft workshops 3·35 m to service zone	Heavy workshops and main factory process 5·2 m min. (but check for special process requirements)

*Typified by: Small machines, small produce and materials, skilled labour, bench work etc, (e.g. tailors, plumbers).

Note: With overhead 2-way cranage the overhead operational zone is occupied and is not available for local services distribution.

STRUCTURAL PLANNING GRIDS

Limited by same factors as under Planning Generally, but in particular maximum sizes of artifacts, transportation requirements, especially long thin bodies, (e.g. timber scantlings or steel sections) and the attitude required for subsequent operations. These may have to be turned and turning positions and radii carefully planned. Fig. 7.13 shows dimensional areas relating to fork-lift trucks.

In general, the larger the span (subject to economic structural engineering considerations and capital cost) provision is made for better flexibility for future use or alterations.

Where process requirements are given, the structural grid will be determined by the need to avoid impediment to the better flexibility for future use or alterations.

Careful analysis and matching of the freedom of the building plan shape and the process should be made.

Fig. 7.14 illustrates a plan showing typical relationship between Process Flow, operational space requirements and structural grid.

NOTE ON STRUCTURAL COSTS

It has always been difficult to generalise on costs, if only because of the difficulty of definition of items included when making comparisons. In the early 1960's several studies were conducted, but these are of limited usefulness today by

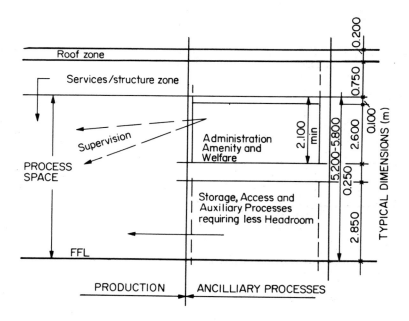

Fig. 7.11   Two-storey ancillary spaces

reason of changes in relative values and of standards. It is possible however to go a little beyond the statement that an increased specification will increase the cost. Very crudely, for a single-storey structure the basic costs, excluding finishes and services and special items, an increase in height will result in an increase in cost at a quite low ratio; e.g. given the basic building, increasing (solely) its height by, say, 50% will increase cost by only, say, 10%. Obviously this will vary by the ratio of vertical elements (particularly external walls), to the plan area.

By contrast, a very much increased proportion of costs can be incurred by sophistication of the roof structure, e.g. by the introduction of monitor rooflights. Similarly, by increasing the span the structural costs will rise in proportion approximately to the square of the span.

LOADING DOCKS

Fig. 7.15 gives dimensions of loading bays for dock levellers and Fig. 7.16 gives dimensions for railway sidings.

Fig. 7.17 gives general settings-out data for road, rail un-loading functions (see also section on Vehicle Turning Data in volume *Planning: Architects' Technical Reference Data*).

TRANSPORTATION

The choice of process transportation system clearly follows the operational process requirements and early consultation with the production engineering advisor is useful. These decisions influence the space and structural (dimensions and superimposed loads) requirements and hence should be defined before the conclusion of the outline design.

Low-level linear systems (e.g. belt conveyors, etc) can provide a continuous barrier to other circulation routes at that level and in particular personnel circulation. Means of Escape may become critical and in the solution of such crossed-circulation problems escape routes may rise only in exceptional circumstances. The supply routes of materials required at intermediate points in the process may also be affected and the total circulation of process and personnel also should be checked at this stage.

Fig. 7.18 illustrates belt conveyors, showing G.A., setting-out limitations effect on other circulation. Fig. 7.19 shows typical setting-out details for overhead unit conveyors.

Table 7.6 PROCESS TRANSPORTATION MATERIALS CONVEYANCE SYSTEMS

1. POWER INSTALLATIONS FOR CONVEYANCE, HANDLING AND CONTROL OF SOLID MATERIALS:	
1.1 *Turntables*	For altering attitude of large or heavy units or vehicles
1.2 *Horizontal linear conveyance* Pallet and unit conveyors Drag-link conveyors Belt conveyors Cradles	Can change level in space and be overhead
Air cushion conveyors	Operate on one level only; free horizontal travel, locomotive
1.3 *Horizontal and vertical conveyance* Gantries	Fixed position; limited horizontal travel
Mono-rails	Unlimited horizontal travel; can be considered as linear conveyor
Gravity feed systems	Do not require power
1.4 *Three dimension conveyance* Fork-lift trucks	Locomotive: limited vertical travel; non-linear horizontal travel
Two-way travelling cranes	As above but system has definite rectangular boundary
Mobile jibs and derricks	Horizontal and vertical travel limits
1.5 *Vertical conveyors* Goods lifts Platform hoists	
1.6 *Automatic stacking, control and retrieval systems* Electronically, computer controlled	Used in automated ware-houses; in principle can be linked to production processes
1.7 *Battery charging systems*	For electric locomotive systems; (strictly speaking a specialised energy distribution point, but necessarily concerned with transportation systems)
2. FINELY DIVIDED SOLIDS, POWDERS, ETC, PNEUMATIC CONVEYANCE SYSTEMS	Linear (See also Fire and Explosion Risks in sub-section on Planning)
3. FLUID CONVEYANCE HYDRAULIC CONVEYANCE SYSTEMS	Piped systems generally, linear

STATUTORY

Table 7.7 ACTS OF PARLIAMENT WHICH CAN INFLUENCE LAYOUT AND CIRCULATION (AND HENCE SPACE REQUIREMENTS)
(See also sub-section on Legislation)

Shops Offices and Railway Premises Act, 1963	Personnel amenities
Factories Act, 1961	Gangways and catwalks; Space round plant; Vessels and pits; Space round self-acting machinery
Noise Abatement Act, 1960	Influence of neighbourhood
Public Health Acts, 1939, 1961	Access to street; Access to stores and warehouses
Clean Air Act, 1956	Grit and dirt extraction
Highways Act, 1959	Access
Water Resources Act, 1963	Taking of water, discharges to natural water courses
Building Regulations, SI, 1972/317	General, especially section E, fire precautions
London Building Acts, 1930 and 1939	Section 20, excess cube, etc, enabling legislation
Health & Safety at work Act, 1974	Increasing future influence (see also sub-section on Legislation)
Petroleum Acts, 1928 and 1936	Use of liquid with flash-point less than 65°C
Explosives Acts, 1875, 1923	Separate buildings, storage and use of explosive substances

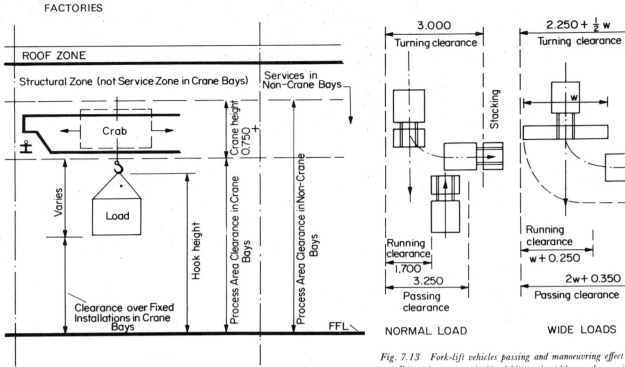

ROOF ZONE

Structural Zone (not Service Zone in Crane Bays)

Services in Non-Crane Bays

Crab

Load

Varies

Hook height

Crane height 0.750 +

Process Area Clearance in Crane Bays

Process Area Clearance in Non-Crane Bays

Clearance over Fixed Installations in Crane Bays

FFL

Fig 7.12   2-way cranage : Effect on production area section

3.000
Turning clearance

Stacking

Running clearance
1.700

3.250
Passing clearance

NORMAL LOAD

$2.250 + \frac{1}{2}w$
Turning clearance

Stacking

w

Running clearance
w + 0.250

2w + 0.350
Passing clearance

WIDE LOADS

Fig. 7.13   Fork-lift vehicles passing and manoeuvring effect on planning (Dimensions are typical). Additional width may be requirement for manoeuvring   (see also Section 8 "Warehouses")

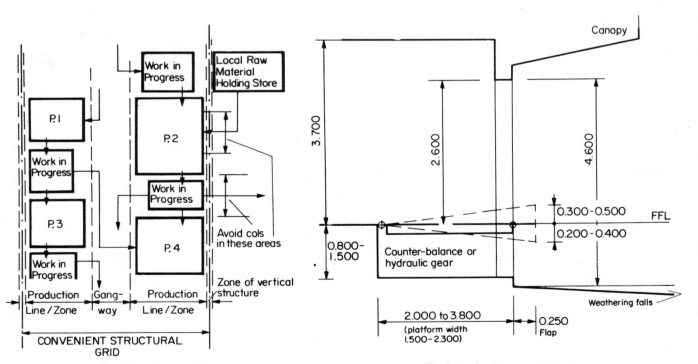

Work in Progress

Local Raw Material Holding Store

P.1

Work in Progress

P.2

P.3

Work in Progress

Work in Progress

P.4

Avoid cols in these areas

Zone of vertical structure

Production Line / Zone

Gang-way

Production Line / Zone

CONVENIENT STRUCTURAL GRID

Fig. 7.14   Structural Grids
Production zone must include space for ; process/machinery ; attendance and operation ; maintenance and access ; safety clearance

Canopy

3.700

2.600

4.600

0.300-0.500

FFL

0.200-0.400

0.800-1.500

Counter-balance or hydraulic gear

Weathering falls

2.000 to 3.800
(platform width 1.500-2.300)

0.250
Flap

Fig. 7.15   Loading bays ; dock levellers

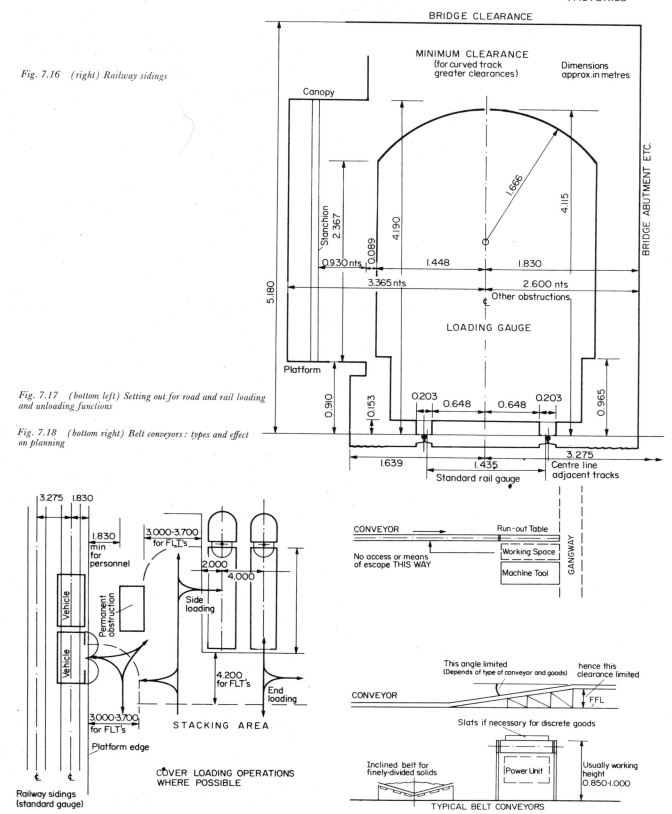

BRIDGE CLEARANCE

MINIMUM CLEARANCE
(for curved track
greater clearances)

Dimensions
approx.in metres

Canopy

LOADING GAUGE

Other obstructions

Platform

Standard rail gauge

Centre line
adjacent tracks

Fig. 7.16 (right) Railway sidings

Fig. 7.17 (bottom left) Setting out for road and rail loading and unloading functions

Fig. 7.18 (bottom right) Belt conveyors : types and effect on planning

COVER LOADING OPERATIONS
WHERE POSSIBLE

1.830
min
for
personnel

3.000-3.700
for FLT's

Side
loading

2.000

4.000

4.200
for FLT's

End
loading

STACKING AREA

Vehicle

Vehicle

Permanent
obstruction

3.000-3.700
for FLT's

Platform edge

Railway sidings
(standard gauge)

CONVEYOR → Run-out Table

No access or means
of escape THIS WAY

Working Space

Machine Tool

GANGWAY

This angle limited
(Depends of type of conveyor and goods)

hence this
clearance limited

CONVEYOR

FFL

Slats if necessary for discrete goods

Inclined belt for
finely-divided solids

Power Unit

Usually working
height
0.850-1.000

TYPICAL BELT CONVEYORS

7—17

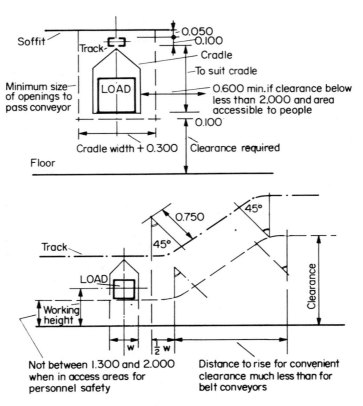

Fig. 7.19   Overhead conveyors: typical details

ASSESSMENT OF FUTURE EXPECTATIONS

The extent to which facilities for future increases and adaptations can be catered for at the initial design stage is limited. Nevertheless this problem should be given serious consideration as many who have attempted the solution of alteration problems can testify. Building-in adaptability is always expensive and its economy is grounded in the probability of correct forecasts. Hence one is in the hands of the factory-owner.

The one cheap facility in the designer's palate is the arrangement on site, which should take account (so far as practical) of possible extensions of area of an additive nature. For this reason linear systems in parallel are often chosen, so that expansion can take place linearly in the perpendicular direction (Fig. 7.20).

The other particular area where capital investment in the future is worth considering is that below ground level, where future changes in design (e.g. drainage) may be very expensive indeed.

The main headings of future expectations to be considered are:

Growth of output or use.

Increased market or external demands.

Administrative or commercial expansion or rearrangements (rationalisation).

New technologies and techniques of production, etc.

Changes in internal use.

Sale of the whole premises (as a capital investment it should be saleable!)

SPECIAL ANALYSIS FIELDS

In connection with the design of factories the following topics will arise in some degree, even if only at a trivial level. Where the problem is a simple one the architect should be able to solve it at a commonsense level in conjunction with the factory management. If problems are complex or involve specialised knowledge, specialist consultants advice should be sought at an early stage.

Activity data analysis
(Referred to briefly under Special Requirements)

Plant layout and operational analysis

Environmental analysis
Where special environmental conditions are required for production processes.

Pollution and waste disposal
Where by reason of quantity or quality of wastes produced they are not disposable by the usual means.

Industrial physics and chemistry
Where advanced technologies are used on a large scale.

Insurance
High risk areas where the costs of additional protective works or installations may result in lower premiums.

Operational safety
In all cases the Health & Safety Executive should be con-

sulted. Where radio-active or explosion risks occur other specialist advice may also be appropriate.

Energy

The efficient use of energy has become topical and is likely to become more important and critical. Fuel tariffs, alternative or duplicate fuel systems and total energy concepts may result in fundamental restrictions or requirements affecting physical planning and services or space requirements.

Stock control and distribution

Shelf-life, identification and onward distribution factors can influence the planning of storage and handling areas.

Noise and vibration control (See under sub-section on 'Planning' following).

PLANNING

PRINCIPLES

By the processes described in the previous sub-sections it will normally have been possible to have established the operational and space requirements including the circulation. The selection and suitability of the site should follow, although this is frequently not the case for reasons beyond the architects' control. Nonetheless the planning of the factory in its dimensional form must take account of the requirements and of the physical and topographical restrictions of the site (see sub-section on 'Siting'). At this stage one must analyse the dimensional limitations of the require-

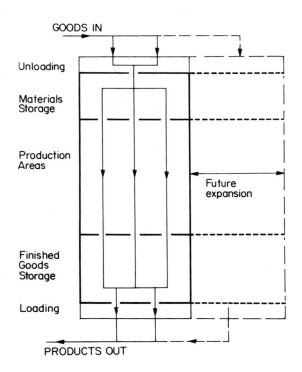

Fig. 7.20 Linear system planning

ments together with the more detailed planning problems. These may be calssified as:
  Site limitations:
    topographical
    neighbourhood planning
  Access:
    working
    maintenance
    emergencies
  Avoidance of nuisance
  Vertical restrictions, processes depending upon gravitation, including drainage.

SEASONAL OR PHASED WORKING

Where parts of the process accommodation are out of use for periods, either seasonally, or on shifts, or perhaps for maintenance, the ancilliary accommodation should be so arranged that the remaining working parts may be reached and serviced, while adequate security is maintained.

FLOORS

Function

In the great majority of factories the floor is the most important and essential tool. It provides, inter alia, the means of efficient transportation for men and materials; the platform for men and machines and work-in-progress; it usually takes heavy wear and because of its constant and varied use, probably receives less maintenance than it is due.

The specification of the floor should be carefully considered in this light, both structure and finish making due allowance for the nature of the loads and traffic, means of transportation (e.g. steel-wheeled vehicles) and not skimped.

Levels

Changes in levels should be carefully thought out, and the effect that they may have upon circulation and efficiency. The tendency since World War 2 at least has been to plan storage and production areas at a single level for this reason and for flexibility. Hence single storey buildings (with perhaps mezzanine offices) have become the general rule.

It may be that with the increasing pressure on land space coupled with a change of attitude to the measurement of 'efficiency' that this tendency has reached its zenith, and more multi-storey buildings may ensue (see also sub-section on Siting).

FIRE AND EXPLOSION RISKS

Flammable materials

Where flammable materials are used or stored, the risk of fire is high. This may seem obvious enough but frequent cases of lack of simple precautions occur, and it is worth examining the risks, actual or potential, at the planning stage, and design precautions where possible. For example, the introduction of fire-walls to form isolated spaces and hence reduce the volume at risk in any one incident is one idea.

There is of course much legislation on this matter (see sub-section on Legislation), and the advice of the Health & Safety Executive, the Fire Officer and the Insurance Company should be sought. Additional means of escape may have to be provided.

Storage areas should be isolated wherever practicable. All liquids of a flash-point lower than 32°C come within the control of the Petroleum Acts.

Explosion

The risks associated with combustible gases are self-evident (Flixborough, June 1st, 1974). Many finely-divided solids and dusts, even of materials not normally considered combustible, can form explosive mixtures with air.

Some processes use substances which are explosive by nature (e.g. organic peroxides). In these cases expert advice must be taken and special precautions designed. Such precautions could include explosion-relief panels, pressure-stat installations, sprinklers or drenchers, precautions against accidental sparking (e.g. timber guards to steelwork near vehicle routes), static earthing, in addition to the normal fire-warning and detection installations.

Sometimes the use of light-weight roofing which will easily break under the pressure of an explosion *before* the other elements of the enclosing structure can be provided. This would add to the inherent safety of the process and structure providing that the roof is isolated externally. This is often done with transformers where they cannot be sited externally.

Personnel safety

The factory will be certified for safety and adequate means of escape by the Health and Safety Executive. Clearly they will consider any abnormal risks to personnel and require additional safeguards, e.g. more than normal exits (see Fig. 7.21).

Storage areas

Under the Building Regulations and London Building Acts, production areas must be separated from storage areas. Where from process requirements this is not possible, relaxation or waivers would be necessary.

NUISANCE

The general problem of nuisance and the means of reducing the risk by planning and site arrangement is dealt with in the sub-section on Siting.

NOISE AND VIBRATION

Prevention

Included in the heading of nuisance is noise and vibration. This is a highly emotive, subjective matter but one in which increasing attention is being paid, and is real enough to

unfortunate sufferers. It is nearly always much simpler and cheaper to avoid the problem or reduce its effects by careful planning in the first instance than to introduce protective measures into the fabric at a late or post-design stage.

The techniques include remote siting, careful arrangements of doors and windows and other openings, and screening, all matters to be considered in relation to the general site arrangement, and the neighbours on all boundaries.

Note that noise and vibration can be a statutory nuisance under the Public Health Acts.

Environmental noise

There is also the aspect of the internal, working environment which can also be a risk to health at high levels of noise and contributary to loss of working efficiency of personnel.

After remote siting, the chief protection against airborne noise is the intervention of massive structure, but any continuous structure will reduce the transmission. To obtain the necessary continuity of an enclosing structure is frequently impossible but, in these cases, carefully designed partial screening with sound-absorbent linings can assist.

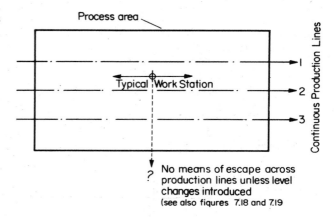

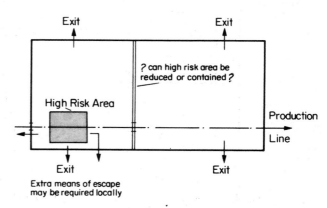

Fig. 7.21   Personnel safety: means of escape

Vibration

Where machinery causing high amplitude vibration is to be installed, isolated bases, anti-vibration mountings, or flexible services connections may be all that is necessary.

Care should be exercised to ensure that the vibrations cannot be transmitted to other parts of the structure or services pipes, which can then propagate the nuisance elsewhere.

Table 7.8a CLASSIFICATION OF WASTE PRODUCTS: HAZARD
(To be read with Table 7.8b)

Type of waste	Possible consequent operations and requirements having effect on design
1. SAFE	Handling; storage and removal
Simple	Packing; incineration
Valuable	Sorting; recycling; packing
2. HAZARDOUS	Monitoring; immediate removal
Hazard to process	
Hazard to personnel	Treatment; safety measures
Explosive	Special storage;
Toxic	Special clothing;
Radioactive	Spillage problem

Table 7.8b CLASSIFICATION OF WASTE PRODUCTS: PHASE
(To be read with Table 7.8a)

Waste	Possible consequent operations or requirements affecting design
1. SOLIDS	Removal; storage; incineration (see 3.2).
1.1 Rejects	
1.2 Off-Cuts	Handling; transportation.
1.3 Swarf	Decontamination.
1.4 Dust	Immediate collection, explosion prevention.
1.5 Sludges	Collection and storage.
2. LIQUIDS	Drainage; storage; dilution.
2.1 Water-borne solids	Monitoring; screening; filtration; sedimentation.
2.1.1 Bio-degradable	Flow control; temperature control.
2.1.2 Non-degradable	Precipitation (to phases 1.5 and 2.2).
2.2 Water-soluble wastes	Flow-control.
2.2.1 Ionising	Ion-exchange.
2.2.2 Non-ionising	Dosage: precipitation (to 1.5 and 2.2)
2.3 Emulsions	Flow-control; separation (to phases 2.2 and 2.4).
2.4 Oils, tars, etc.	Drainage separation; separate removal emulsification.
3. GASES	Immediate removal; ventilation; filtration; scrubbing (to 2.2).
3.1 Dust-bearing	Explosion prevention.
3.2 Fumes	Flue height; precipitation; fan-dilution.
3.3 Noxious	Monitoring; process separation.

Note: The Institution of Chemical Engineers' Code of Practice for Disposal of Wastes (see bibliography) Appendix 1, gives notes on the classification of Industrial Wastes.

EFFLUENTS AND WASTES

Principles

All materials which enter the site, that do not leave it in the form of finished goods, must either accumulate as waste or leave it as effluent. Packaging materials are a typical example.

The accumulation of waste can impair the efficiency of the process, and in time become a hazard, either within the factory or outside. Where it is possible to design for their better handling at the planning stage, the factory is likely to be the more efficient and economic.

Types

Wastes may be classified by their physical phase and by the hazard that they potentially represent. Where they contain constituents worth recovery, the cost of handling plant will pay for itself. See Tables 7.7 and 7.8.

The conversion of energy in the process itself produces waste (usually heat) and is an economic problem which can influence the design of the buildings.

Legislation

There is much legislation concerned with potentially hazardous wastes, and it is likely to grow. Where wastes contribute to an internal environmental hazard they will be controlled under the Factories Act, 1961, and the H & SE should be consulted.

Where wastes may constitute a nuisance to neighbours or the public at large they come under the Alkalis Act (for gaseous discharges), the Water Resources Act, 1963, (discharges to natural water courses) and the Public Health Acts (solids and generally). There are also legal controls for discharges to tidal and sea waters.

Control systems

The design of waste control, handling and treatment systems can be quite complex (see Fig. 7.22) and close collaboration with the production engineers and the public authorities is desirable at an early stage. Specialist Advice may well be necessary.

It is essential to know the production source of each waste and its constituents. In principle, the greater the separation of wastes *before* treatment, the easier the treatment and control of the discharge. Materials can become wastes by reason of spillage, and where the spillage may be large and the material hazardous, the possibility of such an accident should not be ignored.

Solid wastes

Solid wastes in any quantity may require separate consideration, as if they were byproducts or a subsidiary process. They add to the operational flow problem additional transportation and holding storage problems.

With combustible wastes one solution for their disposal worth consideration is incineration. This may be coupled

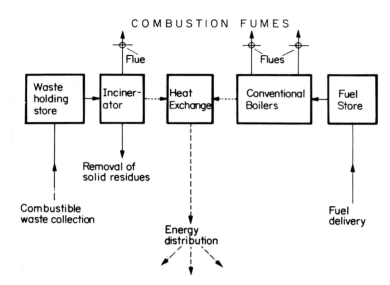

Fig 7.22   *Large-scale incineration. Waste heat use*

with the energy production, using the waste as additional fuel. But all incineration produces wastes in the form of gases and fumes.

Trade effluents

Administratively, these form a special category. The Local Drainage Authority must accept trade effluents to their sewers, if they exist and if there is plant to handle the effluent. They have powers to control the effluent as to quantity, chemical analysis, pH value, and temperature. Typical limits are given in Table 7.9.

The standards of acceptance are likely to become more stringent, particularly in respect of metal ions. It may be necessary to install treatment plant to achieve some degree of control, and the likelihood of this should be determined as soon as possible.

Immiscible liquid wastes

Wastes immiscible with water constitute a particular class of problem in that they may not be acceptable to public

Table 7.9 TYPICAL TRADE EFFLUENT LIMITS
Characteristics of Trade Effluents normally acceptable to Sewers

1.	Volume, Rate of Discharge:	varies according to locality	
2.	pH:	6·0 to 11·0	
3.	Temperature:	43°C (109°F)	
4.	Contaminants	*Content* ppm (mg/l)	*Notes*
4.1	Biological Oxygen Demand	No limits	Amount will reflect in charges made
4.2	Chemical Oxygen Demand		
4.3	Settleable solids	300	Colloidal solids normally acceptable
4.4	Sulphates (—SO₄)	No limits	In special cases or areas limits may be applied
4.5	Chlorides (—Cl)		
4.6	Cyanides (—CN)	2 to 3	Highly toxic
4.7	Metal ions	10	
4.8	Total Metals (incl. 4.7)	30	Varies according to locality; contaminants can interfere seriously with bacteriological treatment methods
4.9	Tar oils	150	
4.10	Grease, Oils		
4.11	Organic Solvents	prohibited	Except from solvent-recovery plant in some cases
4.12	Phenols	50	According to locality
4.13	Soluble Sulphur compounds	50	According to type

Notes:
1. These data are *typical* only: the limits in any case will depend upon the type of effluent, local public treatment plant and capacity available and local aggregate pollution.
2. Guidance and approval obtained from Area Water Authority, normally sought via District Council.
3. These data based on information supplied by courtesy of the Thames Water Authority, Trade Effluent Division, Godalming.

sewers. Liquid wastes containing fine solids in suspension should be carefully considered, as the solids may be deposited at points where the flow velocity is reduced, and there adhere to form blockages. Special note should be taken of points where oils, grease, tars or phenolics are used.

Where degreasing takes place it should be ascertained whether the process is a recovery one or the material goes to waste. Gunks and tars constitute a particular problem for the drainage authorities. Holding ponds, catchpits, interceptors and treatment plants may variously be necessary.

Gaseous wastes

Gaseous wastes once released to the atmosphere are out of control. The Alkalis Acts control the discharges of any noxious fumes and gases, including those of large boilers.

DAYLIGHTING AND OUTLOOK

A few processes, e.g. panel-beating and colour matching are more successfully executed under natural light than under artificial. Most processes however can be carried out under artificial illumination, properly designed. The areal extent of most factories, other than the smaller workshops, means that if daylighting is required it must be provided by means of rooflights. This can be an added safety factor in the event of power failure, but daylight intensity is an uncontrollable phenomenon.

The introduction of rooflights reduces the average thermal insulation value of (probably) the largest portion of the external envelope and introduces heating and maintenance problems. In most cases it is better to omit rooflights where possible.

There seems to be no general opinion on the advantages, psychological or otherwise, of windows in production areas. It probably depends upon the outlook!

WORKS ENTRANCES

Security aspects are dealt with below under Ancillary Accommodation and Functions.

Since World War 2 there has been an increasing tendency in the cleaner industries to design works entrances (as well as recreational accommodation) in a more comfortable and imposing mode than the 'traditional' fair-faced cream-painted brickwork. This has been done in the interests of industrial psychology, to invest employees with a sense of well-being when at work and identity with the factory. Reports have indicated some success with this approach, increased pride, accuracy and efficiency.

USE OF COLOUR

The selection of colour schemes for factories is essentially no different from that for other building types. The following attributes perhaps have greater prominence and should be considered more carefully:

1. The general psychological effect on the environment and the well-being of staff working in the building;

2. The effect on the standards of illumination, especially where safety may be affected, and moving machinery or vehicles occur;

3. The use of colour codes for information, e.g. designating services, danger zones, etc, and the need to prevent confusion between codes and the background.

ANCILLARY ACCOMMODATION AND FUNCTIONS

IMPORTANCE OF ANCILLARY FUNCTIONS

The production area (or areas, there may well be more than one) form the core of the accommodation; the hub of the plan. It functions by courtesy of the auxiliary, ancillary parts, which in turn must be designed for optimum efficiency of the factory considered as a whole.

The accommodation for these ancillary parts is considered where they are particular to industrial works. In many instances they may be simple, or may be designed on general principles without the application of knowledge of the process. Where such general principles are dealt with elsewhere in these volumes, reference should be made to the relevant section. But the brief for the ancillary accommodation flows *ipso facto* from the design of the process.

A Checklist of ancillary functions was given on page 7–13.

OFFICE ACCOMMODATION

The design of offices usually offers no special problems once the type and extent have been decided.

There are two basic types of offices, those needed for the supervision and administration of the process which are usually locally placed; and those dealing with the development, handling and sales of the products, staff administration and welfare, etc, which can be remote.

It is often convenient to place office accommodation at first floor level, releasing the ground floor level for functions more directly related to the process and which require a lesser headroom. This arrangement may sometimes be used to allow office personnel circulation at high level thus segregating flows, and allowing better visual supervision (see Fig. 7.11).

STAFF LAVATORY ACCOMMODATION

The extent of this is controlled by the Factories Act, 1961, and the OSRPA, 1963. However, e.g. in certain industries, food, printing, and metal finishing, there are further regulations providing for facilities additional to these minima. There may also be process needs for cleanliness which require additional facilities.

Generally it is better to have the accommodation dispersed rather than centralised, reducing loss of manhours and crowded conditions etc, for example at change of shifts. In dirty industries there may be need of special cleansing agents (removal of grease, printing inks, etc). The layout should be considered in the light of personnel circulation, the degree of control of staff required, and the possibilities of contamination by staff movement.

No lavatory may be entered directly from any workroom without the intervention of a ventilated lobby. Determine whether showers or slipper baths are needed, which will influence the planning and need for changing accommodation.

CHANGING AND DRESSING ROOMS

Where staff get very dirty during the process work in risky conditions, or there are social reasons, protective clothing may be required, such as overalls, headgear, boots, or other items. Lockers and changing accommodation will then be required, which must be planned in relation to staff movements, especially those at ends of shifts, meal breaks, etc.

It is generally convenient to plan changing accommodation *en suite* with the lavatories (see Fig. 7.23). Where shift working is the rule, the numbers of lockers will be related to the total numbers of staff employed while the changing and lavatory spaces will be related to the maximum number on shift. Sometimes shifts overlap—twilight shifts employing female labour sometimes give rise to this—which must be taken into account. Where catering staff are employed their accommodation must be separate.

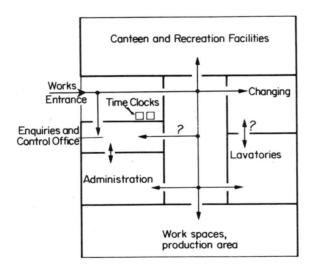

Fig. 7.23   Works entrance. Staff movement

CLOTHING STORAGE

Where protective clothing is provided, some must be centrally stored for periodic (say, weekly) issue and reception of soiled clothes. With the latter, the following questions should be decided. Is the clothing to be laundered on or off the premises, or destroyed? What staff to deal with this will be required and what accommodation will they need?

SMOKING AND RESTROOMS

Is smoking permitted in process areas? If not (because of explosion or contamination risks) then provision should be made for designated smoking areas, with fire safety precautions or anti-contamination precautions as appropriate. In large process areas it is sometimes convenient to provide such smoking and rest rooms distributed locally.

Where processes demanding high concentration or worker fatigue are carried on, the opportunity to relax at intervals is needed and this may be provided by rest spaces; these may be general recreational staff areas such as mess rooms (see Fig. 7.24). Factories employing women should provide at least one restroom for them, including a couch. This may be part of a medical suite where appropriate.

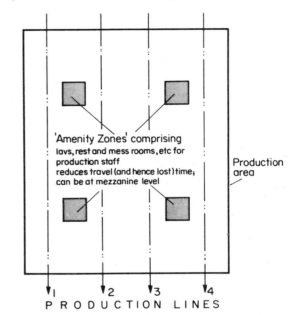

Fig. 7.24   Planning of local amenity zones in large production areas

MEDICAL FACILITIES

All factories must supply first-aid or medical facilities under the Act (Fig. 7.25). The minimum extent is determined by section s.61 of the Factories Act. Many factories provide

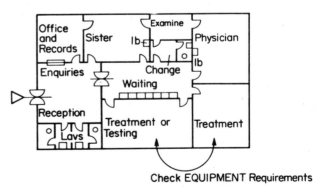

Check EQUIPMENT Requirements
● Doors large enough for stretchers
● Means of escape not shown

Fig. 7.25   Typical medical unit

quite lavish medical accommodation as a social service. In this case the following should be ascertained. Will resident nursing staff be provided? Will a staff physician attend regularly? They would require offices, records, examination rooms, and changing accommodation.

In some processes where dangerous liquids are used emergency showers in the process areas may be needed.

STAFF CATERING

Canteens

Where canteens are provided as part of the staff facilities in a factory they must take account of the pattern of use. Shift working, total staff numbers, types of work and staff employed, and the physical relationship to the works areas may all affect the need. Often the canteen can be an independent building and it would be designed to be operated independently, with its own lavatory and offices, etc. This is often done where the canteen is part of the recreational facilities.

On the other hand where the canteen is conceived to be closely allied to the working pattern of the factory, there are advantages in having it physically and functionally part of the factory. It should then be regarded as a subsidiary function of the workforce.

Messrooms

For many processes, traditionally where small distinguishable groups of specialised workers are employed; messrooms (self-catering or otherwise) may be provided (Fig. 7.26). Such rooms can be used as general staff rest/recreational rooms and become (effectively) a small private club for a specialised group. This is sometimes a good arrangement with floating populations, e.g. transport staff, drivers. Mess rooms may not be entered direct from workrooms.

CLOTHES DRYING

Where wet processes or work are envisaged and a need for drying clothes exists, the drying rooms should be located next to the changing rooms. Where the need arises from outdoor work, drying rooms should be situated next to the entrance lobby leading to cover.

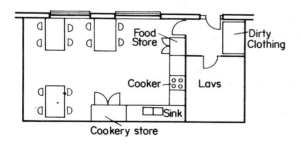

Fig. 7.26 Typical mess room

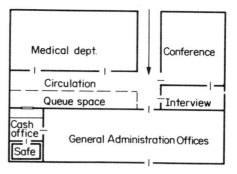

Fig. 7.27 Personnel administration. Typical arrangement

PERSONNEL FACILITIES

Where staff are paid on the premises and cashier/payment facilities are needed, the space must take account of the queueing problem, and the security aspect. Often this is made part of a personnel department which would include Staff Interview, Medical, and possibly Meeting Rooms for staff conferences, union meetings, training and the like. An interface with the administration offices may well be needed (see Fig. 7.27).

PRINTING

Some factories find it worthwhile to have their own small printing shop. This may arise from the need for labelling despatched goods, or for other documentation (e.g. for sampling), development or straightforward administrative matters.

MAINTENANCE FACILITIES

Function

The need can vary from a single Cleaners' Room to quite complex engineering workshops. Such needs should be considered early and as part of the subsidiary process requirements.

Cleaning

Cleaners' Stores will be required for each part of the factory at each level, according to the dirt and waste produced. For production areas this should be considered as part of the waste-disposal problem. The dangers of spillage and droppage must be taken into account. In large establishments machine sweeping and cleaning may be employed and the machines will require their own housing and maintenance.

Equipment

Maintenance for process equipment will again vary widely; from an oilcan to a fullscale workshop plus stores for materials and spares.

Building fabric

Building and building services maintenance will be required and it should be established whether this would be carried out by staff or contractors, and what accommodation will be needed.

External maintenance

Grounds and external spaces also require maintenance and similar reasoning applies.

PROCESS DEVELOPMENT CONTROL

In certain processes differing products may be produced on essentially the same production line. This is particularly so in the craft-based and machine tool industries, e.g. wood-working. As a corollary, it frequently arises that special development is carried out on the production line itself, and there is need for more frequent inspection and supervision.

Visitors may be permitted to inspect the plant, process or embryo product, and space would be needed for the reception of visitors, and inspection of the product. Alternatively, a development area may be provided with requirements similar to a Pilot Workshop.

VISITORS

Visitors to most factories are comparatively few, but should not be overlooked. Apart from persons delivering goods for process and subsidiary functions and contractors staff, etc, there may be sales representatives from other companies, statutory officials, and the like.

Very few factories invite the general public to visit, but those that do usually limit and control the numbers. It is as well, nevertheless to establish the likelihood of visits of all types and the need for special accommodation (Car parking is the usual essential).

TIMEKEEPING

Where time clocks are envisaged they should be situated immediately next to the entrance/exit(s) of those who are required to use them. This entrance is on the line of the security 'cordon sanitaire', a line, formed of normally im-passable construction, dividing the secure area from the rest.

Clocks may be in a free-flow area or lobby, when it should be *immediately outside* the security line; the lobby may be on the line, when it is normal to arrange the clocks as a number of turnstiles. In either case, it is usual for clocks to be under constant supervision.

GATEHOUSES

The gatehouse is situated in the outer security line (if there is more than one) and its prime function is to control the entrance and exit of vehicles and goods to the works (Figs 7.28 and 7.29). It may also control pedestrians and visitors, and possibly staff. Sometimes the time-office is part of the gatehouse.

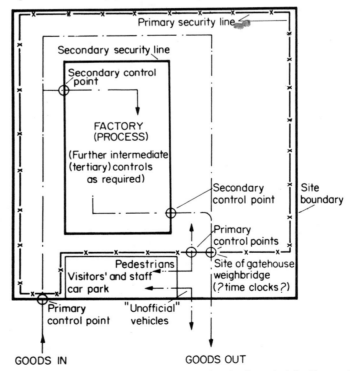

Fig. 7.28 Physical security, controls, gatehouses etc. If primary control points can be reduced to a single locality control is more effective and efficient

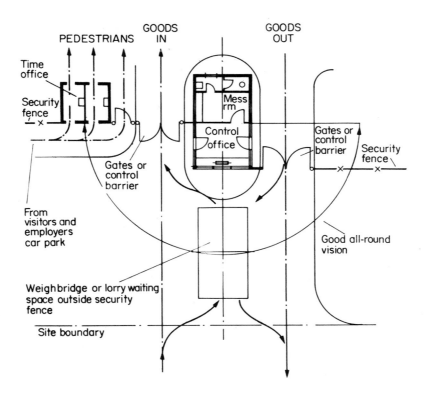

Fig. 7.29 Primary control: typical gatehouse

Gatehouse and security staff will work different hours from the rest of the staff, and thus require independent facilities for clothing, refreshments and communications. Usually a small messroom is attached. The arrangement should be so that gatehouse staff, sheltered from the elements, should have good vision for their supervisory tasks. The gatehouse must be conveniently arranged for dealing with enquiries by visitors and new arrivals, and an enquiry office or window with a convenient lorry-sized lay-by is required. If the whole works is to be secured, the gatehouse is the last part to be locked.

RECREATIONAL FACILITIES

These are usually provided for works staff, can be very varied in range, type and sophistication. Clearly an on-cost of the factory economics they should be designed with two main factors in mind, circulation and security, and maintenance and running costs.

It is important to distinguish between those facilities intended primarily for use within the working day or shift, and those which are for use out of hours. The first type must be within the factory site curtilage, but those in the second category may be remote, e.g. sports grounds.

Where people other than staff are expected to use the facilities, then special care in establishing the circulation to and from them will be needed, taking into account the security question.

PROCESS SERVICES

Certain processes in production may require services normally considered 'specialist'. Insofar that they will require special plant for their production or transduction (which in turn will require housing and maintenance), their basic space requirements should be determined at Outline stage. For detailed specifications specialist advice should be sought (see Table 7.1 for Checklist of Services).

WORKING CONDITIONS

Process requirements

Processes where the products are exposed to the air may require particular conditions of cleanliness (food, paint-spraying), humidity (yarn-spinning), or ambient temperature. Such needs should be determined at an early stage and space provision allowed for the necessary services, equipment, distribution, etc.

Process wastes and effluents

Discharge of wastes is dealt within the sub-sections on Planning and Legislation. Waste products may have a risky effect on the local working environment, which must not be overlooked. Under the Factories Act, 1961, a number

FACTORIES

of processes and substances incur special regulations affecting the conditions or the installation of plant, or the provision of additional facilities for worker welfare.

In principle, the safety and efficiency of the plant is improved, the welfare of workers best secured and the subsequent handling of the waste simplified, if the waste can be collected at the point at which it is produced. Many machine tools, for example, those producing swarf or dust, have built-in collection facilities, or connections.

Control of special environmental conditions is made easier by separation of distinct areas or rooms. This technique however should be carefully employed, considering the economy and technology of the process at the flow-diagram stage. Services requirements consequent should be considered as part of the total production needs.

Normal conditions

Where there is no special process requirement, work rooms must be heated and ventilated to normal working conditions. Where there are large workshops or process areas and staff density is low, or concentrated in one area, there may be problems of uneconomic running costs, by reason of the large volume of the spaces. Local radiant or direct air heating may be the answer, depending on the working conditions.

LABORATORY REQUIREMENTS

Quality control

Where the control is to ensure the exactness of the process, the laboratory should be sited close to the process area so that samples and measurements may be readily taken and rapidly assessed. Rectification measures can then be taken immediately.

Where quality control is post-manufacture, the laboratory may be sited more remotely. Its size and siting will depend upon the process and extent of sampling required, the nature and size of samples to be tested, and the nature of the test equipment. Section 6 'Research Laboratories' in the volume *Planning: Buildings for Education, Culture and Science*.

Development laboratories

For small scale products a development laboratory is likely to be similar to a normal bench laboratory. Otherwise it may be known as a 'pilot workshop'. This could be integrated into the process, or located nearby, for convenience of testing, information feedback and use of common stores.

Design requirements are likely to be more akin to factory production area than a bench laboratory and should be analysed and designed accordingly.

SITING

GENERAL

Successful siting of a factory will follow from its definition, considered with the requirements of transportation to and from the site.

7–28

Where the architect or designer is consulted, he must be aware of the influences that availability of labour (especially key-workers), energy or fuel, and the transport for materials and goods may have on the decisions. Under current legislation these factors may be modified considerably by the subsidies available in Development Areas (see Legislation) and, of course, in its locality, by the operation of the local Development Plan.

CONSIDERATIONS

A set of restrictions may be identified arising from the general requirements of the proposed factory, the legislated planning restrictions, the availability of resources against the requirements, and local environmental matters. These may be enumerated under the following headings:
Site area;
Development subsidies;
Planning restrictions;
Availability of transport: road, rail, water, air;
Availability of resources: Labour, Services and power,
Waste and effluent disposal;
Topography of site;
Potential nuisance to locality.

EXTERNAL SPACES

External spaces should be considered with the same care as the internal spaces, as they can influence the working efficiency of the factory in the same way, and hence should be considered functionally as part of it.

Indeed, any process that does not require shelter from the elements may be external and just as vital as those under cover. Their arrangement moreover may have a significant effect on the matter of security. The main functions usually carried out externally are given below.

VEHICULAR CIRCULATION

Movement and transhipment of goods about the site; this is no different in its requirements but more vital (See volume on *Planning: Architects' Technical Reference Data*, for vehicle and roads requirements).

Special note should be taken of the increased hazard to pedestrians where personnel circulation routes near or cross the vehicular, particularly by fire escapes, or where hazardous loads may be transported.

VEHICLE PARKING

Adequate space for parking of goods vehicles should be allowed. Goods outwards are often loaded and left for their journey to commence during the night or the following morning. The use of detachable good trailers with independant prime-movers should be noted as this may point to special needs for parking and loading facilities.

Car parks for visitors and staff are frequently sited outside the security fence to reduce the likelihood of pilferage of valuable and attractive materials and goods.

EFFLUENT TREATMENT

Plant is normally sited in external spaces, and dependent upon the treatment required can take up considerable ground space. Its position is clearly limited to some extent by the topography of the site and its environs and the positions of discharge available.

GASEOUS DISCHARGES

Smoke, fumes and noisy discharges may of course limit the neighbourhood of the site. Where these are of any proportion they will be controlled under the Alkalis Acts, and plant for reducing its effects required. See sub-section on Legislation and checklist of processes, Table 7.1.

NUISANCE

An important aspect to be watched for potential nuisance is where other buildings, especially dwellings, are nearby. The main types of nuisance are:

Noise;
Shift-working;
Dust and fumes emission;
Smells;

but any effect which may disturb established neighbours in their work or private lives may constitute nuisance under the Public Health Acts—welding flash at night has been such a ground. Where possible it is better and cheaper to avoid the problems by initial good planning (for example, placing the offending department in a remote area), rather than build-in additional plant or material. The former is the best answer. Where distance cannot be provided then other planning solutions, e.g. screening, can help (Fig. 7.30). For legal aspects see legal aspects, see sub-section on Legislation.

TOPOGRAPHY

By and large, factories require a level floor to provide flexibility of internal transportation, especially where this is mainly or largely by means of vehicles. By corollary, the most economical site is the most level. Where sloping sites are to be considered, the gradient may be turned to advantage where a multi-level process can be useful or acceptable, where gravity-feed systems can be used, or where the process may be divided into smaller, independent production areas with transportation betweem them.

With growing pressure on land space, and the single-storey factory becoming less economical in national terms, a steep site could permit the future expansion of a multi-storey factory (Fig 7.31).

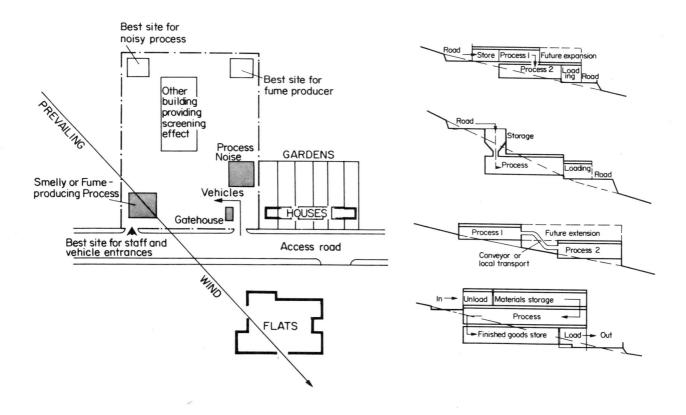

Fig. 7.30 *Siting – nuisance aspects*

Fig. 7.31 *Use of steep sites*

LEGISLATION

GENERAL LEGISLATION

Not unnaturally there is considerable legislation about factories. Apart from general legislation applicable to all buildings there are certain parts of the general Acts which apply specifically to industrial buildings and some of these references are included below.

SPECIFIC LEGISLATION

Specific legislation may be grouped under two main headings; that for Safety Health and Welfare of those employed in factories, and that to protect the public at large from the extraneous effects of industrial processes. Much of this legislation (of either type) refer to particular processes and industries. When any particular process is being considered at the design stage, the extent to which legislation may affect the form of building or installations should be determined. Most legislation in Northern Ireland is separately enacted and is not considered here.

SAFETY, HEALTH AND WELFARE

The principle Act covering this is the Factories Act, 1961, and the various Regulations made thereunder. A synopsis of the Act is included as Table 7.10.

Table 7.10 SYNOPSIS OF FACTORIES ACT, 1961

Part		Sections
I	Health (General Provisions)	1–11
II	Safety (General Provisions)	12–56
III	Welfare (General Provisions)	57–62
IV	Health, Safety & Welfare (Special Provisions & Regulations)	63–79
V	Notification of Accidents & Industrial Diseases	80–85
VI	Employment of Women & Young Persons	86–119
VII	Special Applications and Extensions	120–132
VIII	Home work	133–134
IX	Wages	135–136
X	Notices, Returns, Records, Duties of Persons Employed, and Application of Weights & Measures Acts	137–144
XI	Administration	
XII	Offences, Penalties and Legal Proceedings	145–154
XIII	Application of Act	173–174
XIV	Interpretation and General	175–185

Schedules :

1st Table of *Humidity*
2nd Modification of certain provisions in relation to *Factories occupying parts of building*
3rd Procedure for making *special regulations*
4th Provisions of Factory & Workshop Act, 1901, applicable in *London and Scotland* only and administered by district councils
5th *Transitional provisions*
6th *Enactments repealed*

This important Act came into force on 1st January, 1975. Apart from placing certain obligations on employers, employees and designers for the safety of working conditions, its main provisions are two. The old Factory and Alkalis Inspectorates are amalgamated into the new Health and Safety Executive, under the jurisdiction of a Health and Safety Commission. A list of existing Acts of Parliament are scheduled and may be the subject of repeal and redraft by future Regulations made under this Act. Its immediate effect is slight, but ultimately it is likely to have far-reaching effects on all building design, and especially of factories. Local Authorities will have delegated control over buildings, so that the process of obtaining approvals will probably remain much the same as at present. But it is likely that matters now controlled retrospectively eg. under the Factories Act, 1961, will be brought into the design stage and the Executive would have the prospective powers to enforce standards of safety incorporated in designs.

INDUSTRIAL DEVELOPMENT CERTIFICATES (IDC)

When Planning Permission is sought an IDC must also be submitted for projects situated in the south and east of the U.K. The principal statutory provision on the IDC controls are contained in :

Town and Country Planning Act, 1971 sections 66–70
Town and Country Planning (Scotland) Act, 1972 sections 64–68
Town and Country Planning (Industrial Development Certificates Exemption) (No. 2) Order, 1974 (SI 2028/1974)
Town and Country Planning (Industrial Development Certificates): Regulations, 1972 (SI 904/1972), 1973 (SI 149/1973) and 1974 (SI 1418/1974)

When an IDC is required

IDCs are not required in the Development Areas and Special Development Areas. There is no IDC legislation in Northern Ireland.

An application for planning permission for an industrial development in England and Wales, outside the DAs, must be supported by an IDC if the industrial floor space to be created by that development (together with any related development) exceeds 5 000 sq ft in south eastern England, 15 000 sq ft in the intermediate areas and 10 000 sq ft elsewhere. The statutory provisions about related development are contained in section 68 of the Town and Country Planning Act, 1971. The industrial development to which the control applies are:

(a) The erection or re-creation of industrial buildings;
(b) extensions and alterations to existing buildings;
(c) the change of use of existing buildings from non-industrial and industrial purposes.

ADMINISTRATION AND GENERAL

Public Health Act, 1936

s.53	Requires the *deposition of plans* with Local Authority.
s.54	One may not build on land filled with *offensive material*.
s.107	Requires consent of Local Authority to establish '*offensive trade*'. *Exemptions to the above part of the Act* Smelting of ores and minerals; Calciuming, puddling or rolling of metals; Conversion of pig iron; Annealing Hardening Forging metals Converting Carbonising

P.H. Act, 1961

ss.4–11	Empower Minister to make *Building Regulations*.
s.57	Empowers Local Authority to make conditions for the acceptance of *Trade Effluents* relating to: 1. temperature of discharge; 2. pH value of discharge; 3. provision of inspection chambers; 4. provision of meters

Factories Act, 1961

s.157	Defines factory as premises in which or within whose curtilage persons employed in manual labour in any process for (or incidental to) any purpose for gain. (*Note*: See Table 7.9).
s.79	Plans for *cotton cloth factories* submitted for approval of Local Authority shall be accompanied by Inspector's Certification of compliance with Section 68 'Humid Conditions'.
ss.120-122	Provisions as to *Tenement and Flatted, Factories, etc.* *Note*. 'Tenement' means using common source of motive power. See Schedule (2) of the Act.
s.124	Provisions as to Institutions' Factories.
s.125	Warehouses subject to provisions of the Act.
ss.129–132	Regulations of the use of *lead paint*, etc.
s.173	Act applied to all factories, including Crown factories, subject to exceptions contained within section.
s.170	*Definitions* Includes 'young person' i.e. under 18 years; 'Prime mover' means any machinery for converting other energy to mechanical energy; 'Apprentices' are 'employees' within the meaning of the Act.

Factories Act, 1961. SI. 1964/762

Makes S.40 (Certification of Means of Escape by the Authority) apply to *any factory* situated in a building where aggregate of office *and* factory employees number is:
greater than 20;
greater than 10 per floor above ground floor; or where explosives or high-flammability materials are used or stored.

Town and Country Planning Act, 1962

s.38	Defines IDC as issued by Board of Trade certifying the proposed development can be carried out consistently with the proper distribution of industry.

Noise Abatement Act, 1960

s.1	Noise and vibration becomes nuisance under Part III (ss.91–110) of Public Health Act, 1936.

Petroleum (Consolidation) Act, 1928

s.1	Petroleum spirit shall not be kept without *licence*.

Public Health (Drainage of Trade Premises) Act, 1937

s.9	The Local Authority may require production of plans of *private drainage works* at any time.

Rivers (Prevention of Pollution) Act, 1951

s.4	Prohibits works to beds and banks of streams which disturb the waters.

Public Health (London) Act, 1936

s.137	*Offensive trades* are statutory nuisance.
s.139	GLC has powers to make *by-laws* for the following: manufacturing; brewing; slaughter houses and knackers
s.140	Consent of GLC required for establishment of *offensive trades*.
s.142	GLC has power to make *by-laws for offensive trades*.
s.146	GLC has power to make by-laws for *fish curing*.
s.183	GLC has power to make by-laws for *food preparation*.
ss.187, 188	requires registration of premises used in a manufacture of certain foods.

Highly Flammable Liquids and LPG Regulations, 1972/917

s.2	Highly flammable liquid defined as any giving off flammable vapour under 32°C.
s.3	All premises and operations using highly flammable liquid comes under this Regulation.
s.5	Storage of highly flammable liquids.

PLANNING, LAYOUT AND CIRCULATION

Public Health Act, 1936

s.55	Requires satisfactory means of access to street.
s.59	Requires free and unobstructed access to *stores and warehouses* where public are admitted or more than 20 persons employed.

Clean Air Act, 1956

ss.5–10	Requires *grit and dust extraction* plant to be incorporated.

Factories Act, 1961

s.18*(2)	Requires *gangways, catwalks and ladders* near vessels, structures and sumps to be securely fixed to 3 ft above floor or local platform.
(3)	*Spaces between* vessels, structures and sumps and walls or partitions less than 3 ft shall be fenced off to 3 ft.
s.19	no *gangway* or route shall pass closer than 18 in. to any self-acting machine at its greatest extension in any direction.
s.23 (1)	*Passenger and dual purpose lifts* shall be properly constructed; be securely fenced and gated; protect

	persons from touching moving parts; have automatic overrun protection; have gate interlock.
s.24	*Teagle openings* shall be securely fenced with hand-holds each side.
s.28 (2)	Every *staircase* shall have a *handrail* and one on each open side.
(4)	*Openings* in floors shall normally be fenced.
s.29 (1)	Means of access to any work place shall be safe as far as practical; otherwise secure foot and hand-holds shall be provided.
s.30 (2)	Manholes to confined spaces shall be not less than 18 in. × 16 in. or 18 in. diameter.
s.48 (2)(3)	Doors shall open out from (a) rooms containing more than 10 persons. (b) routes of exit. (c) foot of staircases.
(10)	Rooms shall be arranged so there is free gangway to means of escape.
s.58	*Washing facilities* shall be 'conveniently accessible'.
s.59	*Clothing and drying facilities* shall be provided.
s.60	*Seating* shall be provided where possible at work places.
s.61	*Ambulance* room may, if approved by Inspector exempt from provision for first aid facilities. In factories employing more than 50, a trained person must be in charge of first aid facilities.
s.69	Inspectors empowered to certify limited use for *underground rooms*, i.e. half the height of which is below adjoining street, ground or floor level.
s.75	Where women and young persons are employed in contact with *lead compounds*, cloakrooms, mess rooms and washing accommodation as required shall be provided.
s.92	Women and young persons shall not be allowed to remain in workrooms during work intervals (for exceptions, see part VI).

Offices, Shops and Railway Premises Act, 1963

s.5 (1)	Offices and shops must *not be overcrowded*, and regard must be hard in this respect to *space occupied by functions*, fittings and machinery.
(2)	Minimum space within room: 40 ft²/person or 440 ft³/person, whichever is less.
s.12	Clothing storage shall, and drying facilities should be provided.
ss.13, 14	*Seats* shall be provided where possible, and footrests where applicable. In *sales rooms* one seat for every three assistants shall be provided.
s.16	Handrails shall be provided to stairs at least on one side, on two where both sides open or they are hazardous.
s.29 (5)	No more than the number of persons stated in the Fire Certificates may be employed in the premises.

Water Resources Act, 1963

s.36	Requires River Authority Licence for interference with or obstructed of any natural water or course.

Noise Abatement Act, 1960

s.1	Noise and vibration become nuisance under Part III (ss.91–110) of Public Health Act, 1936.

Building Regulations 1972 (SI. 1972 No. 317)

E.4	Limits of area and volume of factories and storage buildings.
P.3 (2)(c)	No sanitary accommodation shall open directly into a room where any persons habitually employed.

Electricity (Factory and Workshop) Regulations 1908 (SR & O. 1908 No. 1312)

R.17	Switchboards shall have platforms and passageways (measured in feet from bare conductors in case of horizontal dimensions), as follows:

Voltage	Height (Minimum)	Clear width	Conductors both sides
l.t. m.t.	7	3	4·6
R.t.	8	3·6	8

R.19	All r.t. apparatus shall be properly protected.
R.25	All apparatus shall have adequate working space about.
R.30	Substances shall be substantially constructed, arranged to prevent access other than by authorised person by a proper entrance; dry; and ventilated.
R.32	Underground substations shall be provided with adequate means of access with secure ladder out of reach of apparatus, unless easily and safely accessible otherwise, by means of doorway and staircase.

Highways Act, 1959

s.142	Prohibits placing of wires, ropes or apparatus over highway if likely to be danger without all necessary means of warning or danger.
s.144	Dangerous land adjoining street may be required to be made good.
s.157	Restriction of construction of bridges over highways (may grant licence in certain cases).
s.152	Restriction of construction of rails and beams over highways (may grant licence subject to conditions, etc).

STRUCTURAL DESIGN

Where Ministers have power to make special regulations, the section or subsection is marked with an asterisk.

Factories Act, 1961

*s.50	Ministers power to make special regulations as to fire protecting and construction materials.

Thermal Insulation (Industrial Buildings) Act, 1957

*s.1	Ministers power to make regulations and standards (SI.1958 No. 1220).
*s.3	Ministers power to prescribe certain materials (SI. 1958 No. 1220).

Public Health Act, 1936

s.107   Requires impervious floors where *offensive trades* carried on to have washing-down facilities and drainage.

Factories Act, 1961

s.3   Requires floor drainage for wet processes.
s.28 (4)   Openings in floors shall normally be fenced.

Shops, Offices and Railway Premises Act, 1963

s.16   Floors etc, shall be of sound construction and capable of maintenance; openings in floors shall be fenced where practicable.

Public Health Act, 1936

s.107   Offensive trades to have impervious walls, coved corners, easily washed down.

Factories Act, 1961

*s.50   Ministers power to make special regulations for fire-resisting construction and materials.

Thermal Insulation (Industrial Buildings) Act, 1957

*s.1   Ministers power to make regulations (SI.1958 No. 1220).
s.2   Local Authority have duty to inspect and approve plans.

Noise Abatement Act, 1960

s.1   Noise and vibration becomes statutory nuisance under Part III (ss.91–110) of Public Health Act, 1936.

Factories (Cleanliness of Walls and Ceilings) Order, 1960/1974

s.3   Requires painting of walls and ceilings with compact continuous film capable of being cleaned.

Highly Flammable Liquids and L.P.G. Regulations 1972/917

s.10   Workrooms using highly flammable liquids shall be a fire resisting structure, except door, windows and roofs if single-storey.
s.11   Fire resisting structures may have explosion-relieving panels if safe.

London Building (Constructional) By-Laws, 1972

Superimposed floor loads. To standards of CP3, Ch. V, Pt 1, 1967 or worse, if DS requires.
Notice:
Imposed floor loading limits (prescribed form) must be posted permanently.
Table of Fire Resistance Periods
For warehouse trade or manufacture   Classes III and IV

For H.V. electrical equipment   Class V
For housing petrol-driven vehicles   Class VI
Ducts from trade and cooking apparatus
Treated as flues
Minimum thickness of fire resisting construction 50 mm.

ENVIRONMENT

Where Ministers have power to make special regulations, the section is marked with an asterisk.

Public Health Act, 1936

s.92   Defines *insufficient ventilation* as nuisance.
s.107   Requires adequate ventilation in *offensive trades* premises.

Factories Act, 1961

*s.3   Reasonable temperatures shall be maintained.
*s.4   Suitable ventilation shall be provided and for practicable removal of dust and fumes.
*s.5   Suitable lighting (natural and artificial) shall be provided.
s.63 (1)   Injurious dust and fumes shall be removed by mechanical ventilation from as near as possible to source.
s.68   Requirements for humid atmospheres.
*s.69   Underground rooms must be properly constructed, ventilated, be hygienic and have adequate provision of means of escape.

Shops, Offices and Railway Premises Act, 1963

s.6   Reasonable temperatures (i.e. 16°C after 1 hr) must be provided, except in rooms only in use for short periods.
s.7   Suitable ventilation must be provided.
s.8   Sufficient lighting must be provided.

S.R. and O. 1941 No. 94—Factories (Standards of Lighting) Regulations, 1941

s.2 (2)   General standards of illumination shall be not less than 6 ft candles measured at 3 ft level where fittings must be over 25 ft above f.f.l. 2 ft candles measured at 3 ft level provided that at work benches 6 ft candles measured at 3 ft level.
s.2 (b)   Level at other parts where employees go not less than ½ ft candle measured at floor level.
s.3   Cut of angle for fittings brighter than 10 candles/in.² within 100 ft of work places shall be 20° from horizontal. Local lights for illumination of workbenches etc, shall be properly shaded.
ss.3, 4   All possible means shall be taken to avoid shadows and glare likely to cause eye strain.
s.5   Certain processes and works are exempt.

WASTE DISPOSAL AND EFFLUENTS

Public Health (Drainage of Trade Premises) Act, 1937 amends P.H. Act, 1936)

FACTORIES

Administered by Department of the Environment; applies to *England and Wales only (excluding London)*.

Requires arrest of effluents from (inter alia): oil, petrol, garages; pickling vats; tinning; electroplating; dairy, milk products; horticultural products; textiles; radioactive wastes. (Provision to make by-laws repealed by Public Health Act, 1961, q.v.). *Excludes domestic sewage.*

s.2	Occupier who wishes to discharge trade effluent to L.A. sewers must serve notice stating:
	(1) nature and composition;
	(2) maximum daily discharge;
	(3) peak ratio of discharge;
	Exemptions: Laundry effluents (but see s.65 Public Health Act, 1961)
s.7	*Agreements:* The L.A. may agree with occupier to carry out specialist drainage works arising out of the operation of the Act for agreed terms.
s.9	Power to require plans.

Public Health Act, 1936

ss.34–52	Sewage to be purified before discharge to streams.
s.37	Empowers local Authority to require connection to nearby suitable sewer.
s.38	Empowers local Authority to require use of private sewers in certain cases.
s.73	Empowers local Authority to remove trade refuse upon reasonable charge.
s.92	Prevents nuisance due to:
	(1) premises prejudicial to health;
	(2) accumulation or deposit prejudicial to health or nuisance;
	(3) dust or effluvium prejudicial to health or nuisance;
	(4) factories not sufficiently ventilated.

Public Health Act, 1961 (ss.55 to 71)

s.57	Empowers local Authority to make conditions for the acceptance of trade effluents in respect of:
	(1) temperature of effluent;
	(2) pH value of effluent;
	(3) provision of inspection chambers;
	(4) provision of meters.
s.64	Minister may declare any trade effluent not already specified to come under effect of the Acts (1936, 1937 and 1961).
s.65	Laundries may be brought under the Acts in certain circumstances.
s.72	Steam (except from locomotives) is Statutory Nuisance under P.H. Act, 1936.

Clean Air Act, 1956

ss.1, 2	Prohibit emission of dark smoke from chimneys, some qualifications.
s.3	Specifies performance of industrial furnaces.
s.5	Requires that grit and dust shall be extracted from flue gases.
s.10	Local Authority power to approve heights of chimney.
s.11	Prohibits discharge of smoke from unauthorised fuels in Smoke Control Areas.
s.16	Provides that smoke may be statutory nuisance (Part III of P.H. Act, 1936).
s.17	Confirms that extends control of Alkali Act, 1906 in relation to smoke and grit.
s.34	Defines 'industrial plant' as including stills, pots, incinerators.

Rivers (Prevention of Pollution) Act, 1951

s.2	Offence to discharge or permit any poisonous or polluting matter or any other matter likely to pollute or obstruct any stream or natural water course.

Public Health (London) Act, 1936

ss.101–103	

Factories Act, 1961

s.6	Requires wet processes to have *floor drainage*.
s.63	Requires removal or injurious fumes, dust, and exhausts from internal combustion engines.

Alkali etc, Works Regulation Act, 1906

s.1	Hydrochloric acid fumes may not be discharged to atmosphere over certain concentrations (5% maximum or 1 gr./ft^3).
s.2	Noxious and offensive fumes must be removed as far as practicable from exhaust gases.
s.3	Acidic wastes, alkaline wastes and wastes containing sulphides etc, shall not be mixed.
s.4	Alkali wastes may not be discharged without prior practicable means of abating any nuisance which could arise.
s.6	Acid gases and fumes may not be discharged to atmosphere over certain concentrations, i.e.:
	SO_3-equivalent: 4 gr./ft^3.
	HCl: $\frac{1}{5}$gr.·ft^3.
	Applies to:
	Sulphuric Acid manufacture (lead chamber process).
	Hydrochloric acid manufacture.
	Hydrochloric acid used in manufacturing processes.
	Tin plate flux works.
	Salt works (extraction of salt from brine).
s.7	Noxious or offensive gases may not be discharged to atmosphere from *any* works contained in First Schedule.
s.8	HSC powers to require control of discharge from cement works and smelting works in certain cases.

Town and Country Planning Act, 1962

s.12 (3)	Deposit of waste comprises 'change of use', including cases where material alteration of height or spread of existing (approved) waste is involved.

Clean Rivers (Estuaries and Tidal Waters) Act, 1960

s.1	Extends control of trade effluent discharges to estuaries and tidal waters ('controlled waters').
	Schedule defines seawards limits of controlled waters.

Water Scotland Act, 1946: 4th Schedule

s.37	Prohibits discharge to natural courses or land of washing water and liquids used in manufacture of gas and other items including those given below:

gas;	vitriol;
gas by-products;	paraffin;
naphtha;	dyestuffs.

s.38   No gas shall be allowed to foul water belonging to statutory water authority.

Highways Act, 1959

s.142   Prohibits discharge of water (including surface water) into public highway.

WASTE DISPOSAL AND EFFLUENTS

Public Health (Drainage of Trade Premises) Act, 1937

s.1   Local Authority may accept trade effluent.

s.2 (1)   Trade effluent notice shall be served on local Authority stating:
1. nature of effluent;
2. maximum daily quantity of discharge;
3. maximum rate of discharge at any time.

(3)   Local Authority may accept effluents conditionally.

s.7   Local Authority may enter into a particular agreement with occupier for the provision of effluent and/or sewage disposal.

s.9   Local Authority may require plans of private drainage works at any time.

Rivers (Prevention of Pollution) Act, 1951

s.2   Prohibits any matter which does or could pollute being discharge to any stream directly or indirectly.

s.4   Prohibits any works to streams which disturb the bed or banks etc, and so pollute the flow.

*s.5   River Authorities may make by-laws.

*s.6   Minister may extend the Act to cover certain estuaries and coastal waters.

s.7   New or altered outlets to streams shall not be constructed without the consent of the River Authority, who may impose conditions.

Rivers (Prevention of Pollution) Act, 1961

s.5   River Authorities may at any time reasonably vary the conditions for discharge to streams etc.

s.7 (4)   s.5 above applied also to indirect discharges.

Rivers (Prevention of Pollution) (Scotland) Act, 1951

*ss.2, 5   Secretary of State for Scotland may define River Pollution Board Areas.

s.11   Power to make by-laws.

s.22   Prohibits of any solid or polluting liquid matter into streams either directly or indirectly.

s.24   Prohibits works to beds or banks of streams, etc, that could pollute.

s.25   River Pollution Authorities may make by-laws for any stream.

s.28   New or altered discharges to streams etc, may be made only with consent of RPA's, which may be conditional.

*s.29   SoSS may extend Act to Firths of Clyde and Forth.

s.35   Dry water-coursed included in provisions.

Rivers (Prevention of Pollution) (Scotland) Act, 1965

s.1 (1)   All wastes discharging to streams etc, require RPS's consent.

(2)   Application for such consent shall include details of effluent including:
1. nature of composition;
2. temperature;
3. maximum daily volume;
4. maximum possible rate of discharge.

s.7 (3)   s.20 of 1961 Act (q.v.) also applies to indirect discharge.

s.12   Deposit of any solid refuse so that it could pollute any streams etc, is prohibited.

Public Health (London) Act, 1936

s.57   Effluents may not be discharged to sewers if they are:
1. possible cause of nuisance;
2. dangerous or injurious;
3. polluting;
4. at a temperature greater than 110°F.

s.58   GLC may proscribe certain substances prohibited from discharge to sewers.

s.61   Brewery washings are exempt from ss.57, 58 if they are:
1. cool
2. contain less than 3% solids;

s.62   Prohibits discharge to sewers of:
1. petroleum;
2. petroleum-spirit (ref. Petroleum (Consolidation) Act, 1928);
3. calcium carbide.

s.82   Defines accumulations of waste and rubbish as statutory nuisance.

s.92   Local Authority shall remove trade refuse if so required at reasonable cost.

s.101   Gas washings shall not pollute water supply.

ss.181, 188   In food preparation areas: 1. drains shall be separate from sewers; 2. refuse shall be regularly removed.

SERVICES INSTALLATIONS

Minister has power to make specific regulations under these sections or sub-sections marked with an asterisk.

Public Health Act, 1936

s.107   Requires adequate washing-down facilities where offensive trades are carried on.

Public Health Act, 1961

s.72   Empowers Local Authority to declare *discharge of steam* statutory nuisance.

Factories Act, 1961

*s.3   Requires reasonable temperatures to be maintained.

s.4   Requires suitable ventilation to be provided and removal of dust and fumes.

s.5   Requires suitable natural and artificial lighting.

ss.12, 13   Requires all electrical machinery (unless in separate secure accommodation) to be securely fenced. Means of prompt local cut-off shall be provided.

s.31 (1)	Explosive dust-making processes shall be ventilated.
s.32	Steam boilers shall have:
	1. test pressure gauge attachment;
	2. low water protection device;
	3. safety valve;
	4. stop valve on steam main;
	5. steam pressure gauge;
	6. transparent water gauge;
	7. a number.
s.35	Steam receivers construction and safety devices.
s.36	Air receivers construction and safety devices.
s.39	Water sealed gas holders—use and safety precautions.
*s.48 (7)	*Means of audible warning in case of fire* shall be provided in all parts.
*s.50	*Adequate means of fire fighting* shall be provided.
s.57	*Drinking water facilities* shall be provided (drinking fountains implied).
*s.58	Requires provision of warm water for washing.
s.63	Process dust, fumes, exhaust from internal combustion engines must be removed from as near sources as possible.
s.68	In humid atmospheres:
	1. two hygrometers shall be provided in each room.
	2. two tables (as schedule 1) in each room.
	3. two forms for records in each room.
	4. no humidification shall take place over 72½°F, wet, or, in special cases, over 80°F, wet.
	5. no humidification shall take place when wet and dry bulb difference is less than that shown in table (schedule 1 of the Act).
	6. only pure water shall be used for humidification.
*s.75	Where women or young persons are employed in contact with lead compounds, sufficient ventilation shall be provided to remove dust and fumes.
*s.123	*Electrical substations shall be considered as part of factory* (if persons can enter them).

Shops, Offices and Railway Premises Act, 1963

s.6	Rooms shall be maintained at 16°C after 1 hr of occupation.
s.7	Rooms shall be adequately ventilated, either naturally or mechanically.
s.8	Rooms shall be sufficiently lighted either naturally or artificially.
*s.10	Warm water or hot and cold water shall be provided for washing.
s.11	Drinking water facilities shall be provided.
s.34	Audible fire alarms shall be provided to all parts of the premises.

Noise Abatement Act, 1960

s.1	Noise and vibration becomes statutory nuisance under Part III (ss.91–110) of Public Health Act, 1936.
s.2	Loudspeakers shall not operate in any space open to the general public.

Clean Air Act, 1956

*s.11	Smoke from use of unauthorised fuels may not be discharged in smoke control areas.
*s.24	Empowers building regulations to control heating apparatus for the purposes of the Act.

Water (Scotland) Act, 1946

s.11	Water authorities shall supply water provided they are satisfied that it would not prejudice their supplies and current and future obligations.
s.19	Water authorities may contract to supply water in bulk.
.s.34	Provides that water used continuously for purposes other than heating may be required to be metered.
ss.60–65	Local Water Authorities power to make by-laws.

Petroleum (Consolidation) Act, 1928

s.1	Over 3 gal. petroleum spirit shall not be kept without licence.
*s.10	Minister's power to make bylaws for keeping of petroleum spirit.
*ss.12, 19	Ministers power to make regulations to extend definition to other substances.
s.23	Defines 'petroleum' spirit as that which under test gives off an inflammable vapour at temperature less than 74°F (N.B. 2nd schedule specified test apparatus —but *see* page **7** 00).

Electricity (Factories Act) Special Regulations, 1944: S.R. & O. 1944 No. 739)

s.4	Arrangements shall be made for when work is carried out on a section of a h.t. switchboard all other sections shall be separated and secure.

Electricity (Factory and Workshop) Regulations, 1908: S.R. & O. 1908 No. 1312

R.12	Electric motors shall have switch adjacent to hand for operator.
R.15	Switchboards having bare conductors shall be either
	1. in separate and secure accommodation;
	2. fenced or enclosed.
R.26	All places containing electrical apparatus shall be properly lighted.
R.30	Substations shall be ventilated.

Electricity Supply Regulations, 1937

R.32	Electricity Authority may require consumer's installation to be suitable and safe.
RR.27–29	Recognise I.E.E. Regulations as applicable.

Water Act, 1945

ss.19, s.27	Water undertakings shall provide, water supply in providing it does not prejudice their statutory obligations.

Public Health (London) Act, 1936

s.101	Gas washings may not pollute water supply.
s.181	In food preparation areas, water supplies shall be fed from cistern separate from these to sanitary facilities.

MEANS OF ESCAPE AND FIRE AND EXPLOSION
PREVENTION

Factories Act, 1961

s.31 (1)   Explosive dust-making processes shall be (a) enclosed; (b) ventilated and cleaned; (c) protected from all possible sources of ignition.

(2)   Explosives dust making processes shall be either (a) pressure enclosed; or (b) have explosion reliefs, baffles and chokes.

s.40, 45   Factories shall have local Authority *Mean of Escape* if
     1. More than 20 persons are employed
     2. Explosives or highly flammable materials are used or stored.

*s.46   Minister power to make special regulations as to Means of Escape.

s.48 (2) (3)   Rooms containing *more than 10 persons :*   shall have:
     Routes of exits :   doors
     Doors at foots of staircases :   opening out

(4)   Hoists and lifts shall be enclosed with fire resisting materials and doors.

(6)   Every exit *M of E shall be marked unless obvious.*

(7)   Noise of audible warning in all parts shall be installed.

(10)   Access must be arranged so there is free gangway to MoE.

*s.50   Ministers power to make special regulations as to fire precaution, construction and materials.

*s.51   Adequate means for *fire fighting* must be provided and readily available.

Shops, Offices and Railway Premises Act, 1963

s.28   Allowances for MoE must be made to all persons likely to be in shop or office.

s.29 (1)   Fire Certificate must be obtained from Local Fire Authority will be given for the total number of persons in the premises in accordance with this and/or the Factories Act, 1961.

(5)   No more than the number of persons stated in the Certificate may be employed in the premises.

s.34   Audible Fire Alarms shall be provided in all parts of the premises.

London Building (Constructional) By-Laws, 1972

Part XIII : Oil Storage

Rooms containing oil-burning appliances must be fire resistant according to Table 7.10, capacity V, fire resistance.
Floor must be leak-proof.
Rooms must be ventilated with fire-resisting structural standards.
Exemption for daily storage tanks (under 900 litre capacity) in existing buildings.
Catchpits capacity 110% of storage capacity; include a sump for drainage.
Separate storage rooms for oil storage fire resist table capacity—fire resistance. Limit of openings to storage rooms. Situations in lowest storey if capacity 750 gal (certain exceptions).
Valves, warning devices, etc.
External oil fuel storage.
Corrosion proof.
   6 ft (2 m) from any building or boundary if capacity less than 750 gal (3400 litres).
   20 ft (6 m) from any building or boundary if capacity greater than 750 gal (3400 litres).
Catchpits required for capacity greater than 275 gal (1250 litres) if above ground.

Use of Electrical Equipment in Hazardous Areas

Fittings Categories :

division   0   Pressurised in inert gas.
          1   Flame-proof equipment buxher, Cert.
          2   Explosion unlikely for well-designed equipment.
Administration by H & SE.

Explosives Act, 1875

s.3   Defines explosives as materials used to produce an explosion or pyrotechnic display, including:

gunpowder	fog signals
nitro-glycerine	fireworks
dynamite	fuses
guncotton	rockets
colloidal cotton	percussion caps
blasting powders	detonators
fulminates	cartridges
coloured fires	ammunition

   Any processes on explosives.

s.6   Plans of factories, explosives stores or magazine shall be submitted to Home Office with application for licence.
   Note : See Memorandum on Procedure for application for Licenses under Explosives Acts, by H.M. Inspector of Explosives).

*s.10 (1)   Stores and magazines intended for explosives shall only be used for that purpose.

(2)   No iron or steel shall be exposed in any building.

(3)   Each store, magazine or 'danger-house' shall have lightning conductor.

(6)   Notice of the permitted amount of explosive shall be affixed to the building.

s.46   Exceptions for manufacture of small arms ammunition.

s.48   Exceptions for small fireworks manufacture.

ss.97–101   Exceptions for rocket stations etc.

*s.106   Explosives defined by Order in Council come under the Act.
   Note : 'Danger building' defined by Order in Council No. 4, d. 27.11.1875.

Explosives Act, 1923

*s.1   Empowers SoS (Home Office) to prescribe special precautions to be taken in any registered premises.
   Note : For detailed working of Explosives Acts, see 'Guide to Explosives Acts, 1675, 4th Edition', J. N. Thomas, HMSO).

Factories Act, 1961 (Extension of Section 40) Regulations, 1964 : SI. 1964 No. 762.

Buildings ancillary to factories, not themselves factories as defined, shall be considered as under s.40 of the Act for means of escape purposes where :
   1. they come under the terms of the Shop, Offices and Railway Premises Act, 1963 (q.v.)
   2. more than 20 persons are employed therein.

STATUTORY AUTHORITIES

The following bodies may need to be consulted in connection with the design, or their approval may be required for intended processes, installations or activities.

DISTRICT AUTHORITY

Town and Country Planning

In addition to applying the Planning Acts in respect of the external form of the building and the proposed use of the site for its purpose, the planning authority is responsible for official liasion with the Highways and Transport Authorities and the Water Authority;

Building Regulations

Public Health Inspector

Concerned with sanitary and health matters within the premises and general matters of public health in the neighbourhood;

Trade Effluent Inspector

Drainage of Trade Effluents to Local Authority Systems.

INDEPENDENT AUTHORITIES

Local Fire Brigade

All fire-fighting and fire-protection facilities; in some circumstances it could be responsible for issuing certificate under the Offices Shops & Railway Premises Act 1963, permitting occupation, but usually under control of Factory Inspectorate of Health and Safety Executive.

Water Authority

The Statutory Water Supply undertakings also act as agents; Concerned with EXTRACTION FROM AND DISCHARGES TO Natural water courses; also may be interested in external storage areas exposed to the elements; (see Schedule below); where tidal waters are concerned the Sea Fisheries Authorities are the interested bodies.

Health and Safety Executive

Administers Health and Safety at Work, etc. Act, 1974, Factories Act, 1961 (Safety, health and welfare of workers) and Alkalis Acts (fumes and noxious gaseous discharges to the atmosphere), and will play an increasing role in the control and supervision of all places of work, in conjunction with the Local Authorities.

BIBLIOGRAPHY

Allen, W. A., 'Factory design for the future' *Production Engineer*, London (June 1960).

Allen, W. A., 'Modern American factory design' *DSIR/BRS*, Watford, (Oct. 1953).

Department of Employment, *Safety Health & Welfare Booklets* (Several titles). Especially *Booklet No. 25: Basic Rules for Safety & Health at Work*, London.

Factory Building Research Committee, *Factory Building Studies*:
  No. 1 Design of multi-storey factories (1959)
  No. 2 Lighting of factories (1959)
  No. 3 Floor finishes (1959)
  No. 4 Structural loading (1960)
  No. 5 Sites and foundations (1960)
  No. 6 Noise in factories (1960)
  No. 7 Structural framework for single-storey factories (1960)
  No. 8 Colouring in factories (1960)
  No. 9 Fire protection (1960)
  No. 10 Electrical supply and distribution (1962)
  No. 11 Thermal insulation (1962)
  No. 12 Economics of factory building (1962),
(Published by HMSO, London).

Gregory, S. A., *The design method*, Butterworth, London (1966)

Henn, W., *Buildings for industry*, Iliffe, London (1965).

Hertz, R. (Ed) Neufert, E. (Transl), *Architects' data*, Crosby Lockwood Staples, London (1970).

Krull, H., 'Modern trends in industrial building', *Progress*, (March 1961).

Manning, P., 'Industrial production buildings: Design Guide', *Architects' Journal*, London (6/4/66 and 27/4/66).

Mills, E. D., *Factory building* Leonard Hill, London (1967).

Mills, E. D., *The modern factory*, Architectural Press, 2nd ed London (1959).

Mills, E. D., *The Changing Workplace*, George Godwin (1972).

Sliwa, J. A., *(Ed)* and Fairweather, L. *(Ed)*, *A. J. Metric Handbook*, Architectural Press, London (1969).

Stone, P. A., *BRS Factory Building Study No. 12: Economics of Factory Buildings*, HMSO London (1962).

Trickett, K., 'Plant and site Layout' *Better Factories*, published by Institute of Directors, London (1963).

ACOUSTICS

Aldersley-Williams, A. G., *BRS Factory Building Study No. 6: Noise in factories*, HMSO London (1960).

Wilson, Sir Alan *(Chairman)*, *Noise: Report of the Committee on the Problem of Noise*, HMSO London (July 1963).

Department of Employment, 'Noise and the worker', *S.H. & W. Booklet No. 23*, HMSO London.

ANALYSIS

Bailey, N. T. J., 'Statistical methods in architecture and their use in planning', *Bartlett Society Trans.* (1962/3).

Currie, R. M., *Work study*, 2nd edn, Pitman, London (1963, 1968).

Department of Environment (M.P.B.W.), *Research and Development Bulletin N/3. Activity data method*, HMSO London (1966).

Duckworth, W. E., *A Guide to operational research*, 2nd ed, Methuen, London (1964).

COLOUR

Gloag, H. L., *Factory Building Study No. 8: Colouring in Factories*, HMSO London.
Hardy, A. C., *Colour in architecture*, Leonard Hill, London (1967).

COMMUNICATIONS AND SITING

Sargent, A. J., *Seaports and hinterlands*, A. & C. Black, London (1938).

DESIGN METHOD

Bruce Archer, L., 'Systematic method for designers', *Reprint from 'Design' magazine, revised*, Council of Industrial Design, London (1965).
Bruce Archer, L., 'Technological innovation and methodology', *Science Policy Foundation*, Inforlink Ltd. (1971).
Gregory, S. A. *(Ed)*, *The design method*, Butterworth (1966).
Moseley, L., 'A rational design theory for planning buildings based upon the analysis and solution of circulation problems', *Architects' Journal*, (11/9/63).
Stone, P. A., 'Factory buildings, evaluation and decisions' *Better Factories*, Institute of Directors, (1963).
McKown, R., *Comprehensive guide to factory law*, Chantry Publications, London (1961).
Matthews, Ryan and Simpson, 'Schedule of products and processes under legislation', Information Sheet 1837, *Architects' Journal*, London (4/5/66 and 18/5/66).
O'Keeffe, P. and Parlett, D. S. *(Ed)*, *Building Regulations (1972): Checklists and Index*, 2nd edn, House Information Services Ltd. London (1975).
Samuels, H. *Factory Law*, 7th edn, Charles Knight, London (1962).
Department of Employment, *Structural Requirements of the Factories Act, 1961*, S.H. and W. Booklet No. 16.

SECURITY

Fire Protection Association, Booklet No. 30: *Electricity and the fire risk in industrial and commercial premises*, London.
Fire Protection Association, Booklet No. 40: *Planning fire safety in industry*, London (1964).
Fire Protection Association, Booklet No. 24: *Industrial solvents and flammable liquids*, London.
Fire Protection Association, Booklet No. 29: *Fire hazards of static electricity*, London.
Fire Research Station, Fire Note No. F.5: *Fire-venting in single-storey building*, HMSO, London (1965).
Langdon-Thomas, G. J., *Fire protection in factory buildings*, Factory Building Study No. 9.
Ministry of Labour, *Dust explosions in factories*, New Series No. 22, HMSO, London.
Ministry of Labour, *Fire fighting in factories*, New Series No. 100, HMSO, London.

STRUCTURE

Creasy, L. R., 'Economics of Framed Structures', *Proc. Inst. Civil Engineers*, London (March 1959).
F.R.B.C., *Structural loading*, FBS No. 4, London
F.B.R.C., *Structural framework for single-storey factories*, FBS No. 7, London.
Manning, Peter, *Design of Roofs for single-storey General-Purpose Factories*, University of Liverpool, Dept. of Building Service, Liverpool (1962).

WASTES

Matthews, Ryan and Simpson, 'Industrial Wastes & Effluents', Information Sheet 1382, *Architects' Journal*, London (1/6/66).
Southgate, B. A., Treatment & Disposal of Industrial Waste Waters, Water Pollution Research Laboratory, HMSO, London (1948).
Institution of Chemical Engineers (Working Party), *Provisional Code of Practice for the Disposal of Wastes*, Inst. of Chem. E., London (1971).

ENVIRONMENT

Hickish, D. E., 'Thermal sensations of workers in light industry in summer' *Journal of Hygiene*, (March 1955)
Keyte, M. J. and Gloag, H. L., *Factory Building Study No. 2: The lighting of factories*, HMSO, London.
Longmore, J., *Ergonomics for Industry: Booklet 9: Lighting of workplaces*, HMSO, London (1966)
McCollough, W., *Physical working conditions*, Gower Press, London (1969).
Manning, P. *(Ed)*, 'Industrial production buildings: Recommended environmental standards', Information Sheet 1388, *Architects' Journal* (8/6/1966).
Matthews, P., *Workrooms*, Design Centre, London (1969).

ERGONOMICS

Edholm, O. G., The biology of work, World U.P. (1967).
Murrell, K.F.H., *Ergonomics*, Chapman & Hall, London (1965).
Woodson, W. E., *Human engineering guide for equipment designers*, University of California Press, Berkeley, Ca., U.S.A.

INDUSTRIAL MANAGEMENT

George, F. H., *Cybernetics in management*, Pan Books, London (1970)

LEGAL

Central Office of Information, *Incentives for industry in the areas of expansion*, Dept. of Industry, London (1974).
Cooper, W. M., Outlines of industrial law, 5th edn, Butterworth, London (1966).
Fife, I., Machin, E. A. and Horsler, P. G. *(Eds)*, Redgrave's Factories Acts, 20th edn, Butterworth, London (1962).
McKnown, R., *Comprehensive Guide to Factory Law*, Chantry Publications, London.

Fig. 7.32 *Heinz Factory Wigan, Lancs. Two-level production area with intermediate service floor between. Note the 2-storey warehouse and loading bay beyond: raw materials at the upper level and finished goods at lower level. The bridge in the foreground provides access from the administration and employees' amenity building (Architects: Matthews, Ryan & Partners)*

Fig. 7.33 *Mullard television tube factory, Durham. Note conveyors at working and high levels and the underfloor ducting for low-level services distribution. (Consulting Engineers: W. S. Atkins & Partners)*

Fig. 7.34   Park Farm Industrial Estate, Folkestone. Unit factories built in steep terrain, showing terracing to give vehicle access to flatted factory units on two floors. (Owners: McKay Securities Ltd. Architects: Paton Orr & Partners)

Fig. 7.35   International Flavours and Fragrances factory, Enfield, London. A single-storey factory with north-light roof showing 2-storey office block and single-storey laboratory attached. Note also the security fence and external storage. (Architects: Edward D. Mills & Partners)

FACTORIES

EXAMPLES

Parke Davis Pharmaceutical Factory, Pontypool, Wales
Architect: Percy Thomas Partnership
Architects Journal (31st July 1974)

John Player & Sons Cigarette Factory, Nottingham
Architect: Arup Associates
Building (31st March 1972)

Lyon Brush Works, Killingworth, Newcastle-on-Tyne
Architect: Ryder Yates & Partners
Building (31st March 1972)

WD & HO Wills Cigarette Factory, Bristol, Somerset
Architect: Skidmore Owings and Merrill and YRM
Architects Journal (October 1975)

Cigarette Factory, Richmond, Virginia, USA
Architect: Skidmore Owings and Merrill
Architects Journal (October 1975)

Perfumery Factory, Tadworth, Surrey
Architect: Piano & Rogers
Architects Journal (December 1974)

Potash Mine, Baulby, Yorks
Architect: Frederick Gibberd & Partners
Architects Journal (August 1974)

Power Station, Didcot, Berks.
Architect: Frederick Gibberd & Partners
Architects Journal (August 1974)

May & Baker Pharmaceutical Factory, Dagenham, Essex
Architect: Edward D. Mills & Partners
Architect and Building News (26th October 1960).

Pharmaceutical Factories, Hoddesdon, Herts and Eastleigh, Hants
Architect: Edward D. Mills & Partners
Architect and Building News (26th October 1960)

ACKNOWLEDGEMENT

The assistance of Ross Gilhome, R.I.B.A. in providing material and reference is gratefully acknowledged. Much of the research needed to produce this article was originally his.

Paul Darrington, *ARIBA. Paul Darrington received his professional training at Leed's School of Architecture. After qualifying in 1958, he worked as an assistant with J. Douglass Mathews (later, Mathews, Ryan & Simpson) with whom he gained experience in design of laboratory, commercial and industrial buildings. He has worked on buildings for food processing, pharmaceuticals, metal working, finishing and testing, timber by-products, automobiles, electronics, and artificial fibres. He was a member of the team which collaborated with Peter Manning in the preparation of the Architect's Journal 'Design Guide' on Industrial Buildings, published in 1966.*

He is particularly interested in the methodology of architectural design and the interactions between the disciplines contributing to the construction industry, and spent four years with a firm of multi-disciplinary consultants. He is now in practice in Epsom, Surrey. He is an Associate of the Institute of Arbitrators and a member of the Operational Research Society.

8 WAREHOUSES

A. F. BONE, A.R.I.B.A.
Beard Bennett Wilkins & Partners

INTRODUCTION

It is not practical to give here a complete compendium and designer's manual of warehouse and distribution service requirements and solutions. There are as many requirements as there are operators and almost as many solutions.

The purpose of this section is to provide a simplified aide-memoir to the basic thinking involved and further precise details can be found by recourse to the sources of reference given at the end.

The operations considered by most people as 'warehousing' have expanded and changed in content in the last quarter century so that the word 'warehousing' is no longer adequate. This is only a part of a total process of distribution from producer to consumer and, in the simplest definition, is the periodic storage of goods in transit through a distribution network. Consequently it may be preferable to regard a 'warehouse' only as a particular type of goods container used at node points in the network.

SITING

The network of distribution may be simple or complex and the siting of a storage unit is determined, primarily, by
(i) The location of the source of article to be distributed.
(ii) The form of transport employed.
(iii) The particular part of the distribution system being served.

With air and water transport the preliminary storage point is often a local unit on, or near, the airport or quayside. Subsequent movement from this local unit, in most cases, will be by rail, or by road, to another node point in the system. Except when dealing with containerised goods, specially designed carriers, or special contract freight movements, most rail distribution from air/water ports or other sources is to a rail depot where goods in transit remain for a limited time before being moved further by road transport.

Generally speaking, the design team will not be involved in the siting of air/waterport or rail depots and, thus, most siting studies are related to road transport. In other words virtually all consumer goods final transit is by road.

The positioning of storage facilities for road transport when related to air/water/rail transport will be determined by
(i) The road network serving the air/water/rail depot.
(ii) The ultimate goods destination.
(iii) Statutory/union regulations related to loadings, speeds, hours of operation, etc.
(iv) Transport economics.
(v) Site availability.
(vi) Official planning policies.
(vii) Availability of labour for depot operation staff.
(viii) Availability of services for the depot and vehicles.

Inevitably, the evolving motorway network is a major factor in siting studies related to national or very large distribution networks. The motorway network is often a considerable factor in dealing with regional or purely local distribution studies. However, in studies relating to storage facilities serving cities or large urban areas the densities and difficulties of road traffic is more often the most important factor. For example, producers of fresh food with long-established factories in a large urban area are frequently faced with very serious transport problems in trying to serve valued customers beyond a certain limit, due solely to traffic congestion causing delays resulting in loss of freshness. This problem can inhibit the producers' business to such an extent that business failure can result.

Other factors to be considered in storage unit siting are:
(i) National, regional and local planning policies, the effects of which can have an enormous impact on a distribution system beneficially or harmfully (it is often crucial that planning policy aspects are ascertained as the first task of a study both in relation to the actual storage unit siting and to the transportation and distribution volume changes which might accrue from planning proposals or changes),
(ii) Probable or forecast changes in demand over a period of time resulting from possible population changes, consumption pattern changes, manufacturing changes, etc. As considerable capital is ventured in establishing a new storage unit demand variations are a most important factor and one where, in most cases, the design team is not trained to contribute materially.

(iii) Hazards from, or to, adjoining sites, e.g. it is thought generally that food storage units should avoid areas subject to severe air pollution by industry. Similarly, most authorities are hesitant to permit hazardous materials storage where a resulting hazard would be difficult to control.
(iv) Personnel problems, e.g. differential union rates in adjoining areas, local political difficulties, social or industrial tensions. These are all matters which can give rise to problems with which distributors may have to deal and which may need serious consideration in siting studies.

PLANNING

A distribution system may be for:
(a) Simple movement from source to user, e.g. egg farm to consumer.
(b) Source to processer or manufacturer, e.g. metal ore to foundry.
(c) Manufacturer to wholesaler, e.g. automobile manufacturer to main franchise holder.
(d) Wholesaler to retailer, e.g. bulk groceries dealer to shopkeeper.
(e) Retailer to customer, e.g. bookseller to customer.

A system may cover one or more of these stages in any particular study. In principle, a complete system will incorporate all five stages. The detailed arrangement of a system will depend upon:
(a) The article to be moved.
(b) The method of movement.
(c) The distance of movement.
(d) The quantity to be moved in a given time.
(e) In certain instances, the time limit between source and use (e.g. eggs, milk, butter, etc.) or the time limits of seasonal availability (e.g. strawberries, game, etc.).

In the above examples not all the items need a warehouse in the previously accepted sense. Nevertheless, even open storage requires the same discipline to achieve an orderly flow from source to user.

Usually it is not necessary to consider the total distribution system as few organisations require to establish a complete new system. Invariably it is a question of extending an established system, refining part of such a system, or grafting in a new sequence.

The simplest operation is not likely to require the services of distribution specialists (e.g. egg farmer selling direct to the public). On the other hand, distribution operators exist who are unaware, or unappreciative of the prime importance to their profit margins and sales of an efficient system of movement and storage.

In considering a distribution problem and, therefore, any warehousing requirement, the following questions are fundamental:
(a) What is being moved?
(b) Why is it being moved?
(c) Which part of the distribution system is the particular operation to serve?
(d) In what form is the item received?
(e) Is storage really necessary?

In the case of question (e), if the answer is 'yes' then the following additional questions need to be answered:

(i) In what form must/can it be stored?
(ii) For how long is storage required?
(iii) What form of storage is most effective and/or most economical?
(iv) What means of movement is used at the receiving point?
(v) What means of movement is used in the storage area?
(vi) In what form will the item leave the storage area?
(vii) What means of movement will be used in delivery to the next stage?

The answers to these questions will produce further questions, for example:

(a) Delivery vehicle by water / air / rail / road	what type and size of vehicle, what are its movement / servicing / harbouring / parking requirements?
(b) Storage requirement to be	open/closed, warm / temperate / chilled/frozen, dry/humid/wet, long term/short term, bonded/hazardous, etc?
(c) Storage method to be by	pallets/containers, block stacking/racking, silos/tanks, etc?
(d) Movement in/out of storage by	hand/hand trolley, powered fork lift, mechanical picker, conveyor belt, automated trailer, pipe/elevator, etc?
(e) Security facilities required for	smoke prevention, fire prevention, dust prevention, corrosion prevention, escape routes, fire fighting, theft prevention, vermin control, customs and excise control, stock checking, etc?
(f) Ancillary facilities required for	operators amenities, (toilets / mess room / first aid / rest room / warm-up room), supervision, vehicle maintenance etc?

Throughout the design study, the testing question of true economy must be posed. Many operators are unable to give an accurate operational cost per item of the distribution and storage on-costs. This gives rise to casual thinking on efficiency and service, and will be reflected in the performance of profit margins.

The reduction of distribution and storage costs must be the constant endeavour and this requires thought, study, care and effort. Economic distribution and storage are not necessarily synonymous with cheap vehicles and cheap installations. When the advice of a building team is sought it is part of the team's responsibility to guard the distribution operator against false economy. This may make it necessary

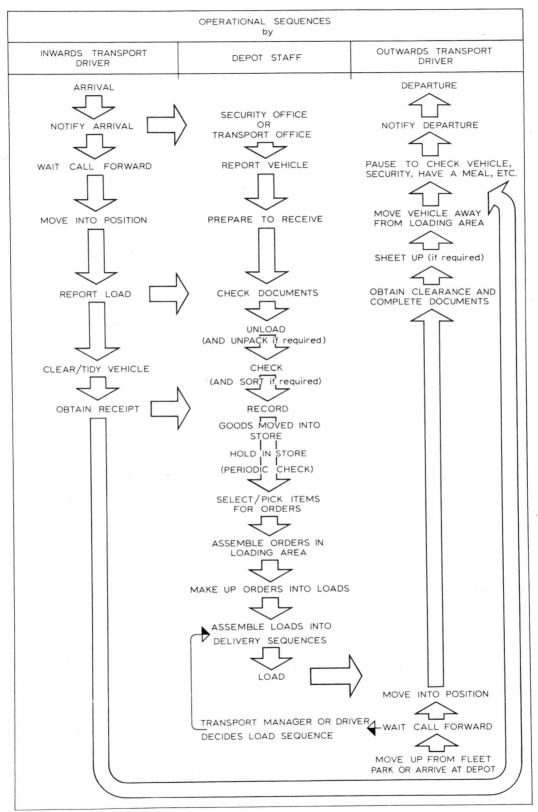

Fig. 8.1 Line diagram of basic normal sequence of operations. Based on road transport; other forms of transport have similar sequences.

for the design team's advice to include suggestions for modifying packaging since the packaging of articles is often crucial in determining the selection of transport and storage methods.

Cheap warehousing is available (almost always) for rent, purchase, or construction. Such units will suit many operators, but when an operator, or a producing company, seeks the services of a design team, it means that a particular problem requires to be solved or that suitable facilities are not available at the capacity/cost/location sensible and acceptable to the user. It is not unknown for an operator to be unable to specify his particular problem; he just knows that his competitors are winning and he is looking at all aspects of his business.

In practice every operator has special requirements, due solely to:
(a) The articles involved.
(b) The means of transport used.
(c) The area of operation.

The question of selecting the means of transport to and from a point of storage is beyond this brief and is a matter seldom within the jurisdiction of the building design team.

Storage of the articles will be of two basic forms:
(a) Open air storage.
(b) Enclosed (or covered) storage.

The same operational sequence applies to both forms of storage (see Figs 8.1 and 8.2).
(a) Access/arrival system
(b) Arrival sorting process, e.g.
  Vehicle to vehicle
  Plane/train to vehicle
  Ship/train/vehicle to store.
(c) Storage
  Short term e.g. open staging yard,
             covered staging yard.
  Longer term e.g. covered staging yard,
             enclosed or covered storage.
(d) Despatch, i.e.
  Order assembly and checking, shipment packaging, loading system.
(e) Departure.

The term 'staging' in this context means the transfer of a load, or part of a load, or several loads from one, or more, vehicles to other vehicles without an intervening storage period. It is applied normally to road vehicles but could be carried out with any combination of transport forms.

All distribution systems involve administrative recording and, in the main, this is done on paper covering accounting for goods received in storage, and delivered, transport, returnable containers, breakages, sales, wages, insurance, etc. Sufficient facilities must be incorporated to enable operational staff to deal with this essential work, and these may include such special facilities as computer rooms, computer terminals, telex, etc.

Similarly, some staff facilities will be required in all depots to provide rest, refreshment, comfort, toilet, and first aid arrangements. Special arrangements may be required for security patrols, police or fire service access, customs and excise control, etc.

In both open and closed storage the following require the most careful consideration:
(a) The access and manoeuvring space for incoming and outgoing transport, together with the construction techniques needed to cope with these, and,
(b) The size, shape, and environment of the storage area.

It is bad design, bad economics, and bad management to skimp these two studies. The advent of larger and more sophisticated forms of transport and handling means that greater care is needed than hitherto.

In closed storage it is essential to provide a first class, soundly constructed floor (having a surface suited to the operation) together with a roof of equal performance. The design of walls, or vertical enclosure, will be dictated by a variety of factors, not the least important of which being the ability to withstand the usage (and abusage) of the operating staff.

Increasingly, security is a considerable factor. Apart from the annoyance and inconvenience of petty theft, the loss of stock and buildings through fire, or the damage of stock by water or smoke, can be disastrous to the operating company and to the insurers. For example, smoke can cause irreparable damage to micro-circuit electrical equipment such as television sets, pocket calculators, tape recorders, etc.

Understandably, the insurers demands have become very stringent. The more experienced and deep thinking insurers are aware that the present construction and protection codes used by them can be (and are) applied by less experienced, or more rigidly minded, assessors not only to the detriment of the insured but to the insurers in general. For example, it is quite useless to insist on sprinklers to the standards in the latest code (29th) in warehouses full of grain, soluble powders, salt, and similar materials where water is a greater hazard than fire or smoke.

Nevertheless, forms of storage have been developed where fire prevention and fire fighting are extremely difficult, if not actually impossible. It is essential that all the risks are considered with the greatest care (at the outset of any project) by all those involved.

The advice and guidance of the building inspectorate, the fire service, and insurers should be sought at the beginning. Certain limitations and controls are mandatory but, it is only fair to remember that inevitably insurers' assessors, fire service advisors and local authority inspectors are human and capable of honest error especially if over-worked, as many often are. Should the building team consider such a case to have arisen it is best managed with patience, tact and understanding.

Such situations are likely to occur mostly in projects involving new, unfamiliar, or untried forms of operating. The last decade has seen the development of very high forms of enclosed warehouse using very sophisticated arrangements of mechanical handling. Some projects under consideration rise to more than 50 m and a number are in operation at about 30 m. It is considered by their designers and owners that these forms are the best available solution where multiplicity of types and sizes of items are to be handled in very large quantities.

It is too early perhaps to determine whether these high rise forms are genuinely efficient and economical—their use is growing, particularly in the advanced technological countries and especially in Europe; it must be stressed that the UK Fire Research Station has carried out tests which show clearly the fires in these forms of storage are extremely difficult to control with existing resources. The same tests have shown that sprinklers are far from satisfactory unless fitted at every level of every bay—the cost of such a solution

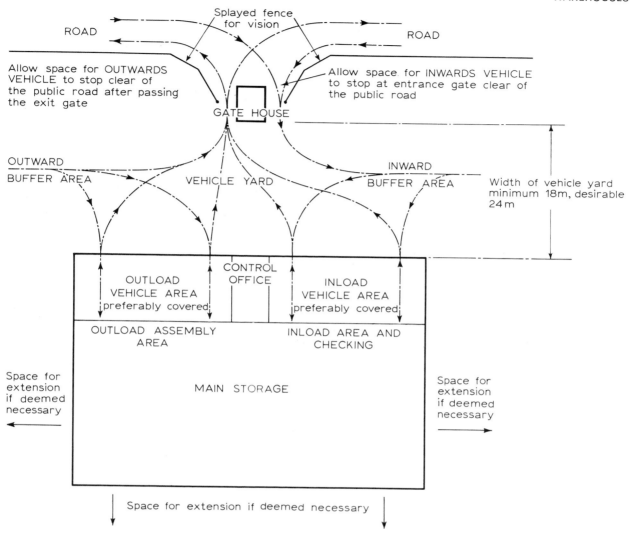

Fig. 8.2 Simplified diagram of basic unit for most uses. Based on road transport to and from a medium-sized depot.

would be prohibitive for most operators.

Other factors which need most careful consideration in high rise warehouses, and others, is the choice of racking and mechanical equipment. The ranges available are considerable and growing, and are also becoming more sophisticated.

The persistence of energy difficulties and of human and mechanical errors in the design construction, and installation of the more advanced equipment has engendered:

(a) The increase of fail/safe arrangements (e.g. standby private generators).

(b) An increase in reliance on methods less susceptible to mechanical failure.

However, computers and mechanical equipment will improve and be better understood and employed with experience. Increased goods movement and rising labour rates in a labour intensive operation will mean that operators of large distributive systems will be forced to undertake very careful cost effectiveness studies in conjunction with the building team before determining which method to adopt.

A further factor to be considered in distribution studies is the advancement of transport systems. The so-called 'continental juggernaut' is the beginning only of a considerable change. It is likely that the 'road train' (i.e. a motorised tug vehicle with two linked trailers) will be permitted in Britain before long. 'Swop-body' systems (i.e. interchangeable motorised tugs with interchangeable container units) are available and in use as are containers for sea/rail/road/air multiple use. Sea 'train-' and sea 'swop-body' systems are being examined and, at the same time, airship/balloon movement of heavy loads is being considered seriously once more. Helicopter and land/sea hovercraft freight movement exist. Pipe distribution of powdered and liquid items is feasible (this is apart from the obvious examples of oil, water, gas, concrete, etc.)

In consequence, some operators are being cautious about their long term policies as capital investment on a system which is quickly out-dated could be commercial suicide. From the designer's point of view it is clear that a close and continuing study will need to be made of transport methods, movement routes, movement aids, packaging systems, handling equipment, storage techniques and equipment, security requirements and techniques, human requirements.

SPACE REQUIREMENTS

These considerations are of real concern to large national and international companies. However, for the smaller operator the type of storage arrangements required can be seen in Figs 8.3 and 8.4.

Fig. 8.3 is fairly typical of many of the units available throughout the country and usually erected by developers for rental. The design and construction are basic and the tenant is responsible in many cases for installing his own lighting, heating, storage equipment, and security facilities.

Fig. 8.4 is fairly typical of a number of relatively larger units employed by many national and international firms and usually such a unit forms part of a network of similar units sited strategically throughout the country. Sometimes

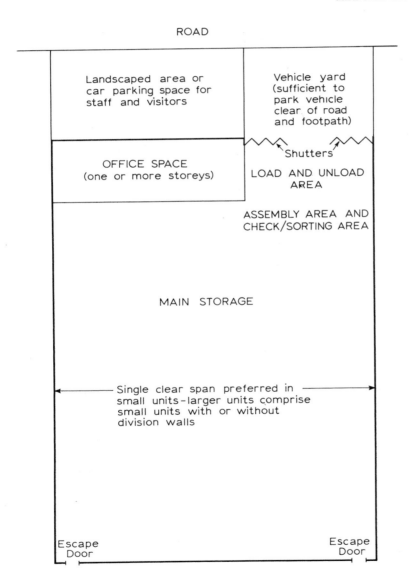

ROAD

Landscaped area or car parking space for staff and visitors

Vehicle yard (sufficient to park vehicle clear of road and footpath)

Shutters

OFFICE SPACE (one or more storeys)

LOAD AND UNLOAD AREA

ASSEMBLY AREA AND CHECK/SORTING AREA

MAIN STORAGE

Single clear span preferred in small units - larger units comprise small units with or without division walls

Escape Door

Escape Door

Note: Police and Fire Authorities usually require reasonable access around the unit, particularly to the rear

Fig. 8.3 Typical layout of small unit often offered by developers for rental.

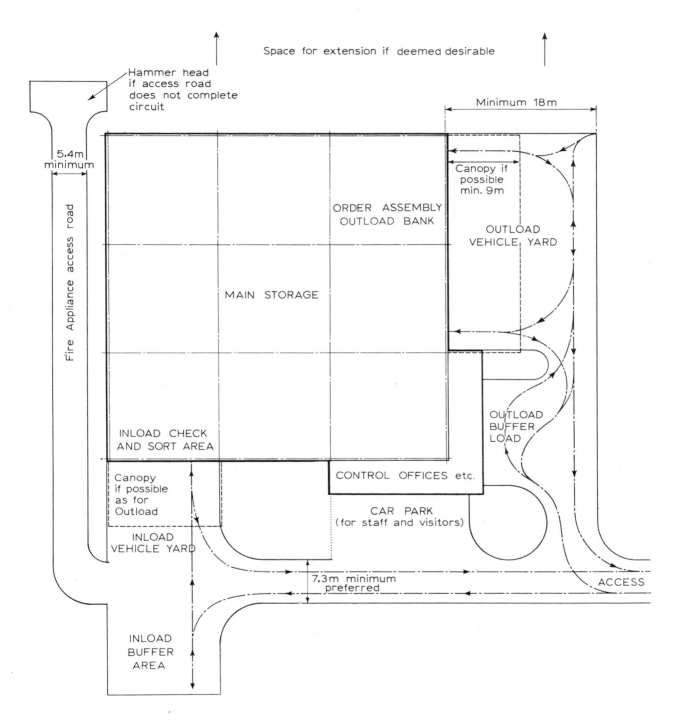

Space for extension if deemed desirable

Hammer head
if access road
does not complete
circuit

Minimum 18m

5.4m
minimum

Fire Appliance access road

Canopy if
possible
min. 9m

ORDER ASSEMBLY
OUTLOAD BANK

OUTLOAD
VEHICLE YARD

MAIN STORAGE

OUTLOAD
BUFFER
LOAD

INLOAD CHECK
AND SORT AREA

Canopy
if possible
as for
Outload

CONTROL OFFICES etc.

CAR PARK
(for staff and visitors)

INLOAD
VEHICLE YARD

7.3m minimum
preferred

ACCESS

INLOAD
BUFFER
AREA

Fig. 8.4 Example of type of layout preferred by a number of larger operators.

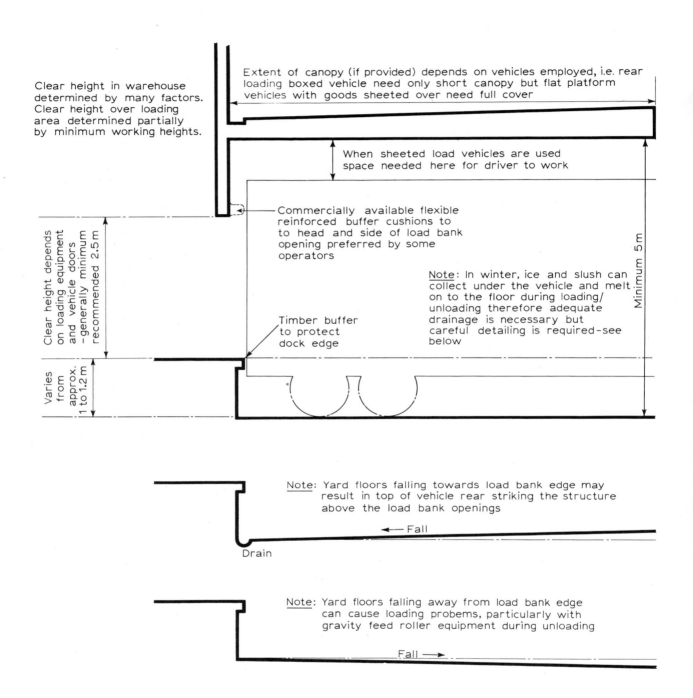

Clear height in warehouse determined by many factors. Clear height over loading area determined partially by minimum working heights.

Extent of canopy (if provided) depends on vehicles employed, i.e. rear loading boxed vehicle need only short canopy but flat platform vehicles with goods sheeted over need full cover

When sheeted load vehicles are used space needed here for driver to work

Commercially available flexible reinforced buffer cushions to to head and side of load bank opening preferred by some operators

Note: In winter, ice and slush can collect under the vehicle and melt on to the floor during loading/ unloading therefore adequate drainage is necessary but careful detailing is required–see below

Timber buffer to protect dock edge

Minimum 5 m

Clear height depends on loading equipment and vehicle doors –generally minimum recommended 2.5 m

Varies from approx. 1 to 1.2 m

Note: Yard floors falling towards load bank edge may result in top of vehicle rear striking the structure above the load bank openings

← Fall

Drain

Note: Yard floors falling away from load bank edge can cause loading probems, particularly with gravity feed roller equipment during unloading

Fall →

Fig. 8.5 Points of importance in relation to load banks and canopies.

such units have integral, or adjoining, chill or cold room facilities either because some of the operator's goods require it or because the operator has links with another operator dealing in chilled or frozen goods and they have combined their distribution networks for mutual benefit.

The necessity or not of providing a raised load bank or dock will depend on the type of transport vehicle being used to and from the distribution unit, the type of mechanical handling equipment used in the distribution unit and, finally, on the operator's experience—sometimes this experience might be called bias, or even blind prejudice! See Fig. 8.5. The same comments apply to the method of storing the goods within the unit. In open storage without cover the goods may be parked side by side in groups or in closed containers or stacked in blocks of one or more layers.

DATA

In closed storage within a building (that is, within a warehouse in the original meaning) the methods of storage are almost legion. The following brief definitions will give an indication of possible variations.

Block stacking: The stacking of loads (boxes, sacks, drums, blocks of items corded or banded together in defined loads, etc) one on top of another in groups one or more loads in width and length. Not suitable for goods or packaging subject to crush damage.

Stillage: A variety of stillages is available but in its simplest form it comprises a timber and/or metal platform (designed to carry an assortment of loads) which may be fitted with wheels or may require to be lifted and moved by other mechanical equipment. Not specifically constructed for movement by fork lift equipment.

Pallets: (see BS 2629; parts 1 and 2). Timber, or metal, or cardboard and plastic platforms of a variety of plan size (1016 × 1219 being a commonly used size) designed to support a unit load and specifically constructed for handling by fork movement equipment. Properly loaded pallets of suitable goods can be block stacked effectively.

Post pallets: Specially designed load platforms, usually of steel, supported on posts at the four corners (often with metal mesh sides between the posts), the posts having feet designed to sit on the floor or on another similar post pallet. Useful for protecting items which may be crushed and for coping with the handling and storage of heavy and awkwardly shaped items not easily handled by other means.

Pallet racking: Steel framing with parallel rails sited to support the edges of pallets at a number of levels above floor level. Framing is designed to allow fork lift equipment to move through the racking to deposit or select loads at various levels and can be used up to approximately 10 m high. Care is needed to ensure accurately levelled floor surface and to ensure floor structure capable of withstanding the heavy point loads resulting, care is also required to ensure the racking structure does not slew due to uneven or incautious loading.

Dead racking: Steel or timber framing supporting a number of platform levels or 'floors' on which goods are stored in recorded sections available for immediate selection. The length, height, capacity, modules, and load carrying ability being infinitely variable.

Live racking: Similar to dead racking but platforms or 'floors' set at a slope which allows items deposited at the upper end of the sloped rack to flow by gravity or powered movement to the lower, selecting, end.

Mobile racking: Dead or live racking units mounted on floor rails and moved sideways on the rails by hand or electric power to enable the operator to reach any particular section at will. Main advantage is the reduction of order selection gangway needed; cost effectiveness needs careful evaluation.

Containers: Specially manufactured metal boxes 2438 wide × 2590 high × 6090/9144/12192 long, capable of enclosing securely a variety of boxed or palletised goods for movement by road, rail, sea, or air and capable of being stored in the open in one or more layers (it is dangerous to stack more than 3 No. containers high); available with completely enclosed sides or with some flexible cover sides and tops for special purposes.

Similarly, the equipment for handling goods during the various operations grow in number, variety, and complexity with every year. Some of the most common are:

Manual pallet truck: A pedestrian-operated mechanism for the movement of palletised goods up to 1500 kg; vertical movement is restricted; horizontal movement determined by the strength of the operator!

Powered pallet truck: Pedestrian, or rider, controlled battery operated truck for carrying palletised goods. Only capable of lifting pallet clear of the floor sufficient for horizontal movement.

Platform truck: Similar to the last item but having a fixed long flat carrying bed instead of fork. Can be used for transit of palletised goods but other equipment is needed to place the pallets on the truck and to remove them at the end of the journey.

Powered or manual stillage truck: Similar to a platform truck but not suited to pallet movement (see notes on stillages earlier).

Manual stacker truck: Pedestrian controlled manually operated truck fitted with forks and capable of lifting a single load up to 1·8 m.

Pedestrian controlled lift and reach truck: Similar to the manual stacker truck but powered (usually battery operated) for carrying and lifting up to 3–6 m. Forks are normally fitted but other attachments are available.

Power-operated lift and reach truck: A very large range available for carrying and lifting a wide variety of loads in all sorts of shapes and sizes. Can be pedestrian, or rider, controlled, battery or liquid fuel powered. Certain types are designed for specific operations (e.g. barrel handling) and are not suited for general use.

Mobile picking platforms: Boxed platforms in which picking operators travel horizontally and vertical between racking in the goods selection process ('order picking'). Equipment may be free or fixed travel horizontally, vertically, or both. Floor and crane/ceiling mounted versions available with either simple, or automated, travel control.

Conveyors: Powered or manual chain, roller, plate, or belt tracks for controlled, or free, transit of goods in the storage area, or off/on to transit vehicles. Free roller systems suited only to horizontal or downward sloping use. Powered belts and chains suited to upward moderate slopes; plates suited to vertical movement. Right-angled and curved tracks available with, or without, special tote boxes, hanging frames, etc.

Pneumatic conveyors: Continuous tube pneumatic system for movement of goods in special tube containers form station to station. Commonly used for movement of documents. Very sophisticated systems are now available but limitations of permissible bends sometimes cause problems.

Tow trains (or tug trains): Rider controlled, or automated, tugs towing trains of wheeled trucks of light/heavy construction and capacity. They require reasonably clear routes. Automated systems follow a fixed, sunken, floor track.

In addition to the special terms used in equipment description the distribution trade has developed a vocabulary of its own. This vocabulary is growing but the following glossary covers the main items:

Active store: Store place of goods in constant use, i.e. the items held move quickly and are replenished frequently. (Sometimes called *working area store*).

Aisle: The gangway space between blocks or racks, etc along which the stockman or order picker moves to deposit or select goods.

Aisle width: The minimum distance between opposed blocks, racks, etc; in existing systems the aisle width helps to determine the type and size of mechanical equipment which may be selected, whereas in planning new systems the mechanical equipment may determine the aisle width.

Buffer area: An area adjoining vehicle loading and/or unloading positions where vehicles can stand without interfering with the work of loading or unloading. It is desirable to have such an area in large depots so that a delivery vehicle can wait its turn clear of the work area or an outward bound vehicle can stand whilst the driver completes his documents, has a meal, etc.

Buffer area: internal: A space adjoining the loading or unloading bank where goods can be stacked pending sorting.

Buffer store: A separate store room or area where bulk storage of particular heavy demand items can be provided to guard against shortage of stock caused by uneven manufacture/delivery, etc.

Bulk sorting: The inspection, checking, and categorising of goods received in quantity prior to depositing in specific storage groups.

Bulk store: Area devoted to storage of large quantities of the same items pending demand. May be used as a Buffer Store.

Dock (raised): The area incorporating the leading edge of the warehouse floor against which vehicles stand to be unloaded or loaded. Normally the term is used where the floor is raised above the yard level on which the vehicle stands, the difference in level being designed to accommodate the height of the vehicle load platform above ground level (usually between 1066 and 1219) (rail docks require between 838 and 965 above rail level). See Fig. 8.5.

Dock leveller: A hinged metal platform manually or mechanically operated, designed as a ramp to take up the difference between a fixed dock level and road vehicle platform level, both to allow for the height variations between different makes of vehicle and to accommodate the changing height of the vehicle platform (as it is unloaded or loaded) due to changing wheel spring tensions and tyre pressures.

Goods inwards: The process of receiving goods into store or, more usually, the point at which those goods are received, unloaded, and checked before being put into store.

High security store: A separate enclosed store with a ceiling or roof, the total enclosure of which store is constructed to prevent unauthorised entry. Often required in general storage units for certain items of small, attractive, easily pilfered items.

Order assembly: The process of marshalling all the items needed to complete an order, or batch of orders, prior to loading on the delivery vehicle. A generous area should be allowed for movement and accumulation of the items comprising the orders.

Order load: This may comprise one or more order assemblies to be delivered by one vehicle to one or more customers. If more than one delivery has to be made by that vehicle during its run then the driver (or transport manager) determines the sequence of loading the order assemblies so that the last order to the loaded is the first to be delivered and so on, in sequence.

Order picking or retrieval: The process of collecting from the storage area each individual item contained in an order and depositing it on the load bank for order assembly.

Promotions Store: A separate storage area for advertising display material, free offers, gifts, etc, used in sales campaigns. May be allied to, or form part of, a high security store and be constructed the same way.

Re-coup store: A separate store or area (preferably covered and reasonably secure) for the collection of returnable pallets or containers, damaged goods needing replacement, and, sometimes, incorrect deliveries waiting return to the supplier.

Slow movers: Items of stock for which there is little or patchy demand, and hence remain in store for considerable periods. Usually relegated to the furthermost point of the storage unit.

Fig. 8.6(a) High bay automatic warehouse, with conveyor belt for collecting selected orders

Fig. 8.6(b) (right) Interior of typical high bay automatic warehouse

Small lines: Items similar to slow movers in that they are an occasional demand (sometimes brisk) or periodic demand in small quantities. Again usually relegated to the less immediate area of storage units.

Stock balance: The process of maintaining stocks of items in store sufficient to meet the normal, or forecast, demand.

Stock movement time: The average time that any item of stock remains in store. Used in calculating delivery periods for restocking.

Throughput: The volume of goods flowing through a storage unit. Expressed in monetary, weight, quantity, terms depending on which is easier to evaluate.

Turn round time: The time required to unload or load vehicle from arrival to departure.

UCR: ('Unpack, check, re-pack') The process carried out on receipt of goods and before putting into store or order assemblies.

Unsold returns: Where delivery vehicle drivers also act as salesmen the items unsold at the end of their trading period are taken back into store and accounted.

Variety: Also called stock range, being the total inventory of the different items held in store. Certain stores have very limited variety (perhaps only one type of articles) others have a multiplicity of articles (e.g. pharmaceutical or general grocery warehouses).

STATUTORY REQUIREMENTS

The following Acts of Parliament relate to requirements which may be needed in the design and building of warehouses.

Town and Country Planning Acts.
Public Health Act: Including Building Regulations.
Offices, Shops and Railway Premises Act.
The Factories Act.
Road Traffic Act, Transport Act, Transport (London) Act.
Highways Act.
Fire Act.
Clean Air Act.
Rights of Light Act.
Law of Tort.
Prevention of Damage by Pests Act.
Restriction of Ribbon Development Act.
Health and Safety at Work Act.

EXAMPLES

Modern Art Glass Warehouse, Erith, Kent
Architects: Foster Associates
Building: 14th June 1974

Warehouse at Runnymede, Surrey
Architects: Farrell/Grimshaw Partnership
Building: 22nd February 1974

Warehouse for Penguin Books Ltd., Harmondsworth, Middx.
Architects: Arup Associates
Architects Journal: 20th November 1968

WAREHOUSES

Hoffman-Laroche Warehouse, Welwyn, Herts
Architects: James Cubitt, Fells Atkinson and Partners

REFERENCES AND BIBLIOGRAPHY

ADVISORY INFORMATION

1. 'Better factories'. Published by the Institute of Directors.
2. 'Comprehensive guide to factory law'. (Robert McKown) Published by George Godwin.
3. Department of the Environment Bulletin No. 43 'Safety in mechanical handling'. Health and Safety at work No. 22, 'Dust explosions in Factories'.
4. 'Factory building studies'. HMSO
5. Fire Officers Committee Notes and 'Rules for automatic sprinkler installations' (29th ed.).
6. 'Industrial storage'. Architects Journal (contains a wealth of detailed information and advice).
7. 'Materials handling with industrial trucks' (K.E. Booth and C.G. Chantrill) published by British Industrial Truck Association.

USEFUL INFORMATION

1. 'British commercial vehicles for the World'. Published by 'Commercial Motor' for the Society of Motor Manufacturers and Traders Limited.
2. Fire Prevention Association Journal.
3. 'Materials handling and management'. Journal of the Institute of Materials Handling.
4. 'Materials Handling News'. Published by IPC Industrial Press Limited.
5. 'Stock control and storekeeping'. Published by Management Publications Limited, for the British Institute of Management.
6. 'The costing of handling and storage in warehouses—part 1; conventional warehouses'. Department of Trade and Industry, HMSO.

Bone, A. F., *A.R.I.B.A., trained at the Brighton School of Architecture and qualified externally in 1958. Joined Farmer and Dark in 1951. From 1956 until the present day, Mr. Bone has been a member of the London office of Beard Bennett Wilkins & Partners and is now a partner.*

In addition to the many other types of project this practice has carried out industrial work comprising process plants, warehousing, cold stores, laboratories, offices and facility buildings for many nationally known companies. Work for these companies has provided much experience in the problems of warehousing, and storage and distribution processes.

9 AIRPORTS—PASSENGER & CARGO TERMINALS

JOHN VULLIAMY, RIBA
Partner, YRM. Architects and Planners

INTRODUCTION

Over 500 million passengers travelled on scheduled flights during 1974; ten years ago a comparable figure was 135 million. Air transport, despite the fuel problem, will undoubtedly continue to increase and this dynamic expansion is reflected in the unprecedented growth of the Airport—keeping pace, but only just, with the technology and scale of aircraft development and the increase in passenger traffic. Although this section is primarily concerned with passenger terminals, there has been an equally spectacular growth in the volume of air cargo carried and this will undoubtedly continue.

The fundamental characteristic of airport planning is simple; the airport is a means of transferring from one form of transport to another. The methods of achieving this transfer are, however, somewhat complex and there are certainly no standard solutions for the design of an airport terminal. An article of this length can do little more than introduce the subject and give the designer an indication of what his job will involve: it is also intended to ensure that he knows the principal questions to ask. The need for a comprehensive, authoritive and highly detailed brief is essential before the architect can begin his work. The airport designer must see himself as a member of a team upon whose knowledge, in disciplines often unfamiliar to him, he will be dependent. No other building form has developed and changed so rapidly as the Airport; this will continue to be the case and undoubtedly the architect's greatest skill is to be able to meet, within the inevitable restrictions of economy and time, the demands of the present without inhibiting the inevitable changes of the future.

Once a site is established it is essential that the airport authority, from the outset and with the best available knowledge at its disposal, initiate a strategic Master Plan. This plan should be on the principle of non-finite zoning to allow for changes in the concept of the Airport terminal. The strategic plan should be able to accommodate not only changes in the form of the terminal buildings, but also changes in landside transport access systems. The speed with which these changes can take place are well illustrated in Paris Charles de Gaulle No. 1 and No. 2, where the master plan was able to accommodate the planning of a completely different concept for the second terminal system before the first stage was even completed. (See section on 'Planning').

The plan should establish, probably within zones defined by runway and taxiway layouts, the possibility of varying the relationships between the three fundamental systems in the terminal area. These systems are landside transport access, the terminal unit and aircraft access. It must be assumed that all three systems are subject to unforeseen change. For example a shift in emphasis from private to public landside transport, radical changes in passenger processing techniques and the introduction of much larger aircraft could have a significant bearing on these relationships.

The majority of examples in this article are major international airports. It is, however, apparent that there will be an increasing need for regional airports and for airports in the developing countries, often on a comparatively modest scale. The principles of terminal design apply regardless of size—and this point is referred to in more detail in the section on Space Requirements.

SITING

The siting of a new airport or the extending of an existing one will be primarily determined by political, economic, regional planning and environmental considerations, in addition to the technical factors involved. Airports are inevitably unpopular neighbours, except for those employed by them and the ever increasing number of passengers who use them and expect them to be easily accessible. The siting would undoubtedly have been established before the terminal area designer is briefed.

Technical factors affecting the siting of an airport would include availability of airspace, contours of surrounding

Note. This article was prepared at the end of 1974. Since this date new airports have been opened and many more have been extended despite the repercussions of the recession and the reductions in demand.

Fig. 9.1. (left)   Newark, New York. (The Port Authority of New York & New Jersey)

Fig. 9.2. (below)   Newark. Development plan. (The Port Authority of New York & New Jersey)

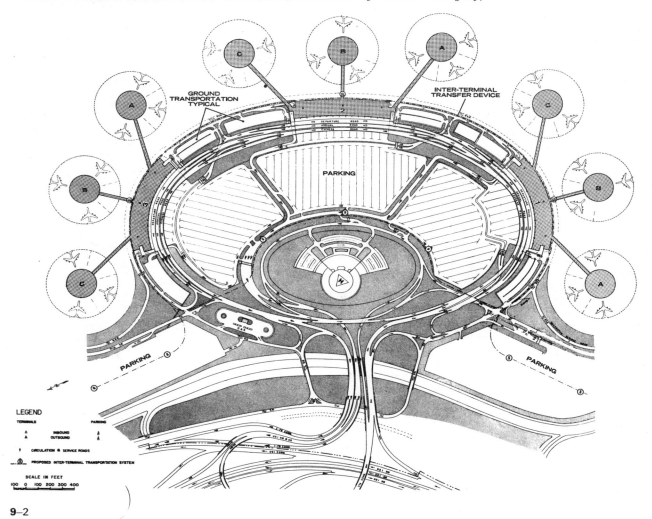

Fig. 9.3. (right) Tampa, Florida. (Hills-borough County Aviation Authority-Canoly)

Fig. 9.4. (below) Tampa, Florida, showing satelite transfer system. Master plan ('Florida Architecture')

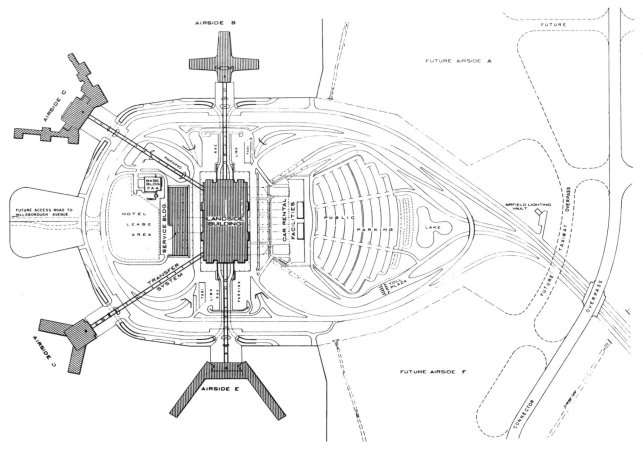

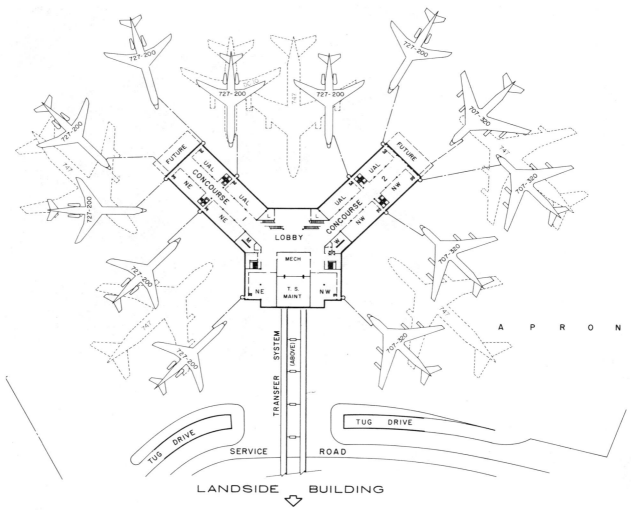

Fig. 9.5. *Tampa, Florida. Airside building No. 4, aircraft parking configuration. (Hillsborough County Aviation Authority)*

C- pier with aircraft stands

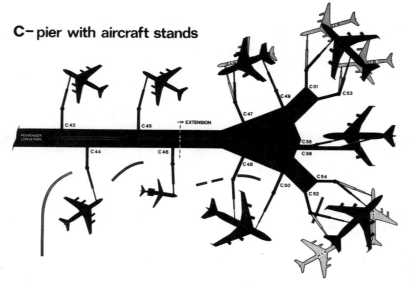

Fig. 9.6. *Schiphol, Amsterdam. Aircraft parking configurations. (N.V. Luchthaven Schiphol)*

Fig. 9.7.   Kansas City, Missouri. (City of Kansas City, Department of Aviation-Commercial Photo Inc.)

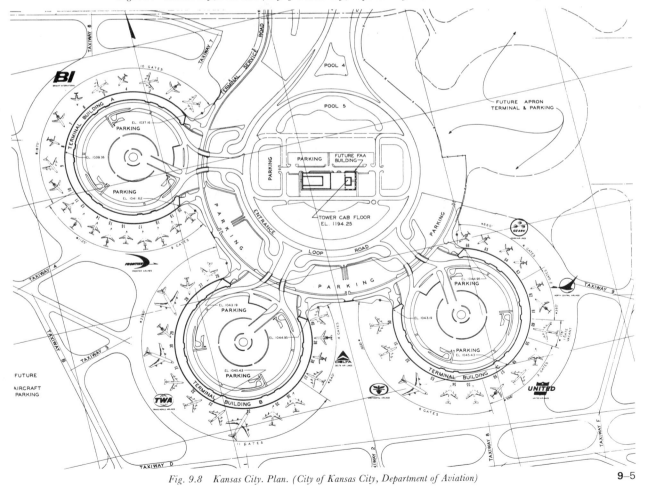

Fig. 9.8   Kansas City. Plan. (City of Kansas City, Department of Aviation)

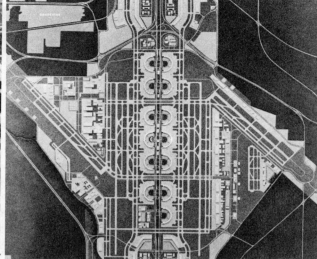

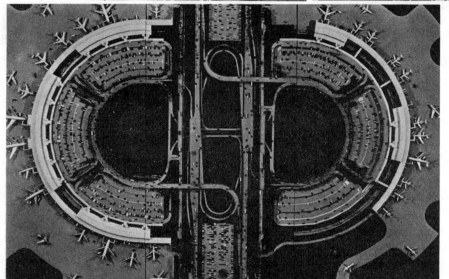

Fig. 9.9. (top left) Dallas/ Fort Worth, Texas. March 1974.

Fig. 9.10. (top right) Dallas/ Fort Worth, Texas, Master plan

Fig. 9.11. (left) Dallas/Fort Worth, Texas. Model of typical units (Dallas/Fort Worth Airport Authority)

Fig. 9.12. Schiphol, Amsterdam (N.V. luchthavon Schiphol)

terrain, climatic and meterological conditions, ground conditions and flood tables, runway alignments and prevailing winds, noise and population distribution, space for industrial and residential supporting accommodation, space for expansion and the availability of ground access systems.

In the section on Accommodation a check list of the individual buildings within an airport is given as an appendix to the accommodation schedule, together with a summary of the principal operational zones. Even if, at the outset, many of these elements are not required the strategic plan should make provision for them; the development of many existing airports has been frustrated by this having not been done. There is inevitably a conflict between land use and master planning of this nature—but there are obvious economic advantages for the future in siting airports where sufficient space for unforeseen expansion is available.

PLANNING

In addition to studying examples of airports, visiting them and using them, it is necessary for the designer to have a very detailed knowledge of the many systems and activities that are combined together in a Terminal Building.

Nevertheless it is essential to bear in mind constantly that a terminal building is a transfer building. The aim is to provide for the movement of people, quickly, simply and directly, between land vehicles and aircraft.

GENERAL

Although there are many combinations and modifications of each category in existence, the following basic airport terminal plan forms can be identified.

1. Central terminal and open apron (direct access).
2. Central terminal and pier access.
3. Central terminal and pier access with gate rooms.
4. Central terminal and attached satellites.
5. Central terminal and island satellites, with tunnel or bridge access.
6. Linear central terminal(s) with direct access, single or double sided, with spinal landside approach.

These categories are in an historical sequence and, as would be expected, also in a scale sequence.

Examples are illustrated in Figs 9.1 to 9.43. It is interesting to notice that the early concept of the open apron central terminals is now being repeated again, although often on a vast scale, in the latest linear terminals. The aim being to revert to the short passenger walking distances of the former era. The allocation of sectors to individual airlines is an important factor in linear concepts.

BASIC PLANNING FACTORS

There are four basic components in a terminal, each with departure and arrival functions.

1. Landside access systems.
2. Landside activities within the terminal.

3. Airside activities within the terminal.
4. Airside access systems.

There are two principal movement activities within the building towards which airport terminal planning should be solely directed:

1. Passenger processing
2. Baggage handling

There are five groups essential to the operation of an airport terminal:

1. Airport managers.
2. Airline operators.
3. Control Authorities (Immigration/Port Health/Customs/Security).
4. Operational controllers.
5. Amenity concessionaires.

The following are the principal considerations in terminal planning.

1. Immediate proximity of land transport access, particularly car parking, to the terminal.
2. Early separation of the passenger from his baggage.
3. Short walking distances for the passenger from check-in to aircraft access and from the aircraft to leaving the terminal.
4. Direct and simple routing for passenger movement with minimal directional and level changes.
5. Reliable and accessible baggage handling systems with adequate airside handling areas.
6. Disposition of management, airline and control units to allow maximum effective use of staff.
7. Provision of amenities for passengers that will satisfy varied needs in appropriate locations as well as contribute to airport revenue.
8. Facilities for invalid, infirm, handicapped and very young passengers.
9. Resolving the inevitable conflict of requirements demanded in a building with so many differing users—at the same time maintaining an economic scheme.
10. Ability to expand capacity and modify existing facilities with minimal disruption—airports do not close down.

BASIC FLOW FACTORS—INTERNATIONAL

DEPARTURES

Passengers Landside	Supporting Requirements. (see Accommodation schedule for details)
Arrival at terminal	Kerbside/check-in.
Parking	Check-in.
	Access (covered) to terminal.
Check-in	Check-in desks.
	Baggage conveyor to handling area.
	Airline offices, information, ticket sales etc.
	Departure indicators.
Post Check-In	Landside amenities.

Airside

Immigration control	Immigration staff offices. etc.
Customs outbound	Customs staff offices, etc.
Airside waiting	Buffet/Duty Free.
	Airline information desks.
	Departure indicators.
Aircraft access	Boarding control/security.
	Gate room control/security.

ARRIVALS

Airside

Access from aircraft

Port health	Check desks.
	Port health suite.
Pre-immigration buffer	
Immigration	Immigration channels/desks.
	Immigration staff offices etc.
Pre-baggage reclaim buffer	Reclaim belt indicator system.
Baggage reclaim	Reclaim units with indicator systems.
Customs examination	Examination channels. (Red/green indicator system) Customs offices/etc.

Landside

Arrivals concourse	Arrivals indicators.
	Arrivals information sources.

DOMESTIC PASSENGERS

These passengers obviously omit the control systems and require separate baggage reclaim facilities. Technically they remain 'landside' passengers until boarding.

FLOW PLANNING

There are two basic rules:

1. Separation must be completely secure between airside and landside activities. (Airport staff operate pass systems. The combination of airside/landside catering preparation facilities requires approval.)

2. Departure and arrival flow systems must be separated within the terminal. The communal use of piers and aircraft access systems is an exception, when all passengers are international. Departures and arrivals concourses do not require physical separation.

Some of the methods of flow separation are shown in Figs 9.50 to 9.55. In all but small airports it is advisable to place the principal amenities and administration office above (or below) the passenger flow system; this usually produces a more economic layout and will facilitate subsequent expansion. The planning of both departure and arrival functions on the same level is usually associated with smaller terminals because of the resulting limitation of kerbside access to this one level. It is obviously preferable to separate, by level, this access for departing and arriving passengers.

SUPPLEMENTARY CONSIDERATIONS

Communication

In addition to normal facilities the following are indispensible:

Sign systems. Simplicity, legibility and accurate placing essential. (The better the plan the fewer directional signs required). See page **9**–22.

Indicator systems. Split-flap or equivalent systems should be used for landside departure, airside departure, gates or gate rooms, baggage reclaim buffer lounges, reclaim units and the arrivals concourse. Television systems can be used as a more economic alternative. See page **9**–23.

Public Address systems must be audible in all areas used by public, with the provision of zone selection. Central control for use by trained announcers for all airlines preferable.

Public telephones. See page **9**–24.

Toilet facilities

Owing to airside/landside movement restrictions and holding locations these must be planned for passengers in the following areas.

Landside concourses/amenity areas.
Airside waiting.
Piers/gate room areas (but no direct access to toilet after security check).
Pre-Immigration waiting areas.

Building Services

Although the characteristics of airport services are similar to other comparable building types the following points should be noted:

Air conditioning should be considered and because of high occupancy rates the space requirements will exceed the norm.

Twenty-four hour occupation will effectively increase the demands made on service installations including water storage.

The provision of telephone exchange facilities (internal and external) with computer links will be required.

Sub-station accommodation will be above the norm.

GENERAL AVIATION

General aviation terminals are not described in this article. In many airports private (or privately hired) aircraft use the normal facilities of the passenger terminal. Where a separate terminal is provided, as at Gatwick–London, it is in essence a miniature international terminal—with facilities for the control authorities to operate and crews to be briefed.

Airside/landside restrictions must be properly observed and domestic/international separation maintained. Where the terminals are used for domestic flying only, these restraints are, of course, unneccessary. G.A. terminals are usually associated with separate apron accommodation.

GROUND AND AIR TRAFFIC CONTROL

(This item is referred to only in this section, Data and Accommodation)

Functions : Nomenclature may vary in different countries.
Approach Control—from radar room.
   Controls aircraft approaching or leaving airport within 10–30 mile area.
Aerodrome Control—from visual control room.
   Controls aircraft approaching or leaving airport and use of runways.
Ground Movement Control—from visual control room.
   Controls aircraft and vehicles on manoeuvring areas and order of departing aircraft.

Planning : Siting determined by vision requirements.
Avoid morning/evening sun within vision lines.
Radar control usually below approach control cabin.
Associated equipment room sited on ground level below tower: facilities for expansion and equipment change.
Ground movement control room can be sited independently.
Visual control rooms virtually impossible subsequently to increase in size. Allow for any foreseen future requirements initially.
Special characteristics
Acoustics: absorbent materials on floors/ceilings.
   Maximum internal sound level 55dBA. (usually involving reduction of about 40–45dBA)
Lighting: visual control rooms—dimmer for individual control.
   No window reflection. All surfaces non-reflective. Subdued lighting for radar rooms.

METEOROLOGICAL, AIS, FLIGHT CLEARANCE

(This item is referred to only in this section, Data and Accommodation) Note that ICAO (International Civil Aviation Authority) sets out recommendations.

Functions : *Meteorological.*
   Weather at point of departure, destination and along route.
AIS (Aeronautical Information Service).
   Navigational warnings, statutory requirements, political situations, military (air force) exercises, airfield data, runway conditions, accidents.

Flight clearance.
   The 'arm' of flight control, relaying data to the Control Tower.

Planning : Meteorological, AIS and Flight Clearance must be located together.
Direct apron-level aircrew access.
Associate with crew and aircraft boarding customs facilities.
Landside access required for staff and airlines.

Appropriate amenities for 24 hour occupation. All three services have counters for common access from crew 'concourse'.
Environment.
   High level of illumination, insulation from external sound: vocal contact essence of operation. Air-conditioning essential.

SPACE REQUIREMENTS—GENERAL

This section indicates the factors that will determine the size of a Terminal Building. The information is intended to cover a major international airport. The principles of the space standards given would also apply to a smaller regional airport, but an obviously important factor has to be taken into account in designing such terminals: the lower the number of passengers in the busy hour the more significant in passenger areas is the impact of large aircraft loads.

There are no established rules for these calculations; they will vary with the status of the airport, available finance and national or local custom. The Airport Authority will advise on these matters and, indeed, many will have their own planning department to provide information for the designer.

Normally a terminal would be constructed initially to handle, without extension, traffic growth for about 5 years. Depending upon provisions in the strategic Master Plan, the design should be capable of expansion to accommodate a further 5 years of traffic growth. (See previous section on Planning). The Airport Authority will provide the aircraft and passenger movement forecasts – and will convert these into the selected busy hour rates required by the designer.

There are two aspects to consider:

(a) the facilities and spaces required for the passengers and their friends;
(b) the accommodation needed for the many organisations which run and service the airport terminal.

Much detailed information is required *before* space requirements can be worked out: this is scheduled in the next section.

SPACE REQUIREMENTS. BASIC DATA: PASSENGER MOVEMENTS

Aircraft movements
Aircraft types envisaged/number of stands for each category. (The stand numbers will be calculated from the absolute peak of movements incorporating expected stand occupancy times).
Average loads and peak (charter) loads.
Proportion of scheduled/charter.
Selected peak hourly movement (the 'busy' hour).

Passenger forecast
International/domestic.
Ratio arriving/departing/transfer and transit in both categories.
(Passenger throughputs are usually taken as approximately 80% of the absolute peak—to produce the selected busy hour rates).

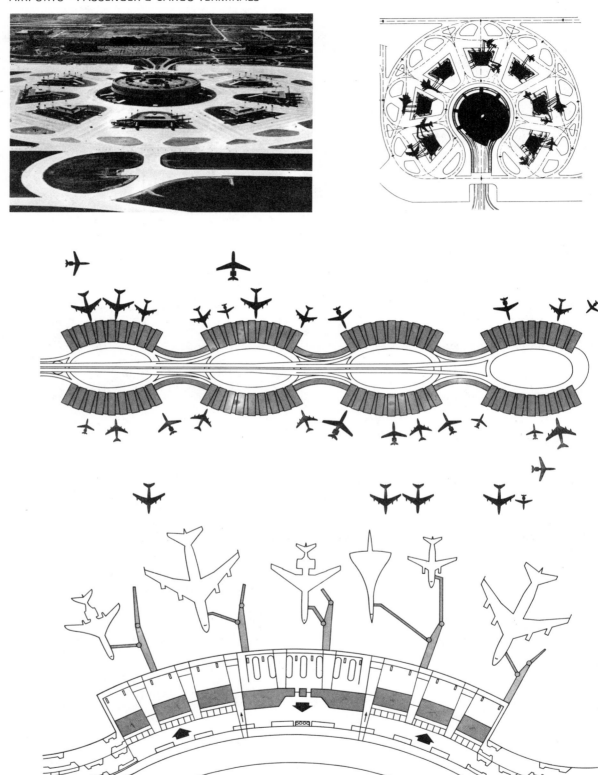

Fig. 9.13. (facing page, top left)   Charles de Gaulle, Paris. Terminal No. 1 (Aéroport de Paris-J. Moreau)

Fig. 9.14. (facing page, top right)   Charles de Gaulle, Paris. Plan. Terminal No. 1 (Aéroport de Paris)

Fig. 9.15. (facing page, centre)   Charles de Gaulle, Paris. Master plan Terminal No. 2 (note change of concept from Terminal No. 1) (Aéroport de Paris)

Fig. 9.16. (facing page, bottom)   Charles de Gaulle, Paris. Plan of a unit in Terminal No. 2 (Aéroport de Paris)

Fig. 9.17. (above)   Toronto. Terminal 1 ('Transport Canada'-Baxter)

Fig. 9.18. (below)   Toronto. Expansion (central portion completed). Note change of concept from original terminal. ('Transport Canada')

Fig. 9.19. (left)   Heathrow Airport, London (British Airports Authority)

Fig. 9.20. (centre, left)   Gatwick Airport, London. Expansion 1975. (British Airports Authority-Handford)

Fig. 9.21. (centre, right)   Gatwick Airport, 1935. The world's first satellite terminal, with tunnel access and telescopic gangways to the aircraft.

Fig. 9.22. (below)   Gatwick Airport, London. Expansion of airport 1975. Arrivals terminal to right and new car parks on left. (British Airports Authority)

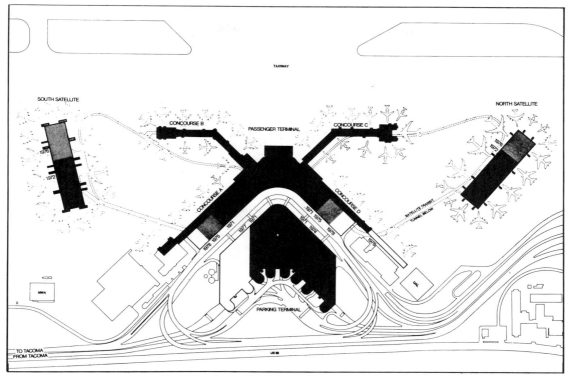

Fig. 9.23.   Seattle, Washington. Master plan. ('Airport Forum')

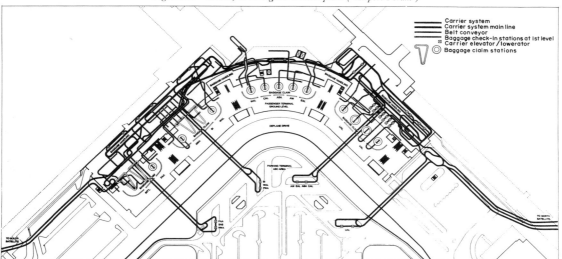

Fig. 9.24.   Seattle. Baggage handling systems, central terminal. Note car park check-in. ('Airport Forum')

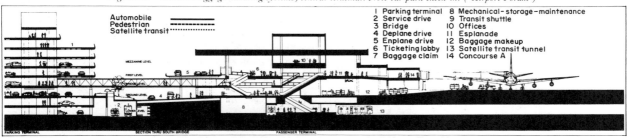

Fig. 9.25.   Seattle. Section through concourse A. ('Airport Forum')

Traffic categories:
   Scheduled/charter/other (e.g. trooping).

Accompanying persons:
   International/domestic: arrival and departure.

Landside transport:
   Percentages. passengers and friends. arriving/departing by:
      private car—owner/driver
      private car—otherwise driver
      coach or bus
      taxi
      rail or other means

Town terminal check-in:
   Percentage of each passenger category (International/domestic and charter) using this facility.
   Transport method used to reach airport.

Baggage:
   Number of pieces/passenger/international/domestic;
   Baggage handling: by one agent or by individual airlines;
   Check-in locations/car-park/kerbside/central terminal/gate.

SPACE REQUIREMENTS. BASIC DATA

Airport administration
   General office accommodation.
   Conference/overnight/etc.
   Specialised accommodation: Police/security/maintenance/cleaners.
   V.I.P. requirements.

Airline operators
   Schedule of known and anticipated airline operators.
      Check-in: Airline check-in/common check-in/group check-in/other.
            No. of desks for passenger and/or baggage check-in.
            Check-in location: car park/kerbside/central terminal/gate.
            Method of check-in: manual/electronic/etc.
            Preferred conveyor systems.
   Sales and information/desks/counters/locations.
   Offices for airline staff.
   Anticipated reporting times pre-flight departure.
   C.I.P. requirements.
   Staff amenity requirements.
   Employee forecast/terminal population by sex.
   Aircrew accommodation.
   Staff car parking.

Control authorities

Immigration
   No. of departure examination desks.
   No. of arrival examination desks.
   Aircrew examination requirements.
   Supporting administrative offices/etc., with locations.
   Staff amenity requirements.
   Employee forecast by sex.

   Staff car parking.
(The last three items above are grouped subsequently as 'Staff Information'.)

Port Health
   Accommodation schedules.
   Estimate percentage flight examination.
   Requirements for full flight examination.
   Staff information.

Customs
   Departures examination requirements, including currency control.
   Arrivals examination.
      Use of Red/Green systems.
      No. and length of channels required.
      No. of examination points/channel.
      Use of baggage conveyor system at examination point.
   Supporting accommodation/locations.
   Staff information.

Operational
   Information will be required on all items noted in accommodation check-list.
   Staff information.

Concessionaires
   (See also accommodation check-list).

Retail sector:	Shops/duty-free/advertising space/other.
Catering sector:	Buffets/bars/grills/coffee shops/restaurants/delay catering/vending/other.
Passenger Services:	Banks, post office, insurance, car hire, hotel information, etc.

CALCULATING CAPACITY

The use of mathematical models for this activity, for large terminals, which could well become an established approach, is beyond the scope of this article.

Initial assessment

A very crude method of assessing the total gross area of an international terminal (excluding landside access) is to allow $18\,000m^2$ for every $1\,000$ passengers in each direction. This area will include all support activities and include 12% of the gross area for building services plant. For example, a terminal with $3\,000$ passengers in each direction would have an approximate gross area of $54\,000m^2$.
   Domestic terminals require about 60–70% of the area.
   It must be emphasised such calculations are a rough starting point only: detailed assessment is essential.

Areas not occupied by passengers

Using the basic data noted above and with the aid of the accommodation check-list, these can be established in the normal way.

The Airport Authority would usually provide this information: if they do not, it must be obtained from the individual sources. In a large terminal, these areas will equal about 55% of the total gross area, including baggage handling areas.

Passenger areas

It must be stressed that there are no universally accepted standards in this sector—variations in individual airports can be considerable. The areas given are maximum.

Landside access

Car Parking: Normal space standards—but allow in check-in and check-out systems for very high rate of hourly turnover.
Long haul passengers tend to use taxis/hire cars/public transport; short haul and domestic tend to use own car. An average mix requires 70–90% of the hourly peak in each direction. Calculate car parks 85% full at peak demand.
Note proportional reduction made if rail or other efficient public transport service available.

Kerbside set down/pick up. 10% of hourly movement in metres should be considered a minimum. (100m/1 000p in both directions).

TERMINAL AREAS—DEPARTURES

Time factors: Check on average airline pre-flight departure check-in time—this might be 60 minutes (charter can be up to 2 hours, domestic 30 minutes). Passengers tend to allow considerable margins. The time may be spent as follows, assuming one hour period:

Check-in (including queuing)	6 minutes
Landside wait	15 minutes
Immigration (including queuing)	2 minutes
Departure lounge	20 minutes
*Departure to gate/security and boarding	17 minutes
	60 minutes

*The current need for individual security checks, especially where large aircraft are involved, will considerably increase this time. This is either met by longer pre-departure check-in and/or reduced time in the departure lounge.

Check-in: Desk numbers are determined by the method of check-in, the number of passengers and the number of operators (and there can be a purely commercial 'frontage' consideration

here). An average check-in time is $1\frac{1}{2}$m/passenger and allowance should be made for a peak of $\frac{1}{4}$ total hourly rate in 15 minutes.
e.g. 2 400 p/hour
therefore peak = 3 200/hr
= 4 800 minutes
= at $1\frac{1}{2}$ mins/p
80 desks.

This is a somewhat theoretical calculation—the number of desks will normally be stipulated.

Deciding the average number of bags/passenger is important for both departure and arrival conveyor capacities. IATA use 1.7, whilst in the UK 1.5 is the average, although current experience suggests this is reducing to 1.3. With good feed control and sorting facilities one conveyor should handle between 900 and 1 200 bags/hour.

Allow an overall area, including desks, conveyors and circulation of 1.5m²/p/hour.

Immigration: Each control channel requires approximately 25 m² given a width of 1.5 m. Allow 6 desks/channels/1 000 passengers/hour.

Airside waiting: The scale of this area relates to the way the airport is operated and the use of gate rooms. (See sub-section on Planning). Assume a 20 minute wait and provide about 80% seating. At 1.5m²/passenger this will give 0.5 m² × hourly passenger peak.

Duty-free shop: Will vary with type of traffic and, in Europe, with EEC rules. The sales area can be up to an additional 25% of the area allocated to airside waiting lounge.

Buffet/bar: Provision will vary with passenger handling method, e.g. use of gate room assembly, trickle feed, etc. Allow for additional 25% on the airside waiting lounge.

If duty-free shop and buffet are provided, allow for passengers using them when calculating airside lounge area.

Access to aircraft gates or gate room:
Pier or corridor—2 way movement.
Minimum width 7.0m.
If two-way passenger conveyor 10.0–11.0 m width required.
Ignore pier systems in capacity calculation.

Gate rooms

The provision of gate-rooms, if proper use is made of early flight call, will reduce airside lounge capacity.

An 80% load factor should be used for the largest aircraft served at the gate: seating should be provided for 50% of the passengers.

Allow: 0.9 m² for standing passengers
1.4 m² for seated passengers
∴ 1.15 m²/passenger required

Add 10% for circulation/airline requirements.

e.g.   wide-bodied aircraft—capacity 450 passengers
80 % load factor = 360 passengers
= 415 m²
+ 10 % circulation = 450 m²/say.
etc.

∴   calculation can be achieved thus:

Aircraft capacity × 1.0 m = total gate room area.

Information on aircraft sizes using particular stands would be provided by the Authority.

Toilet facilities are excluded from this calculation—for security reasons not accessible from gate rooms.

Terminal areas—arrivals

Time factors: mean figures.

Disembark and move to immigration (dependent on planning)	12 minutes
Immigration queue and check	4 minutes
Baggage wait and reclaim	12 minutes
Customs	2 minutes
Arrivals concourse	5 minutes
Waiting to leave airport	5 minutes
	40 minutes

Port health

Considerable variation—check authorities' requirements. Approximate area for average airport is 15 % of hourly rate of passengers × 1 m².

Immigration

Channel areas as for departures. Desks/channels, allow 12/1 000 passengers.

Overall area, allowing pre-immigration assembly and including channel area, 60 % of hourly peak × 1 m².

Baggage reclaim—buffet lounge

Allow 30 % of hourly rate × 1 m².
Seating for 10 % of passengers.

Baggage reclaim—conveyors

Reclaim belts—continuous.

Assume ⅓ of peak hour in 15 minutes and sustain peak for one hour.

Assume passengers will off-load 700 bags/hour from each belt and allow 1.5 bags/passenger.

e.g. 3 000 passengers/hour
∴   1 000 passengers peak in 15 minutes
=   4 000 passengers/hour
=   6 000 pieces of baggage/hour

No. of belts required = 6 000 ÷ 700 = say, 8 belts

The same calculation method is used for carousels of other devices—these will have a lower bags/hour capacity.

Note the critical effect of increasing the baggage allowance /passenger. If security measures preclude hand-baggage being carried, this could be critical. In the above example, increasing the rate from 1.5 to, say, 2.2 increases the number of belts from 8 to 12.

For belt dimensions see Data sub-section.

Baggage Reclaim—areas

Reclaim hall areas are difficult to analyse mathematically because there is no known method of presenting baggage to the right passenger at the right time. Space has to be allowed for an incalculable number of passengers to await presentation (see Data sub-section).

Assume peak as for conveyor calculation. (The introduction of the passenger baggage trolley is a factor to be considered).

Allow 80 % of the hourly peak total × 1 m².

Customs examination

Assume Red/Green system.
Allow 400 m²/1 000 passengers.

Arrivals concourse

Assume ratio of friends/passengers 1 : 2 or 3 long haul (less, say, 1 : 4 short haul). Average passenger wait is 4–5 minutes after clearing Customs, but note that their friends (possibly 50 % of the passenger total) may wait on average 30 minutes.

Allow 80 % of hourly rate × 1 m².

CATERING

Since the aim of airport planning and management is to get passengers through a terminal as quickly as possible, the provision of full-scale restaurants can be seen as something of an anachronism. The use of limited menu grills (call-order) should become increasingly predominant. Restaurants, in the main, are used by non-passengers.

Users: Passengers, friends, visitors and staff.

Assume: 70 % of the total will make use of a catering facility.

Arriving passengers will rarely use catering systems.

Four categories of catering:

Buffet/bar	(1.3 m²/P)
Grill/coffee shops	(1.6 m²/P including counters)
Restaurant	(1.6 m²/P)
Delay catering	(1.4 m²/P)

Total area for public use requires an additional 50–60 % for delivery, storage, preparation, serving staff facilities, etc.

Demand for catering:

The following percentage may be used as a guide:

Buffet/bar	65 %
Grill	25 %
Restaurant	10 %

Delay catering is not normally allocated for this sole purpose; if it is, it should be able to accommodate about 5–7 % of the hourly departure rate.

Note that catering areas (together with the retail concession areas) absorb the landside waiting passenger capacity surplus to the check-in concourse capacity.

Fig. 9.28. Dulles International, Washington D.C. Airside of terminal with mobile lounges. (Department of Transportation, Washington)

Fig. 9.27. (above) San Francisco. The initial master plan. ('Architecture d'aujourd'hui')

Fig. 9.29. (left) Houston Intercontinental, Texas. (City of Houston)

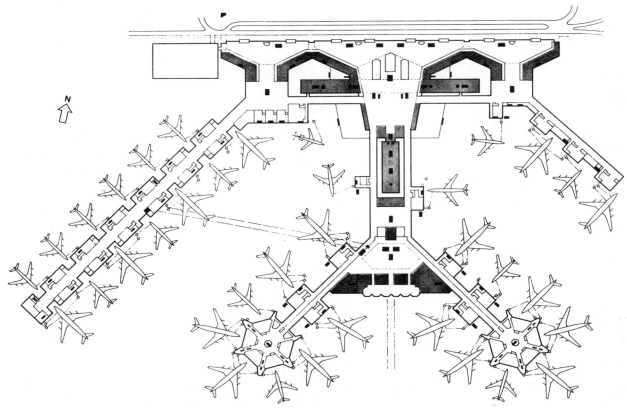

Fig. 9.30. Frankfurt/Main. Plan at departures and gate-room level. (Bauern & Wohnen)

Fig. 9.31. Frankfurt/Main. Aircraft access from central pier system. (Frankfurt/Main A.G.)

Fig. 9.32. Dusseldorf. Control tower and aircraft access from Pier B. (Flughafen Dusseldorf, GmbH)

Fig. 9.33. Dusseldorf. (Flughafen Dusseldorf; Walter Moog)

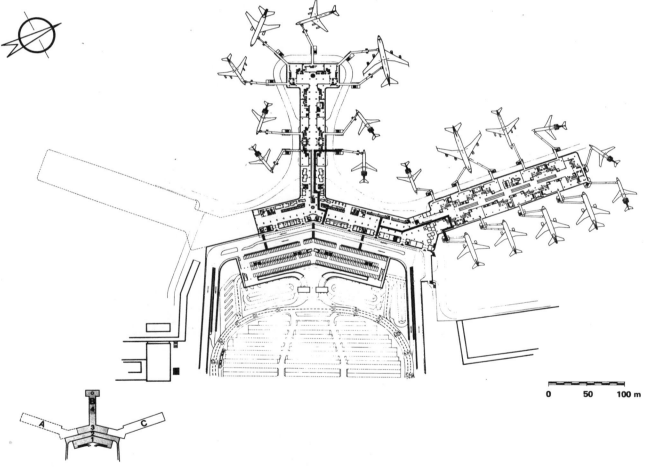

DEPARTURE-LEVEL

Fig. 9.34. Dusseldorf. Plan at departures and gate-room level. Central pier completed. ('Airport Forum')
1. Parking lot.
2. Departures.
3. Main hall (counters; baggage check-in; information; bank; Port Office; shops)
4. Pier B—Transfer (waiting room and check-in; passport and customs control)

Fig. 9.35. *Berlin-Tegel. The initial master plan. ('Architecture d'aujourd 'hui')*

Fig. 9.36. *Pan-Am Terminal, John F. Kennedy, New York. The problem of expansion. Note parking over gate-rooms in extension. (Pan American World Airways)*

Fig. 9.37. *Laguardia, New York. ('Port of New York Authority—L. Johns')*

Fig. 9.38. Cologne/Bonn. (Flughafen Koln/Bonn GmbH)

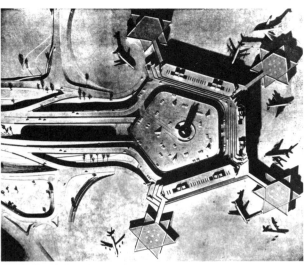

Fig. 9.39. Cologne/Bonn. The initial master plan. ('Architecture d'aujourd'hui')

Fig. 9.40. Hamburg-Kaltenkirchen. The present development model (1974). ('Flughafen-Fotodienst Doring')

Fig. 9.41. Hamburg-Kaltenkirchen. An earlier development model. ('Flughafen-Fotodienst Doring')

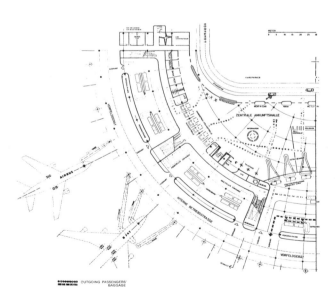

Fig. 9.42. Hamburg-Kaltenkirchen. Plan of terminal segment, arrivals level. (Flughafen Hamburg)

Fig. 9.43. Hamburg-Kaltenkirchen. Plan of terminal segment, departures level. (Flughafen Hamburg)

DATA

GENERAL

There are a number of specific data and planning problems peculiar to airports, some of which are described below. Data requirements that also have an application outside airports are not described; e.g. car parking, catering amenities, offices and normal passenger and staff amenities.

BAGGAGE HANDLING (see Figs. 9.56–9.70, 9.74–9.79)

The baggage handling system is by far the most vital equipment in a terminal and requires examination from the outset of design. It is a highly specialised subject and the installation will have a considerable impact on the whole operation of the airport and the operators' staff costs.

There are many extremely sophisticated automated handling systems, involving the use of electronic control systems and coded bag-tags, which are beyond the scope of this article. However, the direct methods, some of which are illustrated, are frequently the most trouble-free in practice.

The basic operations are as follows:

Departures: Conveyor system at check-in. Secondary conveyor, usually 3-stage, for weighing, transfer to labelling position and thence to primary conveyor.

Departures: Conveyor systems at baggage flight assembly area. These may be straight feed with straight line accumulation, multiple sorting onto a series of straight line feeds or direct feeds onto circulating accumulation devices. There are many variants to these methods.

Arrivals: Baggage delivery area. If reclaim is on same level baggage can be off-loaded from container or vehicle directly onto a continuous reclaim belt, (preferred system). Otherwise off-loading is onto straight-line conveyors. Layouts are determined by container dolly train systems, other vehicles used and plan configuration.

Arrivals: baggage reclaim. Carousel (rotating turn-table)—fed from above or below, continuous reclaim belt ('race-track'), or straight linear conveyors—the least satisfactory.

Transit and transfer: This requires a direct airside interchange system. This can be done by vehicle transfer or a conveyor system, depending on the building plan.

In planning the flight assembly areas and baggage delivery areas it is essential to know the vehicle and/or container dolly train types that the operators use or intend to use in the future. Details of parking and storage requirements must also be established, together with the loaders accommodation.

Conveyors between loading and off-loading locations should always have the minimum number of changes in direction and level. Blockages, damage and label tearing usually occur at these changes. Adequate space for maintenance and replacement of conveyors is essential.

SIGNS

The movement of passengers within the Terminal is largely dependent on signs.

The fundamental principle is that the sign makes an essential statement clearly visible and correctly located. Most airport authorities (including the BAA) have standardised sign systems: if this is not the case a system must be devised by a graphics specialist. Departures from the accepted system can cause misunderstanding and confusion.

Methods of displaying flight information come into a different category; proprietary systems would normally be used and are described briefly below.

CATEGORIES OF SIGN

1. *Flight information.* (See Figs 9.81 to 9.83)
    Flight departures: in check-in area and departure lounges.
    Gate information: on gate routes and gate location.
    Baggage reclaim: in buffer lounge if appropriate and at reclaim belts.
    Arrivals baggage handling area: over each reclaim belt off-loading position.
    Flight arrivals: in arrivals concourse.

    Other locations will depend on the scheme: e.g. where kerbside and car-park baggage check-in systems are used.

    The systems most commonly used are the following:
    Split-flap mechanically operated electronically controlled systems. These are almost ubiquitous in major terminals allowing input from tape, computer or keyboard.
    Alphanumeric display cathode ray monitors, using character generation methods. These allow variation of character size and have replaced earlier T.V. systems. Input from tape, computer or keyboard.
    Light matrices, based on the use of incandescent lamps. Similar input systems can be used and the characters can be static or flowing.

    All three systems can be electronically controlled together in one combined installation.

    Flight information systems do not exclude the use of public address installations.

2. *Movement signs*
    These are the principal flow guidance signs and should be illuminated. They state all passenger routes and must confirm them at changes of direction or points of divergence. They use both words and symbols.

3. *Location signs*
    To identify a location. Normally illuminated and use of symbols (pictograms) should be considered.

4. *Emergency signs*
    Fire exit signs must be illuminated from public areas and located in agreement with the Fire Officer(s).

5. *Room identification signs*
    Signs on or adjacent to doors. Note that administrative areas require identification.

DESIGN OF SIGNS

The following factors must be taken into consideration:

1. All signs in an area must be considered together.
2. Only one letter size should be used on a sign.
3. Where signs vary in size they should be hung to the same underside height: about 2.8 m.
4. Choice of x height: 25 mm per 15 m viewing distance, but relate to space in which sign hangs.
5. Colour: colour coding systems are not usually effective, colour being used to make signs conspicuous.
6. Standardisation: internationally accepted symbols (pictograms) are suggested by IATA and should be used.

AIR JETTIES (See Figs. 9.86–9.87)

The air-jetty, loading bridge or air-bridge is a means of establishing a direct connection between the aircraft doors and the terminal (or pier), with obvious advantages to passengers, operators and control authorities. It also avoids the hazard of passengers walking on the apron.

Location. This will depend on the type of bridge selected, the range of aircraft served and the stand layout adopted. Bridges can accommodate aircraft in parallel, oblique or nose-in configurations, the last being the most economical. The parking configuration will usually be determined by the airport authority.

Factors. The following factors influence siting and selection:
1. *Gradient of bridge to cill height of aircraft.* 1:8 is a maximum. (Variations in current aircraft cill heights: BAC 1-11 2.03 m. Boeing 747 5.36 m.)
2. *Apron service road.* If adjacent to terminal or pier the jetty will require a fixed bridge with adequate clearance for all vehicles envisaged, including fire tenders.
3. *Apron drive bridges.* Require space to swing clear of aircraft to allow push-tractor access. These bridges, with telescopic sections, allow greater versatility in the range and location of aircraft served.
4. *Fixed bridges.* Although more economical these bridges (also referred to as nose-docks) have an application for 1 on 1 parking configurations only. Other configurations, e.g. 2 on 1 or 3 on 2, require apron drive telescopic systems.
5. *Number of bridges.* Wide-bodied aircraft (B 747, DC 10, L 1011 and A 300B) require a minimum of two access points; a third can be provided by an overwing system, but this is not usual. Two access systems are also used frequently on the larger conventional aircraft. To avoid interfering with servicing and loading aircraft starboard access is usually avoided.

Manufacturers. The makers of air jetties have in most instances an advisory planning service on stand configurations in relation to bridge design. Collaboration with the selected firm is advisable in the early planning stage and in subsequent detail design.

CHECK-IN DESKS (See Figs. 9.56–9.59.)
See also sub-section on Baggage Handling, page **9**-22

Layout. The layout of check-in desks will determine the departure conveyor system and usually takes one of the following forms:

1. Linear groupings with a single conveyor.
2. Double sided linear groupings with single or twin conveyor.
3. Island groups with a 'pass-through' system: 4 to 6 desks per unit.

Linear systems are most common and they permit greater flexibility in allocating groups of desks to airlines.

Information and ticket sales counters should be kept apart from the check-in system to avoid wasting conveyor frontage.

Factors. Although overall design will be standardised individual airline requirements must be checked for the following:

Document compartments within desk and back-up storage.
Power and telephone requirements.
Electronic data processing facilities (see below).
Baggage weighing methods.
Staff access to offices, etc.
Coupon conveyor requirement (if no EDP).
Sign requirements, e.g. split flap or light matrix sign for flight Nos.

Processing systems. Electronic processing systems are now frequently used, with links to control ticketing locations, town terminals, parking and kerbside check-in, and boarding gates. They may have the following facilities:

C.C.T.V. monitor
Ticket reader and boarding pass issuer
Credit card reader and ticket printer
Coded bag-tag printer

Identification. Illuminated identification signs are essential over all check-in desks.

MOVING WALKWAYS (PASSENGER CONVEYORS)
(See Figs. 9.49 and 9.71–9.73)

An early decision on the use of moving walkways is essential in view of structural requirements and the depth of the machine rooms below. They are normally used in pier/gate-room access systems where walking distances exceed 200–250 m.

VISUAL CONTROL ROOMS (See Figs. 9.84 and 9.85)

The size of air traffic control cabins will vary with the scale of the airport. No design work should be undertaken without prior consultation with those responsible for air traffic control at the airport and with the telecommunications engineers. The diagrams shown give basic data only.

Control authorities (see Figs 9.96–9.99)
The diagrams illustrated show typical accommodation requirements for:

Immigration and customs—departures.
Port health—arrivals.
Immigration—arrivals.
Customs—arrivals.

The accommodation required by these authorities will vary according to local custom and the scale and nature of the traffic envisaged.

Met, AIS and flight control (see Figs 9.92–9.95)
Meteorological Office, Aeronautical Information Service and Flight Clearance. These facilities are not necessarily incorporated within the terminal building but crew movement is simplified if they are. The data shown in the diagrams are indicative of the accommodation required, but, before planning, consultation with the appropriate authorities is essential.

ACCOMMODATION

GENERAL

Obviously there is no standard schedule of accommodation for an airport terminal, and the scale and nature of the project will determine the spaces required. The following is a check-list covering all the principal accommodation for an international airport. Ancillary items are noted due to the particular demands of airside/landside restrictions.

The schedule is divided into the following categories:

Departures—landside
Departures—airside
Arrivals—airside
Arrivals—landside
Support accommodation—landside
Support accommodation—airside

At the end of the schedule a check-list is given of the principal buildings associated with the total airport.

DEPARTURES—LANDSIDE

Parking	cars coaches taxis	Baggage/ticket check-in

Kerbside	set-down	Cars/coaches/taxis—Baggage/ticket (check-in)

Car park links to terminal

Other transport terminal access	Public transport

Check-in concourse	Airline check-in desks Airline information & ticket sales Airport information

Landside waiting	Waiting lounge Departure flight indicator

Newsagent, tobacconist
Chemist, gift shops
Post Office, bank, bureau de change
Public telephones
Buffets, bars
Coffee shop, restaurant
Delay catering
Duty-free ordering desks
Vending machines
Left luggage lockers
Insurance sales
Airline/club lounges
Rest rooms/air-wait
Tele-cinemas

VIP/CIP accommodation (arrivals or departures)	Lounges Press Interview rooms Catering Communications Car access

Invalid facilities
Nursing mothers/creche
Chapel
Toilets, powder rooms, hairdresser

Departure lounge (Domestic) unless part of landside wait area.

DEPARTURES—AIRSIDE

Immigration control comb	Immigration desks Office accommodation Detention Amenity facilities

Customs departure check	Customs desks/counters Office accommodation Secure store Amenity facilities

Airside waiting lounge(s)	Information desks (airline) Departure indicator Buffet/Bar Duty-free shop Duty-free stores Toilets

Aircraft access:	Direct access—air jetty/apron access Pier—air jetty/apron access Gate-room—check-in facility security check facility waiting area/toilets

(Domestic/international separation)

Fig. 9.44. *Gatwick Airport London. Immigration Hall. (British Airports Authority; Brecht-Einzig.)*

Fig. 9.45. *Gatwick Airport London. Immigration Desks. (British Airports Authority; Brecht-Einzig.)*

Fig. 9.46. *Gatwick Airport London. Arrivals Concourse—Flight Information. (British Airports Authority; Brecht-Einzig.)*

Fig. 9.47. *Gatwick Airport London. Baggage Reclaim Hall. (British Airports Authority; Brecht-Einzig.)*

Fig. 9.48. *Boston-Logan International, John Volpe Terminal. 1st floor concourse. (Boston-Logan Airport Authority)*

Fig. 9.49. *Charles de Gaulle Airport—Paris. Glass covered moving walkway from Departure to Transfer levels. ('Airport Forum')*

9–25

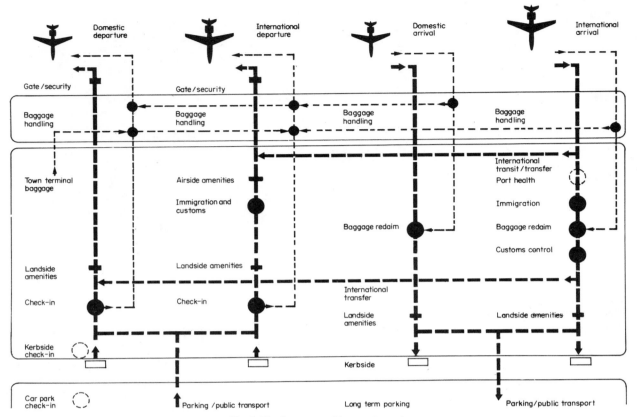

Fig. 9.50   Passenger and baggage processing

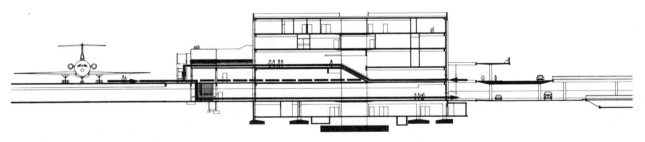

Fig. 9.51.   Basel-Mulhouse. Section

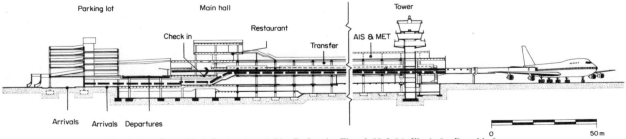

Fig. 9.52.   Duesseldorf. Section through Pier B. See also Figs. 9.32-9.34. Flughafen Dusseldorf

ARRIVALS—AIRSIDE

Access from aircraft	As for departures/gate room by-pass
Interline information desks	(Domestic/international separation)
Immigration hall	Toilets
Port health	Waiting Examination, Doctors' rooms Nurses' room/X-ray/Vaccination Office(s)/ambulance bay Amenity accommodation
Immigration control comb	Immigration desks Offices, interview rooms Passenger waiting rooms Detention, Police (Special Branch) Amenity accommodation
Pre-baggage reclaim area	Toilets
Baggage reclaim hall	Reclaim and indicator systems Out of gauge baggage facility
Customs examination hall	Examination benches/desks Offices, interview rooms Search rooms, merchandise examination Lock-ups, Cash office Amenity accommodation

ARRIVALS—LANDSIDE

Arrivals concourse	Arrivals indicator Car-hire, taxi information Hotel reservations Tourist information Customs enquiry office
Baggage reclaim (domestic)	

SUPPORT ACCOMMODATION—LANDSIDE

Airport administration	Offices, Conference Overnight accommodation
General management, operational, engineering and maintenance	Airport police, porters Engineering stores and M/shops Maintenance stores, cleaners Lost property, general stores
Airlines	Offices—associated with check-in Offices—remote from check-it Staff and air-crew accommodation:

	rest rooms, changing amenity facilities Computer terminals Operation and duty rooms
Catering and concessions	Delivery, receiving, storage Liquor stores Normal preparation/kitchen/serving facilities (including delay catering systems) Staff dining, changing, lockers, toilets, showers.
Control authorities	See Departures and Arrivals—airside. (Note that landside access required to airside facilities.)
Police	Office(s), detention, amenity facilities
Porters	Porters' rooms, amenity facilities
Common use	Staff canteen and associated ancillaries (see concessionaires above) Medical centre, first-aid Women's retiring rooms
Services	Normal building services requirements Additional facilities: Public address systems Flight information sign control systems Telephone exchanges Telex terminals Pneumatic tube system Public telephones Airline computer terminals
Spectators	Admission systems Viewing galleries (open/enclosed) Buffets/bars/restaurants Gift shops, other concessions Amenity facilities

SUPPORT ACCOMMODATION—AIRSIDE

Baggage handling areas (Departure and arrival)	Vehicle, tug, dolly and container parking Advance, mishandled and transfer baggage stores Covered and protected handling areas Loaders' lockers, restrooms Amenity facilities
Aprons	Engineering offices Workshops and spares stores Apron staff offices

Typical flow sections

One level

Departure

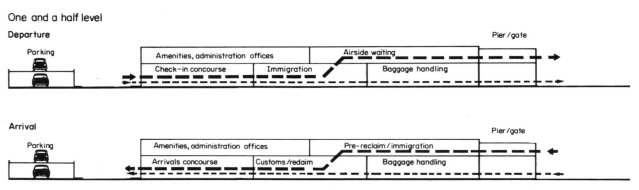

Parking — Amenities, administration offices — Check-in concourse — Immigration — Airside waiting

Arrival

Parking — Amenities, administration offices — Arrivals concourse — Customs/reclaim — Immigration

Fig. 9.53.

One and a half level

Departure

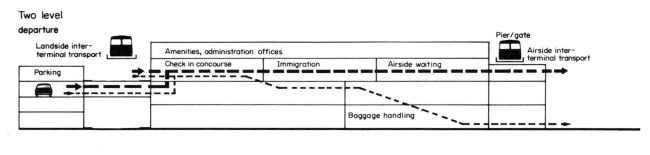

Parking — Amenities, administration offices — Check-in concourse — Immigration — Airside waiting — Baggage handling — Pier/gate

Arrival

Parking — Amenities, administration offices — Arrivals concourse — Customs/reclaim — Pre-reclaim/immigration — Baggage handling — Pier/gate

Fig. 9.54.

Two level

departure

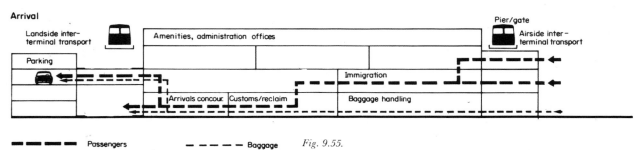

Landside inter-terminal transport — Parking — Amenities, administration offices — Check in concourse — Immigration — Airside waiting — Baggage handling — Pier/gate — Airside inter-terminal transport

Arrival

Landside inter-terminal transport — Parking — Amenities, administration offices — Arrivals concourse — Customs/reclaim — Immigration — Baggage handling — Pier/gate — Airside inter-terminal transport

━ ━ ━ ━ Passengers   – – – – Baggage   *Fig. 9.55.*

Check-in desks

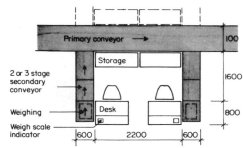

Primary conveyor →

2 or 3 stage
secondary
conveyor

Weighing

Weigh scale
indicator

Storage

Desk

100

1600

800

600   2200   600

Front access   *Fig. 9.56.*

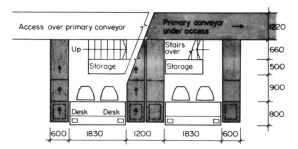

Access over primary conveyor

Primary conveyor
under access

Up

Storage

Stairs
over

Storage

Desk   Desk

1220

660

500

900

800

600   1830   1200   1830   600

Back access: Gatwick Airport, London   *Fig. 9.57.*

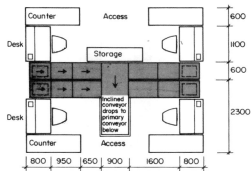

Counter   Access

Desk

Storage

Desk

Inclined
conveyor
drops to
primary
conveyor
below

Counter   Access

600

1100

600

2300

800   950   650   900   1600   800

Island   *Fig. 9.58.*

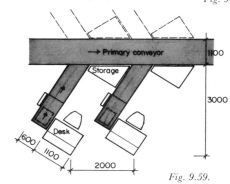

→ Primary conveyor

Storage

Desk

1100

3000

600
1100   2000

Fig. 9.59.

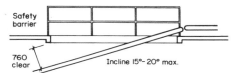

Deposit
conveyor

Weighing and
and
labelling   Waiting
conveyor   conveyor

Primary
conveyor

Weigh scale
indicator

Illuminated sign
with storage under

Section of check-in: Orly Airport, Paris   *Fig. 9.60.*

Chevron

Safety
barrier

760
clear

Incline 15°- 20° max.

Fig. 9.61.

Inclined baggage conveyor, section

Flight assembly area baggage sorting

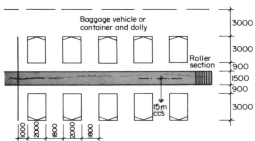

Baggage vehicle or
container and dolly

Roller
section

15m
ccs

3000

3000
900
1500
900

3000

1000   2000   1800   2000   1800

Straight feed: straight line accumulation   *Fig. 9.62.*

Typical dimensions using containers

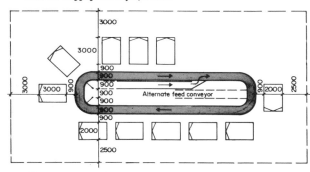

From check in

Controller

Alternate feed conveyor

3000

3000

900
900
900
900
900
900
900

3000

2000

2000

2500

900   2000   2500

Multiple sorting with circulating accumulation   *Fig. 9.63.*

Typical dimensions using containers

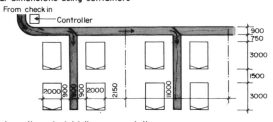

From check-in

Controller

900
750

3000

1500

3000

2000   900   900   2000   2150   1100

Multiple sorting: straight line accumulation   *Fig. 9.64.*

Typical dimensions using containers

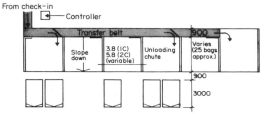

From check-in

Controller

Transfer belt

Slope
down

3.8 (1C)
5.8 (2C)
(variable)

Unloading
chute

Varies
(25 bags
approx.)

900

900

3000

Multiple sorting to chute accumulation   *Fig. 9.65.*

Typical dimensions using containers

Baggage: off-loading and reclaim.

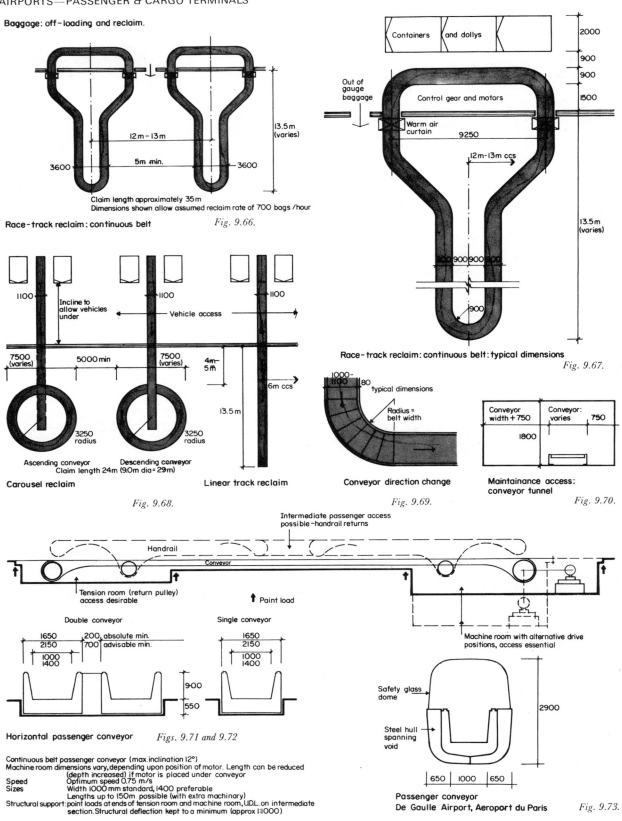

12m–13m

5m min.

3600   3600

13.5m (varies)

Claim length approximately 35m
Dimensions shown allow assumed reclaim rate of 700 bags/hour

Race-track reclaim: continuous belt   *Fig. 9.66.*

Containers   and dollys   2000
                                            900
                                            900
Out of gauge baggage   Control gear and motors   1500
Warm air curtain   9250
                          12m–13m ccs
                                            13.5m (varies)
900 900 900
900

Race-track reclaim: continuous belt: typical dimensions
                                            Fig. 9.67.

1100   1100   1100

Incline to allow vehicles under   Vehicle access

7500 (varies)   5000 min   7500 (varies)   4m–5m

6m ccs

13.5m

3250 radius   3250 radius

Ascending conveyor   Descending conveyor
Claim length 24m (9.0m dia = 29m)

Carousel reclaim   **Linear track reclaim**

Fig. 9.68.

1000–1100   80   typical dimensions
Radius = belt width

Conveyor direction change

Fig. 9.69.

Conveyor width + 750   Conveyor: varies   750
1800

Maintainance access: conveyor tunnel

Fig. 9.70.

Intermediate passenger access possible – handrail returns

Handrail

Conveyor

Tension room (return pulley) access desirable   ↑ Point load

Machine room with alternative drive positions, access essential

Double conveyor   Single conveyor

1650   200 absolute min.   1650
2150   700 advisable min.   2150
1000   1000
1400   1400

9·00
550

Horizontal passenger conveyor   *Figs. 9.71 and 9.72*

Continuous belt passenger conveyor (max. inclination 12°)
Machine room dimensions vary, depending upon position of motor. Length can be reduced (depth increased) if motor is placed under conveyor
Speed   Optimum speed 0.75 m/s
Sizes   Width 1000 mm standard, 1400 preferable
             Lengths up to 150m possible (with extra machinery)
Structural support: point loads at ends of tension room and machine room, UDL. on intermediate section. Structural deflection kept to a minimum (approx 1:1000)

Safety glass dome

Steel hull spanning void

2900

650   1000   650

**Passenger conveyor
De Gaulle Airport, Aeroport du Paris**   *Fig. 9.73.*

Duty Rooms
Amenity facilities
Sanitation/waste disposal
systems

Met., AIS and Flight clearance
(concourse in common to all three units)

Meteorological:
Concourse, counter
General office
Senior officer's office
Library, store
Reproduction/photo-copying
room
Teleprinter room (International
airports and met. central unit
link)
Staff amenities

Aeronautical Information Service:
Concourse, counter
General office, teleprinter (International airports and central
AIS units link)
Senior officer's office
Storage
Staff amenities

Flight clearance:
Concourse, counter
General office, teleprinter—control tower link
Storage

Customs
Offices: aircraft boarding and
crew
Examination
Crew examination areas
Crew search rooms
Amenity facilities

Airlines
Operational offices
Bonded stores
Catering facilities

Security
Police unit accommodation

Port health
Isolation unit

PRINCIPAL AIRPORT BUILDING AND FACILITIES

Terminal area

Landside access/car parks/public transport
Terminal buildings/aircraft access
Spectator provision
Staff catering
Hotels/shopping centres
Conference/exhibition centres
General office accommodation
Police
Control building
Air-crew briefing

General Aviation Terminal
Fire station/ambulance station
Power house/plant buildings/electrical distribution
Sanitation buildings
Aircraft catering
Aircraft fuel depot(s)

Maintenance area

Landside/airside access
Hangars/including general aviation
Airline offices/training facilities
Airport maintenance buildings
Motor transport depot(s)
Plant building/electrical distribution
Fire station
Parking/staff amenity/canteen

Cargo area

Landside/Airside access
Cargo handling building(s)
Cargo Agents' building(s)
Customs offices
Administration offices
Parking/staff amenity/canteen
Plant building/electrical distribution
Fire station
Aircraft fuel depot

Navigational buildings

On and off airport

LEGISLATION, STATUTORY REQUIREMENTS AND AUTHORITIES

GENERAL

Legislation and Statutory requirements differ between countries. However, the principles are likely to be similar, since the operation of air transport and the design of operational facilities at airports is largely affected by the minimum requirements laid down by ICAO (International Civil Aviation Organisation).

Where the UK is concerned, matters under this heading affecting terminal buildings differ very little from other building types. Reference should be accordingly made to the relevant paragraph dealing with legislation and the recognised authorities listed below.

The siting of an airport and other similar fundamental questions which require to conform to specific Acts of Parliament will normally have been cleared by the Airport Authority with the Planning Authorities before terminal planning begins. In the formulation of the brief the client will also have sought the advice of special departments such as the Civil Aviation Authority, Customs, Immigration, Port Health and Police, which are themselves are controlled by Acts of Parliament and other legislation.

As planning develops from this stage, normal approvals will be required from the Planning and Building Authority and the Fire Officer, all of whom operate with powers vested in them by Acts of Parliament. Under the Civil Aviation Act 1949 (Air Navigation Order 1972) the Planning Authority are required to obtain approvals from the Department of Trade and Industry to ensure navigational aids are not infringed.

BUILDING REGULATIONS

In applying Building Regulations to terminal buildings, some difficulties may be experienced and it is vital that their interpretation is clearly established with the Planning, Building and Fire Authority at the outset.

An example of this is the matter of building category which will affect the fire compartmentation required (Building Regulations 1972 Part E) since no special category exists for an airport terminal building in the Building Regulations.

The importance of early consultations with the Building and Fire authorities cannot be overstressed, with regard to compartmentation, structure and materials, fire detection, fire-fighting and means of escape.

LEGISLATION

Airports Authority Act 1965
Civil Aviation Act 1949 and amendments 1968, 1971 (Air Navigational Order 1972)
Offices, Shops and Railway Premises Act 1963
Factories Act 1963
Town and Country Planning Act 1971
Fire Precaution Act 1971
Building Regulations Act 1971

AUTHORITIES

The Airport Authority
The Civil Aviation Authority
HM Customs and Excise
HM Immigration (Immigration and Nationality Dept. of the Home Office)
Port Health Authority
The Local Authority

International Civil Aviation Organisation (advisory)
International Air Transport Association (advisory)

EXAMPLES

The prime source of initial information on international airport developments is the journal. A list of foreign journals which are available in the UK is given in the Bibliography. Further detailed information can be obtained from the airport authorities. The following is a list of the Airports referred to in the preparation of this article, and to whom acknowlegement is made for making available detailed information. Many authorities and consultants are involved in airport development but only architect/planners are noted below.

Full information can be obtained from the airport authorities.

EUROPEAN AIRPORTS

Basel-Mulhouse, Basel.
   Suter & Suter.

Berlin Tegel Airport.
   Van Gerkan, Marg, Nickels & Niedballa.

Charles de Gaulle Airport, Paris. No. 1 and No. 2
   H. Vicariot and J. Bachelez, Aeroport de Paris.

Cologne-Bonn International Airport.
   Esleben & Schneider.

Copenhagan International Airport, Kastrup.
   Knud Harboe; Ostenfeld & Jonson.

Dusseldorf International Airport.
   Rosskotten & Tritthart; G. C. van Wageningen.

Frankfurt-Main Airport.
   Giefer, Mäckler & Kosina.

Gatwick Airport London.
   YRM

Hamburg International Airport.
   Dorsch, Gerlach, Freese, Weidle & Howell.

Heathrow Airport London.
   Frederick Gibberd & Partners; Pascall & Watson.

Lisbon International Airport. Competition design for new Terminal.
   YRM

Luton International Airport. Bedfordshire.
   YRM

Munich II.
   Manfred Steffen; Dorsch, Gerlach, Weidle; Becker, Kivett & Myers; Projektgemeinschaft für Flughafenplanung; von Gerkan, Marg & Partners.

Newcastle International Airport.
   YRM

Orly Airport, Paris.
   M. Vicariot.

Schiphol Airport, Amsterdam.
   Netherlands Airports Consultants Office. (N.V. Naco)
   F.C. de Weger & Professor M. Duintjer, Interiors: Kho Liang le, Associates. Freight building: E.A. Riphagen.

U.S.A. AND CANADIAN AIRPORTS

Boston-Logan International Airport.
Volpe Terminal.
   Kubitz & Pepi; Desmond & Lord; Amsler & Hagenah.

Chicago, O'Hare International Airport, Illinois.
C.F. Murphy & Associates.

Dallas/Fort Worth Airport, Texas.
Hellmuth, Obata, Kassabaum, Brodsky, Hopf & Adler;
Thomas Sullivan.

Dulles International Airport, Washington D.C.
Eero Saarinen (Roche Dinkerloo Associates) Ammon
& Whitney.

Greater Cincinnati Airport, Ohio.
Heery & Heery; Robert A. Keefe.

Houston Intercontinental Airport, Texas.
Goleman & Rolfe; Pierce & Pierce.

Kansas City International Airport, Missouri.
Burns & McDonnell.

La Guardia Airport, N.Y., New York.
Harrison & Abramovitz.

Los Angleles International Airport, California.
Charles Luckham Associates with William Pereira &
Associates and Welton Becket & Associates.

Montreal International Airport.
Illsley, Templeton, Archibald; Larose & Larose.

New York, J.F. Kennedy.
American Airlines.
Kahn & Jacobs.

Pan American World Airways.
Tippetts-Abbett-McCarthy & Stratton.

Trans World Airlines.
Port of NY. Authority Aviation Planning Division.
Eero Saarinen.

United Airlines.
Skidmore, Owings & Merrill.

Newark International Airport, New York.
Port of New York Authority & New Jersey.

San Francisco International Airport, California.
Carl Warnecke & Associates; Desmond & Lord.

Seattle International Airport, Washington D.C.
Richardson Associates.

Tampa Airport, Florida.
Leigh Fisher Associates; J.E. Greiner & Co., Reynolds,
Smith & Hills.

BIBLIOGRAPHY

There are few general publications on airport terminal
planning, possibly because they would become quickly out
of date. One of the best sources of information are the journals. In addition the airport authorities themselves are almost
always prepared to provide detailed information on request.

PUBLICATIONS

Airports Terminals Reference Manual, 5th edn (amendments
1974) IATA, 1155 Mansfield Street, Montreal 113, P.Q.,
Canada.

Airport Masterplanning, ICAO manual, Doc. 8796/AH/891.
1080 University Street, Montreal 101, P.Q., Canada.

'Airports for the 80s'. *Conf. Proc. Inst. of C.E.*, (1973)
Blankenship, E.C., 'Der Flughafen', *Verlag Gerd Hatje*,
Stuttgart English and German text (1974)
Commission on the Third London Airport. HMSO, London
(1969–70)
Fruin, J.J. 'Environmental factors in Passenger Terminal
Design', *ASCE Transportation Engineering Journal* (Feb.
1972)
Masefield, P. 'An Airport system for airport services', *Aero.
Journal*, 76 (1972)
Perrett, J.D., 'The capacity of Airports; Planning Consider-
ations', *Proc. Inst. C.E.*, 50 (1971)
Planning and Noise. D. of E. Circular 10/73, HMSO (1973)
'World Airports, the way ahead', *Conf. Proc. Inst. C.E.* (1970)

JOURNALS

Airport Forum, (German and English text). Bauverlag
GmbH. Wiesbaden. W. Germany.
Airports International, (Journal of ICAO) Published in UK
by W.H. Smith & Son.
Flight International, Published by IPC
The Aeronautical Journal, Royal Aeronautical Society,
4 Hamilton Place, London W.1.
Air Transport World, 115, 15th St., Suite 1000, Washington
D.C. 20014.
Airport World, P.O. Box 5800, Washington D.C. 20014.
Interavia (Geneva), Published in UK by Derek Wood,
149 Fleet St., E.C.4.
ICAO Bulletin, 1080, University St., Montreal 101, P.Q.,
Canada.

ARCHITECTURAL JOURNALS

Numbers devoted to airports or descriptions of particular
airports appear in the following journals:

The Architectural Review, Architectural Press Ltd., 9 Queen
Anne's Gate, London SW1H 9BY.
The Architects' Journal, Architectural Press Ltd.
The Architect, Building & Contract Journals Ltd. 32
Southwark Bridge Road, London SE1.
Building, Building (Publishers) Ltd., The Builder House,
PO Box 135, 4 Catherine Street, London WC2B 5JN.
Design, Design Council, 28 Haymarket, London SW1Y 4SU.
L'Architecture d'Aujourd'hui, 5 rue Bartholdi, 92100
Boulogne, France.
Bauen + Wohnen, Vogelsangstrasse 48, 8006 Zurich,
Switzerland.
Domus, via Monte di Pieta 15, 20121 Milan, Italy.

Fig. 9.75.   Tampa, Florida. Racetrack continuous belt baggage reclaim units. ('Florida Architecture')

Fig. 9.74.   Heathrow London, No. 1 Terminal Domestic baggage reclaim carousels. (British Airports Authority; Henk Snoek)

Fig. 9.76.   Pan-Am Terminal, J. F. Kennedy, New York. Carousel reclaim units, high level feed. (Pan American World Airways)

Fig. 9.77.   Pan-Am Terminal, J. F. Kennedy, New York. Baggage flight assembly, automated straight line selection. (Pan American World Airways)

Fig. 9.78.   Copenhagen. Baggage flight assembly, multiple sorting from chute accumulation. (Copenhagen Airports Authority)

Fig. 9.79.   Heathrow London, Terminal 3. Baggage flight assembly, circulating accumulation, (British Airports Authority)

Fig. 9.80. Heathrow London, No. 1 Terminal. Island check-in. (British Airports Authority; Henk Snoek)

Fig. 9.81. Heathrow London. Split flap baggage reclaim sign over carousel. Baggage controller kiosk beyond. (British Airports Authority, Solari-Telesign. Fox).

Fig. 9.82. (above) Heathrow London. Split flap domestic departures indicator, No. 1 Terminal. (British Airports Authority. Solari-Telesign. Fox).

Fig. 9.83. (above right) Gatwick London. British Airports Authority standard signposting—black on yellow ground, illuminated. (BAA—Kinneir, Calvert, Tuhill)

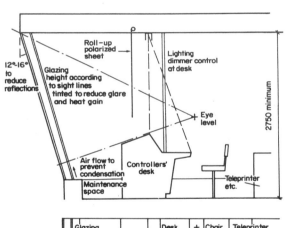

Part-plan/section visual control room (typical dimensions)

Fig. 9.84. Basel-Mulhouse. Control room. (Weyermann-Heiber)

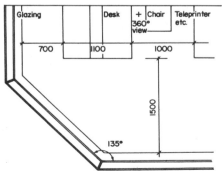

Fig. 9.85. Control room: typical data

CARGO TERMINALS

INTRODUCTION

This section is a brief summary of a complex subject. The ultimate building envelope may, and indeed should, be simple. The factors that determine its final form will be the reverse.

During the last ten years air cargo has had an average growth rate of about 15%. The fastest growth is in Europe followed by the US and Japan. In 1972/73 some 68 million tonnes of freight were carried by air, representing over 13 000m tonne kilometres. As with passenger traffic there are current indications (1974) of a reduction in the growth rate. The introduction of wide-bodied aircraft has obviously increased greatly carrying potential: a B.747F has a payload of 119 tonnes compared with 42 tonnes in a B.707 320. The wide-bodied aircraft also have considerable freight capacity when used on passenger services.

As with passenger handling, the fundamental characteristic of the cargo terminal is simple; it is a means of transferring freight from land transport to an aircraft and vice versa. This process is however influenced by several factors, i.e.

The great range in the size and weight of individual items.
The diversity of destinations.
The complexity of documentation.
The need for substantial handling and sorting systems.
The increasing costs of ground processing.

It is important for the designer to appreciate that ground handling activities at cargo terminals are a prime contributor to total air cargo costs. Although the real costs of air cargo have fallen over the last ten years this has been mainly due to the increased productivity of aircraft—terminal costs have risen as a proportion of the total.

Air cargo is in a relatively early stage of development and the terminals should be designed not only for expansion but to permit considerable changes in their layout and equipment, both within the building and on the aprons. Early cargo terminals were little more than open warehouses; there followed the development of increasingly complex systems for the handling of individual packages. These are now giving way to systems for dealing with cargo in containers and pallets, coupled with mechanised aircraft loading systems.

Operators prefer to carry bulk loads to reduce handling procedures and lower costs: this could lead to off-airport clearance depots where the shipper can make up his container/palletised loads. If this procedure could be linked with local customs clearance the terminal function will be greatly simplified. Documentation is not only a cost factor but can be a delaying factor and the automation of these complex procedures is now becoming accepted practice. Automated information systems can prove more economic and amenable to change than automated handling systems. (At Heathrow the London Airport Cargo EDP system deals with inventory control, customs control, calculates duty, taxes and fees and handles accounts.)

In the not too distant future it is possible to imagine cargo terminals reverting to the open warehouse or dock area for handling only containers—like a seaport. Specialised individual high value items could then be segregated and handled separately as a part of the passenger aircraft combination load.

SITING

Reference has been made to the strategic master plan in the introduction to the section on Terminal Buildings. The Cargo Area is an important element in this plan and should be sited on the non-finite zoning principle, allowing sufficient land for expansion for the anticipated maximum cargo aircraft movements related to the runway capacities envisaged. Only the Airport Authority can advise the planner on this matter.

There are seven principal factors in siting the cargo area:

1. Road access for land vehicles or other landside transport systems.
2. Space for the cargo terminal buildings, including expansion.
3. Space for the cargo aircraft aprons, including expansion.
4. Minimum taxying distances for aircraft to the runway(s).
5. Airside road access to the passenger terminal area aircraft stands.
6. Airside taxying and vehicle access to the maintenance area.
7. Adequate landside road system to the rest of the airport.

The buildings that may be included in a Cargo Area are noted at the end of the accommodation schedule in the previous section (see page **9**-31).

PLANNING

GENERAL

There are four basic movements of cargo: export (outbound), import (inbound), interline transfer and direct transfer (aircraft to aircraft). Export and import cargo is in two categories: domestic and international. Export cargo is normally bonded after customs examination and pre-flight assembly; import cargo is placed in bond after pallet break-up and sorting and before customs clearance.

Domestic handling, with simpler documentation, has a faster throughput than international freight and less warehouse space in proportion to the volume of cargo handled.

There is inevitably a requirement for administrative accommodation and staff amenities. These should not occupy premium warehouse level space.

CARGO FLOW (See Figs. 9.100. and 9.101.)

The items below indicate the principal cargo movement/operations but exclude documentation procedures.

Export/outbound

1. Unloading from landside vehicles
2. Identification and checking

3. Weighing, measuring and labelling
4. Domestic cargo:
    pre-flight assembly and storage
    flight assembly (container, pallet or free)
    staging for despatch
    loading onto aircraft.
5. International cargo:
    as domestic, but customs clearance/bonding after
    initial sorting.
6. Cargo for passenger and cargo aircraft is separated in
flight assembly area or staging area.

Import/inbound

1. Aircraft off loading (by vehicle from passenger terminal
if non-cargo aircraft)
2. Holding, pre check-in
3. Sorting and check-in
4. Domestic:
    pre-delivery holding area
    delivery to landside vehicles
5. International:
    bond storage
    customs examination and clearance
    pre-delivery holding area
    delivery to landside vehicles.

Transfer

Direct transfer: If containerised, this can take place on the apron if international/international or domestic/domestic. If international/domestic or vice-versa the cargo may require customs clearance within the terminal.

Interline

Interline transfer will be processed within the terminal.

BUILDING AND EQUIPMENT

There are five fundamental factors to bear in mind:

1. Handling and storage equipment will probably change within the life of the building.
2. The information control procedures, in parallel to the cargo movement systems, will also change.
3. Expansion of both systems must be achieved without disruption, and each should be able to expand independantly of the other.
4. Administrative and amenity accommodation should not be at handling level.
5. Barriers between export/import should be moveable —to allow for pattern changes.

BUILDING SHAPE

Research carried out by IATA has suggested that a near-square plan gives a sound proportion for accommodating the handling systems, with a maximum rectangle ratio of 1:1.3; the airside/landside frontages being the larger.

Airside and landside frontages must be continuous—a requirement greatly simplified if there is only one user.

SPACE REQUIREMENTS

GENERAL

There is no established formula for calculating the size of a cargo terminal building. This is due mainly to the variety of operating methods, different handling techniques, the nature of the freight to be handled—especially the degree of container/palletised loads—and the varying storage times anticipated. Another varying factor will be the documentation and customs control procedures to be adopted.

The Airport Authority will almost certainly provide the designer with a highly detailed brief, which should have been prepared in close collaboration with the carriers and their agents.

FACTORS

It is usually necessary to construct some form of mathematical model, developed from projected daily and hourly anticipated busy periods, taking into account all the categories of cargo noted in the sub-section on Planning above.

To get an economic building the carrier wants to avoid high peak/trough ratios, small consignments and long storage periods—all of which will increase building size.

A major factor in determining the scale of the building is the number of users. The most economical scheme will be where one user only is involved. If there is more than one, and they vary in size, an economic building shape will be more difficult to achieve.

Anticipated requirements would normally be based on 5, 10 and 15 year increments.

DATA

Design data will depend in every instance on the handling and storage systems adopted. In addition to the forecasting of traffic demand and determination of capacity the following is a check-list of the principal items on which data is required during brief-formulation and the design process:

1. Cargo characteristics:
    percentages of loose, containerised and palletised cargo.
    percentages of bulk and heavy piece cargo.
    extent of express, perishable and mail cargo.
2. Ratio of import, export, transfer and interline.
3. Landside patterns:
    load characteristics of vehicles for delivery and collection.
    requirement for dock levelers or equivalent.
    door requirements associated with off-loading and loading.
4. Airside patterns:
    stand configurations for freight aircraft.

Air bridges and nose loaders

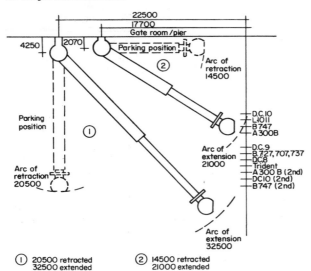

Type 1 apron drive

Min. retracted length 11500
Max. extended length 55000
Vertical height adj. 1330 to 6100
Arc. of travel 190°

Type 2 non telescopic rotation bridge
Gate room/pier

Max. length 20000
Vertical height adj. 1330 to 6100
Arc. of travel 190°

Type 3 nose loaders

(a) Gate room/pier — Fixed tunnel, First telescopic tunnel, Second telescopic tunnel, Pivot point

(b) Gate room/pier — Fixed tunnel, Pivot point

(c) Gate room/pier — Fixed tunnel, Vertical lift

Fixed tunnel 9100 to 15200
Min. retracted length of telescopic tunnel 5200
Max. extended length of telescopic tunnel 6700
Vertical height adjustment 2100 to 5200

Note: fixed tunnel can be dispensed with if adjustable tunnel is attached directly to gate room/pier

Approximate internal dimensions of all tunnels (fixed or telescopic):
Min width 1,500
Min height 2200

① 20500 retracted 32500 extended   ② 14500 retracted 21000 extended

Note: apron service load bridge not shown
Information: N.V. Aviobridge, Fokker–VFW

Fig. 9.86.

Fig. 9.87. Schiphol, Amsterdam. Air bridges on C Pier showing fixed apron service road section and over-wing loader. (Fokker-VFW N.V.)

Fig. 9.88. Dulles International, Washington D.C. Mobile passenger vehicle. (Boothe Airside Systems Inc., USA.)

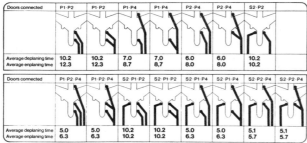

Doors connected	P1·P2	P1·P2	P1·P4	P1·P4	P2·P4	P2·P4	S2·P2
Average deplaning time	10.2	10.2	7.0	7.0	6.0	6.0	10.2
Average enplaning time	12.3	12.3	8.7	8.7	8.0	8.0	10.2

Doors connected	P1·P2·P4	P1·P2·P4	S2·P1·P2	S2·P1·P2	S2·P1·P4	S2·P1·P4	S2·P2·P4	S2·P2·P4
Average deplaning time	5.0	5.0	10.2	10.2	5.0	5.0	5.1	5.1
Average enplaning time	6.3	6.3	10.2	10.2	6.3	6.3	5.7	5.7

Fig. 9.89. Schiphol, Amsterdam. Study of loading and unloading times with different air bridge configurations on a B.747. (Airports International/Fokker-VFW N.V.)

Fig. 9.90. Tampa, Florida. Transportation system, landside terminal to airside satellites. (Hillsborough County Aviation Authority/Westinghouse Electric Corporation)

Fig. 9.91. Tampa, Florida. Transportation system, landside terminal to airside satellites. ('Florida Architecture')

Met. A.I.S. and flight clearance

Fig. 9.92.

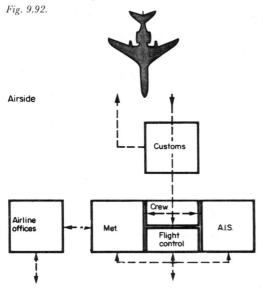

Airside

Landside

Met. backup

Fig. 9.93.

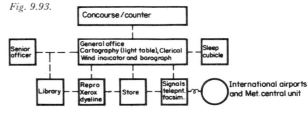

A.I.S. backup

Fig. 9.94.

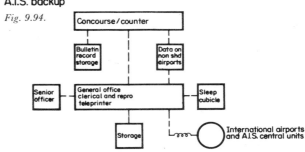

Flight control backup

Fig. 9.95.

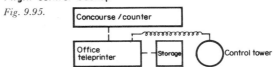

Port health control -arrivals

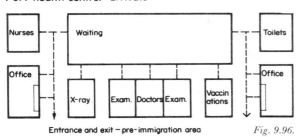

Entrance and exit – pre-immigration area

Fig. 9.96.

Immigration control accommodation- arrivals.

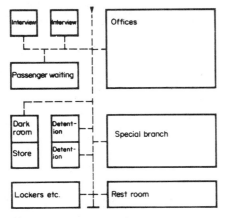

Entrance adjacent to immigration comb
Secure exit to landside

Fig. 9.98.

Customs accommodation–arrivals

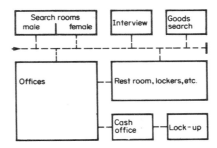

Entrance from examination hall
secure entry (staff) from landside

Fig. 9.97.

Customs and immigration accommodation–departures

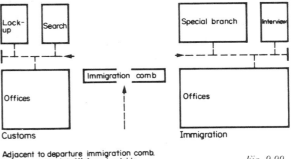

Adjacent to departure immigration comb.
Secure entries (staff) from landside

Fig. 9.99.

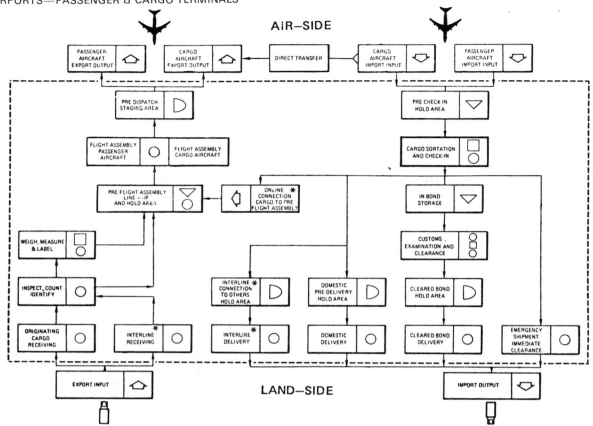

American Society of Mechanical Engineers (ASME) symbols.

KEY TO SYMBOLS

OPERATION ○ — An *operation* occurs when a unit of cargo is lifted up or put down or moved during a process. Marking and labelling is considered an Operation. An 'Operation' also occurs when information is given or received or when planning or calculating takes place (e.g. input or extraction of information from/to EDP Systems).

INSPECTION □ — An *inspection* occurs when a unit of cargo is examined to determine proper packaging, acceptability for carriage, weighed, measured, etc.

TRANSPORTATION ▷ — A *transportation* occurs when a unit of cargo is moved from one place to another beyond the limited movements which occur during some Operations and Inspections.

DELAY ◗ — A *delay* occurs to a unit of cargo when it is prevented from progressing to its next planned activity.

STORAGE ▽ — A *storage* occurs when a unit of cargo is staged, prior to assembly, assembled, pending dispatch to aircraft, or held pending breakdown and/or Customs examination and/or delivery.

Fig. 9.100. Example of cargo flow in a Terminal. (International Air Transport Association)

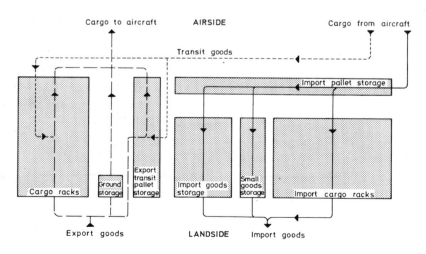

Fig. 9.101. (left) KLM Cargocentre, Schiphol, Amsterdam. Diagram of automated cargo handling and storage system. (Schiphol Airport Authority)

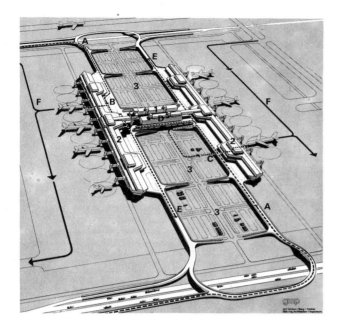

Fig. 9.102. Munich II. First development stage. A, approach. B, Passengers, kerbside to aircraft. C, Passengers, carpark to aircraft. D, central building. E, Exit. F, Aircraft taxi-route. 1. central building and station. 2. passenger terminal building and gates. 3. car parks. (Airport Forum)

(Note: the material relating to this airport was published after the article was prepared, but in the author's view it's significance justifies its inclusion.)

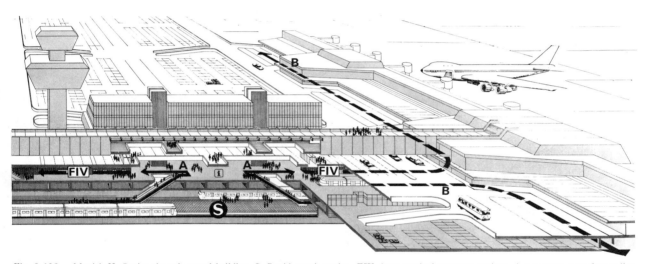

Fig. 9.103. Munich II. Section through central building. S, Rapid transit station. FIV, inter-terminal transport stations. A, passenger route from rail to FIV stations. B, FIV routes to check-in locations. ('Airport Forum').

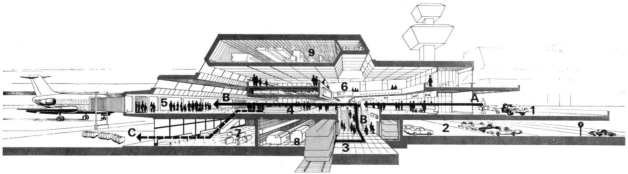

Fig. 9.104. Munich II. Section through a passenger terminal. A, Passenger route: kerbside/aircraft. B, passenger route: inter-terminal transport to aircraft. C, baggage route. 1. curbside. 2. car park. 3. Inter-terminal transport. 4. check-in. 5. lounge. 6. offices and connecting level. 7. Baggage. 8. Utilities. 9. Plant. ('Airport Forum')

access routing for combination aircraft.
aircraft loading systems.
ramp vehicle parking requirements.
door requirements for cargo access.
canopy requirements.
5. Internal handling:
systems for handling containers, pallets and loose cargo.
requirements for by-pass system for containers.
6. Internal storage:
types and height of racking, import and export. (Usually determinant of building height.) Floor loadings.
7. Customs operation:
requirements for import/export examination and clearance.
8. Automation of handling (if envisaged):
details of control systems for automated handling and related accommodation.
9. Automation of documentation (if envisaged):
details of control systems for automated document handling and related accommodation.
10. Administrative requirements, including staff amenities.
11. Security and policing requirements.

ACCOMMODATION

It will be understood from the above paragraphs that, until the brief for a specific terminal has been established, it is not possible to produce a schedule of accommodation.

STATUTORY REQUIREMENTS, AUTHORITIES AND LEGISLATION

In the UK Legislation is confined to the various Acts listed on page **9**–32. Otherwise there are no regulations applying specifically to cargo terminals, and normal building regulations are appropriate.

Requirements regarding fire-hazard are particularly stressed and early consultation with the fire authorities and the user's (or the airport's) insurers is imperative. The degree of compartmentation required may have a very significant effect on the ultimate plan. Although not in themselves peculiar to cargo terminals the following items must be cleared at the outset of the design process:

Compartmentation
Means of escape
Sprinkler installations

Detection systems
Alarm systems
Fire-fighting equipment
Combustibility of internal and cladding materials.

EXAMPLES

In the fast-moving development of cargo terminals the designer would be well advised to seek information on new projects currently being undertaken. This can be provided through IATA. It should be noted that Customs procedures vary from country to country with marked repercussions on design. It can also be misleading to examine plans without knowledge of the brief.
Typical examples are:
Schipol Cargo, Amsterdam. KLM.
Montreal Cargo. Air Canada.
Cargocentre Europe, Heathrow. British Airways.
Cargo Terminal, Frankfurt. Lufthansa.

BIBLIOGRAPHY AND REFERENCES

Airport Terminals Reference Manual. IATA. Revised cargo section (Jan 1974)
Bey, Dr-Ing. Inguard, *Analysis of Air Cargo Handling,* University of Karlsruhe, (1973)
British Airports Authority *Future of air cargo in the South-East* (1974)
Devenish, A.F. 'Cargo terminals'. Conference: 'World Airports—the Way ahead'. *Inst. C.E.* (1970)
Koster, A.D. 'Cargo handling'. Conference: 'Airports for the 80's'. *Inst. C.E.* (1973)
Smith, P.S. *Air cargo ground facilities,* Cranfield Centre for Transport Studies (June 1974)
Wiley, J.R. 'Air Cargo Terminals of the 80's'. Conference: 'Airports for the 80's', *Inst. C.E.* (1973)

John Vulliamy, *is an executive partner of Yorke Rosenberg Mardall and he has been involved in all their airport projects. YRM were commissioned in 1954 to design the first stage of Gatwick Airport London, and they have been working continuously on the expansion of this airport up to the present time. At Heathrow Airport, London they designed the principal agents' and customs buildings in the cargo area. They designed at Luton Airport the Terminal Building and a hangar for Britannia Airways; they have also planned a new passenger terminal for this airport. Other airports by YRM include the Terminal Buildings at Stanstead Airport London and Newcastle Airport— for which expansion plans are being produced. Schemes have been prepared by them for an airport in British Honduras and for an invited competition design for a new Terminal at Lisbon Airport.*

10 GARAGES AND PETROL STATIONS

ALFRED J. ROWE, A.R.I.B.A

INTRODUCTION

This section is concerned with data and planning for motor vehicles. It is divided into three parts: Public Service Vehicles, Public Garages and Filling Stations.

For the purpose of this section the term 'Public-service Vehicle' (P.S.V.) should be taken as referring to motor buses, motor coaches and taxis, but not to motor-cars which are used for private hire.

BUS STATIONS

The bus station which is specially planned is a relatively new development brought about by a general increase in public-service traffic. Its provision is also due to the desire to increase public safety by the reduction of obstructions in streets and to avoid traffic delays arising from vehicles stopping to pick up and set down passengers, change crews, etc. in any but recognised and authorised locations. It is probable that fuller planned bus-station facilities will be regarded as a necessity in all urban areas in the near future.

It cannot be stressed too strongly from the initial conception of any scheme that bus stations may be concerned with the operation of both local and long distance services and in some areas also with sight-seeing and similar tourist traffic. The latter may occur not only in seaside and similar holiday resorts, but in towns possessing historical and architectural interest and beauty which must be preserved, not marred, by provision of public-service vehicle facilities.

GARAGES

Garages can be divided into public garages for letting for a period of time and garages which are provided as ancillary to other building types such as department stores, hotels, etc. Basic requirements are common to both types, their main difference being the method of payment.

FILLING STATIONS

This section covers facilities provided for refuelling vehicles. It does not cover large garages and petrol stations although some of the data given may be relevant to these.

SITING

BUS STATIONS

For local services and those serving small towns and villages in the locality, it is desirable that the site for a bus station be found within 400 m to 500 m of the main shopping and commercial centres of the town. Wherever possible bus stations should be close also to the main railway station, although it is realised that this full combination of shops and stations may not always be possible.

Bus stations should not be planned near dwellings, churches or schools. The noise can be a considerable source of annoyance and discomfort to the occupiers, especially during early or late hours of the day. For stations concerned with long-distance express services, close proximity to shopping centres is of less importance.

The areas required for bus-station sites are entirely dependent on the various local circumstances which will dictate the volume and frequency of traffic. However, as it would seem that the use of buses is constantly increasing, ample sites should be sought at the commencement of any scheme, if only to meet the possibility of the future extensions required for more frequent buses or the establishment of new services. Unless some such policy is pursued it may mean that an urban bus station may have to be moved to a new or larger site or have to be duplicated elsewhere purely as a result of demand.

Site areas again are affected by the need to meet peak-traffic loads on market or on special mid-week shopping days. Through services may make similar demands for site area, especially if they are well spread out throughout the day. If, however, many such services arrive or leave about the same

GARAGES AND PETROL STATIONS

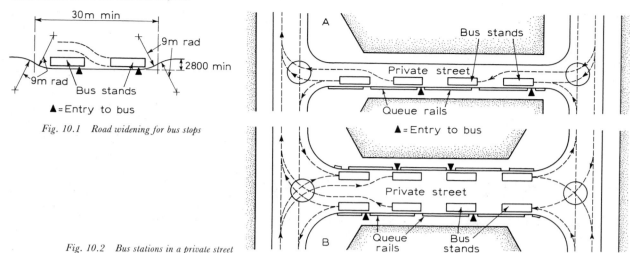

Fig. 10.1 Road widening for bus stops

Fig. 10.2 Bus stations in a private street

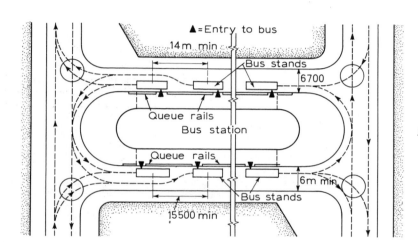

Fig. 10.3 Bus stations. Central concourse

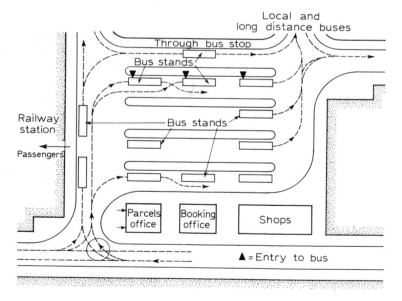

Fig. 10.4 Bus stations. Open standing

10–2

time and form connecting services, much more standing-space may be necessary. Terminal stations involving long waits for vehicles will also need large areas especially set aside for parking.

An important planning factor in the selection of a site is its relationship to the roads and traffic flow of the surrounding area. The concentration of vehicles using the station must not impede normal street traffic or in any way increase danger for any other road user, vehicular or pedestrian.

Where traffic is heavy, bus stations may be provided by acquiring land suitable for the planning and construction of what amounts to a wide private street with one-way or straight-through traffic. In towns with more frequent P.S.V. traffic, much more elaborate station schemes naturally become necessary, and will affect larger areas of the urban layout around the actual station site.

In smaller towns it may be possible to provide bus-station facilities by widening a portion of a main street, if the number of vehicles is small and few stop for long or at any one time; such a scheme should not cause cross-traffic. Widenings, therefore, are usually needed on both sides of the street, although possibly not exactly opposite one another.

GARAGES

The siting of a garage is dependent on its nature. A public garage will, of course, be sited close to town centres and direct pedestrian links can often be provided. Sites which are rectangular, or nearly so, are best, as awkward shapes make economical parking difficult. Sloping sites can often be used to advantage to provide access from the street to several floors.

A central control point should, however, be provided in those garages where a charge is made if the control point is manned. Garages which serve hotels, department stores etc can often be sited in basements but access should be planned in such a way as to facilitate pedestrian access to and from cars.

FILLING STATIONS

The selection of a site for a filling station should be considered very carefully from the point of view of traffic in the surrounding streets and from the point of view of advertising advantages. It is essential to be able to see a station some time before reaching it in order to have sufficient time to make a decision on the question of stopping.

The best sites for filling stations are frequently too expensive, consequently less satisfactory ones at low costs have to be used, with the result that site conditions are often very difficult. Town planning and traffic conditions, however, should be very carefully considered in order to avoid damaging amenities and causing traffic congestion, with the consequent avoidance of the station by motorists.

The important factors in the design of filling stations are quickness of service, elimination of danger to passing traffic, pedestrians, or users of the station, distant visibility for passing motorists and a clear view of passing traffic for those leaving the station. Thought should be given to provision for the display of accessories in showcases or windows and for the installation of a repairing depot with all stores and equipment.

SPACE REQUIREMENTS AND ACCOMMODATION FOR P.S.V.s

VEHICLE BAYS

Fig. 10.1 illustrates the essential widening of a roadway to provide a bus stopping-place which will not interfere with the normal traffic flow of the street. Such a layout requires a set-back in the road width of 2800 and preferably up to 3000. It is also important that there should be no reduction but, if possible, an increase in the pavement width in order to allow for covered waiting-space for queues and to avoid pedestrian congestion.

The length required for this type of vehicle bay is based on the number of vehicles likely to use the stop at any time; the allowance should be at least 14 m per vehicle, with a minimum of 30 m. As shown on the illustration these dimensions will allow each vehicle to move away into the main traffic flow without moving any other vehicle in the bay.

SITING OF BUS STATIONS

Fig. 10.2 illustrates two examples of the 'private-street' type of stopping-place or station. In each example the length can be anything needed to provide standing-places for the anticipated number of vehicles and waiting passengers. Congestion at the ends where junctions with the main roads occur may become serious, however, if any P.S.V.s are to be catered for within such a scheme. However, if adjoining space, more than is required for the traffic-ways and the passenger queuing-spaces, is acquired, other and more complete bus-station facilities can be provided on one or both sides of the road, in either of the two examples.

Scheme A (Fig. 10.2) is planned for vehicles to wait on one side of the street only and consequently involves one-way traffic and requires, in addition, suitable roadway layout and traffic conditions in the surrounding streets, a circumstance which may not always be found. Both examples require that the streets at each end do not carry very heavy traffic, as 'cross-overs' are involved, through buses entering and leaving the station to go in any direction in the main street, and these may cause serious intermittent delays.

Scheme B makes provision for traffic in both directions and the roadway, therefore, provides for four separate traffic-lanes. At each out-going end, the corner buildings must be designed so that proper vision is possible of the traffic using the street to be entered.

It is almost essential that schemes of this type should not be used also by ordinary traffic.

Schemes based on Type B are apt to cause inconvenience to strangers using the station, as they may not know from which stand a bus is leaving and may therefore need to cross busy traffic-ways quickly.

The layout shown in Fig. 10.3 has a central concourse around which all the bus stands are planned. The traffic proceeds in a one-way direction round the central unit. The central unit allows concentration of all passenger facilities in one unit of building. If the roads of such a scheme are used for normal traffic, in addition to the bus traffic, bridges or subways for access to the central concourse are likely to be needed.

10–3

The openings in the passenger guard-rails will have to be related closely to the position of entrances to the vehicles using each stance; or, alternatively, the guard-rails must be adjustable or movable. It should be noted that the width of traffic-ways influences the spacing of the bus stands, as shown in Fig. 10.3. If roads are only 6000 wide, an additional length of 1500 over the minimum of 14 m will be needed for vehicles to enter and leave stances without disturbing adjoining vehicles in the process.

LAYOUT AND CONSTRUCTIONAL DATA

Fig. 10.4 illustrates a type of bus station with a large open standing-space, slightly raised passenger waiting-spaces or platforms and a concourse and booking-unit on one side. The scheme is based on a single entry; normal road traffic can be taken, however, through the scheme if extra roadway widths are provided as shown on the left and top of the plan.

As the layout is based on one-way traffic, the platforms or passenger waiting-spaces need to be at least 6000 apart and are used on one side only for access to vehicles. Provision is made for through services to stop on the left and top sides of the scheme, leaving the central platforms free for vehicles which may wait for longer periods.

The concourse is planned on a normal street frontage.

inconvenience in the main roads. This may be reduced if the road width is increased to form an unloading stance on the lines of that indicated in Fig. 10.1. The differences between Schemes (a) and (b) (Fig. 10.5) is, that in the former, the vehicles back in after driving past the stand, and in the latter, drive straight into the stand and then back out to leave.

In layouts of this type vehicle stands should be based on 4000 centres to provide a minimum of 1500 between standing vehicles. The set-back of the pavement or platform needs to be such that the roof will provide cover to entrances placed near the front of the vehicles. The planning of the stances at an angle, as shown, facilitates driving in or out and occupies far less space than parking at right angles to the main traffic routes.

Fig. 10.6 shows three variations of a typical layout which is economic on street frontage and makes good use of a deep site. A central concourse is shown directly entered from the main street footway; at the same time a part of the frontage may be used for shops in the one position on the site which would carry the highest rental values. Round this concourse is arranged a number of bus stands. To provide the same number of stands in any other way as, for example, that shown in Fig. 10.4, would involve a much larger site.

Each variation shows one-way traffic round the concourse and either backing in or out of the stands, according to

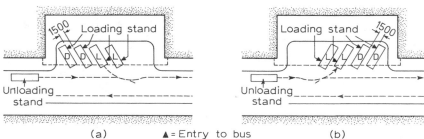

(a)   ▲ = Entry to bus
        L. Long distance buses
        D. Local buses

(b)

Fig. 10.5   Bus stations. Small set-backs

If schemes of this type are adopted it will probably be found to be uneconomical to roof the whole area. Covering may be provided over the platforms to protect the passengers, although such roofs are apt to be unsatisfactory in driving rain. This scheme is based on a one-way entrance but it should be noted that it has exits in three directions.

It will be seen that in the schemes shown in Figs. 10.1, 10.2 and 10.3 vehicles drive through and do not have to back into or out of a stand either on arrival or departure. The lengths of the stands, however, must be based on maximum vehicle lengths with an additional allowance for entering or leaving without disturbance of other vehicles; these lengths may involve very large site areas for the larger stations. Such sites may not always be available and an alternative layout shown in later diagrams may become necessary.

Schemes involving backing in or out of stands, although more economical in site area land can be more troublesome in operation. They also tend to slow up the handling of vehicles, especially in peak periods.

Fig. 10.5 illustrates a smaller type of bus station formed by making a set-back in a street frontage into which the vehicles are turned. The whole area may be covered. The need in such plans to back vehicles at some stage may cause traffic

whether the vehicle entry is at the front or back of the vehicles. Backing is not so serious a matter within a station used exclusively by buses and coaches as it would be within the confines of a public street or square.

Diagram (a) (Fig. 10.6) is for front-entrance vehicles which drive into the stand and back into the traffic-way when leaving.

Diagram (b) is based on back-entrance vehicles and makes it necessary for the vehicles to back into the stands. Diagram (c) provides for both front- and back-entrance types by keeping one side of the control unit for each type, for example, local and long-distance.

Developments of the type shown in Fig. 10.6 can often make good use of any available backland after the necessary number of stands have been provided for, by planning laybys for waiting vehicles, repair and servicing spaces and even for covered garaging. The scheme shown provides protective covering for waiting passengers over all entrances to the buses.

Fig. 10.7 illustrates detailed requirements for the type of bus station shown in Fig. 10.6. Passengers ways giving access to bus stands should not be less than 1800 wide. If there are doors dividing concourse from platforms (desirable for

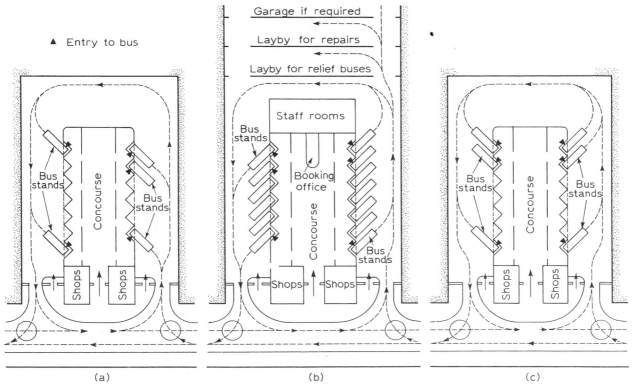

▲ Entry to bus

Fig. 10.6   Alternative bus stations   (a) Long distance   (b) Local   (c) Local and long distance

comfort in bad weather) this minimum width of 1800 should be increased by the amount of the doorswing. Any supports needed for roofs, upper storeys or marquises projecting over the platforms are best and more safely placed as indicated on the plan, since in this position the least obstruction is created, both for the pedestrians and for the vehicles themselves.

The width of the bay at the end of the vehicle stand should be at least 3400 in order to provide not less than

900 clear space between adjacent buses having the maximum permitted width of 2400. In order that platform spaces may be protected as far as possible from rain, it is desirable to provide cover at least up to the line of the bus entry, as indicated on the diagram. The effective protection will be improved if the covering, whether roof, marquise or upper floor, is extended further as indicated.

A similar arrangement is possible for vehicles having front entry and the alternative conditions are indicated in Fig. 10.6.

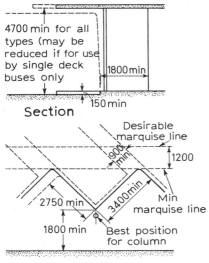

Fig. 10.7   Passenger ways

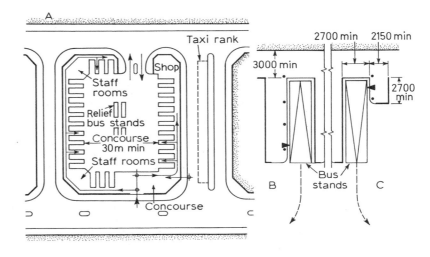

Fig. 10.8   Alternative bus station and platform arrangements

10–5

It will be noted on the diagrammatic section included in Fig. 10.7 that platform heights are indicated to a maximum of 150. This will correspond with normal kerb heights of footpaths above traffic ways, as it should be remembered that bus stops are designed in order to fit this height.

All roofs or marquises should be designed to provide a clear height of 4700 above the level of the roadway. This height may be reduced if it is certain that only single-deck vehicles will ever be used.

If vehicles are to be backed into specially shaped platforms (as in Fig. 10.6) wheel-stops should be provided to avoid damage to coachwork. The positions of these stops may, however, need to be altered from time to time as the design of vehicles changes and to make the stops adjustable should present little difficulty.

Diagram A (Fig. 10.8) illustrates a further type of bus station in which all movement of vehicles takes place in the centre and the pasenger facilities are provided round the outside. As in the type shown in Fig. 10.6, this scheme requires vehicles to be backed either in or out of stands. This is somewhat difficult and may be even very inconvenient in rush periods owing to the probability that the central turning-space is likely to be relatively small and crowded; this central space cannot in any case be less than 30 m across.

The arrangement of passenger accommodation round the perimeter has, however, its advantages. The most important ones are that passengers need never cross traffic-ways to reach a bus and passengers are also well protected while waiting for a vehicle. Additional staff or passenger accommodation may be planned both over the bus stands and the general entrance and concourse accommodation. The entire layout provides ample opportunity for good lighting and also for good ventilation to the open air.

Diagrams B and C (Fig. 10.8), show alternative platform arrangements for the 'perimeter' type of station. Type B is based on berthing the bus bonnet inwards, and here either front- or back-entry types can be accommodated in every berth. Type C, however, provides only for rear-entry types and the vehicles must be backed into the stand, an operation difficult to achieve satisfactorily. This type of 'closed berth' must be at least 2700 wide, even though the buses are only 2300, or at the most, 2400 wide, to give reasonable latitude for the manipulation of the vehicles.

The main perimeter circulation space for passengers should never be less than 3000 wide and the platform bays for access to vehicles should not be less than 2700 wide. Guard-rails may be provided, or alternatively the passengers bays may be partially closed (or screened) and roofed as suggested in diagrams A and B.

The scheme shown in Fig. 10.8 may be used on any site which has one suitable street frontage (for example, that at the top of the diagram) and need not be an island site as shown. The suggested passenger entrance from a main street may be advantageous, as indicated, as it can be planned together with the suggested taxi facilities. The latter are often needed if long-distance services use the station. It is obvious also that any island site may assist in achieving better circulation of vehicles to and from the station and ease traffic congestion in streets adjoining the station.

The spaces needed for drawing out buses from station or parking stands for the two most common conditions are shown in Fig. 10.9. It will be seen that the 45° stands allow for roads of considerably less width, an important consideration where

site-space is limited.

In addition to the stands and the space required for the movement of vehicles, facilities must be provided for the use of passengers and staff.

Passengers need queueing space, waiting rooms, a booking-office where long-distance services are involved, an inquiry office, left-luggage room, parcel office, and sanitary accommodation for both sexes.

Shops or kiosks for papers, tobacco, etc., and in many schemes light refreshment facilities also are required. These additional elements may have to be planned so that they may be let to separate tenants as concessions rather than operated by the bus company. In either case the use of space for such purposes helps to reduce the overhead or running costs of the bus station and is obviously of assistance to and therefore popular with, passengers. A general analysis of essential station accommodation is shown in Fig. 10.10.

There are advantages in planning passenger arrivals in positions well away from queues of passengers waiting to be picked up, mainly to avoid congestion and confusion. Several of the diagrams indicate separate setting-down positions.

Difficulties for casual users may, however, arise if departures are from two sides of a parking area as shown in Figs. 10.2, 10.3 and 10.6 as any of these examples may necessitate crossing lines of moving traffic or passenger queues in addition to parked vehicles. Central waiting, as shown in Fig. 10.6, or a continuous perimeter platform as shown in Fig. 10.8 is, therefore, probably the best arrangement wherever the size of the station justifies such layouts.

Stations which are entirely enclosed from the weather are obviously to be preferred but may be difficult and costly to provide. Roofed spaces unenclosed or only partially enclosed on the sides are apt to be very draughty. Roofed shelters over narrow queueing-spaces or platforms can be dry only if enclosed or screened with the necessary entrances and exists properly planned.

The type of shelter which seems generally preferable is one which is parallel to the traffic-ways (Figs. 10.11 and 10.12). Alternatively, the whole station may be based on a central and covered concourse as shown in Fig. 10.6.

The problem of providing accommodation for waiting passengers satisfactorily is an exceedingly difficult one. Many schemes have been tried but all seem to have greater or lesser disadvantages. Standing queues are suitable for all healthy people but are very unsatisfactory for old or infirm persons and for mothers with young children unless associated seating can be provided.

It is almost impossible to provide seating for all, even in 'off-peak' periods, nor would all use it if provided. Priority arises between those standing, those seated, and those who wait in a waiting space or room.

In all stations, except those catering only for very frequent local services, some type of waiting room or concourse is essential. The waiting space, of whatever type, should be spread out, if there are many routes to be served; although, if all are long-distance services, the problem becomes

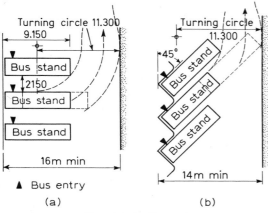

Fig. 10.9 Parking roads

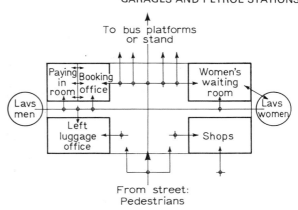

Fig. 10.10 Analysis of essential bus-station accommodation staff rest rooms, administrative offices, etc., may be on the first floor

similar to that of a railway station, where queue spaces at various points and a number of small waiting rooms may be preferable to one large room.

Waiting spaces should be based on peak loads which may arise on market days or at holiday periods, but may have to exclude exceptional loads occurring for example, on Bank Holidays.

Seating should be based on an allowance of 530 run per person. It is best of an open slatted type; the underseat space should be kept as clear as possible for easy cleaning.

BOOKING AND INQUIRIES

The booking-office should be the most prominent of all the passenger facilities. Its position must be immediately obvious from whatever direction passengers may approach. It should be independent of, and, in fact, well away from waiting rooms and similar accommodation; where there is a central concourse it should form an important part of it.

Booking-offices are not usually necessary for local services, but most express services arrange that passengers book and pay for seats prior to the commencement of a journey, as even if there is a conductor on the vehicle, money is not taken *en route*. Similarly sight-seeing and trips are pre-booked. Stations catering for these latter types of traffic need considerable space on both sides of the counter; for passengers waiting to book and making enquiries on the staff side for working-space, charts, timetables, tickets and cash.

The essential element of an enquiry office is an ample counter to allow for an adequate number of clerks working at the same time, based on the needs of an average demand. Counters with an allowance of at least 1500 run of serving space per clerk, are usually adequate for all purposes. Counters should be planned with adequate space between them and all entrance and exit doors so that enquiries and their luggage do not impede normal circulations to and from the bus stands. Booking and enquiry offices should be under cover, i.e. indoors, not merely hatches in external walls. At least 5 m² of passenger space is necessary to each clerk's space.

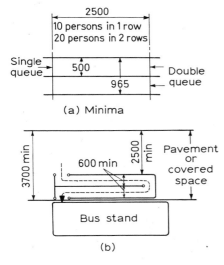

Fig. 10.11 Bus queues

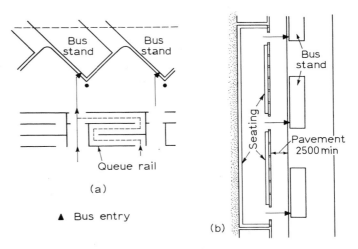

Fig. 10.12 Under cover bus queues

Counters for enquiries or bookings should be 1070 high and 450 wide for enquiries and 600 wide for booking. The space behind the counter need not be wide unless it is also used as general office space. The latter arrangement is generally undesirable, as office workers are less disturbed if provided with separate offices, possibly approached by doors from the clerk's space. It should be noted that passengers often take longer at booking-counters than at enquiry counters and the clerk's space and circulations should be planned accordingly. There should be plenty of wall space in all public spaces for orderly and well-planned displays of posters, timetables and notices.

LEFT-LUGGAGE OFFICE

Facilities should be provided at all bus stations for left luggage and parcels. Normally most of the articles are reclaimed within a few hours and very few remain for more than 24 hours. Articles may be left for longer periods and unclaimed articles have to be kept for several months; space should be allotted accordingly.

A lost-property office is necessary and is usually associated with left-luggage facilities. Left-luggage offices are generally equipped with a counter to divide passenger space from storage- and working-spaces. This counter need only be 450 to 600 high, as all luggage has to be lifted on to and over the counter. Though the counter length may be short (one or two clerks only) there should be plenty of passenger waiting-space adjoining the counter. It should be borne in mind that bus passengers generally have less bulky luggage than railway passengers; the most common article is the suitcase with a maximum size of 600 long × 400 high × 200 wide and most of the storage racking should provide all-purpose racking in multiple units of 600 × 600 × 600.

A clerk's desk is needed for making out the passengers' checks for goods handed in. Luggage offices in large stations sometimes have separate incoming and out-going traffic.

Parcel offices are often needed, either associated with left luggage or as a separate unit, as many bus companies undertake the delivery of parcels on rural routes. Mostly such parcels are of relatively small dimensions and light weight but racking needs to be based on keeping parcels for each route together. Parcel offices need space for a weighing machine and desk space for the clerk in addition to the counters. Counters should be at least 450 wide and preferably 600.

Luggage and parcel offices must be kept dry and reasonably warm in winter but not enough to damage perishable contents of parcels (13° to 15°).

INDICATORS

An important aid for passengers is efficient, clear and distinct indication of when and where departures of vehicles will take place. Berths or stands should be clearly marked with numbers; detailed destination boards are also desirable. All important signs should be illuminated at night.

It is becoming usual at all large stations, to install a loudspeaker system for the direction of passengers. The loudspeakers should be placed very carefully in relation to the queue and waiting spaces so that audibility is not too much affected by engine noises. The controls should be placed in the inspector's or controller's office.

GENERAL EQUIPMENT

Stations should be adequately equipped with rubbish bins and baskets in or adjoining waiting rooms and queueing-spaces. Drinking-fountains should also be provided.

A service room with sink facilities for filling and emptying buckets, racks for brooms, etc., is essential for cleaners of both the buildings and open yards.

ARTIFICIAL LIGHTING

It is most important for bus stations to be well lighted in all parts used by passengers and vehicles; but care must be taken that lights do not shine in the eyes of drivers. Internal lights should be screened from yards, and yard lights should be installed at least 4500 above roadway level.

At busy stations 'in' and 'out' ways into public streets may have to be controlled by traffic-lights. If these are installed, careful placing is required to avoid the possibility of confusion by normal road users with any adjacent public street traffic-lights.

INTERNAL ROADWAYS

Roadways should be as level as possible excepting for the falls needed to provide quick drainage of all surfaces. Steep cambers towards kerbs or platforms should be avoided, to reduce the risk of vehicles sliding or skidding toward the kerb. A camber of 1 in 40 should be the maximum and it is better to make the surface fall away from kerbs and platforms used by passengers.

Road surfaces should be selected to provide a non-skid surface which will not be affected by oil patches. Where falls along kerbs or platforms are necessary these should be so arranged that kerbs are an average of 150 high and not less than 100 or more than 200 mm.

LAVATORIES

All bus stations, regardless of size, should provide sanitary accommodation for male and female passengers.

Lavatories should, if possible, be planned on the same level as the platforms and in fairly close association with passengers' waiting-spaces. At stations used by long-distance express services, washing facilities may be required for both sexes.

Lavatories should be readily accessible also from the bus stands. Separate accommodation for passengers and staff should be planned.

CAFES AND RESTAURANTS

Facilities (at least for light refreshments) are desirable at all bus stations except for those catering only for very local traffic. Where the station is a stopping- and inter-change station for long-distance services, the service of main meals may be necessary, and in these cases self-service or waitress-service at tables is desirable.

Counter-service is becoming more generally acceptable, but where it is adopted consideration must be given to the fact that many customers have luggage or parcels which they wish to keep near them during a meal.

KIOSKS AND SHOPS

Shops, or more frequently, kiosks are desirable for the sale of newspapers and magazines, sweets and confectionery and also for tobacco. They are often leased as concessions rather than operated by the bus company. Whenever there is a suitable street-frontage as much of the adjacent ground-floor area and frontage as possible should be used for shops. It is wise to ensure that the selling-space is indoors, or at least under very adequate cover, as a protection from rain and wind, for both passengers and the goods on open-fronted stalls or kiosks.

Very small kiosks or stalls usually require additional space for some bulk storage in positions reasonably accessible to the selling space.

The essential needs of these kiosks are: a counter (which may include a flap or wicket gate for access), shelving, some storage and as much display space as possible. Shutters or gates are necessary to secure the stalls or kiosks when required. No separate sanitary facilities are needed as shop staff usually use the general station accommodation or that of the station staff. Kiosks can be as little as 1200 wide and 1500 deep but more space is obviously desirable.

STAFF ACCOMMODATION

The staff accommodation roughly divides itself into two groups, one needed for the operating of the vehicles and the other for administration. The latter may be of considerable extent if the organisation has a Head or Area Office at the station, or quite small if it is only to administer the traffic of the particular station. Offices for administrative staff may, with advantage, occupy upper floors of any station building. The detailed planning should follow the recommendations given in Section 4 'Office Buildings and Banks'.

The following accommodation is needed for the operating staff of an average-sized bus station: offices for manager, controller and inspectors; offices for cashiers and ticket clerks; a conductors' paying-in room, locker rooms, sanitary and rest-room accommodation; canteen; storage for staff cycles may be needed. Facilities for clocking-on may have to be provided either inside a building or under external cover. Recording clocks should not be installed closer together than 1500 centre to centre and should be in a position where waiting staff do not impede passenger movements.

Rooms for inspectors and controllers should have good visibility of all the bus stands if this is possible. Some stations have a controller who acts as starter and who is placed in such a position that he overlooks the station from a high level and controls the movements of the buses by light signals, and the passengers by loudspeakers.

The cashiers' room and conductors' paying-in room should adjoin and have connecting hatches for intercommunication.

In planning the cashiers' room it must be remembered that there are at times, especially at night, large sums of money in the room; proper provision should be made, therefore, for the safety and storage of cash and, in a measure, for the safety of the cashiers themselves. The cashiers' room should be planned on an allowance of at least 4·7 m² per person. Paying-in hatches at about 1500 centre to centre should be provided. Night safes, similar in principle to those used by branch banks are sometimes installed. Many conductors' rooms are equipped with racking for the storage of the conductors' ticket-boxes and equipment, which vary considerably in size and shape, according to the requirements of different operating companies; in some cases, where the station is a terminal, these rooms may also act as rest rooms.

Locker rooms providing accommodation for all personnel using the station are essential; in many cases personnel change in or out of uniform on starting or leaving duty and adequate space for changing may be required in, or additional to, a locker room. Full-length lockers to hold an overcoat are desirable, together with some drying facilities, although with the modern closed types of buses drivers and conductors no longer get excessively wet.

Canteens must be designed to give quick service, as the breaks for meals may be of short duration for drivers and conductors and other outside staff.

PARKING OF BUSES

Temporary parking of vehicles is often needed, and if garages are not planned in connection with or as part of the bus station some parking facilities are essential in the station itself. These may be under cover, but as vehicles are only likely to stand for relatively short periods open-air parking may be quite adequate.

Parking spaces should be designed so that any vehicle may be moved without disturbing others. It is important that the parking does not in any way impede the free movement of vehicles into and out of bus stands. Reference to Figs. 10.2 to 10.9 will show the data required to plan suitable parking of this kind.

FUEL AND WATER-FILLING

Vehicles are usually operated for 12 hours or more per day and may, therefore, be dependent on replenishments of petrol or fuel oil and water several times during a working-day. These supplies, for all but long-distance vehicles, are usually provided at garages or terminal points; public-service vehicles must not be filled with petrol while carrying passengers. It is also undesirable to have vehicles filled within station buildings or near passenger platforms.

The storage of petrol is controlled by the Petroleum Act, 1928, and Petroleum Spirit Regulations 952/29, which require storage places to be licensed. Storage tanks are better placed outside buildings and cut off from buildings by fire-resisting construction, or placed underground; they must be at least 6000 from public highways.

Filling sometimes takes place in an open (often roofed) space in front of or behind the garage, or in some space adjoining a station in a position to which the public does not normally have access. More often filling occurs just as the vehicle enters or leaves the garage building. The storage tank may be at a distance from the delivery pumps which are generally electrically operated (see Fig. 10.13).

GARAGES AND MAINTENANCE BUILDINGS

Buildings are needed for vehicles when not in use and for cleaning and other daily services. This work is distinct from major repairs and overhauls, for which more fully-equipped and centralised workshops may also be needed; these may be associated with, or be part of, a garage.

Garages and repair shops are usually separate from bus stations; the latter are normally planned on relatively extensive urban sites, whereas garages and, particularly, repair shops, also needing considerable site areas, may, with advantage, be planned on less central, and therefore less costly, sites.

BUS STOPPING PLACES

Stopping places to pick up and set down passengers, other than at bus stations, fall into the following classes:
(a) Terminal and interchange stops for local and country services.
(b) Urban street stops.
(c) Rural road stops.

At all these stops space must be available for varying numbers of passengers; this may or may not necessitate arrangements for queueing. All stopping-places should be clearly marked so that they may be seen both by pedestrians and bus passengers for a considerable distance. If possible, stops should be arranged so that a driver can see them at least 100 m ahead, and twice this distance would be advantageous.

It is desirable at many stops to display timetables. In exposed and wet districts main stopping-places should provide covered and if necessary enclosed waiting-places.

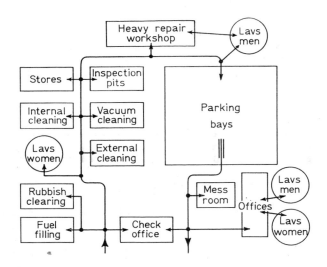

Fig. 10.13   General analysis for maintenance garages

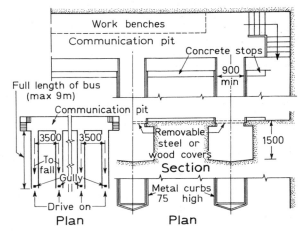

Fig. 10.14   Inspection pits

Some garaging is in the open air, but in exposed districts and in winter this is undesirable as vehicles need to be kept warm.

The essential planning-requirement for garages is a large floor area with the minimum of supports to cause obstruction. The area should be based on an allowance of 28 m² per vehicle, although with the increasing legal overall sizes space allowances can well be increased to 30 m² for each vehicle. A clear height of at least 4900 below trusses or tie bars is essential and preferably rather more. Good daylight from roof lights is also essential, together with carefully arranged artificial lighting, as much cleaning and servicing is carried out at night.

With normal circulation, vehicles enter the garage and are refuelled near the doors, while the cleaners clear the rubbish. The buses then pass through a washing-area and after being cleaned externally move to a space where they are polished and vacuum-cleaned internally. After cleaning they pass on to the inspection pits for inspection and repairs.

TERMINAL STOPS

It is essential that these be planned to provide sufficient space for the vehicles to turn without reversing. If they are used by many vehicles there should be special sanitary facilities for drivers and conductors.

Many terminal stopping-places are associated with public houses and because of this special accommodation is frequently omitted. A covered waiting-shelter for passengers and staff, together or separated, is almost a necessity for a terminal stopping-place unassociated with a bus station.

URBAN STREET STOPS

In busy streets and on roads carrying heavy traffic-loads buses should not stop in the traffic stream and thus delay or slow down the traffic; consequently the placing of stopping-bays is desirable.

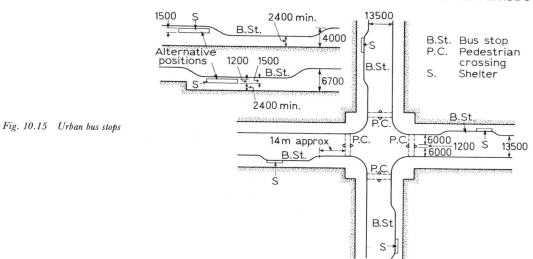

Fig. 10.15 Urban bus stops

B.St.   Bus stop
P.C.   Pedestrian
        crossing
S.   Shelter

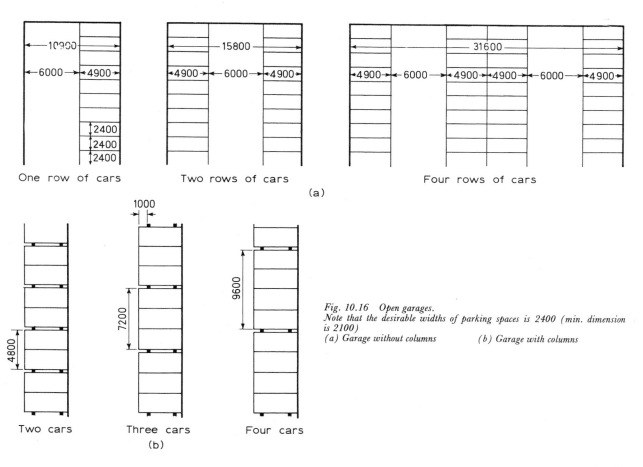

(a)

One row of cars

Two rows of cars

Four rows of cars

Two cars

Three cars

Four cars

(b)

Fig. 10.16 Open garages.
Note that the desirable widths of parking spaces is 2400 (min. dimension is 2100)
(a) Garage without columns   (b) Garage with columns

The set-back in the footway or the increased road width should be not less than 2700 mm and probably 3000. The lengths are dependent on the number of vehicles expected to be at a stop at one time, allowing 15 m run per vehicle to provide for pulling in and out without waiting for other vehicles to move. These set-back stops should not be too near to cross-roads or to traffic lights (Fig. 10.15).

When set-back stops of this type are used and queueing, especially in covered spaces, may take place, the width of the footway needs to be such that there is at least 2400 of free space between the queue and any adjoining building or fence.

SPACE REQUIREMENTS AND ACCOMMODATION FOR PUBLIC GARAGES

In cities and towns land values prohibit separate lock-up garages and, in many instances, they are not particularly necessary. Open garages provide large undivided floor spaces on one or more floor levels where cars are arranged in rows.

As the majority of car users often come and go in rush periods of short duration, easy access to and from car berths is essential. Therefore planning has to be based on single rows of cars placed on either side of driving aisles. These aisles must be of such widths as to allow for driving a car in and out of a berth between two other vehicles without risk of damage. The berths are usually based on a width of 2400 and a depth of 4900 which is sufficient for all but exceptionally long cars which may be placed together either in a special part or a special floor of the garage.

The width of berth is arrived at by taking the width of a car as 1800 and allowing 300 for manoeuvring and opening of doors, etc. The best method of parking cars is to have the bonnets towards the driving aisle. The width of the aisles should be at least 6000 although there are examples where only 5500 width has been allowed.

Fig. 10.16 shows typical spacing of car berths based on these dimensions together with widths of buildings necessary to accommodate various numbers of rows. Cars should not be placed in double rows with access on one side only as the time required to move cars from the front row for the removal of a vehicle at the back is too great and confusion is created. In cases of extreme necessity, however, double-row parking has been adopted, and considerable saving of space has been effected in this way, as in this case one aisle serves four rows of cars.

Any columns required to support superimposed floors or roofs should be placed at least 1000 within the 4900 allowed for the length of the cars to permit easier turning. The space between columns should be either 4800, 7200 or 9600 which accommodates, two, three or four cars respectively. Any spacing between these dimensions is obviously uneconomical.

MULTI-FLOOR GARAGES

Where several floors are to be used, methods of rapid inter-floor communication have to be considered. Firstly, by means of ramps or sloping ways, and secondly, by use of lifts; the former, although requiring more actual floor space per car stored, has generally been found to work more satisfactorily in practice owing to the time and trouble saved in getting each vehicle in or out of its berth, especially in rush

hours. Ramps are cheaper than lifts in first cost and require very little maintenance, both of which are highly important factors; the ramp system involves no cost in moving vehicles, as they pass from floor to floor under their own power.

A number of schemes have been put forward, and some have been built for automatic mechanical handling of cars in 'auto-silos' and the like. Most projects rely on centralised push-button or even electronic controls and result in the planning of highly specialised buildings individually fitted to accommodate the system adopted. No single type seems yet to be generally approved by use or economy of operation and therefore the planning of such buildings is not dealt with in these notes.

RAMPS

The slope of ramps may be as steep as 1 in 6 but they are generally 1 in 7 (or 15°). Turns on the ramps should be slightly banked and the whole surface treated to give a good hold for tyres. The floor heights of garages should give 2600 in the clear between beam casings and floor level.

Ramps for smaller buildings may be as narrow as 2600 but they are better if 3000 is allowed and if vehicles have to pass one another in opposite directions a width of 6000 is considered to be the minimum. Also, if one wide ramp is to be used for traffic travelling in opposite directions, up and down ways should certainly be separated by a kerb or, more thoroughly, by a railing, although such precautions are frequently not taken. If only one narrow ramp is to be used for up and down traffic some system of signalling should be provided, to avoid cars meeting between floors.

The radius of outside kerbs on all curved ramps should be not less than 6000 based on the turning circle of the average-size cars, but it is better to allow a radius of 7500 to avoid risk of damage to wings.

Fig. 10.17 (a), (b) and (c) show three different methods of arranging double-track ramps in buildings. The hatched areas represent the space available for car berths, and it should be noted that certain of these spaces are not readily accessible, as that in the top left-hand corner of Fig. 10.17 (a).

Type (a) is the simplest type, where each floor is level across the building; the ramp may easily be turned (at the lower end in the diagram) for continuation from floor to floor. Type (b) is somewhat more complicated, but has only one long ramp serving all floors at various points in its length as shown on the section. Type (c) is a continuous concentric curved ramp; the corners as shown are difficult to utilise, as are also the spaces enclosed by and around the ramps. This system is frequently used for long sites, the ramps sometimes being placed near the entrance or at the extreme ends. The central spaces within the ramps in type (c) are seldom useful for storing cars owing to the difficulty of access, but they are, however, useful for motor cycles and sidecar combinations. One fault of type (b) is the necessity, on leaving or entering a floor, of crossing the main traffic lines on the ramp.

Type (d) has a single ramp used for traffic in both directions, and is only suitable for garages where the possible number of car berths is not greater than approximately 300, otherwise congestion is likely to result. This type is not very satisfactory except on small sites where space does not permit double ramps. Even in such circumstances a considerable amount of floor space is wasted, as may be seen from the

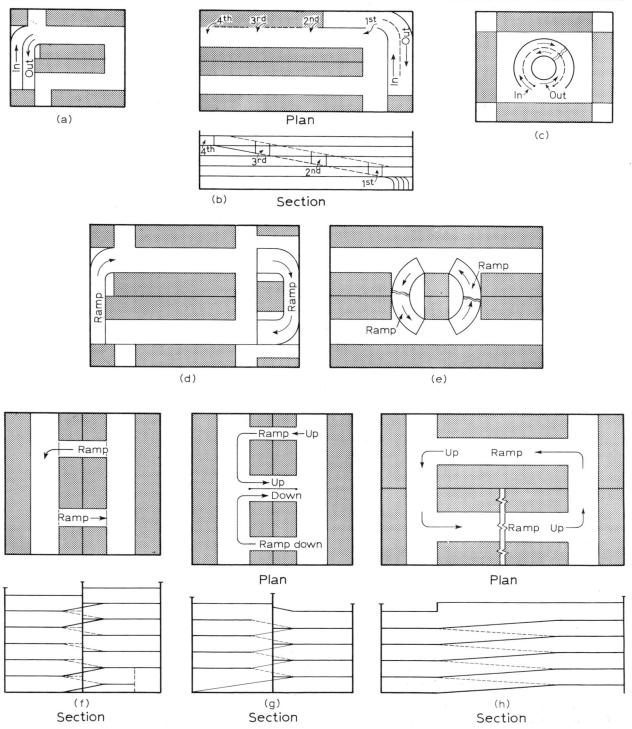

Fig. 10.17 *Types of ramp*

(a) Double-track ramps
(b) Single long ramp
(c) Central spaces within ramps
(d) Single ramp
(e) Double spiral ramp
(f) Staggered floor
(g) Double ramp. Staggered floor
(h) Ramped floor (warped)

figure and the alternative use of lifts may be justifiable on central urban sites.

Diagram *(e)* illustrates a double-spiral type of ramp on which traffic cannot meet; this type is satisfactory in space economy and ease in controlling the traffic. This ramp is designed on the principle of a double-thread screw, up-traffic driving on one thread and down-traffic on the other, both ramps using the same space as is needed for a single ramp of the same diameter.

Type *(f)* is divided vertically into two blocks, one block of floors being set half a ceiling-height higher than the other; the floors are connected by short ramps. This system is very efficient, as regards proportion of floor space available for car storage to total floor area, and as regards handling of traffic. This applies more especially when the ramps are doubled and separate tracks provided for traffic in each direction as in Fig. 10.17*(g)*. One half of the ground floor or basement will have a greater height, as shown on the right-hand side of diagram *(f)*. This additional height is useful for showrooms, parking of commercial vehicles, or for a pressure-greasing department where hydraulic car-lifts are used. One disadvantage of the staggered floor type of building is its uselessness for other purposes should the building not be required as a garage at some future time, whereas in other types the ramps may be removed and replaced with normal floors comparatively easily.

A further development of the ramp is the 'warped' floor type of garage as illustrated in Fig. 10.17 *(h)*. In this example the floors are laid throughout the building at a pitch similar to the ramped approaches which they adjoin. There are many factors favouring this system but, at the same time, there are three disadvantages, namely: long sites which are not too wide for more than four berths and two aisles are needed to give sufficiently small gradients; secondly, cars are parked on a sloping surface (although it is very slight—only similar, in fact, to the curve of a normal road surface from crown to gutter), and cars stand across the slope; and thirdly, the building cannot be converted for other purposes.

The benefits of the 'warped' system are the low gradients utilised, good visibility for drivers and the parking areas are each easily accessible, though the largest possible areas are utilised and easy turning-radii planned. Construction costs are lower in this system than with ordinary ramps, due to the constant pitch of the floor without sharp banked curves, and consequently it is little more expensive than level floors in normal buildings.

LIFTS

Many multi-floor garages are served by lifts in preference to ramps, probably owing to the fact that lifts waste less floor area than do any of the ramp systems and consequently more cars can be stored to any given site area. Lifts are particularly useful for high buildings and for buildings on small sites.

There are also examples in which lifts are used to serve the upper floors only while ramps are installed for the service of the two or three lower floors where cars are parked for short periods and therefore must be handled more rapidly. Lifts for private cars are usually about 3000 wide and 6000 long.

Lifts are sometimes run in open wells surrounded by wire enclosures only. In larger buildings a fire-resisting enclosure is essential, together with automatic fire-resisting cut-off doors or shutters at each floor level so as to avoid the risk of fire spreading from one floor to another.

The number of lifts required for a garage building presents a difficult problem. Two should be considered as essential to permit dealing with rush periods, and also to guard against a possible breakdown. Generally, it should be assumed that two lifts will handle up to 250 cars. Lifts are usually run at speeds of about 15 m per minute; high speeds facilitate rapid handling of vehicles, and they should be designed to carry at least 30 cars in one direction per hour to the highest floor level. Sometimes lifts are designed to carry two vehicles side by side, but it is doubtful if this is, in fact, a real advantage over two separate lifts, except in initial cost and possibly in running costs; the benefits may be offset by delay in handling vehicles.

PASSENGER LIFTS

In addition to any lifts installed for moving vehicles from floor to floor, passenger lifts are desirable, and in the case of many-floored buildings are necessary to convey owners to the floors on which their cars are parked, or to convey garage drivers to the car berths in order to hasten delivery to owners waiting at the entrance to the garage. These lifts need not be of very large capacity but should be of fairly high speed.

LAVATORIES

Lavatories are required for the use of male and female visitors, chauffeurs, garage and office staffs. Those for the use of visitors should be placed near the public waiting room, and those for the chauffeurs adjoining the chauffeurs' room.

Accommodation for the garage staff should be grouped together in small buildings, preferably near the workshop or repair department, but in large garages provision is desirable on each floor to save loss of time. Office staff lavatories should be attached to the office. It is, of course, advantageous to plan lavatory accommodation in similar positions on each floor in order to group plumbing services together.

Each lavatory should provide wash-basins and W.C.s. Attached to visitors' lavatories, changing rooms and baths are occasionally installed for use of out-of-town customers who wish to change into evening dress. The staff lavatories should also provide space for the installation of lockers for outdoor clothes, overalls, uniforms, etc.

OFFICES

Administrative offices, other than the control and pay offices at the entrances and exits, may be placed anywhere in the building, though preferably within easy access of the customers' enquiry office and sales counters. The office staff is generally small, even for a very large garage and therefore only about three or four rooms are usually needed; these generally consist of a manager's office, typists' room and a book-keeper's room.

Small offices for superintendents are usually needed on each floor in large buildings. These are often tucked away quite satisfactorily in any odd corner useless for car parking, but should be so placed as to have good visual control of the whole floor area.

STORE ROOMS

Store rooms are required for spare parts, accessories, cleaning materials, etc. and should be generally planned where communication can easily be provided by lifts to sales counters or to repair departments. Space usually does not permit stores on ground floors, therefore they are usually placed in basements or on top floors.

The equipment of the rooms consists of suitably designed racks, bins and shelving, made of wood or metal, one or more workbenches and a storekeeper's office.

BATTERY SERVICE

All garages require facilities for storage and recharging of batteries, and in many areas the accommodation for this has to be separated from the normal work of the garage by fire-resisting materials and in some cases has to be approached from the external air. The actual charging of batteries and the storage of recharged batteries, together with spares, are sometimes separated into two rooms connected by doors or, if on different floors, by small service lifts.

The recharging room is best placed on the lowest floor of the building, so as to provide a solid base for motors when these are required. Care has to be taken to provide proper benches with lead or other acid-proof tops. The batteries are charged on benches or racks, usually placed against walls on which the leads from the motors or mains are fixed. Low racks are needed for the storage of acid and distilled water containers and further racks and bins for spare parts and new batteries.

SERVICES

Compressed air is required for the operation of many types of petrol and oil pumps, as well as for tyre service. For the latter purpose outlets should be provided in the entrance forecourt and also on each floor level. The motors and compressors for all purposes should be located together, preferably on the ground floor or in the basement and be in a separate room adjoining the garage, cut off by fire-resisting materials. The plant should be duplicated to obviate breakdown.

Water should be provided on each floor for filling radiators and it is also needed for car washing. In order to get adequate water pressure for car washing, it may be necessary to provide pumps or, alternatively, be dependent on the height of the storage tank above the car washing department floor level. If sufficient pressure is available, and it is permitted, connection may be made direct from the supply company's mains. Pumps, if required, should be placed in the basement, though portable machines with flexible connections to water points are now in use.

A sprinkler system is installed in many garages; the water discharged by such a system has the advantage of smothering petrol fires by the elimination of the air necessary for combustion. Sprinkler outlets should be at ceiling level and each should cover not more than 10 superficial metres of floor area. Water supply for a sprinkler system may be taken directly from local supply mains or through high-level storage tanks, dependent on conditions of the supply and its pressure.

In addition to sprinklers, fire-fighting apparatus, especially suitable for dealing with petrol fires (sand buckets, foam sprays, etc.), should be distributed at frequent intervals throughout garage buildings, particularly near petrol and oil storage and filling departments. Petrol and oil must not be fed into vehicles inside the garage building or on the various floors, but should be supplied from pumps installed at the entrances or exits of the building.

CAR WASHING, ETC.

This is an important department in most garages and is usually placed either on the ground floor or in the basement. In modern establishments rising and revolving car lifts are used for easy accessibility to the under-sides of the cars in conjunction with high-pressure water guns to speed up the process of cleaning.

The floors of washing spaces should be formed of metal grids through which the water and dirt passes on to cement floors laid to falls discharging into proper gullies designed to collect petrol and oil. The metal grids allow workmen to stand on a comparatively dry and clean surface. The rotating car-lifts are generally 5500 long for private cars and consequently need the area of a circle of 5500 in diameter for their installation. The lifts are raised either electrically or hydraulically.

Adjoining the washing space should be several berthing spaces for waiting cars and for economy these may often be shared by greasing and oiling departments.

Rotary car lifts are also installed for greasing purposes but sometimes alternatives such as raised tracks with inclined approaches or inspection pits are used. Lifts or racks with inclined approaches eliminate the use of inspection pits and tend to facilitate better work and service. Care has to be taken with raised tracks and similar fittings, so that suitable illumination is available for the undersides of raised vehicles.

REPAIR SHOPS

These may be planned either in basements or on ground floors, but are seldom placed on upper floors except top floors. Badly damaged vehicles or those not running under their own power are difficult to move to higher floors.

Car lifts are also useful in repair shops so that the work in hand may be lifted to a comfortable working level. Inspection pits are still used in many garages and involve little up-keep cost and low initial expenditure as compared to lifts or raised tracks. It should be remembered that lifts require a clear height of 3600 to 4300 above floor level, as well as space below for the ram, whereas pits do not necessitate extra floor height but can only be used on the lowest floor.

Workbenches and machinery should have ample space and good daylight if possible, while the whole repair shop should be cut off from the garage itself by solid partitions and large sliding doors or shutters. If painting or cellulosing is to be undertaken, a separate department should be formed adjoining, but cut off from the repair room by fire-resisting partitions and doors, and should be approached from the external air. Motors and compressors should also be in a separate compartment cut off from the paint shop. Special ventilation is required for paint-spraying rooms by Government Regulations.

10–15

INSPECTION PITS

The width of a pit is dictated by the width of the track of the smallest cars, and is consequently 900 maximum; this is narrow, and difficulty is experienced in working under cars of much greater track widths. Therefore, if two pits are being installed, one only needs to be the minimum width, and the other may be as much as 1100 wide.

The depth required for pits is fairly constant, since all cars are, within a few inches, the same height above the roadway to the undersides of the chassis. The usual depth of a pit is 1500 below the floor level, which allows a man of average height to stand upright and work comfortably under a car. The bottom of a pit should have a slight fall to a drain for removal of water, oil, etc.

It is an advantage to have a raised curb of metal fixed round the opening in the floor, and which projects, say, 75 above it. This partially guides cars and prevents tools being kicked into the pit. It is advantageous to have the pit walls set back from the opening in the floor, in order to provide space for tool racks, etc.

Sometimes fixed artificial lights are installed in boxes in the sides of the pit and are arranged to throw the light upwards, thus illuminating the underside of the car. Such a system avoids the possibility of electric shock, as the rubber insulated flex trailing from portable lamps may become perished by contact with oil.

PETROL STATIONS

These notes are confined to roadside filling stations and the information is not intended to apply to the sale of petrol connected with large garages, although many points are common to both. Important factors to be considered in planning of filling stations are, firstly, relation to surrounding streets; secondly, circulation and layout of roadways and buildings on the site together with the placing of petrol and oil pumps; thirdly, whether any sales are to be made in addition to petrol and oil, and if provision for the execution of repairs is to be made. Toilet facilities for both sexes should be provided, if possible, in all types of petrol station regardless of size, although this is sometimes difficult to achieve in small stations in rural areas.

Entrance roadways should be about 6000 wide and driveways between buildings and pumps or between rows of pumps should be at least 3600 wide. When planning driveways from the street to pumps, sharp curves must be avoided and consideration should be given to the turning spaces required for the largest cars and particularly lorries. Driveways must be constructed to receive heavy loads without damage to the surface. Surfaces should be paved for cleanliness and ease of upkeep. The most suitable paving materials are concrete, asphalt and tarmacadam; they should be laid to falls to remove water quickly in wet weather.

All pumps and buildings should be raised above roadway levels on islands with kerbs about 100 to 150 high to eliminate the possibility of damage. Canopies over islands and driveways are useful as a protection in wet weather, but care should be taken that the driveway on one side of the pumps selling purely commercial-vehicle grades of petrol should be left uncovered so that high lorries may use the pumps. The latter is a point frequently forgotten, and it is found that high-loaded lorries cannot approach covered pumps. Canopies should leave a clearance of 2800 over driveways and should have supports of minimum dimensions to reduce obstruction of pavements. Toilet accommodation should have external approaches in small stations, but in large buildings where waiting rooms are provided the approaches may be from these rooms. It is better if the approach doors do not face the driveways or working spaces, although this is sometimes unavoidable. Entrances and exits on main roads are better if separated, and should be very clearly marked.

Roadside filling stations seldom have covered driveways, but the whole island on which the buildings and the pumps stand might be easily and cheaply placed under one roof. Signs are an essential part of the design of a filling station and must be properly considered as part of the layout scheme and in the detail of the building. Signs have to indicate the existence of the station, its name, entrances and the type of petrol sold. Main signs should be visible at least 200 m before reaching a station.

Fig. 10.18 shows typical petrol pumps and spacing. It will be found, however, that an island on which pumps stand should be about 900 wide, to allow space on which mechanics may stand without risk of being caught by moving vehicles. Islands, or bases for pumps, should be 150 above driveways.

Pumps are sometimes placed singly or in pairs. Pairs should be placed about 900 apart centre to centre and at least 1800 should be allowed between single pumps or between pairs to allow further standing space both for mechanics and cars. The height of pumps varies according to type.

Storage tanks for pumps must be placed either under driveways or may be enclosed tanks on the lowest floors. Tanks are usually of ungalvanised steel, cylindrical or rectangular in shape. They must be underground or enclosed in a fire-resisting container which will hold a quantity of liquid nearly equal to the tank capacity in the event of leakage. A manhole cover for access is necessary, together with a filling and a ventilation pipe, the latter carried up well above the ground and fitted with gauze covers. Tanks for petrol vary in size from 250 gallons to 2,000 gallons.

Fig. 10.19 illustrates six typical filling station sites with their relationship to traffic in the adjoining streets. In regard to site planning those shown in Diagrams 1 and 2 are similar in relation to the streets, but the essential difference lies in placing buildings on the site. In Diagram 1 the buildings are towards the back of the site, leaving the front part of the site open, which is good from an advertising point of view and for visibility when entering or leaving the site. The fault, however, is that this type of layout is apt to become untidy in appearance unless the design is well handled and the premises well looked after. Type 2 has the advantage of having the road frontage partially closed by the station building. Traffic can circulate more easily on the site because the radii of curves are greater; but the visibility of passing traffic on the road to vehicles leaving the station is bad.

Diagram 3 illustrates two sites placed on the curve of a street. Site A is bad from the traffic visibility viewpoint as well as for advertising purposes, whereas site B is really ideal in every way because both traffic on the road and vehicles entering and leaving the station have a clear view of one another. Also, this site is very good from the advertising aspect as it may be seen from long distances before vehicles reach the station. Diagram 4 shows a good site for an important station at a road junction; the entrances and exits are

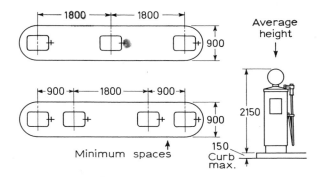

Fig. 10.18 Spacing for single and pairs of pumps

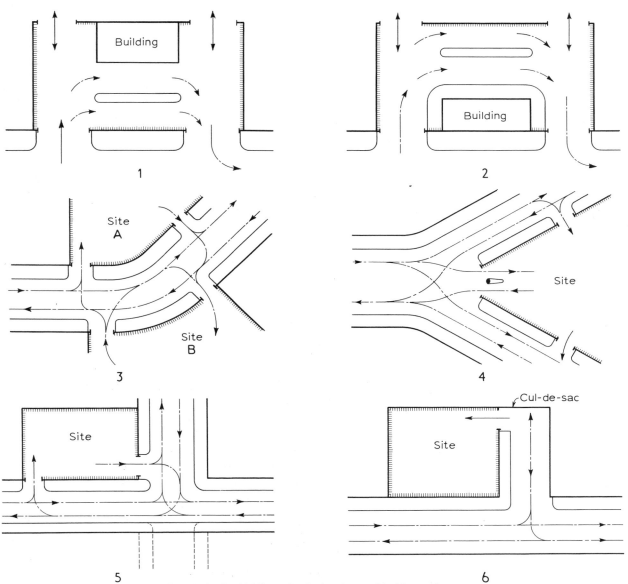

Fig. 10.19 Considerations to be taken into account when siting petrol pumps.
1. Building to the rear of site   4. Junction site for an important filling station
2. Building on street frontage   5 and
3A. Poor visibility   6. Conditions to be avoided at street corners
3B. Ideal visibility

P. Petrol pumps
L. Oil pumps
A. Air points
St. Stores
S. Sign

B. Parking bays
W. Water
Ao. Admin office
R. Roadway

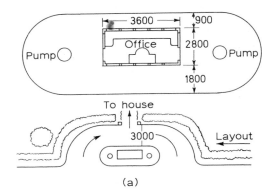

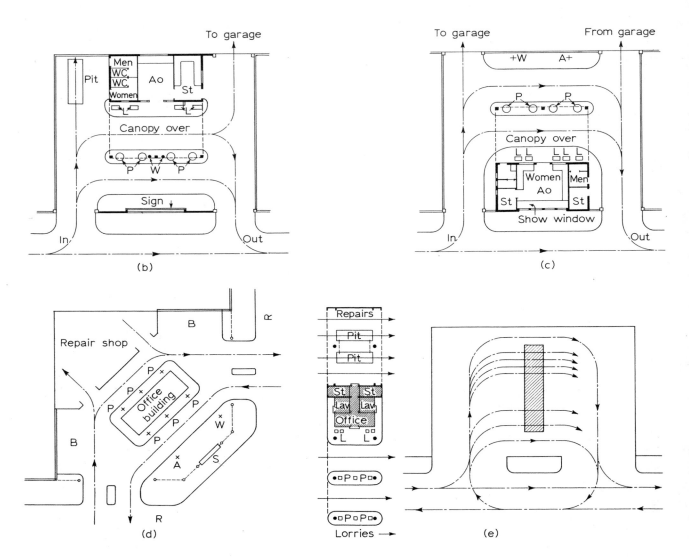

Fig. 10.20 Layout of petrol filling stations and service garages
(a) Wayside filling station with adjoining house
(b) Filling station with buildings at rear of site
(c) Filling station with buildings at front of site
(d) Filling station on a corner site
(e) Station with buildings placed symmetrically at right angles

(b) and (c) show two different planning solutions for identical sites

easy in relationship to the traffic in all directions. Types 5 and 6 illustrate points which should always be avoided. In the former example the vehicles are discharged from the station in a position which is very disturbing to other traffic, especially if there is a likelihood of the traffic of one road having to wait for that of the other to pass; congestion is almost certain to take place.

Type 6 is unsatisfactory as vehicles entering and leaving the cul-de-sac may obstruct one another and cause a hold-up to the main road traffic at the junction. Also visibility of the main road traffic is bad for the cars leaving the station.

Figs. 10.20 (b) and (c) illustrate alternative schemes for the same site. The site is a normal roadside type with other property, either built-up or with open land on either side. Diagram (b) shows the buildings placed at the back of the site, and Diagram (c) with buildings adjoining the main road. In type (b) the pumps are visible from the road; but this has to be well arranged and carefully kept up to avoid an untidy appearance. The petrol pumps must be set some distance back to permit sufficient turning space for cars to draw up alongside pumps. Both schemes suggest covering one driveway but leaving the other uncovered for use of high vehicles.

Type (b) has the advantage of having a suitable space— as shown on the plan by the pit—for the temporary parking of cars while small repairs are made without interruption of the traffic circulation. This space may be doubled if a garage is not placed behind the filling station and may, in either case, be covered if desired. In both examples, petrol pumps, water and air supplies, may be placed on an island between drive-ways, while oil may be stored in bins placed under cover in front of the office. Alternatively, in type (c) air and water supplies may be separated from the petrol at the back of the site, thus causing less interference with petrol pump users— especially if tyres need attention which may take some time to carry out. The buildings provide similar accommodation, but the toilet facilities are better in type (c) the entrance doors for men and women being separate.

Type (c) has a show window on the street, but its value is somewhat doubtful and, except for the fact that attention may be drawn to the station by means of a large sign on the roof of the office building, a station where the pumps are mostly hidden from the road by buildings does not attract the attention of the passing motorist very easily.

Fig. 10.20 (d) illustrates an example of the treatment of a station placed on a corner site. The building is placed on the diagonal of the site with driveways passing on each side of it; if the building is placed more forward on the site it obstructs the view of traffic on the main road. It is important for entrances and exits to the site not to be placed too near the corner, as they may interrupt the easy flow of traffic in the street.

This plan also provides a building at the back of the site, and parking space for a repair shop with good access to driveways.

Fig. 10.20 (e) illustrates a type of filling station plan in which the buildings, pumps and protective roofs are placed at right angles to the street on which the site abuts. Such an arrangement produces a very compact building, which is easy and economical to construct, organise and maintain. It should be placed sufficiently far back on the site to allow space for large commercial vehicles to draw in easily to the outside of the first row of pumps, which is the only driveway

not roofed over. The office is conveniently placed for service both to the pumps and to the repair department, and at the same time has full control of the approaches to the station from the street. The toilets are well placed, being convenient but not too prominent. This plan, when placed on a rectangular site, as in the illustration, leaves ample room at the back corners for car parking and washing, as well as for such repairs and oiling as are not executed under the cover of the canopy.

The corners of the site may also be used for store rooms, compressors and lighting-plant rooms—an arrangement which keeps these units well away from the normal traffic areas. It is also helpful to have such back spaces for tank lorries bringing petroleum supplies to stand while they are discharging their load into the storage tanks which serve the pumps.

Fig. 10.20(a) illustrates the 'wayside station' often attached to a cottage in outlying areas, and is, consequently, very small, providing only the minimum accommodation in the form of buildings, together with one or two petrol pumps. The office building is just large enough for a desk and one or two chairs, and has accommodation for storage of a few tins of oil, etc., but no space for spare parts or accessories. A water point is necessary, although this may only be a pump or a tap fed from a storage tank filled by a small pump.

The positions illustrated for the pumps are well separated so that two vehicles may stand one on each side of the island near each pump.

CANOPIES

In most districts canopies are not permitted over the public highway or footpath, but this does not affect use on land in private ownership. It is a great advantage to have both pumps and those parts of the roadways on which vehicles stand during the process of filling, covered during wet weather so as to keep both the station employees and customers dry.

The canopies may take either the form of flat or pitched roofs, according to the design and locality of the station, but it is generally easier to collect and remove rainwater from flat-roofed types, as falls may be laid to supporting piers or to the building against which down-pipes may be placed. It is very desirable that the water be collected and not simply allowed to drip off the roof on to vehicles or customers. When cantilever types are designed it is essential to bear in mind that they must either be properly tied back to a building or be balanced by similar loads.

It is important that supply connections between pump and vehicle do not have to cross one traffic way to reach another. Accessibility of the pumps is of the utmost importance and is the primary factor in planning the layout of a filling station. Quality and rapidity of service are important, but count for much less in the eyes of a casual user of a station than does a simple and well-arranged layout.

The maintenance of the good appearance of a station may be facilitated by the proper designing of surroundings such as lawns, flowerbeds and trees. Signs and lighting are of the utmost importance because they can aid the commercial value of a station very considerably and must be designed as part of the whole scheme, which should have an appearance of efficiency, clean lines and tidiness.

STATUTORY REGULATIONS, LEGISLATION AND AUTHORITIES

LEGISLATION RELATING TO MOTOR VEHICLES

Petroleum (Consolidation) Act, 1928.
Public Health Act, 1961.
Factories Act, 1961.
Road Traffic Acts.
Town and Country Planning Acts.
Building Regulations, 1972.
Building (Scotland) Acts.
London Building Acts.
Offices, Shops and Railway Premises Act, 1963.
Highways Acts.
Transport Acts.

AUTHORITIES AND ORGANISATIONS CONCERNED WITH MOTOR VEHICLES

Department of the Environment,
Marsham Street,
London, S.W.1.

Road Research Laboratory,
Crowthorne,
Berkshire.

British Road Federation Limited,
26, Manchester Square,
London, W.1.

Society of Motor Manufacturers and Traders,
Forbes House,
Halkin Street,
London, S.W.1.

Much detailed information and advice can be obtained from oil companies, vehicle manufacturers and suppliers of specialist equipment (pumps, parking barriers, car park and workshop equipment, etc).

EXAMPLES

Bus station and car park, Preston, Lancs.
Architects: Building Design Partnership (Keith Ingham).
Architects' Journal (6th May, 1970)

Garage and service station, Preston, Lancs.
Architects: Building Design Partnership (F.K. Lord & C.J.R. Ratcliff).
Architects' Journal (1st April, 1964)

Car Park, Cwmbran.
Architect: Gordon Redfern, Chief Architect Cwmbran Development Corporation.
Architects' Journal (24th March, 1965)

Multi-storey car park and service station, Leicester.
Architects: Oscar Garry & Partners.
Architect's Journal (6th July, 1966)

Car park building at Young Street London, W.8
Architects: Roy Chamberlain Associates.
Architect's Journal (18th August, 1971)

Car park building at Welbeck Street, London, W.1
Architects: Michael R. Blampied & Partners.
Architect's Journal (18th August, 1971)

Car park building at Minories, London, E.C.3.
Architect: E. G. Chandler, City Architect, Corporation of London.
Architects' Journal, (18th August, 1971)

Multi-storey car park, Birmingham University.
Architects: Casson Condor & Partners.
Architects' Journal (21st September, 1966)

BIBLIOGRAPHY

Burchett, Dennis A., 'Garages and Service Stations' *A. J.* (15th April 1964)
Klosk J., *Multi-storey car parks and garages.* Architectural Press.
MOHLG Design Bulletin. *12 Cars in Housing, 2.* HMSO.
Queenborough, J. (ed) '*Garage and Service Station Handbook*' published by George Newnes Ltd. (now out of print).

Architects' Journal Design Guides and Information Sheets
    Car Parking Buildings
    Garage and Service Station Buildings

Alfred J. Rowe *ARIBA Has been responsible for many housing projects both for a large commercial undertaking and in private practice. He was previously with Edward D. Mills & Partners and worked with them on the National Exhibition Centre at Birmingham. He is now in private practice on his own account and has been responsible for many schemes of housing rehabilitation and projects involving the motor car.*

INDEX

1